WHO'S WHO OF LIV

'Believe me, you don't need much motivation when you play for Liverpool. Just pulling on that famous red shirt is motivation enough . . . Just walking out at Anfield beneath the famous sign above the tunnel is a great inspiration . . . Just listening to the roar of the crowd spurs you on. And when they sing "You'll Never Walk Alone", well, it gets you right in the old heart strings. I know all that may sound like a load of footballing clichés, but they all happen to be true. Ask anyone at Anfield.'

Robbie Fowler (1996)

WHO'S WHO OF
LIVERPOOL

Tony Matthews

MAINSTREAM
PUBLISHING
EDINBURGH AND LONDON

First published in Great Britain in 2006 by
MAINSTREAM PUBLISHING COMPANY
(EDINBURGH) LTD
7 Albany Street
Edinburgh EH1 3UG

ISBN 1 84596 140 4

A catalogue record for this book is available
from the British Library

Typeset in Caslon and Gill Condensed

Printed and bound in Great Britain by
William Clowes Ltd, Beccles, Suffolk

CONTENTS

ACKNOWLEDGEMENTS

First and foremost I must say a special big thank you to Bill Campbell, managing director of Mainstream Publishing (Edinburgh), and his colleagues Graeme Blaikie and Debs Warner, and my copy-editor Nick Davis.

Also thank you to Liverpool statistician and historian Stephen Done for clarifying details of certain players' personal records, and a big thank you too, to John Russell (Waterlooville, Hampshire) for his statistical input and to George Hayes (Widnes), Arthur Richardson (Warrington) and Andrew Kellock (Runcorn) for supplying various facts and figures and also photographs from their personal collections. And I can't forget my darling wife Margaret for all her help, support and encouragement as always.

NOTE
The majority of pictures used in this book have come from scrapbooks, photograph albums and old programmes owned by ex-players, avid Liverpool supporters and serious collectors of football memorabilia. I have been unable to establish clear copyright on some of these pictures and therefore both myself and/or the publishers – Mainstream Publishing – would be pleased to hear from anyone whose copyright has unintentionally been infringed.

INTRODUCTION

Today Liverpool FC is, without doubt, one of the top clubs in world football. They were certainly the best in England (and at times in Europe) between 1963 and 1995 when they won prizes galore including 13 League championships, five FA Cup and five League Cup final victories, four European Cup, two UEFA Cup successes and gaining wins in the European Super Cup, the League Super Cup and eight FA Charity Shields, also sharing the latter trophy on five other occasions. And they claimed several runners-up awards as well. As yet they have still to win the coveted Premiership title – but that will come in due course!

Liverpool have been continuous members of the top division in English football since 1962, having previously spent eight years in the Second Division and prior to that had served in each of these two sections on and off since their election in 1892.

Formed in 1892, the club certainly boasts a long and colourful history and over the years literally hundreds of players (some of them the greatest the game has seen) have worn the famous red shirt with pride and passion, whether it be for a considerable length of time, on loan or even briefly as a substitute . . . and there have also been some quality managers at the club.

Each player's individual playing record for the club (appearances made and goals scored, if any) is complemented (if known) with his birth place and birth year, other clubs he played for, international honours, transfer fees . . . all in an easy-to-read and potted biography.

This book will, I am sure, be appreciated by every Liverpool supporter, old and young, male and female, and, indeed, will certainly benefit soccer historians and statisticians, and soccer reporters and commentators, all over the world.

Hopefully the answer to any question asked regarding a Liverpool player, past and present, is here somewhere in this book . . . Where did he come from? When did he join the club? Where did he go to after leaving Anfield? Did he gain international recognition? Was he a defender, midfielder or forward? Did he play in a Cup final? . . . etc.

I know, as you, the reader does, that many arguments have raged in pubs, clubs, offices, on trains and coaches and in cars (travelling to an away game), inside the ground, even walking home after a match, about Liverpool FC and its players. All these, I hope, can now become a thing of the past as you refer to this Who's Who of Liverpool Football Club.

Enjoy it.

Tony Matthews, May 2006

NOTES ON THE TEXT

On the following pages you will find multitudinous, authentic personal details of every single player who has appeared (and scored) for Liverpool FC in a competitive first-team match since the club was formed 114 years ago and the statistics cover fixtures in the Premiership, Football League First and Second Divisions, the FA Cup, the Football League Cup (various guises), the European Cup/Champions League, the European Fairs Cup, the UEFA Cup, the European Cup-Winners' Cup, the European Super Cup, the World Club Championship, the 1895 and 1896 Test matches, the Mercantile Credit Tournament, the FA Charity Shield, the Screen Sport Super Cup and the Football Alliance, the latter being the first major tournament that the club took part in (1892–93), the same season they also entered the FA (English) Cup for the first time. All the statistics are believed to be correct up to the end of the 2005–06 season.

The details of certain players (including several guests from other clubs) who served Liverpool during the two major world wars of 1914–18 and 1939–45, and those of the managers who have been in charge at Anfield, through thick and thin, plus information on other personnel who have, at some time or another, been involved with the club, are also listed in the book.

I will confess that it has been impossible to ascertain every player's exact date of birth or the date of his death (if deceased). But in most cases all the necessary details are there, the exceptions being covered by using the words circa or deceased accordingly.

Throughout this book, where the name of the club is likely to have appeared or been used, I have referred to it as simply Liverpool or the Reds (the nickname) and not the Merseysiders!

Certain abbreviations have also been used, among the common ones being: Apps (appearances), AWS (Auto-Windscreen Shield), cs (close season), FAC (FA Cup), FACS (FA Charity Shield), FC (Football Club), FLC (Football League Cup), FRT (Freight Rover Trophy), FWA (Football Writers' Association), LDV (Leyland Daf Vans Trophy), N (North), NASL (North American Soccer League), PFA (Professional Footballers' Association), q.v. (*quod vide*: which see), S (South), SVT (Sherpa Van Trophy), sub (substitute), v. (versus), WW1 (World War One), WW2 (World War Two), YTS (Youth Training Scheme), ZDS (Zenith Data Systems Cup).

Figures after the + sign in respect of a player's personal record indicate the number of substitute appearances made for the club.

Where a single year appears in the text (when referring to an individual player's career) this indicates, in most cases, the second half of a season, i.e. 1975 for 1974–75. However, when the figures (dates) appear thus: 1975–80, this means seasons 1975–76 to 1979–80 inclusive and not 1974–75 to 1980–81.

If you spot any discrepancies, errors, even omissions, I would appreciate it very much if you could contact me (via the publishers) so that all can be amended in any future publications regarding Liverpool Football Club. If you have anything to add, this would also be appreciated and most welcome, as people often reveal unknown facts from all sources when football is the topic of conversation.

WHO'S WHO OF LIVERPOOL 1892—2006

ABLETT, GARY IAN
Left-back: 141+10 apps, 1 goal
Born: Liverpool, 19 November 1965
Career: Liverpool junior football, LIVERPOOL (apprentice, October 1981; professional, November 1983), Derby County (loan, January–March 1985); Hull City (loan, September–October 1986), Everton (£750,000, January 1982), Sheffield United (loan, March–May 1986), Birmingham City (£390,000, June 1996), Wycombe Wanderers (loan, December 1999), Scunthorpe United (on trial), Blackpool (free, January 2000, retired, injured, May 2001)

A composed left-sided defender, calm under pressure, unfussy with his clearances, Gary Ablett made over 300 appearances for the two Merseyside clubs – 151 for Liverpool and 156 for Everton. He gained one 'B' and one under-21 cap for England and was twice an FA Cup-winner, with Liverpool in 1989 and Everton in 1995. He also won two League titles with the Reds in 1988 and 1990 and played in two FA Charity Shield winning sides: Liverpool 1988 and Everton 1995. Ablett, who made his League debut whilst on loan as a Derby County player in 1985 and could well have joined the Rams for a six-figure fee, was also the target of Middlesbrough three years later. They offered £700,000 for his services but Liverpool boss, Kenny Dalglish, said: 'He's not for sale – we're keeping him.'

A'COURT, ALAN
Outside-left: 382 apps, 63 goals
Born: Rainhill, Lancashire, 30 September 1934
Career: Liverpool County Schools, Prescot Celtic (August 1950), Prescot Cables (July 1951), LIVERPOOL (professional, September 1952), Tranmere Rovers (£4,500, October 1964), Norwich City (player/trainer-coach, July 1966), Chester (assistant manager/coach, October 1968), Crewe Alexandra (assistant manager/coach, February 1969), Stoke City (coach, July 1969–April 1972), Ndola United/Zambia (coach, May–July 1972), Stoke City (coach, assistant manager, seasons 1972–78, also caretaker-manager for two games, January 1978), Crewe Alexandra (assistant manager, late 1970s)

An elusive outside-left, fast and tricky and an excellent crosser of the ball, Alan

A'Court – described as being 'a natural' by *Daily Express* reporter Henry Rose – gained five full England caps as a Liverpool player over a 12-month period from November 1957, scoring on his debut against Northern Ireland and completing three matches in the 1958 World Cup finals in Sweden (v. Brazil, Austria and USSR). He also played in seven under-23 internationals and helped the Reds win the Second Division championship in 1962. He made his League debut in February 1953 and went on to average 38 first-team appearances per season over a ten-year period after taking over from the great Billy Liddell on the left flank. His last outing for Liverpool was against the Icelandic side Reykjavik in a European Cup first-round second-leg encounter at Anfield in August 1964 (won 6–1 for an aggregate 11–1 victory). When dressing room morale was at a low ebb A'Court's sense of humour certainly perked his colleagues up on several occasions. He also encouraged many of the younger players in the camp.

AGGER, DANIEL
Defender: 4 apps
Born: Denmark, 12 December 1984
Career: Rosenhoj/Denmark (March 2001, semi-professional, August 2002), Brondby IF/Denmark (August 2004), LIVERPOOL (£5.8m, January 2006)
Danny Agger was Liverpool manager Rafael Benitez's second signing when the transfer window opened in January 2006. Preferring the centre-half position, he can also fill in at full-back and at 21 certainly had years ahead of him in the professional game. A Danish international, capped initially against Finland in June 2005 when he marked the former Liverpool player Jari Litmanen and also had Sami Hyypia playing against him, he is now a valuable member of his country's senior squad. Indeed, he had an excellent game when the Danes beat England 4–1 in a friendly in August 2005, helping diminish the dual strike-threat of ex-Red Michael Owen and Wayne Rooney. Entering competitive League football as a 19 year old (v. B1909 Odense) Agger helped Brondby win the Danish Superliga in his first season (2004–05) and at the same time was voted the 'Find of the Year' in all sports in Denmark. Standing 6ft 2in. tall, he is strong in all aspects of defensive play and when he moved to Anfield he was regarded as Denmark's most exciting discovery since Michael Laudrup's heyday in the late 1980s/early '90s. Agger made his debut for the Reds against Birmingham City on 1 February 2006.

AITKEN, ANDREW LIDDELL
Goalkeeper: 1 app.
Born: Newcastle-upon-Tyne, 25 August 1909 – *Died*: Newcastle-upon-Tyne, October 1984
Career: Wallsend FC (from August 1927), Liverpool (March 1930–April 1931); returned to the North-east where he later worked in the steel industry
Ten months after Charlie Thompson had left Wallsend for Liverpool, Andrew Aitken joined him at Anfield. A well-built goalkeeper, he played his only first-team game for the Reds in a 3–3 draw with Blackburn Rovers at Ewood Park two days after Christmas, 1930, deputising for the injured Arthur Riley.

ALDRIDGE, JOHN WILLIAM
Forward: 90+16 apps, 65 goals
Born: Liverpool, 18 September 1958
Career: South Liverpool, Newport County (professional, April 1979), Oxford United (£78,000, March 1984), LIVERPOOL (£750,000, January 1987), Real Sociedad/Spain (£1m, September 1989), Tranmere Rovers (£250,000, July 1991, player-manager, April 1997, retired as a player, June 1998, remained as manager until April 2001); later a football summariser/analyst on Sky TV

One of the great marksmen of the latter part of the twentieth century, John Aldridge netted 412 goals in 739 senior appearances for his four Football League clubs. He also netted 21 goals for Real Sociedad in Spain and slotted in another 19 in 69 full internationals for the Republic of Ireland – a joint record at the time with Don Givens which was later bettered by Tony Cascarino, Niall Quinn, Robbie Keane and Frank Stapleton. Positive in his approach and style and ever-alert inside the danger-zone, he won the Welsh Cup with Newport in 1980 and the Second Division championship and League Cup with Oxford United in 1985 and 1986 respectively before going on to gain three prizes with Liverpool: the First Division championship and FA Charity Shield in 1988 and FA Cup in 1989. He knows full well he should have given Liverpool a chance of winning the 1988 FA Cup final, but disappointingly he had his penalty saved by Wimbledon keeper Dave Beasant and the underdogs went on to lift the trophy 1–0. At the age of 39 years and 227 days, he became Tranmere Rovers' oldest player when he appeared in his last game for the club against Wolves at Prenton Park on 3 May 1998, scoring both goals in a 2–1 win to celebrate the occasion. He also holds the record of being Tranmere's most-capped player with 30 to his name. 'Aldo' could not match either the ball skills or the pace of several of his teammates but there was no doubting his marksmanship – it was phenomenal and one wonders what he might have achieved had he remained at Anfield instead of going to play in Spain.

ALLAN, GEORGE HORSBURGH
Centre-forward: 97 apps, 60 goals
Born: Linlithgow Bridge, West Lothian, 23 August 1875 – *Died*: Liverpool, 9 October 1899
Career: Broxburn Shamrock (August 1891), Bo'ness (September 1893), Leith Athletic (semi-professional, August 1894), LIVERPOOL (£100, professional, September 1895), Celtic (£50, May 1897), LIVERPOOL (April 1898, retired through ill health, July 1899)

Scottish international centre-forward George Allan arrived on Merseyside at the age of 20 with no real soccer experience behind him. However, he quickly made his mark with Liverpool and was a key member of the club's Second Division championship-winning side of 1895–96 when he netted 25 goals plus three more vital ones in the end-of-season Test matches and another in the FA Cup. Strong and aggressive, he certainly knew where the posts lay and often chose to shoot from distance. He was Liverpool's top scorer in his first two seasons and after returning from Celtic with whom he won the Scottish League title, he claimed 12 more goals. In January 1897, Allan was involved in a famous incident at Anfield where he charged into Sheffield United's giant 19st. goalkeeper Billy Foulke who, in his opinion, had fouled him. The keeper's retribution was swift, simple and painful as he grabbed Allan by his ankles and dumped him head first into the muddy goal area . . . no penalty! Sadly, illness ended Allan's career and he was only 24 years of age when he died.

ALLMAN, MESSINA WILSON
Inside-forward/right-half: 1 app.
Born: Burslem, Stoke-on-Trent, 1883 – *Died*: Croydon, Surrey, 1943
Career: Burslem Park Boys (1901), Burslem Port Vale (professional, April 1903), Reading (June 1905), Portsmouth (May 1907), Plymouth Argyle (November 1907), Stoke (briefly, no first-team games, March–April 1908), LIVERPOOL (July 1908), Wrexham (September 1909), Grantham (May 1910), Ton Pentre (July 1911), Leicester Fosse (November 1911), Croydon Common (June 1912), Arsenal (guest, during 1916–17 season, retired, August 1917)

'Dick' Allman was 20 when he made his senior debut for Port Vale, in a qualifying round of the FA Cup v. Nantwich in November 1903. He settled into the Vale side well and was leading scorer in 1904–05 before transferring to Reading. After that he was on the move regularly, having his best spell with Wrexham, scoring 19 goals in 34 outings. His only League game for Liverpool was at right-half against Bristol City (home) in March 1909 when he deputised for Ted Parry in a 2–1 defeat. An earthenware painter by profession, he went back to that line of business after WW1.

ALONSO, XABI
Midfield: 73+11 apps, 8 goals
Born: Tolosa, Spain, 25 November 1981
Career: SD Eibar/Spain (1997), Real Sociedad/Spain (junior, 1998; professional, April 1999), CF Eibar/Spain (loan, September–December 2000), LIVERPOOL (August 2004)

A 6ft tall Spanish international midfielder with well over 20 full caps to his credit, Xabi Alonso, after a rather slow start, went on to have a sound first season at Anfield, scoring 3 goals in 32 senior appearances and gaining a Champions League winner's medal. Prior to moving to Merseyside he had played in 115 La Liga games for Real Sociedad and 14 for the minnows of Eibar. Able to orchestrate play in midfield, he has a terrific engine . . . clearing from inside his own penalty area one minute, 30 seconds later he is seen trying to get on to a cross at the other end of the field. Playing against Luton Town in a third-round FA Cup tie at Kenilworth Road in January 2006, Alonso scored a goal from 70 yards – one of the longest ever recorded by an outfield player in open play. He then went on to gain a winner's medal in the epic final win over West Ham United ahead of the World Cup in Germany.

ANDERSON, ERIC
Inside-forward: 76 apps, 21 goals
Born: Manchester, 12 July 1931 – *Died*: Cheshire, July 1990
Career: Army football (from 1948), LIVERPOOL (amateur, December 1951; professional, January 1952), Barnsley (£4,000, July 1957), Bournemouth and Boscombe Athletic (£1,000, June 1959), Macclesfield Town (March 1960)
A lightly built forward able to occupy at least three different positions, Eric Anderson was 22 years of age when he made his League debut for Liverpool against Charlton Athletic at Anfield in March 1953 (lost 2–1), coming into a much-changed front line in the absence of Billy Liddell. He scored his first goal for the club the following season (v. Charlton) and had his best spell at the club in 1954–55 when he netted 9 times in 32 League outings. He failed to make headway at Barnsley (nine League games) or Bournemouth (nil).

ANDERSON, PAUL
Midfield: yet to make his senior debut for Liverpool
Born: Leicester, 23 July 1988
Career: Hull City (apprentice, July 2004; professional, November 2005), LIVERPOOL (trial, December 2005, signed January 2006 in exchange deal involving John Welsh)
Highly rated wide midfielder able to play on both flanks, Anderson joined the Reds after impressing during a trial at Anfield. Spotted while plying his trade with the Tigers' Academy side, he completed his move to Anfield on New Year's Day 2006 as part of the deal that saw John Welsh move in the opposite direction.

ANELKA, NICOLAS
Striker: 15+7 apps, 5 goals
Born: Versailles, France, 14 March 1979
Career: Paris St Germain/France (amateur, August 1995; professional, May 1996), Arsenal (£500,000, March 1997), Real Madrid/Spain (£22.9m, August 1999), Paris St Germain/France (£12m, August 2000), LIVERPOOL (loan, December 2001–May 2002), Manchester City (£13m, July 2002), Fenerbahce/Turkey (£7m, January 2005)
There was no doubting Nicolas Anelka's ability in front of goal – he was top notch – but his attitude let him down badly and in truth he left most of his clubs under a cloud of disappointment! A French international, capped 28 times at senior level, he made only 10 League appearances in his first spell with PSG, netted 28 times in 90 outings for Arsenal (helping the Gunners complete the treble by winning Premiership, FA Cup and Charity Shield in 1998), had a mixed season with Real Madrid (only 19 outings in the Spanish La Liga), did better second time round with PSG (11 goals in 49 League matches) and then had a moderate loan spell with Liverpool, when he averaged a goal every four games, the first coming in his tenth game – a 1–1 draw with Everton in the Merseyside derby in February 2002. He probably played his best football with Manchester City (45 strikes in 193 appearances) but he left that club after comments made to the French newspaper *L'Equipe* back-fired on him!

ARMSTRONG, THOMAS
Goalkeeper: 1 app.
Born: Preston, Lancashire, 1898 – *Died*: Preston, *circa* 1967
Career: Army football, Preston junior football (1919), LIVERPOOL (amateur, January 1920), Preston North End (amateur, June 1920–May 1921)
An amateur all his life, Tom Armstrong made only one League appearance in his brief career. That came with Liverpool against Sheffield Wednesday (away) in March 1920 when both regular keepers Ken Campbell and Elisha Scott were playing on opposite sides in an international match between Scotland and Ireland. Looking nervous in the first half, conceding two sloppy goals, he did well after the break as the Reds fought back to earn a 2–2 draw.

ARNELL, ALAN JACK
Centre-/inside-forward: 75 apps, 35 goals
Born: Chichester, 25 November 1933
Career: Worthing Boys, Sussex Youths, LIVERPOOL (amateur, April 1953; professional, March 1954), Tranmere Rovers (February 1961), Halifax Town (July 1963), Runcorn (July 1964, retired, injured, May 1966)
A strong, energetic, well-built striker who could also play on the wing, Alan Arnell was excellent in the air and had a good first touch but perhaps lacked aggression when it mattered most. Nevertheless, he still averaged a goal every two games for Liverpool for whom he scored on his League debut in December 1953 against Blackpool at Anfield, a match which the Reds won 5–2 in front of 47,320 fans. He also weighed in with a brave hat-trick against Huddersfield Town in 1956. After leaving Anfield, he netted 34 goals in 68 League games for Tranmere and claimed 6 in 14 outings for Halifax.

ARNOLD, STEPHEN FRANK
Midfield: 1 app.
Born: Willesden, North London, 5 January 1951
Career: Wembley Boys Club, Crewe Alexandra (apprentice, April 1967; professional, January 1969), LIVERPOOL (£10,000, September 1970), Southport (loan, January–April 1972), Torquay United (loan, August–October 1972), Rochdale (June 1973), Weymouth (seasons 1974–76); out of football for about two years, later with Connah's Quay Nomads (season 1978–79), West Kirby (season 1979–80)
Half-back Steve Arnold made only 76 League appearances during his professional career – one for Liverpool v. Manchester City at Maine Road in April 1971 when he deputised on the right wing for Ian Callaghan in a 2–2 draw. He played as a central defender for Rochdale.

ARPHEXAD, PEGGUY MICHAEL
Goalkeeper: 5+1 apps
Born: Abymes, Guadeloupe, 18 May 1973
Career: FC Brest/France (amateur, August 1989), Racing Club Lens/France (professional, September 1993), Leicester City (free, August 1997),

LIVERPOOL (free, July 2000), Stockport County (loan, September–October 2001), Coventry City (free, August 2003), Notts County (loan, March–April 2004), released by Coventry City (May 2004)

Signed as cover for goalkeeper Sander Westerveld at Anfield, Pegguy Arphexad was never going to become first choice at Anfield. He played in only six senior games – the first against Chelsea (home) in a League Cup tie in November 2000. Prior to entering English football, Arphexad had made only three League appearances for Lens.

ARROWSMITH, ALFRED WILLIAM
Centre-forward/inside-left: 51+4 apps, 24 goals
Born: Manchester, 11 December 1942 – *Died*: Cheshire, 12 May 2005
Career: Ashton United (1959), LIVERPOOL (£1,250, August 1960), Bury (£25,000, December 1968), Rochdale (£5,000, June 1970), Macclesfield Town (July 1972)

Alf Arrowsmith made 47 League appearances for Liverpool, 48 for Bury and 46 for Rochdale. A First Division championship winner with the Reds in 1963–64 after bursting onto the scene during the second half of the campaign alongside Roger Hunt, he was a lively forward and a very useful linkman. He scored 15 goals in 20 League games during that triumphant season after taking over from Jimmy Melia. He also netted four times in a 5–0 FA Cup win over Derby County in the January. A glittering future seemed to be in store for the Mancunian but it all went wrong in August 1964 when he damaged his knee during the FA Charity Shield game against West Ham United. Arrowsmith, who was a very popular and down-to-earth character, was never the same player after that mishap.

ASHCROFT, CHARLES THOMAS
Goalkeeper: 89 apps
Born: Croston, Lancashire, 3 July 1926
Career: Chorley Boys, Eccleston Juniors (1941), LIVERPOOL (semi-professional, December 1943; professional, August 1945), Ipswich Town (June 1955), Coventry City (June 1957), Chorley (July 1958–May 1960)

An England 'B' international, capped against Holland in Amsterdam in March 1952, Charlie Ashcroft – useful with high crosses – was discovered in wartime football and made a handful of senior appearances for Liverpool towards the end of the 1945–46 campaign before battling with Cyril Sidlow and Russell Crossley for a first-team place when League football resumed in earnest in August 1946. Despite spending 12 years at Anfield, he was only a regular in the first XI in 1951–52 (34 League games) and 1952–53 (24). He was reserve to Roy Bailey at Ipswich and shared the duties at Coventry with Graham Spratt.

BABB, PHILIP ANDREW
Defender: 164+6 apps, 1 goal
Born: Lambeth, London, 30 November 1970
Career: London junior football, Millwall (apprentice, April 1987; professional,

April 1989), Bradford City (free, August 1990), Coventry City (£500,000, July 1992), LIVERPOOL (£3.6m, September 1994), Tranmere Rovers (loan, January–February 2000), Sporting Lisbon/Portugal (June 2000), Sunderland (free, June 2002, retired, injured, June 2004)

Republic of Ireland defender Phil Babb retired in 2004 with 463 competitive appearances under his belt (all levels). He won one 'B' and 35 full caps as an international, starring in the USA World Cup finals of 1994, and helped Liverpool win the League Cup in 1995 – his only major club honour. He initially made his mark with Bradford and continued to improve with Premiership side Coventry, before joining the Reds. At Anfield, the tall, well-balanced and pacy Babb partnered Neil Ruddock in a back-line of four and had 34 League outings that season, holding his place until early 1997 when Bjorn Kvarme was introduced. Eventually slipping further down the pecking-order when Sami Hyypia and Stephane Henchoz became the regular centre-backs, he had a loan spell with Tranmere and played in Portugal before ending his career with Sunderland.

BABBEL, MARCUS

Defender: 71+2 apps, 6 goals
Born: Munich, Germany, 8 September 1972
Career: Bayern Munich/Germany (amateur, September 1988; professional, April 1990), SV Hamburg/Germany (August 1992), Bayern Munich/Germany (July 1994), LIVERPOOL (July 2000), Blackburn Rovers (loan, August 2003–May 2004), Vfb Stuttgart/Germany (July 2004)

Cool and composed German international defender Marcus Babbel, who gained 51 full caps for his country, was a key member of the Reds team that won five trophies in 2001 (UEFA Cup, FA Cup, League Cup, European Super Cup and FA Charity Shield). He had an excellent first season at Anfield before going off, 'feeling unwell' at Bolton on August Bank Holiday, 2001. He was subsequently diagnosed as suffering from Guillain-Barre syndrome which seriously weakened his immune system. Taking quite a while to regain full fitness, he was replaced in the right-back position by Jamie Carragher, with John Arne Riise slipping into the left-back berth. Returning to action briefly halfway through 2002–03, he never looked right and after a loan spell with Blackburn, returned to Germany with Vfb Stuttgart. Prior to joining Liverpool, Babbel, who can also play as a centre-back, had scored 10 goals in 242 Bundesliga games in his homeland, helping Bayern win three titles (1997, 1999 and 2000), lift the German Cup twice (1998 and 2000) and carry off the UEFA Cup (1996).

BALMER, JOHN

Inside-forward: 313 apps, 111 goals
Born: Liverpool, 6 February 1916 – *Died*: Liverpool, 25 December 1984
Career: Collegiate School (Liverpool), Collegiate Old Boys (1934), Everton (amateur, March 1935), LIVERPOOL (amateur, May 1935; professional August 1935); guest for Brighton and Hove Albion and Newcastle United during WW2; returned to Anfield (retired, May 1952)

Jack Balmer's uncles, William and Robert, had both played for Everton in the early 1900s, but the Goodison Park club let Jack go after a month's trial as an amateur. Everton certainly regretted their decision, for Balmer went on to score well over 100 senior goals for rivals Liverpool after developing into one of the best inside-forwards of the immediate post-war era. He also claimed 66 in 105 WW2 matches just to emphasise his ability! A schemer and a finisher of the highest degree, he tucked away 24 goals in 39 games when Liverpool won the League championship in 1946–47, including a hat-trick in 3 consecutive League games in November against Portsmouth, Derby County (4 goals) and Arsenal. He actually scored 15 times in 7 matches around that time. His first appearance for the Reds came in September 1935, away at Leeds United, and his last outing was in February 1952 at home to Charlton Athletic. Sadly, Balmer missed out on a full cap but he did play in one WW2 international for England v. Wales in 1939. He also starred in several other representative matches during the hostilities, playing for the Army v. the Football League in 1940, for Northern Command v. Western Command in 1942, for Western Command v. Wales XI twice in 1942 and v. the RAF and the AA Command in 1944, for the Army (England) v. Army (Scotland) in 1943 and 1944, and for the Army against the FA XI and the Scottish Command in 1944. He was a truly great player.

BAMBER, JOHN
Right-half: 80 apps, 2 goals
Born: Peasley Cross, St Helens, 11 April 1895 – *Died*: Peasley Cross, St Helens, 1971
Career: St Helens Recreation (1911), Heywood FC (1913), LIVERPOOL (professional, December 1915), Leicester City (February 1924), Tranmere Rovers (July 1927), Prescot Cables (August 1930–April 1932)
An England international, capped against Wales in March 1921, John Bamber was regarded as one of the best three right-halves in the Football League at that time. Well built, he was a crisp tackler and distributed the ball well, never hoofing it downfield unnecessarily. After scoring 4 times in 85 WW1 appearances for the Reds, Bamber made his Football League debut at the age of 24 against Aston Villa in September 1919, but missed out on a medal when Liverpool won successive League titles in 1922 (eight games) and 1923 (four games). After leaving Anfield, he played left-half for Leicester, whom he helped gain promotion from the Second Division, and centre-half for Tranmere. He twice represented the Football League and played in two games on tour to South Africa with the FA during his time with Liverpool.

BANKS, ALAN
Centre-/inside-forward: 8 apps, 6 goals
Born: Liverpool, 5 October 1938
Career: Rankin Boys (1953), LIVERPOOL (amateur, August 1956; professional, May 1958), Cambridge City (free with Dave Hickson, July 1961), Exeter City (£6,000, October 1963 – then Exeter's record fee . . . with £3,000 going to Cambridge City and £3,000 to Liverpool), Plymouth Argyle

(free, June 1966), Exeter City (free, November 1967), Poole Town (May 1973), Tiverton Town (seasons 1975–77)

Unable to gain a regular place in Liverpool's first team, in later years, as he gained experience, Alan Banks became a prolific marksman, netting 109 goals in 286 competitive games during his two spells with Exeter City and another 5 in 20 starts for Plymouth, plus over 100 more in two seasons of non-League football with Cambridge City. Described as a 'human dynamo' the diminutive Banks scored for the Grecians against the reigning European champions, Manchester United, in a third-round FA Cup tie in January 1969 and was subsequently voted Exeter's 'Player of the Year' that season. He netted on his League debut for Liverpool in a 5–0 home win over Brighton in September 1958 at the age of 19. After retiring he returned to live and work in Exeter and still attends games at St James' Park.

BANKS, WILLIAM
Inside-right: 26 apps, 6 goals
Born: Cramlington, Northumberland, February 1893 – *Died*: County Durham, 1966
Career: Bedlington (1910), Ashington (May 1911), LIVERPOOL (£150, February 1914), Fulham (£600, December 1919–May 1921)

A useful forward, able to play in three positions, Bill Banks was more of a link man than a marksman, although he did find the net occasionally. He missed out on an FA Cup final appearance with the Reds in 1914, having scored on his League debut against Burnley six weeks previously. He lost his place to England international Danny Shea at Fulham, for whom he made 40 senior appearances. He scored 4 goals in 21 WW1 games for Liverpool.

BARKAS, HENRY BROWN
Centre-forward: 5 apps
Born: Wardley Colliery, Northumberland, 21 January 1906 – *Died*: 1974
Career: Wardley Juniors (1924), Spennymoor United (part-time professional, 1927), South Shields (professional, December 1929), LIVERPOOL (£1,500, December 1930, released May 1932)

Harry Barkas scored 23 goals in 40 Third Division (N) games for South Shields (and Gateshead which that club became in 1930) before joining Liverpool. He was basically a reserve during his time at Anfield, making his debut for the club in January 1931 in a 3–1 home League win over Middlesbrough.

His elder brothers, Ned and Sam Barkas, were both professional footballers. Ned captained Birmingham in the 1931 FA Cup final and also played for Norwich City, Huddersfield Town and Chelsea, while Sam served with Bradford City, Manchester City and Workington and won five England caps.

BARMBY, NICHOLAS JONATHAN, MBE
Midfield/forward: 38+20 apps, 8 goals
Born: Hull, 11 February 1974
Career: Tottenham Hotspur (apprentice, May 1990; professional, April 1991),

Middlesbrough (£5.15m, August 1995), Everton (£5.75m, November 1996), LIVERPOOL (£6m, July 2000), Leeds United (£2.75m, August 2002), Nottingham Forest (loan, February–March 2004), Hull City (free, July 2004) Nick Barmby changed clubs between 1991 and 2000 for almost £11 million and he gave every one he played for value for money to a certain extent. He scored 27 goals in 108 appearances for Spurs, 10 in 49 for Middlesbrough, 24 in 133 for Everton and 8 in 58 for Liverpool. He then followed up with 5 strikes in 31 outings for Leeds and scored once in six outings for Forest before joining his home town club, Hull City, in 2004 at the age of 30. With the Tigers he continued to produce the goods, helping them gain promotion to the Championship in his first season at the Kingston Communications Stadium. In fact, he scored after just seven seconds of his Hull debut v. Walsall – the quickest goal in the club's history. Capped by England at senior level on 23 occasions, he also represented his country in two 'B' and four under-21 games having earlier played at both schoolboy and youth team levels. Following his controversial transfer from Goodison Park – the first player since 1959 to move from Everton to Anfield – Barmby, in his initial season with Liverpool, gained League Cup, UEFA Cup and Charity Shield winner's medals but missed the FA Cup final triumph due to a niggling ankle injury. Indeed, the problem seriously affected his game with Liverpool and England. On his day, though, Barmby was a fine competitor who fought to the last – a real never-say-die footballer. He was awarded the MBE in the 1995 Queen's Honours List.

BARNES, JOHN CHARLES BRYAN, MBE
Forward: 404+4 apps, 109 goals
Born: Kingston, Jamaica, 7 November 1963
Career: Sudbury Court (1979), Watford (professional, July 1981), LIVERPOOL (£900,000, June 1987), Newcastle United (August 1997), Charlton Athletic (February 1999), Celtic (head coach, May 1999–February 2000); now works in the media (mainly on TV); also advisory-coach to Northwich Victoria (2006)
In his prime John Barnes was one of the finest ball-playing wingers in the game. Casual looking at times, he could waltz past a defender with ease, using both feet and a splendid body swerve. His crosses were often precise and dangerous and he scored some wonderful goals – including a quite brilliant individual effort for England against Brazil in Rio in June 1984 – a month after appearing for Watford against Everton in the FA Cup final. That was his 10th senior outing for his country . . . he went on to gain 79 full caps while also collecting 3 at under-21 level. Unfortunately injury robbed him of more senior caps in the 1992 European Championships in Sweden. An FA Youth Cup winner with Watford (under Graham Taylor) in 1982, the year he helped the Hornets reach the top flight of English football for the first time, Barnes then helped Liverpool win two League championships (1988 and 1990), the FA Cup (1989), the FA Charity Shield twice (1988 and 1990) and the League Cup (1995). Barnes was also voted FWA 'Footballer of the Year' in 1988 and 1990. When he retired (after spells with Newcastle and Charlton) he had amassed a fine club record of 762 senior appearances and 199 goals.

23

At Celtic, Barnes joined forces with his former Liverpool colleague Kenny Dalglish who was Director of Football at Parkhead. As head coach, he remained in charge of team affairs for barely nine months, losing his job after the Bhoys had suffered a humiliating Scottish Cup defeat at the hands of the minnows of Caledonian Thistle. Dalglish then took over the reins until the appointment of Martin O'Neill in July 2000. His social awareness and involvement with the third world saw him visit Burundi in June 1998 as an unofficial ambassador for Christian Aid. Four months later he was awarded the MBE for services to football. Barnes' father was also a footballer and captained Jamaica's national team.

BARON, FREDERICK JOHN
Centre-forward/inside-left: 20 apps, 7 goals
Born: Prudhoe, Northumberland, 29 December 1901 – *Died*: Durham, *circa* 1979
Career: Prudhoe Castle (August 1919), Mid-Rhondda (May 1923), LIVERPOOL (professional, February 1925), Southend United (March 1927–May 1932)
Fred Baron was a hard-working player who had a decent run in Liverpool's first team during the last quarter of the 1924–25 season when he scored five times in nine League games, including two in a 3–0 home win over Burnley. He did very well with Southend for whom he struck 41 goals in 62 League outings.

BARON, KEVIN MARK PATRICK
Inside-forward: 140 apps, 32 goals
Born: Preston, Lancashire, 19 July 1926 – *Died*: 5 June 1971
Career: Preston schoolboy and junior football, Preston North End (amateur, 1942), LIVERPOOL (amateur, September 1944; professional, August 1945), Southend United (May 1954), Northampton Town (September 1958), Gravesend and Northfleet (August 1959), Wisbech Town (December 1959), Aldershot (July 1960), Cambridge City (April 1961), Bedford Town (October 1961), Maldon Town (player-coach from July 1962)
Former Bevin Boy Kevin Baron, 5ft 6in. tall, was preferred to Jack Balmer in Liverpool's 1950 FA Cup final attack. A smart forward with imagination and skill, he packed a powerful right-foot shot, was a good dribbler and had an eye for goal. He made his first appearance at senior level for the Reds against Chester in a third-round first-leg FA Cup clash in January 1946 and then had to wait until September 1947 before making his League debut. He had his best season with the Reds in 1949–50 when he netted 7 times in 38 First Division matches while partnering Jimmy Payne on the right wing.

BAROS, MILAN
Striker: 66+43 apps, 27 goals
Born: Vigantice, Czech Republic, 28 October 1981
Career: Valasske/Czech Republic (1997), Banik Ostrava/Czech Republic (professional, October 1999), LIVERPOOL (£3.4m, December 2001), Aston Villa (£6.5m, August 2005)

Black-haired striker, strong and forceful, Milan Baros scored 11 goals in 61 League games for Banik Ostrava and was already a respected Czech Republic international at youth, under-21 and senior levels when he joined Liverpool halfway through 2001–02. With Michael Owen and Emile Heskey as the main attackers, he bided his time in the reserves for the remainder of that season, being monitored by the Anfield coaching staff, making his debut as a substitute for Heskey in the Champions League game against Barcelona in March 2002. The following year he appeared in 42 first-class matches (20 as a 'sub') and scored 12 goals. Continuing to make progress, injuries apart, including a niggling hamstring problem, it was hoped he would take over from Michael Owen but after scoring a hat-trick against Crystal Palace in November 2004, he began to lose his way. Baros was a huge disappointment in the European Champions League final in Istanbul and soon afterwards moved to pastures new, joining Aston Villa by which time he had taken his tally of full caps to 39 and his under-21 tally to 19. He won the League Cup and European Champions Cup with Liverpool in 2003 and 2005 respectively.

BARRAGAN, ANTONIO
Defender: 0+1 app.
Born: Pontedeume, Galicia, Spain, 12 June 1987
Career: Seville/Spain (junior, May 2003; professional, July 2004), LIVERPOOL (July 2005)
Highly rated young Spaniard Antonio Barragan made his debut for Liverpool as a second-half substitute against CSK Sofia in a qualifying round of the European Champions League in Bulgaria in August 2005.

BARTON, HAROLD
Outside-right: 101 apps, 25 goals
Born: Leigh, Lancashire, 30 September 1911 – *Deceased*
Career: Whitegate Juniors (Blackpool, 1927), LIVERPOOL (professional, November 1928), Sheffield United (£1,600, June 1934); guest for Bradford Park Avenue, Chesterfield, Lincoln City, Rotherham United and Sheffield Wednesday during WW2; did not play first-class football after 1946
A fast-raiding winger with craft and guile, Harry Barton was a huge favourite with the fans. He worked in his uncle's butcher's shop before signing professional forms for Liverpool at the age of 17. He made his League debut against Blackburn Rovers in October 1929 and had the honour of scoring four goals in an FA Cup tie v. Chesterfield in January 1932 and a hat-trick in the Merseyside derby against Everton the following year – a game the Reds won 7–4 before a 50,000 crowd. He gained an FA Cup runners-up medal with Sheffield United in 1936 and was a key member of the Blades' promotion-winning side in 1938–39. In March 1940 Barton played for an FA XI against a Yorkshire XI.

BARTROP, WILFRED

Outside-right: 3 apps

Born: Worksop, July 1889 – *Died*: France, March 1918

Career: Worksop Town (1907), Barnsley (professional, June 1909), LIVERPOOL (with Phil Bratley, May 1914 until his death in 1918)

Wilf Bartrop had only three first-team outings with the Reds, making his debut against Oldham Athletic (home) in December 1914 when he deputised for John Sheldon on the right wing. Prior to his move to Anfield, he played in two FA Cup finals with Barnsley – losing to Newcastle United in 1910 and beating West Bromwich Albion in a replay in 1912. A soldier in the Army, he was sadly killed in action while serving his country in France. He was just 29 years of age.

BATTLES, BERNARD

Left-back/right-half: 6 apps

Born: Springburn, Glasgow, 13 January 1875 – *Died*: Scotland, 9 February 1905

Career: Linlithgow junior football (Glasgow), Broxburn FC (1891), Bathgate (1892), Heart of Midlothian (professional, August 1894), Celtic (May 1895), LIVERPOOL (March 1896), Celtic (May 1896), Dundee (May 1897), LIVERPOOL (March 1898), Celtic (October 1898), Dundee (June, 1903), Kilmarnock (August 1904–May 1906)

'Barney' Battles was a big, bustling defender who made up for his obvious lack of speed with great anticipation. A fine positional player, he had three spells with Celtic and two each with both Liverpool and Dundee. He was recruited by the Reds towards the end of the 1895–96 season when promotion was in sight. He played in three of the four Test matches (two won, one draw with no goals conceded) and when he returned in 1898 he played in a League game against Bury when John McCartney was out injured. He made 136 appearances for Celtic, helping them win the League title once (1896) and the Scottish Cup twice (1899 and 1900) and collected two runners-up medals in the latter competition (1901 and 1902). Also a League championship winner with Hearts (1895), he represented the Scottish League. His son, also named Barney, played for Hearts and Scotland.

BEADLES, GEORGE HAROLD

Centre-forward/inside-left: 18 apps, 6 goals

Born: Llanllwchaiarn, Newtown, Montgomeryshire, 28 September 1897 – *Died*: Liverpool, 29 August 1958

Career: Newtown FC (August 1912), Army service and football (1915–19), LIVERPOOL (amateur, March 1920), Grayson's FC (amateur, August 1920), LIVERPOOL (professional, June 1921), Cardiff City (May 1924), Sheffield Wednesday (November 1925), Southport (August 1926), Dundalk (player-coach, July 1929–May 1930); returned to Liverpool and became a licensee with Bents Brewery

On leaving school George Beadles went into employment with a furs and mantles company in Newtown, playing football for the local team at weekends. He served in Turkey with the Welch Fusiliers during the Great War and was awarded the Serbian Gold Medal for gallantry. He signed amateur forms for Liverpool in 1920 but chose to get match fit by spending a season with Grayson's. He returned to Anfield as a professional at the age of 23, yet had difficulty getting into the first XI. Disillusioned, he opened his own sports outfitter's shop in the city, believing that he wasn't going to make it as a footballer. He averaged a goal every three games for the Reds in three seasons before moving to Cardiff City with whom he gained two Welsh international caps, playing against Scotland and England in 1925. He also lined up for the Bluebirds in that year's FA Cup defeat by Sheffield United. After a brief spell with Sheffield Wednesday he became a star performer with Southport, for whom he scored 61 goals in 92 Third Division (N) games, netting in 6 successive matches in 1926 to set a new club record. He was regarded as the best header of the ball in the lower divisions at that time.

BEARDSLEY, PETER ANDREW

Forward: 160+15 apps, 59 goals

Born: Longbenton, Newcastle-upon-Tyne, 18 January 1961

Career: Wallsend Boys' Club (1976), Newcastle United (trialist, season 1977–78), Carlisle United (free, August 1979), Vancouver Whitecaps/NASL (May 1981), Manchester United (£300,000, September 1982), Vancouver Whitecaps (May 1983), Newcastle United (£120,000, September 1983), LIVERPOOL (£1.9m, July 1987), Everton (£1m, August 1991), Newcastle United (£1.45m, July 1993), Bolton Wanderers (£450,000, August 1997), Manchester City (loan, February–March 1998), Fulham (loan, March–May 1998), Hartlepool United (December 1998, retired, May 1999); Newcastle United (Academy coach from 2000); still plays in charity matches (Newcastle United over 35s)

Peter Beardsley was a superb footballer with a wonderful technique whose career record was magnificent – almost 1,000 competitive appearances (for clubs and country) and more than 275 goals scored. He won 59 full caps for England (9 goals) and starred in two 'B' internationals. He formed a brilliant strike-force with ex-Liverpool star Kevin Keegan at Newcastle before linking up with the prolific Ian Rush at Anfield and then he figured prominently with Tony Cottee at Everton as well as playing alongside Gary Lineker for his country. During his four years with Liverpool he won two League championships in 1988 and 1990, an FA Cup winner's medal in 1989 and three Charity Shield winner's prizes in 1988, 1989 and 1990 while also playing in the losing FA Cup final of 1988. The first of his 175 outings for the Reds came in a 2–1 League win at Arsenal in August 1987 and his first goal followed in his second game, a 4–1 win at Coventry. He played in Everton's first Premiership game v. Sheffield Wednesday in 1992 and in 1999 was a member of Fulham's Second Division championship-winning side under his former playing colleague Keegan. As a youngster Beardsley turned down both Cambridge United and Gillingham before joining Carlisle United. Besides football, he also enjoys a game of pool and once beat snooker champion Cliff Thorburn in a challenge match.

BECTON, FRANCIS

Inside-left: 86 apps, 41 goals

Born: Preston, Lancashire, 11 May 1873 – *Died*: Liverpool, 6 November 1909

Career: Preston junior football, Fishwick Ramblers (1889), Preston North End (professional, July 1891), LIVERPOOL (£100, March 1895), Sheffield United (October 1898), Bedminster (June 1899), Preston North End (September 1900), Swindon Town (July 1901), Nelson (briefly, March–April 1903), Ashton Town (May 1903), New Brighton Town (August 1904, retired through ill health, October 1904)

A creative footballer with an eye for goal, Frank Becton won two full caps for England (v. Ireland in 1895, scoring twice in a 9–0 win, and Wales in 1897). He also represented the Football League and helped Liverpool win the Second Division championship in 1896, netting 17 goals in 24 games while forming a wonderful left wing partnership with Harry Bradshaw. He died from tuberculosis at the age of 36. Three members of his family all played football at various levels.

BEEBY, AUGUSTUS RICHARD

Goalkeeper: 16 apps

Born: Ashbourne, Derbyshire, 1889 – *Died*: Derby, 1950

Career: Osmaston FC (Ashbourne and District League, 1906), LIVERPOOL (professional, May 1909), Manchester City (May 1911–June 1912)

A capable reserve to the great Sam Hardy, Gus Beeby made his League debut for Liverpool in a 1–1 draw at Arsenal in December 1909. His last 11 senior appearances for the club came during the first half of the following season when he conceded 18 goals. He was also a reserve at Manchester City.

BEGLIN, JAMES MARTIN

Left-back: 98 apps, 3 goals

Born: Waterford, Ireland, 29 July 1963

Career: Shamrock Rovers (August 1980), LIVERPOOL (£5,000, May 1983), Leeds United (free, June 1989), Plymouth Argyle (loan, November–December 1989), Blackburn Rovers (loan, October–November 1990); retired, injured, May 1991); now employed as a football summariser on TV

Jim Beglin fractured his left leg in a tackle with Everton's Gary Stevens during the League Cup quarter-final encounter in January 1987. That was a bitter blow to the Irishman who prior to that had been in excellent form in his preferred left-back position. A League and FA Cup double winner and also the recipient of a Screen Sport Super Cup winner's prize with the Reds in 1985–86, he also played in midfield and was a shrewd reader of the game, fast over the ground, strong in the air and precise with his clearances and passing, often enjoying an occasional excursion upfield. A Second Division championship winner with Leeds in 1990, he was capped 15 times at senior level by the Republic of Ireland and also represented his country in one 'B' and four under-21 internationals. He spent six years at Anfield before moving to Elland Road, signed by manager Howard Wilkinson. After retiring, Beglin found a new niche in broadcasting and is now a regular in the commentary box covering Premiership and Championship matches on Sky Sport. He made 130 senior appearances during his career.

BENNETT, THOMAS SAMUEL
Inside-right: 1 app.
Born: Walton, Liverpool, April 1891 – *Died*: Liverpool, 11 January 1923
Career: Merseyside junior football, LIVERPOOL (professional, November 1916, retired through ill health, November 1919)
Tommy Bennett scored 77 goals in 70 regional games for Liverpool during the last three seasons of wartime football, including 41 in 30 starts in 1917–18. Unfortunately he never got a chance in League action, making only one appearance v. Chelsea before retiring due to health problems. He died of consumption at the age of 31.

BERGER, PATRIK
Forward: 136+60 apps, 35 goals
Born: Prague, Czech Republic, 10 November 1973
Career: Slavia Prague/Czech Republic (amateur, August 1989; professional, November 1991), Borussia Dortmund/Germany (£500,000, August 1995), LIVERPOOL (£3.25m, August 1996), Portsmouth (free, July 2003), Aston Villa (free, July 2005)
Powerful and direct shooting has been the trademark of Patrik Berger over the last decade or so. He was one of the Czech Republic stars in Euro '96 and was immediately signed by Liverpool boss Roy Evans in readiness for the start of the new Premiership season and, tasting English football for the first time, he did very well, scoring 9 goals in 34 games in 4 different competitions. He made his debut against Southampton (home) in September 1996, netted his first two goals in a 5–1 drubbing of Chelsea a fortnight later and gained FA Cup, UEFA Cup and Charity Shield winner's medals in 2001 while also representing his country several times more before moving to Portsmouth on a free transfer in 2003. He added 60 appearances to his tally with Pompey and then left the south coast for Villa Park two years later. The holder of 44 full caps for the Czech Republic (18 goals) and two for Czechoslovakia, Berger was a member of the latter country's under-16 UEFA Championship-winning side in 1990. He scored 24 goals in 89 League games for Slavia Prague and 4 in 25 Bundesliga games for Dortmund.

BERRY, ARTHUR
Wing-forward: 4 apps
Born: Liverpool, 3 January 1888 – *Died*: Liverpool, 15 March 1953
Career: Denstone School (rugby XV, 1904–05, captain 1905–06), Wrexham (March 1907), Wadham College/Oxford University (Blue, 1908), LIVERPOOL (April 1908 and October 1908), Wrexham (March 1909), Everton (August 1909), Fulham (September 1909), Wrexham (December 1909 and November 1911–April 1912), Oxford City (May 1912),

LIVERPOOL (October 1912), Wrexham (October 1912), Oxford City (January 1913), Wrexham (April 1914), Northern Nomads (August 1914, retired, October 1914); called to the bar as a barrister, at Gray's Inn (late October 1914)

One of the most brilliant amateurs of his day, Arthur Berry was capped once by England at senior level v. Ireland in 1909 and on 24 occasions as an amateur between 1908 and 1913. He also gained gold medals at soccer for Great Britain in the 1908 and 1912 Olympics. A direct, clever winger with thought and precision, one contemporary summed up his all-action style as being 'a complete art without tinsel or gaudiness'. He was an FA Amateur Cup winner with Oxford City in 1913 (his only club honour). His father, Edwin, was on Everton's books for a short time and was chairman of Liverpool for five years from 1904 to 1909. He too was a practising solicitor and was certainly responsible in a small way in getting his son a game with the Reds!

BIMPSON, JAMES LOUIS

Inside-right/centre-forward: 100 apps, 40 goals
Born: Rainford, Lancashire, 14 May 1929
Career: Burscough (1951), LIVERPOOL (professional, January 1953), Blackburn Rovers (£6,500, November 1959), Bournemouth and Boscombe Athletic (February 1961), Rochdale (August 1961), Wigan Athletic (July 1963–May 1965)

A totally committed forward, strong in the air, Louis Bimpson's goal-return for Liverpool was exceptionally good. He made his League debut against Aston Villa in March 1953 and was a regular in the side for the first five months of the 1953–54 campaign when he scored some cracking goals including a hat-trick in a 4–4 draw with Manchester United at Anfield. He lost his way somewhat after that (when Billy Liddell was moved to centre-forward) but continued to serve the club splendidly, returning to first-team action with some excellent displays during 1957–58. After moving to Ewood Park, he was switched to the right wing, a position he occupied for Blackburn in their 1960 FA Cup final defeat by Wolves.

BISCAN, IGOR

Midfield/defender: 81+37 apps, 3 goals
Born: Zagreb, Croatia, 4 May 1978
Career: Samobor FC/Croatia (amateur, June 1995; professional, August 1996), Dynamo Zagreb/Croatia (£100,000, March 1998), LIVERPOOL (£3.5m, December 2000), Panathinaikos/Greece (free, July 2005)

A Croatian international (capped 15 times at senior level) Igor Biscan was a member of Liverpool's League Cup, UEFA Cup, European Super Cup and Charity Shield winning sides in 2001. A strong, versatile footballer able to play in a variety of positions, he never produced less than 100 per cent out on the pitch and after some terrific performances he eventually won over the sceptical Anfield supporters. Injury seriously interrupted his final season with the Reds and when his contract ran out he opted for a move to Greece. He made the first of his 118 senior appearances for Liverpool as a substitute against Ipswich Town (home) in December 2000.

BJORNEBYE, STIG INGE
Full-back: 175+9 apps, 4 goals
Born: Elverum, Norway, 11 December 1969
Career: Kongsvinger/Norway (1986), Strommen/Norway (1988), Rosenborg Trondheim/Norway (1990), LIVERPOOL (£600,000, December 1992), Blackburn Rovers (£300,000, June 2000; retired, April 2003); appointed Norwegian national team assistant trainer (July 2004)
Stig Bjornebye, signed by Graeme Souness to replace injury victim David Burrows, was a solid, no-nonsense full-back, clean kicking with good positional sense, who gave Liverpool excellent service for seven and a half years, making 184 senior appearances and gaining a League Cup winner's medal in 1995, a feat he repeated with Blackburn Rovers in 2002. He took time to settle into the English style of play after making his debut for the Reds against Coventry City in December 1992 and was subjected to criticism by certain elements of the Anfield crowd. Shrugging his shoulders, he pulled through bravely and produced some solid performances, his crosses from the left being described as 'inch perfect'. A broken leg, suffered in a freak accident against Southampton when his studs stuck in the turf, causing him to twist awkwardly with no other player involved, put him out of action for quite a while. Replaced by Steve Harkness, he fought hard and long before getting back into the side where he continued to produce the goods to a very high standard. After leaving Anfield he had two fine seasons at Ewood Park before suffering a nasty training ground accident in 2002 which left him with a fractured eye socket. He regained full fitness but a foot injury, which required surgery, laid him low again and this time he failed to recover and was forced to retire at the age of 33. He represented Norway at youth, 'B' and under-21 levels before going on to win a total of 76 full caps.

BLANTHORNE, ROBERT
Inside-right: 2 apps
Born: Birkenhead, 8 January 1884 – *Died*: County Durham, 1965
Career: Rock Ferry (April 1902), Birkenhead FC (August 1906), LIVERPOOL (professional, March 1907), Grimsby Town (August 1907), Newcastle United (£310, May 1908), Hartlepools United (December 1910–May 1911)
Unable to establish himself or, indeed, settle at Liverpool (he played in only two games), Bob Blanthorne was thought by many to be the best marksman in the Second Division in 1907–08, scoring 14 goals in 28 League games for Grimsby. He broke his leg on his debut for Newcastle and was never the same player again.

BLENKINSOP, ERNEST
Left-back: 71 apps
Born: Cudworth near Barnsley, Yorkshire, 20 April 1900 – *Died*: Sheffield, 24 April 1969
Career: Brierley Colliery (1917), Cudworth United Methodists (August 1919),

Hull City (professional, October 1921), Sheffield Wednesday (£1,000, January 1923), LIVERPOOL (£6,500, March 1934), Cardiff City (November 1937), Buxton (August 1939); played as a guest for Halifax Town, Bradford Park Avenue, Bradford City and Hurst FC during WW2; retired 1945 to become a licensee in Sheffield

Ernie Blenkinsop was a superb left-back, rated by far the best in the Football League during the period from 1928 to 1933 when he gained 26 full caps for England. This total stood as a Sheffield Wednesday record for some 30 years until beaten by fellow full-back Ron Staniforth. He also played for the Football League side on eight occasions (1928–34). A player with a polished style, Blenkinsop (nicknamed 'Blenkie') was judicious in tackling, cool and efficient in defence and was exceptional with his clearances, always trying to find a colleague rather than hoofing the ball aimlessly downfield (except when in dangerous situations and under direct pressure from an opponent). He was always perfectly balanced and never seemed to be in a hurry and formed a terrific full-back partnership at Anfield with Tommy Cooper. The recipient of a Second Division championship winner's medal with Wednesday in 1926 (41 games played), three years later Blenkinsop gained a League championship winner's medal and repeated that feat in 1930. Perennially young looking, after captaining the Owls and also England, he joined Liverpool. He made the first of his 71 appearances for the Reds against Birmingham in March 1934 and after that he skippered the side several times. He eventually took his League career appearance record to almost 500 (1921–39). Blenkinsop died just four days after his 69th birthday when still a licensee.

BLORE, REGINALD
Outside-right: 1 app.
Born: Wrexham, 18 March 1942
Career: Liverpool Schools, LIVERPOOL (amateur, April 1957; professional, May 1959), Southport (July 1960), Blackburn Rovers (£6,000, November 1963), Oldham Athletic (£8,500, December 1965), Bangor City (July 1971), Ellesmere Port Town (season 1971–72); later worked in insurance

A Welsh under-23 international, capped whilst with Southport (being that club's first representative player for 30 years), Reg Blore's only senior appearance for Liverpool was against Lincoln City (away) in November 1959 (lost 4–2). He seemed to do better at golf than he did football, winning the Professional Footballers' golf championship in 1968. After leaving football he worked for an insurance company in Maghull, Liverpool.

BOERSMA, PHILIP
Forward: 99+21 apps, 30 goals
Born: Kirkby, Liverpool, 24 September 1949
Career: Liverpool junior football, LIVERPOOL (amateur, then apprentice, September 1965; professional, September 1968), Wrexham (loan, March–April 1970), Middlesbrough (£72,000, December 1975), Luton Town (£35,000, July 1977), Swansea City (£35,000, September 1978, retired,

injured, April 1981); remained in football and became Glasgow Rangers' physiotherapist (1980s), LIVERPOOL (assistant manager/coach, from 1991), Blackburn Rovers (coach, March 2000), Newcastle United (coach, September 2004)

Phil Boersma took his chance in Liverpool's attack in 1972–73 when John Toshack was sidelined through injury. He did well, scored some fine goals and was perhaps unlucky not to have appeared in more matches than he did. However, with competition for places fierce at the time, he chose to leave for pastures new and with his other clubs scored 12 goals in more than 120 senior matches before hanging up his boots at the age of 30. He gained both First Division championship and UEFA Cup winner's medals with Liverpool in 1973. He teamed up with his former Anfield teammate Toshack at Swansea in 1978. One of Liverpool's 'nearly men', Boersma always seemed to be fighting a losing battle, perpetually failing to convince managers Bill Shankly and Bob Paisley that he was capable of producing the goods at the highest level. As a coach, he followed Graeme Souness from Liverpool to Blackburn to Newcastle.

BOVILL, JOHN MCKEOWN

Inside-right: 29 apps, 7 goals

Born: Rutherglen, Lanarkshire, 21 March 1886 – *Died*: Glasgow, 1935

Career: Junior football in Scotland, Glasgow Rangers (season 1907–08), Blackburn Rovers (April 1908), Chesterfield Town (1909), LIVERPOOL (April 1911), Linfield (July 1914, retired 1919); subsequently returned to Scotland where he became a shipyard worker

A clever, scheming inside-forward with good, close control, Jock Bovill played in just two games for Rangers; he failed to get a senior outing with Blackburn and scored 3 goals in 18 League fixtures for Chesterfield before spending three seasons with Liverpool. He made his debut for the Reds at Bolton Wanderers in September 1911 and netted the first of his seven goals against Notts County in early November. However, niggling injuries affected his game after that and in the end he chose to try his luck, with some success, in Ireland, winning the Irish Cup with Linfield in 1915 and 1916.

BOWEN, GEORGE JOHN

Outside-right/outside-left: 2 apps

Born: Walsall, July 1875 – *Died*: Walsall, *circa* 1945

Career: Bridgetown Amateurs (Walsall and District League, 1895), Wolverhampton Wanderers (professional, July 1899), LIVERPOOL (with George Fleming, May 1901), Wolverhampton Wanderers (November 1901), Burslem Port Vale (briefly, semi-retired, April 1905), Bloxwich Strollers (season 1905–06); later worked in a factory in Bilston, West Midlands, and continued to play for several local non-League sides up to 1912

After making more than 50 appearances for Wolves in two seasons, George Bowen was signed by Liverpool along with George Fleming, his Molineux teammate. Fleming settled in well at Anfield, but Bowen didn't and he quickly returned to Wolves having played in just two games for the Reds, the first at outside-right in a 2–2 draw with Everton in September 1901 when Tom Robertson was absent, allowing John Cox to switch to the left. His son, David Bowen, played for Walsall in 1924–25.

BOWYER, SAMUEL
Forward: 48 apps, 16 goals
Born: Northwich, 12 October 1887 – *Died*: 11 April 1961
Career: Earlstown (Lancashire Combination, 1905), LIVERPOOL (July 1907), Bristol City (February 1912), Bedminster (May 1913–April 1915); did not play after WW1

A member of a strong Earlstown side that gained promotion to the First Division of the Lancashire Combination, Sam Bowyer made the rise from non-League football look easy as he quickly settled into his new surroundings, making his Liverpool debut against Manchester United in September 1907. A versatile player who occupied every forward position for the Reds, he was handed only four League appearances that season and fourteen the following year when he also scored his first goal, following up with a brace in a 5–1 home win over Arsenal in January 1910. He appeared in 50 senior games for Bristol City (14 goals).

BRADLEY, JAMES EDWIN
Left-half: 184 apps, 8 goals
Born: Goldenhill, Stoke-on-Trent, 5 May 1881 – *Died*: Blackpool, 12 March 1954
Career: Potteries junior football, Stoke (amateur, February 1898; professional, August 1898), LIVERPOOL (September 1905), Reading (July 1911), Stoke (August 1913–May 1915); guest for LIVERPOOL (season 1916–17); became a part-time coach to Stoke reserves after WW1; also worked for the Stoke-on-Trent Highways Department

A model of consistency, Jimmy Bradley made 256 appearances in his two spells with Stoke (whom he helped win the Southern League Second Division title in 1915), plus 60 for Reading and his 184 for Liverpool. He moved to Anfield after turning down an offer from Plymouth Argyle and gained a League championship medal with the Reds in 1906, missing only two games. He also represented the Football League against the Scottish League in 1906 and was unlucky not to win a full England cap, being passed over in favour of Bob Hawkes (Luton Town). Bradley, who made 13 WW1 appearances for the Reds as a guest from Stoke and was a great practical joker, had his contract cancelled by Reading after tossing the entire first-team kit into the bath in a rage of temper. His brother, Martin Bradley, played for Sheffield United, Grimsby Town and Bristol Rovers.

BRADSHAW, THOMAS

Centre-half: 291 apps, 4 goals

Born: Bishopton, Renfrewshire, 7 February 1904 – *Died*: Liverpool, 22 February 1986

Career: Woodside Juniors (North-West Lanarkshire League, 1920), Bury (professional, July 1922), LIVERPOOL (£8,000, January 1930), Third Lanark (September 1938), South Liverpool (February 1939), Norwich City (chief scout, 1940s); also worked for a Preston-based insurance company

A Scottish international, capped as a Bury player against England in 1928 when the Scots (dubbed the 'Wembley Wizards' and 'Blue Devils') won convincingly by 5–1, 'Tiny' Bradshaw was a strapping six-footer, strong in defence and attack and loved to carry the ball forward over the halfway line. Massively built, he was surprisingly delicate in his overall play (some described him as being as dainty as a ballet dancer) and he certainly gave Liverpool wonderful service for more than eight years. One of the club's finest-ever half-backs, he made his debut for the Reds a week after joining in January 1930, lining up against Manchester United at Anfield (won 1–0).

BRADSHAW, THOMAS HENRY

Forward: 138 apps, 54 goals

Born: Liverpool, 24 August 1873 – *Died*: Tottenham, North London, 25 December 1899

Career: Liverpool Nomads (1889), Northwich Victoria (May 1891), LIVERPOOL (August 1893), Tottenham Hotspur (May 1898), Thames Ironworks, now West Ham United (July 1899, retired through ill heath, November 1899)

Durable 'Harry' Bradshaw started out as an inside- or centre-forward before developing into a wonderful left-winger, fast and tricky with a strong shot. He scored on his League debut for Liverpool in a comprehensive 5–0 home win over Arsenal in October 1893. At the end of that season he scored the crucial opening goal as the Reds went on to beat Newton Heath (now Manchester United) 2–0 in a Test match to gain promotion from the Second Division. Bradshaw then finished up as Liverpool's top scorer in 1893–94, having the pleasure of claiming the club's first-ever goal in the top flight, in a 1–1 opening day draw at Blackburn. Following demotion, he gained a second Second Division championship medal in 1896 and followed that up by gaining an England cap v. Ireland in February 1897 (won 6–0). He twice represented the Football League, against the Scottish League and Irish League in season 1896–97, and played for the South v. the North in an international trial (as a Spurs player). Bradshaw was only 26 when he died and on 2 April 1900, Spurs met Thames Ironworks in a match to raise funds for his dependants.

BRATLEY, PHILIP WRIGHT

Defender: 13 apps

Born: Rawmarsh, 26 December 1880 – *Died*: Batley, Yorkshire, 1962

Career: Rawmarsh FC (1896), Doncaster Rovers (professional, April 1902),

Rotherham County (1904), Barnsley (May 1910), LIVERPOOL (with Wilf Bartrop, May 1914–April 1915); did not play after WW1

Phil Bratley occupied the left-back, right-half and centre-half positions for Barnsley for whom he made well over 100 senior appearances, gaining an FA Cup winner's medal in 1912, along with another future Liverpool star, Wilf Bartrop. A strong tackler, he succeeded England international Tommy Doyle at Oakwell and had been in good form for the Reds (as deputy to Harry Lowe) when his career (like that of so many other footballers) came to a shuddering end owing to WW1. He served in the Army between 1915 and 1918.

BRIERLEY, KENNETH

Left-half/outside-left: 59 apps, 8 goals
Born: Ashton-under-Lyne, 3 April 1926
Career: Range Boilers FC (Oldham, 1942), Oldham Athletic (professional, April 1945), LIVERPOOL (£7,000, February 1948), Oldham Athletic (£2,750, March 1953), Stalybridge Celtic (May 1955), Mossley (August 1956–April 1958)

A strong and willing defender with good control and passing ability, Ken Brierley appeared in 125 League games in his two spells with Oldham, helping the Latics win the Third Division (N) championship in 1953, having 15 outings, the majority at left-half. He did well enough with Liverpool, for whom he made his debut in March 1948 in a 4–0 win over Huddersfield Town, having a hand in two of Albert Stubbins' four goals.

BROMILOW, GEORGE THOMAS

Left-half: 375 apps, 11 goals
Born: Liverpool, 7 October 1894 – *Died*: Nuneaton, 4 March 1959
Career: Fonthill Road School (Liverpool), West Dingle FC (Liverpool and District League), Army football (1915–18), United West Dingle Presbyterian Club (Liverpool), LIVERPOOL (professional, April 1919, retired, May 1930); coach in Amsterdam (season 1931–32), Burnley (manager, October 1932), Crystal Palace (manager, July 1935, resigned, June 1936; in charge again from December 1936 to May 1939), Leicester City (manager, July 1939–May 1945), coach in Holland (season 1945–46), Newport County (manager, May 1946–January 1950), Leicester City (chief scout and trainer, July 1950 until his death)

An England international left-half rewarded with five caps between 1921 and 1926, Tom Bromilow also played six times for the Football League and was the brains of Liverpool's successive League championship-winning sides of 1922 and 1923. A constructive footballer, crisp in the tackle with fine passing ability, he was invalided out of the Army due to septic poisoning. He recovered from that ailment and gave Liverpool wonderful service for 11 years. After playing in one game at the end of the 1918–19 wartime season (with Jim Penman against Stockport County) he made his League debut against his future club Burnley at Turf Moor in October 1919 (won 2–1) and played his 375th and final game for the Reds against Blackburn Rovers at Ewood Park in May 1930 (lost 1–0). In his first season in charge of Burnley they just escaped relegation to the Third Division. He turned things round and in 1935 the Clarets reached the FA Cup semi-final, beaten by Sheffield Wednesday, and he was the man who sold 17-year-old Tommy Lawton to Everton (and not Liverpool) for a huge fee of £6,500. Bromilow resigned as boss of Crystal Palace following a row with the directors but was re-appointed six months later. He then guided the London club to the runners-up spot in the Third Division (S) in 1938–39 before taking over at Leicester City, who won the Midland Cup in 1941 and the Midland League (S) in 1942. He then spent a year coaching in Holland before taking over at Newport County in May 1946. However, County finished bottom of the Second Division in 1947 after conceding 133 goals. Bromilow sadly died on a train at Nuneaton railway station when returning home from watching a game. His brother-in-law was Theo Kelly, Everton's long-serving secretary-manager from 1936 to 1948.

BROUGH, JOSEPH
Inside-right: 10 apps, 3 goals
Born: Burslem, Stoke-on-Trent, 9 November 1886 – *Died*: Stockton Brook, Staffs, 5 October 1968
Career: Burslem Park Boys (1902), Smallthorne FC (1903), Burslem Port Vale (amateur, October 1906; professional February 1907), Stoke (September 1907), Tottenham Hotspur (July 1908), Burslem Port Vale (June 1909), LIVERPOOL (August 1910), Bristol City (January 1912), Port Vale (April 1913); conscripted into the Army, June 1917; re-signed by Port Vale (October 1919, retired May 1922)
After doing well in the Potteries with Vale and Stoke, Joe Brough was signed by Spurs just after the London club had gained entry to the Football League. He was hampered by ill health at White Hart Lane and made only two senior appearances for the Londoners before returning to Vale. He then had a brief spell with Liverpool, for whom he made his debut against Blackburn Rovers (away) in September 1910 and after 15 months with Bristol City he ended his career back in Stoke-on-Trent. He eventually retired with 209 first-team appearances under his belt for Vale, helping them win both the Staffordshire Junior and Senior Cups and share the Staffordshire Infirmary Cup.

BROWNBILL, DEREK ANTHONY
Forward: 1 app.
Born: Liverpool, 4 February 1954
Career: LIVERPOOL (apprentice, March 1970; professional, February 1972), Port Vale (£6,000, February 1975), Cleveland Cobras/USA (May 1980), Wigan Athletic (September 1978–May 1980); later with Stafford Rangers, Oswestry Town, Morecambe, Witton Albion, Warrington Town (player-manager), Curzon Ashton (manager)
A well-built, stocky forward, Derek Brownbill's only League outing for Liverpool came in the 1–1 draw with Birmingham City at St Andrew's in September 1973 when he deputised for Steve Heighway in a re-arranged attack. He scored 19 goals in 108 games for Port Vale and 8 in 53 for Wigan.

BROWNING, JOHN
Left-half: 19 apps
Born: Alexandria, Dunbartonshire, 27 January 1915 – *Died*: 14 August 1971
Career: Bridgton Waverley (1931), Dunoon Athletic (1932), LIVERPOOL (professional, March 1934–May 1939); did not play after WW2

A versatile footballer, John Browning appeared in five different positions during his career but preferred the left-half berth where he made his Liverpool debut (in place of Jimmy McDougall) in a 6–0 home League win over his father's former club, Chelsea. He was basically a reserve during his five years at Anfield, having his best run in the first team during September 1935. His father, John senior, was a Scottish international who also starred for Celtic, for whom he netted 66 goals in 217 games between 1911 and 1919.

BRUTON, LESLIE HECTOR RONALD
Inside-left: 9 apps, 1 goal
Born: Coventry, 1 April 1903 – *Died*: Coventry, 2 April 1989
Career: Foleshill FC (August 1919), Southampton (professional, November 1922), Peterborough and Fletton United (June 1926), Raith Rovers (November 1927), Blackburn Rovers (£10,000, May 1929), LIVERPOOL (February 1932), Leamington Town (July 1933, retired May 1935); later joined Coventry City's training staff

After failing to make an impression with Southampton, for whom he played just seven games, Les Bruton returned to non-League action and then had a spell in Scotland before his big-money transfer to Blackburn Rovers where he linked up with his namesake and England international Jack Bruton. He scored 23 goals in 38 outings for Rovers and then assisted Liverpool briefly, making his debut for the Reds in a 0–0 draw at West Ham United in February 1932 and netting his only goal in a 2–0 win at Chelsea ten months later. He was a member of Coventry's backroom staff for 20 years.

BUCK, FREDERICK RICHARD
Centre-half/inside-forward: 13 apps, 1 goal
Born: Newcastle-under-Lyme, Staffs, 12 July 1880 – *Died*: Stafford, 7 June 1952
Career: Stafford Wesleyans (August 1895), Stafford Rangers (July 1897), West Bromwich Albion (professional, November 1900), LIVERPOOL (May 1903), Plymouth Argyle (January 1904), West Bromwich Albion (April 1906), Swansea Town (May 1914, retired May 1917); served in the Army in France during WW1; later became a licensee in Stafford, remaining in the trade for 24 years

One of the smallest centre-halves ever to appear in an FA Cup final, Fred Buck was 5ft 4in. tall when he lined up for West Bromwich Albion against Barnsley in 1912, collecting a runners-up medal to go with the Second Division championship-winner's medal he gained the previous season. He made 319 appearances and scored 94 goals in his two spells at The Hawthorns, initially serving the Baggies as a forward before being successfully converted into a defender. He represented both the Football League (with Albion) and the South

League (with Plymouth) either side of his association with Liverpool for whom he made his debut at inside-right against Nottingham Forest (away) on the opening day of the 1903–04 season, and scored his only goal for the Reds in a 2–1 home League defeat by Blackburn Rovers on Boxing Day. He never settled on Merseyside and moved south to Devon after seven months.

BULL, BENJAMIN HENRY

Outside-right: 1 app., 1 goal
Born: Leicester, May 1873 – *Died*: Liverpool, *circa* 1933
Career: Loughborough (August 1893), LIVERPOOL (seasons 1895–97)
A reserve team player with the Reds for two seasons, Ben Bull scored in his only game for the club, in a 6–1 League drubbing of Lincoln City at Anfield in January 1896 when he deputised on the right wing for Malcolm McVean. Also able to play on the opposite flank, he netted once in seven outings for Loughborough.

BURKINSHAW, KEITH HENRY

Centre-half: 1 app.
Born: Higham near Barnsley, 23 June 1935
Career: Denaby United (August 1950), Wolverhampton Wanderers (amateur, August 1952), LIVERPOOL (professional, November 1953), Workington (£2,500, December 1957, player-manager, November 1964–March 1965), Scunthorpe United (player, June 1965, retired, May 1968), Newcastle United (assistant coach, 1968, first-team coach, August 1971–May 1975), Tottenham Hotspur (chief coach, June 1975, manager July 1976–May 1984), Bahrain (national team coach, June 1984), Sporting Lisbon/Portugal (coach, 1987–88), Gillingham (manager, October 1988–April 1989), Swindon Town (chief scout, seasons 1989–92), West Bromwich Albion (assistant manager, May 1992, manager July 1993–October 1994), Aberdeen (Director of Football, 1995–97); technical adviser and scout for several clubs (between 1997 and 2005); Watford (assistant manager, from March 2005)
Apart from his one game for Liverpool v. Port Vale at Anfield in April 1955, the rest of centre-half Keith Burkinshaw's playing career was spent in the lower divisions. A hard-working defender, he made over 400 senior appearances in total before becoming a highly respected coach and manager. He assembled a terrific side at Spurs and guided them out of the Second Division in 1978 (they finished in third place), to two FA Cup final victories (in 1981 v. Manchester City and 1982 v. QPR), to the League Cup final of 1982 (beaten by Liverpool) and to UEFA Cup glory in 1984 when they defeated RSC Anderlecht in a penalty shoot-out in the final. He quit his job at White Hart Lane after becoming disillusioned following a boardroom takeover. He later replaced the Argentinian World Cup winner Ossie Ardiles as manager of West Bromwich Albion.

BURROWS, DAVID
Left-back: 181+12 apps, 3 goals
Born: Dudley, West Midlands, 25 October 1968
Career: St Martin's Junior and Alexandra High Schools (Tipton), West Bromwich District and West Midlands County Schools, Bustleholme Boys (West Bromwich), West Bromwich Albion (apprentice, April 1985; professional, October 1986), LIVERPOOL (£625,000, October 1988), West Ham United (£2.5m exchange deal involving Mike Marsh for Julian Dicks, September 1993), Everton (player-exchange deal involving Tony Cottee, September 1994), Coventry City (£1.1m, March 1995), Birmingham City (free, July 2000), Sheffield Wednesday (free, March 2002, retired May 2003), Studley FC (season 2003–04); emigrated to France (summer, 2004); also coached Alexandra FC (Tipton) on Sundays (1987–88)

David Burrows made his Football League debut for West Bromwich Albion against his future club Sheffield Wednesday in April 1986 while still an apprentice at The Hawthorns. He developed fast and in 1988 Kenny Dalglish signed him for Liverpool. He went from strength to strength at Anfield, gaining three England 'B' caps and seven at under-21 level and was rewarded with winner's medals for triumphs in the FA Charity Shield (1989), League Championship (1990) and FA Cup (1992) while making almost 200 appearances for the Reds. Burrows ('Bugsy' to the fans) preferred the left-back position but could also play in central defence. He spent a season with the Hammers before going back to Merseyside to sign for Everton. He never settled at Goodison Park and after that appeared in over 100 League games for Coventry before winding down his career at St Andrew's and Hillsborough. He captained Wednesday on occasions but he suffered injury problems and his experience and leadership were sorely missed as the Owls struggled against relegation. Burrows retired from competitive football with 496 club and international appearances under his belt.

BUSBY, SIR MATTHEW, CBE
Right-half: 125 apps, 3 goals
Born: Orbiston near Belshill, Lanarkshire, 26 May 1909 – *Died*: Manchester, 20 January 1994
Career: Orbiston Village FC (1923), Alpine Villa (1924), Denny Hibernian (1927), Manchester City (professional, February 1928), LIVERPOOL (£8,000, March 1936); guest for Bournemouth, Brentford, Chelsea, Hibernian, Middlesbrough and Reading during WW2; retired, October 1945; Manchester United (manager, initially appointed as player-manager in February 1945, took up the position as manager in October 1945; administration manager, June 1969, acting team manager, December 1970–July 1971, club director, October 1971–August 1980; United president, March 1980); also member of the Football League Management Committee (from June 1973), Football League vice-president (February–July 1982); then appointed Life Member of the Club; also Scotland team manager (1958–59)

Originally a moderate performer at inside-forward, Matt Busby developed into a wonderful right-half who represented Scotland in both peacetime and wartime internationals. He possessed all the skills, used the ball decisively and well and was always totally committed. He made 226 League and Cup appearances for Manchester City before joining Liverpool with whom he remained a registered player until announcing his retirement in October 1945 to take over as boss of Manchester United – a position he had agreed to six months earlier. He made his debut (in place of Bob Savage) for Liverpool against Huddersfield Town in March 1936 – the first of 151 games he played in for the club, including wartime fixtures. He scored his first goal in the red strip in a 2–2 draw at Blackburn a month later and in 1944 gained a League (N) Cup winner's medal after Bolton Wanderers had been beaten 6–3 on aggregate in the final and in all, made 26 WW2 appearances for the club. In fact, during the hostilities, Busby played an awful lot of football. He starred in seven wartime internationals for Scotland, all against England between 1941 and 1946, and in the encounters at Wembley Stadium and Hampden Park in January and April 1942 respectively, his fellow wing-half was Bill Shankly. He represented the British Army v. the French Army, an FA XI versus a Yorkshire XI and a British XI against the Football League, all in 1940; he played for the Scottish League v. the Football League and the British XI against the Football League in 1941; starred for the Army (Scotland) v. the Army (England) in 1941, 1942 and 1944 and was wing-half for the Scottish Command v. the Scottish Select and the Northern Command, also in 1942; he lined up for the Combined Services versus both England and Ireland, the FA Services v. Belgium, the Western Command v. the RAF, the Army v. the RAF and the Combined Services as well as for Scotland v. the RAF, all in 1944; the following year he assisted the South East Command against the AA Command and also a Berks and Bucks XI against the FA XI.

In 1928, Busby was preparing to emigrate to the USA when he was approached by Manchester City manager Peter Hodge. He never looked back after that and had a wonderful life in football, especially as manager at Old Trafford where he worked wonders and became one of the great club managers of modern times.

He played in two successive FA Cup finals for Manchester City (losing in 1933 and winning in 1934), won his only full cap v. Wales in 1933 and as a manager (a brilliant one at that) he guided United to five League championship triumphs (1952, 1956, 1957, 1965 and 1967), to two FA Cup final victories (1948 and 1963) and to European Cup glory (1968). He also saw United lose two FA Cup finals (1957 and 1958 – the first when they were going for the double), win three FA Charity Shields outright and his youngsters clinch the FA Youth Cup a record six times (five coming in succession from 1953). He assembled some terrific sides at Old Trafford – especially the Busby Babes of the 1950s – and his team of 1958 would surely have won the European Cup had not that tragic plane crash on a snowbound Munich runway (in which Busby was seriously injured) taken the lives of most of the star players, including the great Duncan Edwards, skipper Roger Byrne and centre-forward Tommy Taylor. Busby was awarded the CBE in 1958 and a knighthood ten years later. Awarded the Freedom of the City of Manchester in 1967, he was one of the great men of that city and literally thousands attended his funeral in 1994.

BUSH, WILLIAM THOMAS

Half-back/left-back: 72 apps, 1 goal

Born: Hodnet, Salop, 22 February 1914 – *Died*: Liverpool, 20 December 1969

Career: Shrewsbury Amateurs (from August 1929), LIVERPOOL (professional, March 1933); guest for Fulham and Leeds United during WW2; retired May 1947; coach in Holland; LIVERPOOL (junior coach and office staff, 1950s/early '60s)

Tom Bush, almost 6ft 2in. tall, served Liverpool for over 25 years. A competent footballer, he made his League debut against Wolves in December 1933 and played his second game 48 hours later at Newcastle. However, owing to the form of Jimmy McDougall, Norman Low and 'Tiny' Bradshaw, he had to wait two and a half years before his third game v. Huddersfield Town in March 1936. Blessed with an ideal physique for a defender, like so many other players he lost seven years from his career due to war but always came up smiling, no matter what the circumstances. He and Bill Jones, ex-Liverpool centre-half (q.v.), were instrumental in bringing Roger Hunt (q.v.) to Anfield.

BYRNE, GERALD

Full-back: 332+1 apps, 4 goals

Born: Liverpool, 29 August 1938

Career: LIVERPOOL (amateur, August 1953; professional, August 1955, retired, knee injury, December 1969; later worked on the club's coaching staff)

Gerry Byrne was a courageous, solid and uncompromising left-back who played 117 minutes of the 1965 FA Cup final against Leeds United with a broken collarbone following a collision with Bobby Collins. It was well worth the effort and pain as he went up to collect his winner's medal after the Reds' 2–1 extra-time win, having a year earlier helped his colleagues win the League title, two seasons after they had clinched the Second Division championship. In 1966 he added a second League championship medal to his tally and gained a runners-up medal in the 1966 European Cup-Winners' Cup final. In this very same year he was also named in Alf Ramsey's final 22 for the World Cup finals but wasn't selected for any of the matches. An England international at under-23 level, Byrne won two full caps (v. Scotland in 1963 and Norway in 1966) and he spent over 25 years at Anfield as a player and coach. Byrne, a resolute defender who gave nothing away, conceded an own goal in the first of his 333 senior outings for the Reds in a 5–1 League defeat at the hands of Charlton Athletic at The Valley in September 1957 when he deputised for Ronnie Moran, whom he replaced in 1960 before switching flanks to become Moran's partner in 1962. In later years Byrne formed a superb full-back pairing with Chris Lawler. Liverpool boss Bill Shankly said, soon after Byrne announced his retirement: 'When he went, it took a big chunk out of Liverpool. Something special was missing.'

CADDEN, JOSEPH YOUNG

Centre-half: 4 apps
Born: Glasgow, 13 April 1920 – *Died:* Glasgow, 1981
Career: Glasgow Welfare (1938), Brooklyn Wanderers/USA (1938–48), LIVERPOOL (June 1948), Grimsby Town (July 1952), Accrington Stanley (June 1953, released April 1954), New Brighton (briefly from August 1955, retired injured, late 1956)

Joe Cadden, a well-built Scottish-born defender, took the unusual route into the Football League – travelling via America to Anfield shortly after WW2, and signed after starring against Liverpool when they were on tour in the States. He made only four League appearances for the Reds – the first against Fulham, away, in September 1950 – and after leaving Anfield he understudied Duncan McMillan at Grimsby. He suffered a serious back injury early in 1954 and played very little competitive football after that. He only made 22 League appearances during his career.

CALLAGHAN, IAN ROBERT, MBE

Outside-right/-left (midfield): 851+5 apps, 69 goals
Born: Liverpool, 10 April 1942
Career: St Patrick's RC School (Liverpool), Liverpool and Merseyside Boys, LIVERPOOL (£10 signing-on fee, amateur, May 1957; professional, March 1960), Swansea City (September 1978–January 1981); Cork Hibernian (February–March 1981), Sandefjord/Norway (April–June 1981), Crewe Alexandra (October 1981, retired, February 1982); now living and working near Liverpool and is an occasional after-dinner speaker

Described by manager Bill Shankly as 'the model professional', Ian Callaghan served Liverpool superbly well for more than 21 years and is now the club's record appearance-maker (at senior level) with 856 games under his belt (including 676 in the Football League and 88 in Europe). He also holds the national record for playing in most FA Cup ties – 88 – of which 79 came with Liverpool. A very thoughtful yet positive player, confident in his own ability, he made his debut for the Reds as an orthodox outside-right against Bristol Rovers in April 1960 (after starting out as a right-half) and received applause from his colleagues and opponents as well as the fans for an excellent display as his side won 4–0. Later he played as a wide midfielder (on both flanks) and made his final appearance for the club against Nottingham Forest in the replay of the League Cup final at Old Trafford in March 1978. Capped by England four times (twice in 1966, twice in 1977), he also played in four under-23 internationals and he helped Liverpool win the Second Division title in 1962, the League championship in 1964, 1966, 1973, 1976 and 1977, the FA Cup in 1965 and 1974, the UEFA Cup in 1973 and 1976 and the European Cup in 1977. He also starred in two Charity Shield winning sides (plus three shared) and collected runners-up medals for defeats in the European Cup-Winners' Cup final of 1966, in two FA Cup finals of 1971 and 1977 and the 1978 League Cup final. He was voted FWA 'Footballer of the Year' in 1974 and was a member of England's 1966 World Cup winning squad (playing in two group games). With

Callaghan on the right and Peter Thompson on the left, Liverpool boasted the best pair of wingers in top-class football since WW2. After leaving Anfield, 'Cally' was reunited with two of his former colleagues, John Toshack and Phil Boersma, at Swansea and he duly helped the Welsh club gain promotion into the Second Division in 1979. He was awarded the MBE in 1973.

CAMARA, ABOUBACAR SIDIKI

Striker: 24+13 apps, 10 goals
Born: Donka, Guinea, 17 November 1972
Career: St Etienne/France (professional, April 1990), RC Lens/France (£400,000, August 1995), Olympique Marseille/France (£600,000, July 1997), LIVERPOOL (£2.6m, June 1999), West Ham United (£1.5m, December 2000), Al-Ittihad/Saudi Arabia (January 2003)

A Guinea international, fast and direct, 'Titi' Camara has 24 senior caps under his belt. Following his big-money transfer to the Reds, he made a sensational start to his Liverpool career, scoring some stunning goals and producing several excellent performances. Indeed, he netted on his Premiership debut v. Sheffield Wednesday in August 1999 and claimed 10 goals in his first season, finishing second in the charts behind Michael Owen (12). Always seen with a smile on his face, he proved to be a great favourite with the fans and it was perhaps disappointing to see him leave the club after 18 months of some highly entertaining, all-action performances. He was out injured for quite some time at West Ham and made only 14 appearances for the Londoners before moving to Saudi Arabia. Earlier he scored 38 goals in 218 League games in France (16 in 94 for St Etienne).

CAMERON, JAMES

Left-back/half-back/forward: 16 apps, 5 goals
Born: Glasgow, *circa* 1868 – *Died*: Glasgow, 1934
Career: Cardonald Juniors (Glasgow), Glasgow Perthshire (1888), LIVERPOOL (August 1892), Linthouse Rangers FC (March 1893), Glasgow (August 1893), LIVERPOOL (June 1894–May 1895), Pollockshields (August 1895–May 1897)

Jock Cameron had two spells with Liverpool. He did very well for the club during the 1892–93 season, scoring 4 goals in 12 games and gaining a Lancashire League winner's medal. He then returned home before rejoining the Reds in 1894 by which time he had been successfully converted into a defender. He made only four more senior appearances. His brother, John (born in Glasgow, 1868), played inside-left for Renton, Stoke and Hibernian during the 1890s.

There are some conflicting references regarding this player. Some indicate that he may have played for Glasgow Rangers (1883–87) and had only one prolonged spell with Liverpool. Another says he played briefly for Rangers prior to his return to Liverpool.

CAMPBELL, DONALD

Left-half: 58 apps, 3 goals

Born: Bootle, 19 October 1932

Career: Bootle Schools, LIVERPOOL (professional, November 1950), Crewe
  Alexandra (£4,000, July 1958), Gillingham (trial, July–August 1962, signed
  permanently, September 1962), Folkestone Town (August 1964–May 1966)

An England youth international, Don Campbell made his First Division debut
for Liverpool at inside-right against Sunderland at Roker Park in November
1953, but it was in the left-half position he enjoyed playing most. Unable to gain
a regular place in the Reds' first XI, he went on to appear in 149 League games
for Crewe and 29 for Gillingham.

CAMPBELL, KENNETH

Goalkeeper: 142 apps

Born: Cambuslang, Lanarkshire, 6 September 1892 – *Died*: Macclesfield, 28
  April 1971

Career: Rutherglen Glencairn/Glasgow (April 1908), Cambuslang Rangers
  (August 1909), LIVERPOOL (May 1911), Partick Thistle (£1,750, April
  1920), New Brighton (June 1922), Stoke (March 1923), Leicester City
  (November 1925), New Brighton (November 1929, retired June 1931); ran a
  sports shop in Wallasey (opened in 1922) and the business was still going
  strong well into the 1990s

A brilliant Scottish international goalkeeper, popular everywhere he played,
Kenny Campbell was cool, confident and ultra-reliable. A very modest man, he
was adept at dealing with ground shots and was also brave, thinking nothing
about diving at a player's feet or flying, fists at the ready, into a ruck of attackers
at set pieces. He made his debut for Liverpool against Blackburn Rovers (away)
in February 1912 when he deputised for the great Sam Hardy, from whom he
took over on a regular basis later that same year. Capped eight times by his
country during the early 1920s, Campbell also made one appearance for the
Scottish League and helped Liverpool reach the 1914 FA Cup final, later
collecting a winner's medal in the Scottish equivalent with Partick Thistle
(1921). He made 400 club appearances during his career, including another 37
for Liverpool during WW1.

CAMPBELL, ROBERT

Wing-half: 14 apps, 1 goal

Born: Liverpool, 23 April 1937

Career: Liverpool Schools, LIVERPOOL (amateur, May 1952; professional,
  May 1954), Wigan Athletic (June 1961), Portsmouth (£1,000, paid to
  Liverpool, November 1961), Aldershot (July 1966, retired, injured, May
  1967), Portsmouth (coach, August 1967–May 1972), Queens Park Rangers
  (coach, August 1972–May 1973), Arsenal (coach, September 1973–June
  1976), Fulham (chief scout and part-time coach, July 1976, manager
  December 1976–October 1980), Aldershot (assistant manager, November
  1980), Portsmouth (March 1982–May 1984), Arsenal (assistant manager, July

1984), Queens Park Rangers (reserve team coach, 1986), Chelsea (coach, February 1988, caretaker-manager, March 1988, manager, May 1988–May 1991)

An England youth international, Bobby Campbell won more fame as a manager than he did as a player. In fact, during his playing days he mustered only 90 League appearances in 15 years, 61 with Portsmouth. His debut for Liverpool came in November 1953 v. Sunderland (away) and his only goal for the club came in a 4–1 home win over Bristol Rovers in April 1957. He built up a fine reputation as a coach with QPR and Arsenal and then did very well as a manager, leading Portsmouth to the Third Division title in 1983, Chelsea to the Second Division championship in 1989 and to Full Members' Cup glory at Wembley in 1990. He was replaced in the Fulham hot seat by Malcolm Macdonald, at Portsmouth by Alan Ball and at Chelsea by Ian Porterfield.

CARLIN, JOHN

Forward: 34 apps, 8 goals
Born: Liverpool, 1880 – *Died*: *circa* 1950
Career: Merseyside junior football, LIVERPOOL (professional, April 1902), Preston North End (May 1907–April 1909)

A First Division championship-winner with Liverpool in 1905–06, John Carlin was a resolute, dashing versatile forward with an eye for goal. He made his League debut in January 1903 in the centre-forward position against Stoke (lost 1–0) and netted his first goal for the Reds in a 2–2 draw at West Bromwich Albion in January 1904. He netted 5 times in 32 League outings for Preston.

CARLIN, WILLIAM

Inside-forward: 1 app.
Born: Liverpool, 6 October 1940
Career: Liverpool Schools, LIVERPOOL (amateur, April 1956; professional, May 1958), Halifax Town (£1,500, August 1962), Carlisle United (£10,000, October 1964), Sheffield United (£40,000, November 1967), Derby County (£63,000, August 1968), Leicester City (£35,000, October 1970), Notts County (£18,000, September 1971), Cardiff City (loan, October 1973, signed, free, November 1973, retired, May 1974); he later ran a newsagent's shop in Derby and lived for a time in Majorca

Capped by England at both schoolboy and youth team levels, Willie Carlin's only senior outing for Liverpool was against Brighton and Hove Albion (home) in a Second Division match in October 1959 when he set up one of his side's goals in a 2–2 draw. Failing to establish himself in the Reds' side, he subsequently joined Halifax Town and in later years developed into an exceptionally fine inside-forward, amassing 445 League appearances and scoring 74 goals. He helped Carlisle win the Third Division championship in 1965 and both Derby County and Leicester City the Second Division in 1969 and 1971 respectively.

CARNEY, LEONARD FRANCIS

Inside-forward: 6 apps, 1 goal
Born: Liverpool, 30 May 1915 – *Died*: Liverpool, 1996
Career: Collegiate Old Boys (Liverpool), LIVERPOOL (amateur, August 1944–April 1948)

Len Carney spent two seasons as an amateur at Anfield, scoring on his League debut against Sheffield United (away) on the opening Saturday of the 1946–47 campaign to earn his side a 1–0 win. He acted as reserve to several top-line inside-forwards and scored 15 goals in 33 WW2 games for the Reds.

CARR, LANCE LANYON

Outside-left: 33 apps, 8 goals
Born: Johannesburg, South Africa, 18 February 1910 – *Died*: South Africa, 1983
Career: Johannesburg Callies/South Africa (1927), Boksburg FC/South Africa (1929), LIVERPOOL (professional, August 1933), Newport County (October 1936), South Liverpool (August 1937), Newport County (May 1938); guest for Aldershot, Bristol City and Swindon Town during WW2; Bristol Rovers (August 1946, retired May 1947); returned to South Africa

Joining Liverpool around the same time as 'Nivvy' Nieuwenhuys, Lance Carr made his first two League appearances for the club at inside-left against Manchester City and Newcastle United in December 1933, before switching to the wing where he produced some excellent displays. He later starred in Newport County's Third Division (S) winning side of 1938–39. The son of a professional athlete, Carr was one of the fastest players ever to don a Liverpool shirt. He made 98 League appearances during his career (42 for Bristol Rovers).

CARRAGHER, JAMES LEE DUNCAN

Defender: 400+16 apps, 3 goals
Born: Bootle, 28 January 1978
Career: LIVERPOOL (apprentice, April 1994; professional, October 1996)

Jamie Carragher has Liverpool Football Club running in his blood. A real down to earth Scouser, he can and will play anywhere on the pitch, preferring, of course, a defensive position where he performs with great commitment and endeavour. A true professional in every sense of the word, he celebrated ten years at Anfield in 2004 and would love to complete another ten! He passed the personal milestone of 400 senior appearances for the Reds in 2006 – the first coming way back in January 1997 as a substitute in a League Cup quarter-final clash with Middlesbrough when he replaced the injured Rob Jones in a 2–1 defeat. He gained a permanent place in the side in 1998 and hasn't looked back since. An FA Youth Cup winner in 1996, he has since added to his collection of prizes two League Cup, two FA Cup, a UEFA Cup, European Super Cup, Charity Shield and Champions League winning medals and, having represented England at youth team level, he has now gained 27 under-21, two 'B' and more than 20 full caps for his country – with a lot more to come in many ways! A truly great professional, he was named in the England World Cup squad for the 2006 competition in Germany.

CARSON, SCOTT PAUL
Goalkeeper: 4 apps
Born: Whitehaven, 3 September 1985
Career: Cleator Moor Celtic, Leeds United (academy), Leeds United (apprentice, September 2001; professional, September 2002), LIVERPOOL (£750,000, January 2005, with further payments regarding appearances), Sheffield Wednesday (loan March–May 2006)

Signed for the future by manager Rafael Benitez, 6ft 3in. tall England youth and under-21 international goalkeeper Scott Carson only made a handful of appearances in the first team at Elland Road but he was quickly into his stride at Anfield, being handed his senior debut in March 2005 away to Newcastle United, and then soon afterwards he was in European Champions League action against Juventus, giving near-flawless displays in both matches. Interestingly enough, Carson's first touch in senior football was an unusual one for a keeper – picking the ball out of the back of the net! He made his senior bow for Leeds United against Middlesbrough in February 2004 when he came on to the field to replace Paul Robinson, who had been red-carded. His first job was to face the resulting penalty, which he failed to stop. He then made his full debut in Leeds' next match – away to Manchester United. What you might call a baptism of fire.

CARTER, JAMES WILLIAM CHARLES
Winger: 4+4 apps
Born: Hammersmith, London, 9 November 1965
Career: Crystal Palace (apprentice, April 1982; professional, November 1983), Queens Park Rangers (free, September 1985), Millwall (£15,000, March 1987), LIVERPOOL (£800,000, January 1991), Arsenal (£500,000, October 1991), Oxford United (loan, March–April 1994 and December 1994–January 1995), Portsmouth (free, July 1995), Millwall (free, July 1998, retired, June 1999)

Jimmy Carter – nicknamed 'Sanjay' from his love of curry – did not play a single competitive game for either of his first two clubs. He finally made his League debut for Millwall at the age of 21 and went on to make 130 appearances for the Lions before his transfer to Liverpool. Unfortunately he never got to grips with life on Merseyside, despite his undoubted talent, and after just eight outings for the club – the first against Aston Villa (away) when he was substituted – he moved back to his London roots and joined Arsenal for whom he made just 29 senior appearances. Ending his career back at Millwall, he retired with 275 games under his belt and 20 goals.

CASE, JAMES ROBERT
Midfield: 240+25 apps, 45 goals
Born: Liverpool, 18 May 1954
Career: South Liverpool (amateur, July 1970), LIVERPOOL (amateur/apprentice, £500 fee, May 1972; professional, May 1973), Brighton and Hove Albion (£350,000, August 1981), Southampton (£25,000, March 1985), Bournemouth (free, July 1991), Halifax Town (free, July 1992), Wrexham

(non-contract, February 1993), British Wanneroo/Australia (free, May 1993), Darlington (non-contract, October 1993), Sittingbourne (free, November 1993), Brighton and Hove Albion (free, December 1993, retired as a player May 1995, manager November 1995–November 1996)

A ball-winner who tackled hard and true and sometimes vigorously, Jimmy Case had a wonderful career during which time he amassed 795 club appearances (78 goals) and gained one England under-21 cap, while helping Liverpool win four League titles (1976, 1977, 1979 and 1980), the European Cup on three occasions (1977, 1978 and 1981), the UEFA Cup (1976), the League Cup (1981) and the European Super Cup (1977). He also gained runners-up medals in two FA Cup finals (for the Reds in 1977 and Brighton in 1983) and one League Cup final (1978). A professional through and through, he played every game in a wholehearted manner and he could let rip with one of the most powerful right-footed shots in the game. He made the first of his 265 appearances for Liverpool against QPR in April 1975 (won 3–1), scoring his first goal in his second outing v. Spurs in August of the same year (won 3–2). He was four months short of his 41st birthday when he played his last competitive game for Brighton v. Stockport County in January 1995. He served his apprenticeship as an electrician before becoming a professional footballer.

CHADBURN, JOHN LUCAS
Right-back: 2 apps
Born: Mansfield, 12 February 1873 – *Died*: Mansfield, 10 December 1923
Career: Mansfield and District Schools (County level), Leicester Fosse (reserves, 1890), Mansfield Unitarians (1891), Mansfield Greenhalgh's (March 1892), Lincoln City (professional, July 1893), Notts County (August 1894), Wolverhampton Wanderers (March 1897), West Bromwich Albion (January 1900), LIVERPOOL (May 1903), Barnsley (November 1903), Reading (December 1903), Plymouth Argyle (March 1904), Mansfield Mechanics (March 1905), Swindon Town (August 1906), Mansfield Town (July 1907, retired, injured, January 1908); worked as a shop fitter after retiring from football

John Chadburn, who had both speed and stamina, played in the opening two League games of the 1903–04 season for Liverpool against Nottingham Forest and Sheffield Wednesday, leaving the club following the arrival of Alf West. A player with a volatile temper, he had appeared on the right wing for all his previous clubs and lined up for West Bromwich Albion in their first-ever League game at The Hawthorns (v. Derby County in September 1900). He made over 150 senior appearances during his varied career.

CHADWICK, EDGAR WALLACE
Inside-left: 45 apps, 7 goals
Born: Blackburn, 14 June 1869 – *Died*: Blackburn, 14 February 1942
Career: Rising Sun FC, St George's Mission and Little Dots FC (all Blackburn), Blackburn Olympic (season 1886–87), Blackburn Rovers (professional, July 1887), Everton (August 1888), Burnley (May 1899), Southampton (August

1900), LIVERPOOL (May 1902), Blackpool (May 1904), Glossop (May 1905), Darwen (July 1906, retired, April 1908); later coached in Germany and Holland (The Hague and Haarlem sides); also coach of the England amateur team (November 1908–May 1909); returned to Blackburn to work as a baker

One of the best known and respected players of his day (especially during his time at Goodison Park) Edgar Chadwick, 5ft 6in. tall, was a master strategist and dribbler. As an Evertonian, he netted 110 goals in 300 appearances, gained a League championship-winning medal in 1891 and two FA Cup runners-up medals in 1893 and 1897. He then collected a third Cup loser's medal with Southampton in 1902 but gained some consolation by helping the Saints win the Southern League title. One of only eight players to score over 100 goals for Liverpool's arch-rivals, he made his League debut on the opening day of the competition (8 September 1888) and was capped seven times by England, scoring after just 15 seconds against Scotland at Ibrox Park in 1892. Glaswegian newspaper reporter J.H. Catton wrote: 'Chadwick's goal was perfection – perfect in conception, combination and execution. John Southwork kicked off and Johnny Goodall tipped the ball to Billy Bassett who swung a pass towards the left. Chadwick gained possession, dribbled round Arnott and drove the ball past McLeod, the goalkeeper. The trick was done and the Scots had never touched the ball.'

Chadwick, such a clever footballer, also represented both the Football Alliance and the Football League v. the Scottish League at Bolton in April 1892. He was almost 33 years of age when he joined Liverpool for whom he made his first appearance against Blackburn Rovers in September 1902 (won 5–2) and netted his first goal for the club in a 5–0 home win over Middlesbrough three months later. He is believed to have been the first Englishman to coach abroad. Chadwick's cousin, Arthur Chadwick, played for Accrington, Burton Swifts, Southampton, Portsmouth, Northampton Town and Exeter City and later managed Reading, Exeter and Southampton. Arthur also won two England caps.

CHALMERS, WILLIAM GREEN

Outside-left: 2 apps
Born: Aberdeen, 3 April 1901 – *Died*: Scotland, *circa* 1997
Career: Old Aberdeen FC (August 1919), LIVERPOOL (trial, May–June 1923, signed professional, July 1923), Tranmere Rovers (June 1925–May 1926)

Billy Chalmers, tall and thin, impressed all and sundry during a trial period at Anfield but after signing professional forms for the club he had to wait until the end of November 1924 before making the first of his two appearances in the League side (v. Birmingham, away, lost 5–2). Always in the shadow of Fred Hopkin, he left Liverpool after two seasons and spent the next 12 months with Tranmere Rovers, for whom he made 23 League appearances.

CHAMBERS, HENRY
Inside-forward: 339 apps, 151 goals
Born: Willington Quay near Newcastle-upon-Tyne, 17 November 1896 – *Died*:
  Shrewsbury, 29 June 1949
Career: Tynemouth County School, Willington United Methodists (1912),
  North Shields Athletic (1913), LIVERPOOL (professional, April 1915);
  guest for Distillery and Glentoran during WW1; West Bromwich Albion
  (£2,375, March 1928), Oakengates Town (player-manager, June 1929),
  Hereford United (player-manager, January 1933, retired as a full-time player,
  May 1934, remained a registered player and continued as manager until
  retiring in May 1948)
Harry 'Smiler' Chambers – a shipyard worker by trade – is listed as being one of
the great players in Liverpool's history. Decidedly bow-legged and stocky, he was
certainly in brilliant form during the 1920s when he scored at will, producing
some memorable displays as the Reds won successive League titles in 1922 and
1923. Possessing a terrific shot, he went on to average virtually a goal every two
games during his time at Anfield, finishing up as leading scorer on five
occasions. He was capped eight times by England, netting four goals, while
earning the reputation of a schemer as well as a superb marksman. He moved to
the centre-half position on joining West Bromwich Albion and played his last
competitive game in defence for Hereford United in the old Southern League in
April 1948 at the age of 51.

CHARLTON, JOHN BROWELL
Left-back: 3 apps
Born: Leadgate, County Durham, 23 March 1908 – *Died*: County Durham,
  May 1969
Career: Wallsend FC (1925), Bradford City (professional, June 1928),
  LIVERPOOL (October 1929–May 1932)
A competent reserve at Anfield for two and a half years, John Charlton
deputised in each of his three League games for Tommy Lucas. He could also
occupy the right-back berth where he played on many occasions for the second
XI. He did not make a senior appearance for Bradford City.

CHARNOCK, PHILIP ANTHONY
Midfield: 1+1 apps
Born: Southport, 14 February 1975
Career: LIVERPOOL (apprentice, May 1991; professional, March 1993),
  Blackpool (loan, February–March 1996), Crewe Alexandra (free, September
  1996), Port Vale (free, August 2002), Bury (trial, July 2003, signed on free,
  August 2003), Linfield (free, September 2003)
A reserve at Anfield, Phil Charnock made just two senior appearances in three
and half years, his debut coming as a substitute in a 6–1 home win over Apollon
Limassol in the UEFA Cup in September 1992 (aged 17). His first start
followed six days later in a 4–4 League Cup draw with Chesterfield. After
leaving Liverpool he did extremely well at Gresty Road under Dario Gradi and

made 183 appearances for the 'Alex', helping them gain promotion to the Second Division via the play-offs in 1997.

CHECKLAND, FRANCIS JOSEPH
Wing-half: 5 apps
Born: Seaforth, Liverpool, 31 July 1895 – *Died:* Birkenhead, 19 June 1960
Career: Liverpool junior football, LIVERPOOL (amateur, January 1919), Tranmere Rovers (October 1923–May 1925); later worked full time as a schoolteacher at St Xavier's College, Liverpool

An amateur, signed by Liverpool halfway through the last season of WW1, Frank Checkland made his debut against Manchester United in a Lancashire Section Principal Tournament game in January 1919 and followed up with his League bow in September 1921 v. Sheffield United. Reserve to Bill Lacey, Jack Bamber and Jock McNab, he remained at Anfield for two more years before joining Tranmere, for whom he made 17 League appearances.

CHEYROU, BRUNO
Forward: 27+21 apps, 5 goals
Born: Suresnes, Paris, France, 10 May 1978
Career: Racing Club Lens/France (junior, June 1995), Racing Club Paris/France (professional, May 1996), Lille/France (£100,000, August 1998), LIVERPOOL (£4m, July 2002–May 2005), Bordeaux/France (season loan from August 2005)

A League Cup winner with Liverpool in 2003, Bruno Cheyrou, 6ft 1in. tall and 12st. 8lb in weight, never quite reached the form the club expected from him following his big-money transfer from Lille in 2002. A succession of niggling injuries didn't help his cause but when fully fit he did occasionally produce the goods, scoring some fine goals including a beauty against Chelsea that earned the Reds their first win at Stamford Bridge for 15 years. Cheryou, who made his Premiership debut as a substitute v. Southampton in August 2002, has been capped by France twice at senior level and he scored over 30 goals in more than 100 competitive appearances in French football before moving to Merseyside.

CHILDS, ALBERT ROBERT
Right-back: 2 apps
Born: Liverpool, 25 September 1930
Career: Northern Nomads (from 1950), LIVERPOOL (amateur, September 1953–May 1954), Bishop Auckland (seasons 1954–58)

England amateur international right-back, Bert Childs was a registered player at Anfield for one season during which time he played in two League games, the first against Burnley (won 4–0) a week after joining, the second v. Charlton Athletic (lost 6–0). He deputised for Lambert in both matches. He won the FA Amateur Cup with Bishop Auckland in 1957.

CHISNALL, JOHN PHILIP
Forward: 8+1 apps, 2 goals
Born: Manchester, 27 October 1942
Career: Stretford Schools (Manchester), Manchester United (amateur, April 1958; professional, November 1959), LIVERPOOL (£25,000, April 1964), Southend United (£12,000, August 1967), Stockport County (September 1971–May 1972)

Capped by England on six occasions as a schoolboy and once at under-23 level, Phil Chisnall was described as being a 'hungry reserve' at Old Trafford and scored 10 goals in 47 first-team appearances for Manchester United before transferring to Liverpool. Unfortunately he failed to enhance his reputation at Anfield and following a useful start against Arsenal in August 1964, he struggled after that and played in only 8 more first XI games before moving to Southend, for whom he netted 28 goals in 142 Fourth Division matches. In 1971–72 his club, Stockport, finished 91st (out of 92) in the Football League.

CHORLTON, THOMAS
Defender: 122 apps, 8 goals
Born: Heaton Mersey, Stockport, 1882 – *Died*: Manchester, 1952
Career: Heaton Mersey Juniors, All Saints FC (Stockport and District League), Northern FC (Manchester Federation), Stockport County (professional, August 1900), Accrington Stanley (September 1902), LIVERPOOL (May 1904), Manchester United (August 1912), Stalybridge Celtic (August 1914), Manchester City (assistant trainer, November 1919, trainer up to 1939)

A versatile player who occupied all defensive positions during his career, Tom Chorlton commenced his League career with Stockport and then helped Accrington Stanley win the Lancashire Combination title in 1903 and finish runners-up the following season before joining Liverpool. He helped the Reds win the Second Division championship in his first season but then missed out on a championship medal in 1906, due to an insufficient number of matches (six only). He made his debut for the Reds in a 2–0 win at Lincoln in September 1904 and netted two of his eight goals in a 5–0 home win over Grimsby Town a month later. In all, for his four major clubs, he accumulated more than 150 competitive appearances. He had a very long and happy association with Manchester City. His brother, Charles Chorlton, played for Manchester United reserves in 1906–07 and Bury in 1908–09.

CHRISTIE, FRANK
Left-half: 4 apps
Born: Scone, Perthshire, 17 February 1927 – *Died*: Scotland, 1996
Career: Scone Juniors (1946), LIVERPOOL (professional, March 1949), East Fife (£7,750, January 1951, retired April 1958); later Forfar Athletic (trainer-coach)

Although he developed into a tough-tackling defender, stubborn yet reliable, Frank Christie made his League debut for Liverpool at inside-right against Manchester United at Old Trafford in March 1950 when he deputised for Willie

Fagan in a 0–0 draw. His second appearance three weeks later was at left-half v. Charlton Athletic. After leaving Anfield he was the recipient of a Scottish League Cup winner's medal with East Fife in 1954, being a pillar of strength at the heart of that club for many years, making well over 250 appearances.

CISSE, DJIBRIL

Forward: 43+34 apps, 22 goals

Born: Arles, France, 12 August 1981

Career: Auxerre/France (professional, August 1998), LIVERPOOL (£14m, July 2004)

A French international, capped over 25 times at senior level, striker Djibril Cisse joined Liverpool for a club record fee of £14m in the summer of 2004 after scoring 70 goals in 128 League games for Auxerre. Strong and powerful, 6ft tall and 13st. in weight, he suffered a double fracture of the right leg against Blackburn Rovers in October 2004, just three months after his transfer. He was sidelined until mid-April but bounced back in style, scoring twice against Aston Villa on the last day of the League campaign ahead of the Champions League final against AC Milan in Istanbul. With his ever-changing hair colour, he joyfully came off the bench (to replace Milan Baros) and netted the vital second spot-kick in the penalty shoot-out at the end of that game as Liverpool gained a terrific victory – after they had trailed 3–0 at half-time. He also scored in the 2006 FA Cup final, when Liverpool beat West Ham on penalties after a 3–3 draw. France included Cisse in their 2006 World Cup squad in Germany.

CLARK, JOHN ROBERT

Forward: 43 apps, 11 goals

Born: Newburn, Newcastle-upon-Tyne, 6 February 1903 – *Died*: Byker, Newcastle-upon-Tyne, 1977

Career: Spencer's Welfare FC (1919), Hawthorn Leslie (1920), Newburn Grange (1921), Prudhoe Castle (1922), Newcastle United (£130; professional, February 1923), LIVERPOOL (£3,000 January 1928), Nottingham Forest (January 1931), North Shields (player-coach, August 1932, later player-coach, September 1937–May 1939); was not involved in football after WW2

A hefty forward, 6ft tall and weighing 14st., Bob Clark was a very popular Novocastrian figure between the two World Wars, playing for Newcastle alongside the great Hughie Gallacher, the pair being known as 'little and large'. He scored 16 goals in 77 League appearances for the Geordies, helping them win the First Division championship in 1927. An entertaining footballer, always willing to try something unusual, Clark looked a shade slow at times but was strong in the air and always worked hard. He packed a thunderous right-foot shot and during his career scored some cracking goals, some for Liverpool, including two in an 8–0 home League win over Burnley on Boxing Day 1928 – having made his debut for the Reds against West Ham United the previous February. Clark actually played in a friendly for Newcastle before being signed and as a result the club was severely reprimanded by the FA for this misdemeanour. Some reference books list this player's surname as Clarke and also refer to him as James (or Jim).

CLEGHORN, THOMAS
Left-half: 70 apps, 1 goal
Born: Leith, Edinburgh, June 1871 – *Died*: Perth, Scotland, *circa* 1943
Career: Leith Athletic (May 1892), Blackburn Rovers (May 1894), LIVERPOOL (March 1896), Portsmouth (June 1899–May 1903), Plymouth Argyle (season 1903–04)

Tom Cleghorn was rather on the small side, standing barely 5ft 5in. tall, but he was a ferocious competitor who gave nothing less than 100 per cent on the field of play. He made 30 League appearances for Leith and 45 for Blackburn before joining Liverpool for whom he made his debut in March 1896 against Burton Swifts (won 6–1). He scored his only goal for the Reds also against the Swifts in a 4–3 first-round FA Cup victory in January 1897. He made over 100 first-team appearances for Southern League side Portsmouth (all competitions), gaining a Southern League championship medal in 1902 when his teammates included two more ex-Liverpool players, Tom Wilkie and Bobby Marshall.

CLELAND, JAMES WILLIAM
Inside-left: 1 app.
Born: Lanarkshire, February 1870 – *Died*: Glasgow, 1940
Career: Minerva FC (1889), Royal Albert FC (Larkhall, 1893), Edinburgh St Bernard's (December 1894), LIVERPOOL (loan, April 1895), Edinburgh St Bernard's (April 1895–May 1900); worked as an office clerk in Glasgow for many years

Jim Cleland's only appearance for Liverpool came at the end of the 1894–95 season, in a vital Test match against Bury at Ewood Park, Blackburn, which ended in a 1–0 defeat and thus saw the team relegated to the Second Division. He was recruited for this vital game owing to an injury to David Hannah, the Reds' forward line being switched around to accommodate the Scottish international. Cleland also played at centre-half north of the border and was in that position when he won his only full cap against Ireland in 1891, the same year he helped Minerva lift the Scottish Junior Cup. In 1895 he gained a Scottish Cup winner's medal with St Bernard's. He had two brothers, both of whom played for the Royal Albert club, while his son, James Henry, a schoolteacher and former soldier in Yorkshire, played for Preston North End and Hull City between 1912 and 1915.

CLEMENCE, RAYMOND NEAL, MBE
Goalkeeper: 665 apps
Born: Skegness, Lincolnshire, 5 August 1948
Career: Skegness schoolboy football, Skegness Youth Club (1963), Notts County (amateur, non-contract, August 1964), Scunthorpe United (professional, August 1965), LIVERPOOL (£18,000, June 1967), Tottenham Hotspur (£300,000, August 1981, retired, March 1988; later reserve team coach at

White Hart Lane from June 1989, upgraded to first-team coach, May 1992);
Barnet (manager, seasons 1994–96); England goalkeeping coach (from 1997)
Once a deckchair attendant on the beach at Skegness and centre-half for his
local youth club, Ray Clemence developed into a world-class goalkeeper whose
total of 61 full caps for England (the first against Wales in 1972) would have
been far greater had not Peter Shilton been around at the same time. Blessed
with height, strength, agility, confidence, a safe pair of hands, courage and
commitment, he was a master of his own penalty area. He amassed 1,118 senior
appearances at club and international level (748 in the Football League alone)
before announcing his retirement as a player in 1988, five months short of his
40th birthday. He also played four times for his country at under-23 level and
with Liverpool won five League titles (1973, 1976, 1977, 1979 and 1980), the
European Champions Cup on three occasions (1977, 1978 and 1981), the
UEFA Cup twice (1973 and 1976), the FA Cup (1974), the League Cup (1981),
the European Super Cup (1977) and four FA Charity Shield triumphs (plus one
shared). He was also a runner-up in two FA Cup finals (1971 and 1977), the
League Cup final (1978) and the Super Cup (also in 1978). With Spurs he
added a second FA Cup winner's medal to his collection (1982) and gained a
runners-up medal in the same competition v. Coventry City in 1987, the year he
was awarded the MBE for services to football. He was also on the losing side
against his former club, Liverpool, in the 1982 League Cup final.

A bargain buy by Bill Shankly from Scunthorpe in 1967, Clemence, who was
regarded by many as the best goalkeeper Liverpool had had since the great
Elisha Scott (q.v.), made his debut for Liverpool against Nottingham Forest in
January 1970, eventually taking over the duties from Tommy Lawrence during
the second half of that season, having acted as his understudy since moving to
Anfield. He missed only 7 League games out of a possible 477 between his debut
and his last outing versus Manchester City in May 1981. He had one excellent
run of 333 consecutive appearances and conceded only 22 goals in 41 League
games in 1970–71. Then, after signing for Spurs, he continued to tot up his
appearances, missing only 23 competitive games over the next six and a half
years. He actually made his debut for Spurs at Wembley in a 2–2 FA Charity
Shield draw with Aston Villa in 1981. His son, Stephen Clemence, a midfielder,
is currently with Birmingham City (signed from Spurs in 2003).

CLOUGH, NIGEL HOWARD
Forward: 34+10 apps, 9 goals
Born: Sunderland, 19 March 1966
Career: AC Hunters FC (1981), Heanor Town (from August 1982), Nottingham
    Forest (free; professional forms, September 1984), LIVERPOOL (£2.275m,
    June 1993), Manchester City (£1.5m, January 1996), Nottingham Forest
    (loan, December 1996–January 1997), Sheffield Wednesday (loan, September
    1997), Burton Albion (player-manager from October 1998)
An England international, capped by his country at senior level on 14 occasions
(winning his first against Chile at Wembley in May 1989), Nigel Clough also
played in five under-21 matches (1986–88) and in one 'B' fixture, as well as

representing the Football League. He twice won the League Cup with Nottingham Forest, in 1989 when he scored twice against Luton Town in the final and 1990 v. Oldham Athletic. He also helped Forest win the Simod Cup v. Everton in 1989 and the Zenith Data Systems Cup v. Southampton, three years later. He was, however, a runner-up v. Spurs in the 1991 FA Cup final and also against Manchester United in the League Cup final the following season. Forest's leading scorer for four seasons running (1985–89), Clough topped the charts again in 1990–91 and 1992–93 and during his time at the City Ground (two spells) he netted a total of 131 goals in 412 senior appearances. A centre-forward who enjoyed playing a deeper role rather than an out-and-out striker, pestering defenders inside the penalty area, he tried his best with Liverpool but at times seemed lost among the other star players. He averaged a goal every five games for the Reds, scoring twice on his Premiership debut v. Sheffield Wednesday at home in August 1993 (won 2–0). He failed to impress at Maine Road and had only two games on loan at Hillsborough. As a manager, he guided Burton Albion into the Conference (as Unibond League champions) in 2002. He almost caused an upset in FA Cup football when Burton held Manchester United to a goalless draw in a third-round tie in January 2006 before losing the replay 5–0 at Old Trafford. His father was, of course, the late Brian Clough.

COCKBURN, WILLIAM OLD

Centre-half: 67 apps
Born: Willington Quay, Northumberland, spring 1899 – *Died*: 27 December 1958
Career: Rosehill FC (Newcastle, 1919), Stockport County (professional, June 1921), LIVERPOOL (May 1924), Queens Park Rangers (£400, July 1928), Swindon Town (July 1930, retired, May 1931)

Bill Cockburn was the first of two excellent centre-halves who served Liverpool between the two World Wars – Norman Low was the other. Standing just over 6ft tall and weighing over 12st., he was as strong as an ox and actually played 12 of his first 17 League games for the Reds in the right-half position before taking over as pivot on a regular basis in 1925–26, following the departure of Walter Wadsworth and the demotion of David Pratt. He missed only five games that season before Pratt eventually reclaimed the centre-half position, and as a result Cockburn moved to pastures new, joining QPR for a small fee.

COHEN, ABRAHAM

Left-back: 20+3 apps, 1 goal
Born: Cairo, Egypt, 14 November 1956
Career: Maccabi Tel Aviv/Israel (1975), LIVERPOOL (trial, February 1979, signed permanently, £200,000, May 1979), Maccabi Tel Aviv/Israel (£100,000, November 1981), Glasgow Rangers (May 1987–April 1988)

Israeli international left-back 'Avi' Cohen was already an experienced footballer by the time he arrived at Anfield, having made over 150 senior appearances for Maccabi Tel Aviv. A brave, resourceful player, quick over the ground, he never quite bedded into the English game as he would have hoped and after 23 outings for the Reds (the first against Leeds United at Elland Road in September 1979) he returned to Tel Aviv. His only goal in a Liverpool shirt came against Aston Villa at Anfield on the last day of the 1979–80 First Division programme when a 4–1 victory clinched the League title. Cohen, however, missed out on a medal, having made only four appearances that season. He was later recruited to Rangers by former Liverpool star Graeme Souness, but made only 12 appearances in Scottish football.

COLLINS, JAMES HENRY

Inside-/outside-left: 7 apps
Born: Bermondsey, London, 30 January 1911 – *Died*: London, 10 July 1983
Career: Tooting and Mitcham (amateur, 1929), Queens Park Rangers (professional, August 1931), Tunbridge Wells Rangers (July 1933), Rochdale (September 1933), Stockport County (August 1934), Walsall (June 1935), LIVERPOOL (January 1936), Cardiff City (May 1937); guest for Aberaman and Swindon Town during WW2; did not play after 1946

Jimmy Collins was a chirpy character, short, fair-haired, fast, built like a barrel, strong and fearless. He was used as a reserve by QPR, Stockport County and Liverpool for whom he made his initial appearance in a 6–1 defeat at West Bromwich Albion a fortnight after moving to Anfield. He had first Taylor and Roberts and then Hanson to contest with for a place in the Reds' line-up. He had done reasonably well with Rochdale (6 goals in 32 senior appearances) and also with Walsall (15 in 26 starts) and after leaving Anfield became a huge favourite with the fans at Ninian Park, scoring 40 times in 75 outings for Cardiff City, including a hat-trick on his home debut against Torquay United in August 1937. He helped the Bluebirds reach the Welsh Cup final in 1939.

COLLYMORE, STANLEY VICTOR

Striker: 71+10 apps, 35 goals
Born: Cannock, Staffs, 22 January 1971
Career: Walsall (apprentice, June 1989), Wolverhampton Wanderers (non-contract, July 1989), Stafford Rangers (semi-professional, July 1990), Crystal Palace (£100,000, December 1990), Southend United (£100,000, November 1992), Nottingham Forest (£2.2m, July 1993), LIVERPOOL (£8.5m, June 1995), Aston Villa (£6m, May 1997), Fulham (loan, July 1999–January 2000), Leicester City (£250,000, rising to £500,000, February 2000), Bradford City (free, October 2000), Real Oviedo/Spain (free, January–retired, May 2001); later worked in the media

The son of a Barbadian tax officer, also called Stanley, Collymore failed to make headway with any of his first two League clubs. He came out of his shell with Stafford Rangers and his efforts led to a big-money transfer to Crystal Palace but after 2 years and only 20 games for the Eagles he switched his allegiance to Southend, before Nottingham Forest boss Frank Clark splashed out over £2 million for his services in 1992. He scored over 40 goals for Forest, helping them gain promotion to the Premiership and with it a place in Europe. In his first season at Anfield, the 6ft 3in. Collymore gained the first of three full caps for

England and produced some useful displays for the Reds, netting 19 goals as strike-partner, in the main, to Robbie Fowler. He also played in the FA Cup final defeat by Manchester United. Two years on he moved back to the Midlands to sign for Aston Villa and thereafter slowly wound down his career with moderate spells at Fulham, Leicester, Bradford City and in Spain. Linking up with some of the finest strikers in the game – Ian Wright, Ian Rush, Fowler and Tony Cottee – he netted 125 goals in a career total of 317 senior games – and no doubt these figures would have been far better had he not suffered several injury problems, a lot of suspensions and a serious incident involving the TV personality Ulrika Jonsson. Unfortunately 'Stan the Man' – who could have been a world-beater if he'd put his mind to it, according to former manager Graham Taylor – often hit the headlines for reasons other than football. Nevertheless, he was a real character on and off the field.

COLVIN, ROBERT

Outside-right/centre-forward: 3 apps
Born: Kirkconnel, Dumfries, 5 December 1876 – *Died*: Scotland, 1906
Career: Coatbridge (1895), LIVERPOOL (professional, May 1897), Glossop
   North End (July 1898), New Brighton Tower (August 1899), Luton Town
   (May 1901), Queens Park Rangers (August 1902), Swindon Town (August
   1903–April 1904)

A small, compact, elusive footballer with good pace and skill, Bob Colvin made only three League appearances for Liverpool in his only season with the club, the first against Blackburn Rovers (away) in January 1898 when he deputised for Fred Geary on the right wing. Illness caused his premature retirement after he had played in a total of 145 competitive matches for his six major clubs.

COOPER, THOMAS

Right-back: 160 apps
Born: Fenton, Stoke-on-Trent, 9 April 1904 – *Died*: Aldeburgh, Suffolk, 25 June
   1940
Career: Trentham FC (Cheshire League), Port Vale (professional, £20, August
   1924), Derby County (£2,000, March 1926), LIVERPOOL (£7,500,
   December 1934); guest for Wrexham (September 1939 until his death)

Tommy Cooper, always full of laughter, was one of the finest right-backs in the country during the mid-to-late 1930s. Skilful, solid, sound in the tackle and an excellent passer of the ball (some said he fed his forwards better than the half-backs in his team), his all-round play was superb. His only weakness was perhaps his heading but generally he left that to the taller defenders in the side. He captained both Derby County and England before becoming skipper of Liverpool, and eventually teaming up at Anfield with fellow international Ernie Blenkinsop. Capped 15 times by his country at senior level between October 1927 and September 1934, Cooper, in fact, appeared against eight different countries and featured in England's first-ever defeat by a foreign country abroad, losing 4–3 to Spain in Madrid in May 1929. He also played in the 2–1 defeat in Belfast in October 1927 – the last time Northern Ireland had beaten England in

Belfast prior to their 1–0 victory in a World Cup qualifier in September 2005. Cooper made 33 appearances for Port Vale and 266 for Derby before joining Liverpool, for whom he made his League debut in a 4–1 defeat at Chelsea 48 hours after signing (8 December 1934). He appeared in nine WW2 games for the Reds before sadly losing his life in tragic circumstances – killed in a motorcycling accident while serving as an Army dispatch rider with the Military Police in Suffolk.

CORMACK, PETER BARR

Midfield: 169+9 apps, 26 goals
Born: Granton, Edinburgh, 17 July 1946
Career: Tynecastle Boys' Club (Edinburgh), Heart of Midlothian (amateur, July 1961), Hibernian (apprentice, August 1962; professional, July 1963), Nottingham Forest (£80,000, March 1970), LIVERPOOL (£110,000, July 1972), Bristol City (£50,000, November 1976), Hibernian (free, February 1980, retired, injured, early December 1980), Partick Thistle (manager, mid-December 1980–May 1984), Anartosi FC/Cyprus (manager, season 1985–86), Botswana (national team coach, August 1986–May 1987), Hibernian (assistant manager, season 1987–88); purchased some karaoke equipment in 1989 and toured various pubs in Edinburgh before starting up his own painting and decorating business, also becoming a top-line after-dinner speaker; returned to football as Morton's manager (July 2001–March 2002)

A League Cup finalist with Hibernian in 1969 and later the recipient of winner's medals with Liverpool in the UEFA Cup in 1973, the League championship in 1973 and 1976 and the FA Cup in 1974, Peter Cormack was also capped nine times at senior level by Scotland between 1966 and 1972, represented the Scottish League on six occasions, played for his country's amateur side twice and made five appearances for the under-23s. Possessing an abundance of attributes – skill, commitment, stamina, bravery, stealth and flair – he started out as an old-fashioned inside-forward before switching to the left-side of midfield from where he produced some excellent displays, especially for Liverpool. He scored some splendid goals, some of them tap-ins after drifting in unnoticed on the blind side of defenders and some with well-directed headers and powerful shots. He was also a fine passer of the ball and created chances aplenty for his teammates. He made his debut for the Reds against Derby County in September 1972 (lost 2–1) and during his career amassed over 560 senior appearances at club and international level, scoring 140 goals. Unfortunately Cormack didn't have much success as a manager but he did hit the heights on stage as a singer!

COTTON, CHARLES

Goalkeeper: 12 apps
Born: Plymouth, June 1878 – *Died*: Southend, summer 1910
Career: Sheppey United (1897), Reading (professional, August 1900), West Ham United (June 1903), LIVERPOOL (December 1903), West Ham United (seasons 1904–06), Southend United (August 1906, until his death)

Charles Cotton, who was only 5ft 8in. tall, spent most of his career playing in the Southern League with Reading, West Ham and Southend. He was Liverpool's first-choice goalkeeper for roughly half a season, making 12 League appearances, the first against Nottingham Forest at Anfield on New Year's Day 1904, performing very well in a 0–0 draw. He was recruited following an injury to Peter Platt.

COX, JOHN

Outside-right/outside-left: 360 apps, 80 goals

Born: Blackpool, 21 November 1876 – *Died*: Blackpool, *circa* 1946

Career: South Shore Standard (Blackpool), South Shore FC (1896), Blackpool (professional, August 1897), LIVERPOOL (February 1898), Blackpool (player-manager, August 1909, retired, May 1911)

Jack Cox was Liverpool's regular outside-right for four seasons before switching to the opposite flank where he gained international recognition, playing for England against Ireland in March 1901 and twice against Scotland, in May 1902 and April 1903. He also represented the Football League on three occasions. A mercurial footballer, fast and able to centre in splendid style when in the right frame of mind, he unfortunately had the tendency to beat his opponent twice – much to the annoyance of his colleagues and manager! Indeed, a columnist in the *Athletic News* wrote: 'Fast, but inclined to indulge in trickery against a weak opponent.' He certainly did extremely well for Liverpool, whom he served for 11 years. He made his League debut for the club against Notts County in March 1898 and helped the Reds win the First Division championship twice (in 1901 and 1906) and the Second Division once (1905). Outside football, Cox often took part in athletics events and became a champion sprinter over 100 and 200 yards. He was also successful at crown green bowling.

CRAIK, HERBERT CLARK

Left-half: 1 app.

Born: Greenock, *circa* 1880 – *Died*: Glasgow, *circa* 1934

Career: Greenock Morton (1901), LIVERPOOL (August 1903–May 1904); later with Newton Swifts (Glasgow)

A reserve at Anfield for one season, Herbert Craik's only first-team game was against West Bromwich Albion in September 1903, when he deputised at left-half for fellow Scot George Fleming in a 3–1 defeat.

CRAWFORD, EDMUND

Centre-forward/inside-left: 7 apps, 4 goals

Born: Filey, Yorkshire, 31 October 1906 – *Died*: London, autumn 1977

Career: Filey FC (1929), Halifax Town (professional, July 1931), LIVERPOOL (£1,200, July 1932), Clapton Orient (July 1933); guest for Brighton and Hove Albion and Watford during WW2, retired 1945

Several top clubs wanted to sign tough Yorkshireman Ted Crawford after he had scored 21 goals in 30 games for Halifax in 1931–32. In the end it was Liverpool who secured his services for a fee of £1,200 – but the Anfield management team weren't all that convinced he would do the business in the First Division! Crawford started off exceptionally well, netting four times in his first three League appearances including two on his debut against newly promoted Wolves. But after that his form slumped, and with Billy McPherson, Syd Roberts and David Wright all proving their worth as forwards, Crawford languished in the reserves before moving to Clapton Orient in 1933. His form picked up again with the London club for whom he scored 68 goals in 199 League games in 6 seasons, 23 coming in 1935–36 which was a club record that stood for 14 years. In all he struck 82 goals in 263 first-team games for Orient, including 9 in 51 wartime fixtures.

CRAWFORD, ROBERT STUART
Full-back: 114 apps, 1 goal
Born: Blythswood, Renfrewshire, 4 July 1886 – *Died*: Scotland, *circa* 1950
Career: Barrhead Boys' Club (1902), Arthurlie (from 1905), LIVERPOOL (professional, January 1909–May 1915); did not play after WW1
Full-back Bob Crawford, who could occupy both flanks, made his League debut for Liverpool against Leicester Fosse in February 1909 at the age of 22. He remained at Anfield until 1915, amassing 114 senior appearances in that time, his best seasons coming in 1910–11 and 1911–12 when his partners included Tom Chorlton and Eph Longworth. A splendid tackler, he was competent rather than brilliant, simply because his clearances left a lot to be desired. A recurring knee injury marred his career from 1912 onwards.

CROSSLEY, RUSSELL
Goalkeeper: 73 apps
Born: Hebden Bridge, Yorkshire, 25 June 1927
Career: Army football (from 1944), LIVERPOOL (professional, June 1947), Shrewsbury Town (£1,500, with Joe Maloney, July 1954), Kettering Town (November 1959, retired May 1961)
A brave, daring goalkeeper, Russell Crossley made his League debut against Middlesbrough (0–0) in October 1950, well over three years after joining Liverpool at the age of 20. There were two other quality keepers at Anfield at the same time – Cyril Sidlow and Charlie Ashcroft – and as a result Crossley had to bide his time in the reserves. He finally established himself as the club's number one in late December 1952 but when Dave Underwood arrived in the camp he slipped back into the second XI and subsequently moved to Shrewsbury Town, for whom he made almost 200 senior appearances in five years. An elder brother, Roy Crossley, played centre-forward for Halifax Town from 1948 to 1951.

CROUCH, PETER
Striker: 42+7 apps, 13 goals
Born: Macclesfield, 30 January 1981
Career: Tottenham Hotspur (apprentice, May 1997; professional, July 1998), Queens Park Rangers (£60,000, July 2000), Portsmouth (£1.25m, July 2001),

Aston Villa (£4m, March 2002), Norwich City (loan, September–December 2003), Southampton (£2m, July 2004), LIVERPOOL (£7m, July 2005)

At 6ft 7in., one of the tallest players in the Premiership (and the Football League), Peter 'Beanpole' and 'Coat Hanger' Crouch joined Liverpool with high expectations, but it took quite some time before he proved to be the right man to lead the Reds attack. In fact, he didn't score his first goal for the club until his 18th match – when he netted twice in a 3–0 home win over Wigan Athletic in December 2005. First honoured at senior level by England v. Colombia in the USA in May 2005, having previously represented his country at both youth and under-21 levels, gaining six caps in the latter category, he is certainly strong and able in the air and useful enough on the ground, but one feels he lacks that vital cutting edge to be one of the great strikers. Prior to his move to Anfield, he netted 12 goals in 47 games for QPR, 19 in 39 for Portsmouth, 6 in 43 for Aston Villa, 4 in 15 for Norwich City and 16 in 33 for Southampton, being voted Saints' 'Player of the Year' in 2004–05 when they lost their Premiership status. After helping Liverpool win the FA Cup in 2006, he then played his part in England's World Cup campaign in Germany.

CUNLIFFE, DANIEL
Outside-/inside-right/centre-forward: 18 apps, 7 goals
Born: Bolton, 11 June 1875 – *Died*: Heywood, Lancashire, 28 December 1937
Career: Little Lever (1892), Middleton Borough (1894), Oldham County (1896), LIVERPOOL (professional, July 1897), New Brighton Tower (May 1898), Portsmouth (May 1899), New Brighton Tower (May 1900), Portsmouth (May 1901), New Brompton/Gillingham (May 1906), Millwall Athletic (June 1907), Heywood (September 1909), Rochdale (May 1912–May 1914); did not play after WW1

A forward of stocky, sturdy build, hard to knock off the ball, Danny Cunliffe, with his short-cropped hair, was an admirably persistent player and frequent scorer. He was 22 years of age when he joined Liverpool, making his League debut in September 1897 away at Stoke (2–2). He netted 7 goals in 18 games that season (the first in the 3–1 Merseyside derby win over Everton) before losing his place when the front-line was reshuffled. After assisting New Brighton Tower, he played for Portsmouth in their first season in the Southern League and went on to claim 157 goals in 284 competitive games in his two spells at Fratton Park, helping Pompey win the Southern League title in 1902. An England international, capped against Ireland in Dublin in March 1900, Cunliffe competed in over 400 senior football matches during his 17-year career.

CUNNINGHAM, WILLIAM
Half-back/wing-forward: 3 apps
Born: Radcliffe, 27 October 1899 – *Died*: circa 1964
Career: Blyth Spartans (August 1919), LIVERPOOL (£50, May 1920), Barrow (January 1924), Mid Rhondda United (September 1925–May 1927)

Willie Cunningham's three senior outings for Liverpool were made in different positions: outside-left v. Middlesbrough in March 1921, outside-right v. Arsenal in May 1921 and left-half v. Bolton Wanderers in March 1922. A reserve at Anfield, he later did well with Barrow for whom he scored once in 39 League games before returning to non-League football.

CURRAN, JOHN
Right-back: 24 apps
Born: Belshill near Glasgow, March 1864 – *Died*: Glasgow, 1933
Career: Glasgow Benburb (August 1890), Celtic (professional, April 1892), LIVERPOOL (1894), Motherwell (January 1896), Celtic (briefly, 1897)
Jock Curran learnt his football with Celtic's nursery side, Glasgow Benburb. Regarded initially as a wing-half, he was successfully converted into a full-back and during his first spell at Parkhead, helped the Bhoys win the Scottish League title in 1893 and 1894 and finish runners-up in the 1894 Scottish Cup final. He made only 26 senior appearances for the Glasgow club before making his debut for Liverpool during the club's disastrous 1894–95 season against Burnley (home) in the November. However, early in the next campaign he lost his place to fellow Scot Archie Goldie.

DABBS, BENJAMIN EDWARD
Full-back: 56 apps
Born: Oakengates, Salop, 17 April 1909 – *Died*: Hertfordshire, 1980
Career: Oakengates Town (Birmingham League, 1930), LIVERPOOL (professional, June 1932), Watford (June 1938, retired August 1941)
The wavy-haired Ben Dabbs had his best season with Liverpool in 1936–37 when he made 32 appearances after taking over at left-back from Ernie Blenkinsop. Able to occupy the right-back position equally well, he became surplus to requirements at Anfield in 1938 and his career came to an abrupt end when he was wounded during the war, having made only a handful of League appearances for Watford before the hostilities.

DALGLISH, KENNETH MATHIESON, MBE
Forward: 492+19 apps, 170 goals
Born: Dalmarnock, Glasgow, 4 March 1951
Career: Glasgow Schools, Drumchapel Amateurs (August 1965), Celtic (schoolboy trialist, July 1966), LIVERPOOL (trialist, August 1966), Glasgow United (February 1967), Celtic (apprentice, August 1967), Cumbernauld United (loan, September 1967–March 1968), Celtic (as a professional, August 1968), LIVERPOOL (£440,000, August 1977, appointed player-manager, June 1985, retired as a player, February 1991), Blackburn Rovers (manager, October 1991–1995), Newcastle United (manager, season 1997–98), Celtic (Director of Football Operations, May 1999; later returned as manager, February–May 2000); thereafter a football pundit on both TV and radio
When Kenny Dalglish joined Liverpool the fee involved was a record between two British clubs at that time. He had already done the business north of the border with Celtic, for whom he scored 167 goals (112 in the League) in 320

first-class matches, helping the Bhoys win the Scottish League championship four times (1972, 1973, 1974 and 1977), the Scottish Cup also on four occasions (1972, 1974, 1975 and 1977) and the League Cup once (1975). He also received runners-up medals for defeats in one Cup final (1974) and four League Cup finals (1972, 1973, 1974 and 1977). He made his debut for the Glasgow club as a second-half substitute against Hamilton Academical in a League Cup tie in September 1968, having spent six months developing his game with Cumbernauld United – all this after playing as a trialist for Liverpool's 'B' team in a 1–0 defeat by Southport in August 1966.

After his big-money move to Anfield he added further honours to his collection with Liverpool, helping the Reds win the European Cup three times (1978, 1981 and 1984) and finish runners-up once (1985), clinch the First Division championship on six occasions (1979, 1980, 1982, 1983, 1984 and 1986), capture the FA Cup (1986); gain four successive League Cup final victories (1981, 1982, 1983 and 1984) and finish runners-up once (1978), triumph in the European Super Cup (1977) and finish runners-up twice (1978 and 1985), win the Screen Sport Super Cup (1986) and lose in two World Club championship matches (1981 and 1984). 'King Kenny' as he was known, scored 170 goals in 511 competitive games for Liverpool – and his total of 118 in First Division action gave him the distinction, and honour, of claiming a century of League goals both north and south of the border. He guided Liverpool to the double in his first season in charge (1985–86) . . . thus becoming the first man to achieve this feat as a registered player-manager. Indeed, he was also Liverpool's first official player-manager. In 1990 he guided the club to the League title once more, following this up by leading Blackburn Rovers to the Premiership glory in 1995 following promotion from the First Division, as champions, in 1992. And then, after returning to his first club, Celtic, as Director of Football (with ex-Liverpool star John Barnes appointed as the club's head coach), he took over as team manager in February 2000 and inside three months the Bhoys won the League Cup and finished runners-up to Rangers in the Premier Division, thus gaining a place in the next season's UEFA Cup competition.

Dalglish won a record 102 full caps for Scotland (scoring 30 goals, a record he shares with Denis Law). He also represented his country in four under-21 internationals, in five youth games and four schoolboy matches. In total, he participated in almost 950 matches at various levels and scored 375 goals . . . some record. He was handed the Freedom of Glasgow (for his achievements and service in football), was twice voted the FWA Player of the Year in 1979 and 1983, was awarded the PFA Footballer of the Year prize, also in 1983, and received the Manager of the Year award three times in 1986, 1988 and 1990. He took over from Kevin Keegan as manager of Newcastle United in 1997.

Author Ivan Ponting wrote this about Dalglish in the Hamlyn's *Liverpool Player By Player* book, published in 1996 . . . 'Endowed with magnetic control and a deadly instinct for releasing the ball with nigh-perfect precision and timing, he brought the best out of teammates, often creating for them precious extra seconds in which to capitalise on his skills . . . Wriggling like a muscular eel, he would feint one way, turn another and squeeze a vicious shot or exquisitely weighted pass through the narrowest of gaps . . . the on the field glory of the man who could justly be called the greatest footballer in Liverpool's history.'

When he was manager of Liverpool in 1988, Dalglish said: 'Sure we get our fair share of penalties. But then we get into the penalty area more often than most teams.'

DAVIDSON, DAVID LEIGHTON
Centre-half/left-half: 62 apps, 2 goals
Born: Aberdeen, 4 June 1905 – *Died*: Tynemouth, 30 May 1969
Career: Garthdee FC (Aberdeen), Aberdeen Argyle (1922), Forfar Athletic (professional, August 1923), LIVERPOOL (£1,500, July 1928), Newcastle United (£4,000, January 1930), Hartlepools United (£50, June 1937), Gateshead (free, October 1937, retired, May 1938), Whitley Bay (manager, August 1945), Ashington (manager, April 1955–June 1963); later worked as an attendant in a mental hospital and also ran a masseur's business in Whitley Bay; resided at Monkseaton on Tyneside for many years, becoming a respected local personality

Dave Davidson was all set to sign for Newcastle United when Liverpool stepped in and secured his services for a moderate fee. Not the tallest of defenders, he was a real stopper centre-half who tackled fiercely and had a good attitude. He made his debut for the Reds in August 1928 against Bury and missed only six games in his first season at Anfield, helping the side climb to fifth place in the table. He was injured halfway through the following campaign and struggled after that to regain full fitness and, indeed, his place. With Morrison and McDougall being joined in the half-back line by 'Tiny' Bradshaw, Davidson finally moved to Newcastle! He made 145 first-team appearances during his seven years at St James' Park, gaining an FA Cup winner's medal in the famous 'ball over the line' final of 1932 when Arsenal were beaten 2–0. As manager he turned Ashington into a formidable non-League side.

DAVIES, JOHN OSCAR
Forward: 10 apps
Born: Liverpool, July 1881 – *Died*: Liverpool, *circa* 1941
Career: Liverpool schoolboy football, LIVERPOOL (professional, May 1900), Blackpool (August 1903–March 1904)

A versatile forward, Jack Davies occupied four different positions in Liverpool's front-line during his time at Anfield. He made his League debut in a 1–0 home win over Wolves in March 1901, lining up at outside-right in place of John Cox (away on England duty). He did not get a senior game with Blackpool.

DAWSON, JAMES MAXWELL
Inside-right: 14 apps, 3 goals
Born: Edinburgh, 13 August 1890 – *Died*: Edinburgh, *circa* 1933
Career: Edinburgh Emmett (1910), LIVERPOOL (professional, March 1913;

engaged in war from May 1914); did not play senior football after the hostilities

An adaptable forward, Scotsman Jim Dawson made his League debut for Liverpool in November 1913 against Manchester United at Old Trafford and scored his first goal in a 2–1 home win over Tottenham Hotspur later in the month. After that he battled hard to keep his place in the side, eventually being whisked away to war.

DEVLIN, WILLIAM ALEXANDER

Centre-forward: 19 apps, 15 goals
Born: Bellshill, Lanarkshire, 30 July 1899 – *Died*: Scotland, July 1972
Career: Glasgow junior football, Clyde (professional, May 1921), Kings Park (loan, season 1921–22), Cowdenbeath (October 1923), Huddersfield Town (£4,200, February 1926), LIVERPOOL (May 1927), Heart of Midlothian (December 1927), Macclesfield (November 1928), Cowdenbeath (June 1929), Mansfield Town (June 1930), Burton Town (March 1931), Shelbourne (June 1931), Bangor (August 1932), Boston United (August 1933), Ashton National (August 1934), Olympique Marseille/France (player-coach, August 1935–May 1936)

A football nomad, Willie Devlin served with 14 different clubs from 1921 to 1936. He was a prolific marksman both north and south of the border and during his first spell with Cowdenbeath he netted over 100 goals, including 40 in 1925–26, which remained a club record until beaten by Rab Walls with 54 in 1938–39. Nicknamed 'Demon' he was not a great success at Leeds Road (14 goals in 32 games) but during his short stay at Anfield he certainly made his mark, netting 15 times in only 19 starts, the first coming in the third minute of his debut against Sheffield United in August 1927. He then struck two four-goal hauls in double-quick time, versus Bury (in his second outing) and against Portsmouth on the first Saturday in October. He surprisingly left Liverpool on New Year's Eve and returned to Scotland. He continued to do well with Hearts (12 goals in 15 appearances) and later with Mansfield Town (15 strikes in 21 starts). In fact, the Stags reportedly paid him the highest wage outside the Football League (around £8 a week). During his career Devlin is believed to have netted over 250 goals at various levels.

DEWHURST, GERALD POWIS

Centre-forward: 1 app.
Born: London, 14 February 1872 – *Died*: Wrexham, 29 March 1956
Career: Repton School (first XI, season 1889–90), Cambridge University (Blue, seasons 1892–93–94), Corinthians (from August 1892 to May 1895); also played for Liverpool Ramblers (briefly in 1893) and LIVERPOOL (amateur, March 1894); later worked as a cotton merchant in Liverpool, moving to Wrexham in the 1930s

An amateur throughout his career, Gerald Dewhurst represented England at that level over 20 times. Well built and fast, he tended to hold on to the ball far too long, to the annoyance of his colleagues. He was out of his depth, especially in the first half, in the only League game of his career for Liverpool in a Second Division encounter with Crewe Alexandra in March 1924. He took over at centre-forward from Matthew McQueen – who played in goal – in a 2–0 victory.

DIAO, SALIF ALASSANE
Midfield: 35+26 apps, 3 goals
Born: Kedougou, Senegal, 10 February 1977
Career: Epinal FC/Senegal (May 1996), AS Monaco/France (professional, August 1997), FC Sedan/France (September 2000), LIVERPOOL (£5m, August 2002), Birmingham City (loan, January 2005), Portsmouth (loan, August 2005)

Salif Diao failed to find the net in French football in 75 appearances. However, he was a regular in the Senegalese national side and netted some crucial goals, eventually going on to win almost 40 full caps (up to 2006). A strong, powerful footballer, he had a decent first season at Anfield but after that became something of a bit-player and a niggling calf injury interrupted his routine considerably. He made his Premiership debut as a substitute against Blackburn Rovers at Ewood Park in August 2002 and scored his first goal for the Reds in a 5–0 Champions League win over Spartak Moscow the following month. Diao was a member of Liverpool's League Cup winning side in 2003.

DICK, DOUGLAS CHARLES
Utility: 10 apps, 2 goals
Born: Greenock, Scotland, December 1868 – *Died*: Kilmarnock, June 1950
Career: Greenock Morton (professional, April 1891), Glasgow Rangers (August 1893), LIVERPOOL (October 1893), Third Lanark (season 1894–95); later Kilmarnock (director, then chairman for two years, 1930–32)

A determined all-action player who could occupy several positions, when performing as a winger Douglas Dick produced excellent dribbling skills and crossed the ball well, as an inside-forward he was smart and penetrative and when used in defence he was solid and uncompromising. A jack-of-all-trades but master of none, he had done very well with his first club, Morton, but made only two appearances for Rangers before joining Liverpool for whom he played at centre-half, right-half, inside-right and on the right wing. He made his League debut in a 5–0 win at Arsenal in October 1893 and scored the first of his two goals in his next outing at home to Newcastle United (won 3–1). After serving as a director with Kilmarnock for several years, Dick took over as chairman at Rugby Park in 1930. His brother, Alec Dick, played right-back for Kilmarnock and Everton during the 1880s.

DICKS, JULIAN ANDREW
Left-back: 28 apps, 3 goals
Born: Bristol, 8 August 1968
Career: Washwood Heath School (Birmingham), Birmingham City (apprentice, August 1984; professional, August 1985), West Ham United (£400,000, March 1988), LIVERPOOL (£2.5m deal in exchange for David Burrows and

Mike Marsh, September 1993), West Ham United (£1m, November 1994, retired, injured knee, May 1997); returned with Canvey Island (August 2000–May 2001); changed sports and became a professional golfer

No one doubted Julian Dicks' footballing credentials. He was a fine, rugged defender with a powerful left foot, but his temper let him down so often . . . he was sent off eight times during his career (including a dismissal in his first England under-21 match) and received well over 40 yellow cards as well. He made his League debut for Birmingham City at the age of 17 and appeared in over 100 senior games for the Midlands club before joining West Ham in 1988. Three years later, having by now established himself as a fiercely competitive left-back, he helped the Hammers win the Second Division title. He scored 40 goals in 203 appearances in his first spell at Upton Park and then spent 14 months at Anfield during which time he suffered injury and suspensions. His debut for the Reds came in the Merseyside derby against Everton in September 1993 as partner to Rob Jones. He was injured in his fourth game, struggled off and on after that, and made only 28 appearances for the club before returning to West Ham – not the greatest bit of business done by the Liverpool manager Graeme Souness. Dicks played in two 'B' and four under-21 internationals for his country and when he retired to become a golfer, he had made 450 appearances at club and international level and netted 64 goals, making him one of the highest-scoring full-backs of all time in senior football.

DICKSON, JOSEPH JAMES MARCH
Inside-forward: 6 apps, 3 goals
Born: Liverpool, 31 January 1934 – *Died*: Liverpool, 1992
Career: Liverpool Schools and local junior football, LIVERPOOL (professional, June 1952, released, May 1958)

An England youth international, inside-forward Joe Dickson spent six seasons at Anfield, acting mainly as reserve to the likes of Eric Anderson, Alan Arnell, Louis Bimpson, Johnny Evans, Jimmy Melia, Johnny Wheeler and others. He had to wait until the end of February 1956 for his League debut, starring in a 1–0 home win over Leeds United. He scored the first of his three goals ten days later in a 5–0 home win over Barnsley.

DINES, JOSEPH OSCAR
Left-half: 1 app.
Born: King's Lynn, 12 April 1886 – *Died*: France, 27 September 1918
Career: Local schoolboy and junior football, King's Lynn FC (1907), Ilford (August 1911), LIVERPOOL (amateur, July 1912), Millwall (amateur, August 1913), Walthamstow Avenue (amateur briefly)

Left-half Joe Dines' only game in the Football League during his short career was for Liverpool against Chelsea at Stamford Bridge in September 1912 when he deputised for Jack Scott in a 2–1 win. An England amateur international, capped 27 times, he won a gold medal for Great Britain at soccer at the 1912 Olympic Games. Described as being a 'master dribbler', he was the son of a blacksmith and a schoolteacher by profession. He served in the Royal Ordnance

Corps during WW1 and transferred to the Liverpool Regiment before sadly losing his life on the Western Front in 1918, aged 32.

DIOMEDE, BERNARD
Midfield: 3+1 apps
Born: Saint Doulchard, France, 23 January 1974
Career: FC Bourges/France (professional, April 1991), Auxerre/France (April 1992), LIVERPOOL (£3m, July 2000, released, March 2003), Ajaccio/Italy (free, June 2003)
A French international midfielder, capped eight times at senior level, Bernard Diomede had an unfortunate time at Anfield, knee and cartilage injuries ruining his career on Merseyside – although it must be said that prior to that he hadn't been all that convincing out on the park. He made only four appearances for the Reds, the first in the UEFA Cup encounter with Rapid Bucharest in September 2000. He scored 30 goals in 176 League appearances for Auxerre, helping them win the French League title in 1994 and the domestic double of League and Cup in 1996.

DIOUF, EL HADJI OUSSEYNOU
Striker/midfield: 61+19 apps, 6 goals
Born: Dakar, Senegal, 15 January 1981
Career: Sochaux/France (professional, April 1998), Rennes/France (July 1999), Racing Club Lens/France (August 2000), LIVERPOOL (£10m, July 2002), Bolton Wanderers (loan, August 2004, signed for £3.5m, July 2005)
A Senegalese international with over 30 caps and 15 goals under his belt, El Hadji Diouf had already appeared in almost 100 League games in France before joining Liverpool in 2002. After a very good first season at Anfield when he netted 6 times in a total of 47 games, collecting a League Cup winner's medal in the process, the decision to convert him from a will-of-the-wisp striker into a left-sided midfielder was not a success and he struggled to maintain his form. Indeed, after assisting his country in the African Nations Cup in Tunisia from January 2004, he returned to Merseyside completely out of sorts. Subsequently, after falling out with Liverpool boss Rafael Benitez, he proved to be a shrewd loan signing by Sam Allardyce, scoring nine vital Premiership goals in 2004–05 to clinch a place in Europe via the UEFA Cup for Bolton Wanderers. The Lancashire club then secured his services on a permanent basis in readiness for the 2005–06 campaign.

DOIG, JOHN EDWARD
Goalkeeper: 53 apps
Born: Letham, Forfarshire, 29 October 1866 – *Died*: Liverpool, 7 November 1919
Career: Dunnichen FC/Forfar (1883), Arbroath (August 1885), Blackburn Rovers (loan, November 1889), Sunderland (£50, September 1890), LIVERPOOL (July 1904, retired May 1908); returned with St Helens Recreationalists (March 1910, at the age of 43)

Rated among the best goalkeepers ever produced by Scotland, 'Teddy' Doig was strong in all aspects of his craft and he retained his resource and agility right up to his retirement in 1908 at the age of 41. Capped six times by his country between 1887 and 1903, he made 153 appearances for Arbroath, one for Blackburn (in a 9–1 League win over Notts County) and 457 for Sunderland (417 in the First Division, 35 in the FA Cup), helping the latter club win four League titles (1892, 1893, 1895 and 1902). He established a record for unbroken service with a single club (Sunderland) which was later bettered by Sheffield Wednesday's Andrew Wilson. In fact, his first outing for Sunderland was surrounded by controversy and it cost the club two points and a £50 fine because he was selected to play against West Bromwich Albion before his registration/transfer had been completed. Aged 37 when he joined Liverpool, he immediately became first choice at Anfield and he added a Second Division championship-winning medal to his collection before handing over his duties to another great goalkeeper of the future, Sam Hardy, who had been his understudy and pupil.

DONE, CYRIL CHARLES
Inside-/centre-forward: 109 apps, 37 goals
Born: Liverpool, 21 August 1920 – *Died*: Formby, Liverpool, 24 February 1993
Career: Bootle Boys Brigade, LIVERPOOL (professional, January 1938), Tranmere Rovers (May 1952), Port Vale (£2,000, December 1954), Winsford United (July 1957), Skelmersdale United (manager, seasons 1959–62)
A big burly, forceful player, hard but fair, Cyril Done averaged a goal a game for Liverpool in peacetime football and netted a staggering 148 in 135 regional matches during WW2, including 45 in only 34 matches in 1943–44 when he helped the team win the League (N) Cup final, scoring in the second leg of a 6–3 aggregate victory over Bolton Wanderers. Brilliant at his job – hitting the target – he was certainly not a pretty player but he was a forward every defender feared. He scored on his senior debut for the Reds in a First Division game against Charlton Athletic in October 1946 (aged 26) and at the end of that season duly collected his League championship winner's medal. Unfortunately he missed the 1950 FA Cup final, having lost his place to Albert Stubbins. Done was leading scorer with Port Vale in 1954–55 and again in 1956–57, despite suffering leg injuries during the latter season. He secured all Vale's goals in a 4–3 League win over his former club, Liverpool, in April 1955.

DONE, ROBERT
Full-back: 155 apps, 13 goals
Born: Runcorn, Cheshire, 27 April 1904 – *Died*: Chester, 6 September 1982
Career: Runcorn FC (1922), LIVERPOOL (amateur, February 1926; professional, April 1926), Reading (May 1935), Chester (June 1937), Accrington Stanley (June 1938), Bangor City (November 1938); did not play after WW2
Able to play equally well in both full-back positions, Bob Done loved to attack down the flank. He made his League debut on New Year's Day 1927 against

Bolton Wanderers at Burnden Park and became Liverpool's chief penalty-taker, converting three kicks in the 1928–29 season and missing only once from the spot during his Anfield career. He helped Bangor City finish runners-up in the Lancashire Combination in 1938–39. A railway worker before taking up professional football, Done returned to that line of employment after the war.

DONNELLY, WILLIAM WALTER
Goalkeeper: 8 apps
Born: Edinburgh, Scotland, 1872 – *Died*: Glasgow, December 1934
Career: Hibernian (April 1890), Clyde (August 1894), Celtic (briefly, early 1896), LIVERPOOL (May 1896), Clyde (June 1898)
Acting as reliable cover for Harry Storer, Bill Donnelly's eight senior appearances (six League, two FA Cup) for Liverpool were made consecutively between Boxing Day 1896 and 16 February 1897. He conceded four goals on his debut v. Burnley and six in his last outing v. Stoke. He made over 100 competitive appearances in Scottish football.

DRUMMOND, JOHN
Outside-left/centre-forward: 18 apps, 1 goal
Born: Edinburgh, 1870 – *Died*: Lancashire, *circa* 1947
Career: Partick Thistle (professional, August 1887), Preston North End (£100, August 1890), Sheffield United (February 1891), LIVERPOOL (August 1894), Barnsley St Peter's (May 1895)
A smart and extremely useful footballer, fast over the ground, Jack Drummond scored 4 goals in 11 League games for Preston and 9 in 40 for Sheffield United, netting on his debut for both clubs. He spent one season at Anfield, making his first appearance in a Liverpool shirt v. Blackburn Rovers (away) in September 1894 when he partnered 'Tiny' Bradshaw on the left wing. His only goal for the club came against his future employers, Barnsley St Peter's, in an FA Cup first-round replay in February 1895 (won 4–0). He was not related to 'Geordie' Drummond, the former Preston North End forward who was at Deepdale at the same time.

DUDEK, JERZY
Goalkeeper: 177+2 apps
Born: Rybnik, Poland, 23 March 1973
Career: GKS Tychy/Poland, (junior, 1991), Sokol Tychy/Poland (professional, August 1995), Feyenoord/Holland (August 1996), LIVERPOOL (£4.85m, August 2001)
Before joining Liverpool, Polish international goalkeeper Jerzy Dudek, 6ft 2in. tall and the son of a miner, made over 150 appearances in five years for Feyenoord, gaining a Dutch League championship medal in 1999 when he was an ever-present, conceding 38 goals in 34 games, as well as a runners-up medal in 2001. An excellent shot-stopper, he took over the regular duties from Sander Westerveld and made his debut in the Premiership against Aston Villa in September 2001 – the third different keeper used by Reds' Gerard Houllier in

the opening three matches. Star of the show when Liverpool beat AC Milan in the penalty shoot-out to win the 2005 European Champions League final in Istanbul, he was then replaced between the posts at Anfield by new signing Jose Reina at the start of the new campaign. Dudek now has more than 50 full caps under his belt and was a League Cup winner with Liverpool in 2003. Gained an FA Cup winner's medal (as a non-playing sub) in 2006. Named in Poland's World Cup squad for the 2006 competition in Germany.

DUNDEE, SEAN WILLIAM

Striker: 0+5 apps
Born: Durban, South Africa, 7 December 1972
Career: Bay View/South Africa (1990), D'Alberton Callies/South Africa (1991), FC Ditzingen/Holland (May 1993), Stuttgarter Kickers/Germany (December 1994), Karlsruhe Sport-Club/Germany (July 1995), LIVERPOOL (£2m, June 1998), Vfb Stuttgart/Germany (July 1999)

A 6ft 1in. tall South African-born striker, Sean Dundee never fitted in at Anfield. He looked out of his depth at times and made only five substitute appearances for the Reds, the first (on for Michael Owen) coming against Fulham in a League Cup tie in October 1998 (won 3–1). He was, in effect, fourth in line for a first-team place and left after one season on Merseyside. Prior to moving to Anfield, Dundee had scored 36 goals in 85 Bundesliga games for Karlsruhe.

DUNLOP, WILLIAM THEODORE

Left-back: 358 apps, 2 goals
Born: Hurlford, Ayrshire, 14 July 1871 – *Died*: Sunderland, 1945
Career: Sandyford FC (1888), Hurlford (1890), Annbank (1891), Kilmarnock (1892), Paisley Abercorn (1893), LIVERPOOL (£35, January 1895–May 1909); later Sunderland assistant trainer (January 1922–May 1927)

For a decade and a half, left-back Bill Dunlop was the backbone of Liverpool's defence. A fine tackler and splendid in the air, he was also a clean kicker of the ball, always seeking to find a colleague rather than heaving his clearance 80 yards downfield in hope rather than judgement. Twice a League championship winner with the Reds in 1901 and 1906, he also gained Second Division winner's medals in 1896 and 1905 and made well over 350 senior appearances for the club, the first against Sunderland in March 1895 and the last against Bury in April 1909. He was capped by Scotland against England in his benefit year of 1906, and in the official Liverpool programme, published soon after that international, the editor commented: 'There are some men who perform brilliantly in their various positions on the field, but there was never one who year in year out has given such wholehearted service as Dunlop has to Liverpool.' Dunlop also appeared in two international trials and would surely have gained more caps had he been with one of the top Scottish clubs! His younger brother, Harry, joined Liverpool from Hurlford in 1909, but failed to make the grade, while his cousin, Tommy Dunlop, played right-half for Port Glasgow, Annbank, Small Heath (Birmingham) and Dundee Harp during the 1890s.

DURNIN, JOHN PAUL

Forward: 1+1 apps
Born: Bootle, 18 August 1965
Career: Bootle and Merseyside District Schools, Waterloo Dock FC (Liverpool, 1981), LIVERPOOL (apprentice, July 1983; professional, March 1986), West Bromwich Albion (loan, October–November 1988), Oxford United (£275,000, February 1989), Portsmouth (£200,000, July 1993), Blackpool (loan, January 1999), Carlisle United (free, December 1999), Kidderminster Harriers (free, October 2000–May 2001), Rhyl Athletic (August 2001), Port Vale (free, December 2001–April 2002), Accrington Stanley (free, August 2003)

One of the few players to make just one start for Liverpool, lining up against Arsenal in the Mercantile Credit Tournament in September 1988, John Durnin later came on as substitute against West Ham United in a League Cup tie in November of that same year. He was on the losing side both times. After leaving Anfield he did very well with Oxford and Portsmouth and when he quit top-class football in 2003 he had appeared in 501 competitive games and scored 95 goals. He was known as 'Johnny Lager' because of his love for that drink!

EASDALE, JOHN

Centre-half: 2 apps
Born: Dumbarton, 16 January 1919 – *Deceased*
Career: Scottish junior football, LIVERPOOL (professional, February 1937); guest for Brighton and Hove Albion during WW2; Stockport County (September 1948–May 1949)

Reserve centre-half at Anfield for over a decade, John Easdale's two senior appearances for Liverpool were made at Stoke on Christmas Day, 1946 and at home to Derby County in March 1947, deputising each time for Lawrie Hughes. He made ten appearances in wartime football and had only a handful of outings for Stockport.

EASTHAM, HENRY

Forward: 69 apps, 4 goals
Born: Blackpool, 30 June 1917 – *Died*: Bolton, 1998
Career: Blackpool junior football, Blackpool (amateur, September 1933; professional July 1934), LIVERPOOL (February 1936); guest for Blackpool, Bolton Wanderers, Brighton and Hove Albion, Distillery, Leeds United, Leicester City, New Brighton, Newcastle United and Southport during WW2; Tranmere Rovers (free, May 1948), Accrington Stanley (July 1953), Netherfield FC (July 1955), Rolls Royce (Lancashire Combination, seasons 1956–58); later became a licensee of a pub near Bolton

A League championship winner with Liverpool in 1947 (making 19 appearances), Harry Eastham could occupy any forward position. A polished footballer with two good feet and neat skills (endowed with all the traditional Eastham ball-playing techniques) he was perhaps too much of an individualist for Liverpool's liking, although at times he certainly turned the course of a game.

He made the first of his 69 senior appearances for the Reds against Arsenal in October 1936, starring in a 2–0 win before a 45,000 crowd. He also played in 17 WW2 games (2 goals scored) before appearing in 154 League games for Tranmere Rovers and 42 for Accrington, also guiding Stanley's reserve team to the Lancashire Combination League and Cup double in 1955. He was the brother of George R. Eastham senior (ex-Bolton Wanderers, Brentford, Blackpool, Swansea Town, Rochdale, Lincoln City, England and Accrington Stanley manager) and uncle of George junior (also an England international and formerly of Newcastle United, Arsenal and Stoke City – manager also of the latter).

EDMED, RICHARD ALFRED

Outside-right: 170 apps, 46 goals
Born: Gillingham, Kent, 14 February 1904 – *Died*: Gillingham, 1983
Career: Chatham Centrals (New Brompton and District League, August 1919), Rochester FC (May 1921), Gillingham (professional, October 1923), LIVERPOOL (£1,800, January 1926), Bolton Wanderers (May 1932, retired, injured, April 1933); later assistant trainer with Gillingham for many years

Dick Edmed was a fast, direct and stylish right-winger who took over from Cyril Oxley. He loved to take on his full-back on the outside and his form in the early 1920s brought the scouts flocking to watch Gillingham's matches. Consequently, it came as no surprise when he joined Liverpool early in 1926. He had to wait some time before making his debut but soon drew up an excellent partnership with the South African Gordon Hodgson. Three of Edmed's finest displays for the Reds came against Lancashire clubs – a 4–2 triumph over Manchester United in his first outing in August 1926, an 8–0 victory over Burnley on Boxing Day 1928 (two goals) and a 7–2 win over his former employers Bolton Wanderers in September 1930 (scoring twice more and having a hand in three other goals). Obviously he played brilliantly in several other matches and scored some cracking goals while laying on a multitude of chances for his colleagues. Just 24 hours after leaving Anfield, he found the net on his debut for Bolton in an emphatic 8–1 win over Liverpool at Burnden Park on the last day of the 1931–32 campaign. A cartilage injury ended his career. Initially a fitter's mate in a Chatham dockyard before turning professional, Edmed spent over 20 years on the training staff at Gillingham.

ENGLISH, SAMUEL

Centre-forward: 50 apps, 27 goals
Born: Coleraine, County Londonderry, July 1910 – *Died*: Ireland, April 1967
Career: Yoker Athletic (1929), Glasgow Rangers (professional, July 1931), LIVERPOOL (£8,000, August 1933), Queen of the South (£1,700, July 1935), Hartlepools United (free, July 1936, retired, May 1938); later coach with Duntocher Hibernians and Yoker Athletic in the 1950s; also worked at a shipyard

Unfortunately, centre-forward Sam English was involved in one of football's most tragic accidents when, as a Glasgow Rangers player, he collided with the Celtic goalkeeper John Thomson in the Old Firm derby in front of 80,000 fans at Ibrox Park in September 1931. Thomson, who had dived bravely at the striker's feet, suffered a fractured skull and died from his injury, leaving English distraught. The Irish international never fully recovered from the trauma of Thomson's death although he went on to score a club record 53 goals that season (44 in the League). He later described the last part of his career (1931–38) as being 'seven years of joyless sport'.

Strongly built, hard and courageous, he scored 64 goals in 72 games for Rangers with whom he won the Scottish Cup (1932) and the League title (1933) whilst also gaining two full caps for his country. He made an excellent start with Liverpool, netting 13 times in his first 16 games and claimed 21 in the season, but he couldn't maintain his form and returned to Scottish football after spending two years on Merseyside.

EVANS, ALUN WILLIAM
Inside-forward: 105+6 apps, 33 goals
Born: Stourport, Worcestershire, 30 September 1949
Career: Stourport Junior and Bewdley Council Schools, Mid-Worcester Boys, Birmingham and District Schools, Aston Villa (trial, August–September 1964), Wolverhampton Wanderers (apprentice, July 1965; professional, October 1966), LIVERPOOL (£100,000, September 1968), Aston Villa (£72,000, June 1972), Walsall (£30,000, December 1975), South Melbourne/Australia (trial, June 1978, signed for £10,000, July 1978), Hellas/Australia (April–July 1979), South Melbourne/Australia (August 1979, retired, May 1981); now resides and works in Cheltenham near Melbourne, Australia

The son of the former West Bromwich Albion and Wales wartime international wing-half of the same name, blond mop-haired forward Alun Evans became Britain's costliest teenager when he joined Liverpool in 1968. After winning England caps at schoolboy, youth and under-23 levels, he was regarded as the 'star of the future' but sadly never reached the heights expected of him. Clever, strong and fast with an eye for goal, Evans scored 4 goals in 22 appearances for Wolves and then did the business to a certain extent with Liverpool, averaging almost a goal every three games, including a strike on his debut in a 4–0 win over Leicester City and a brace in a thumping 6–0 victory over his former club Wolves at Molineux. An FA Cup finalist in 1971 (v. Arsenal), Evans' career at Anfield was marred by a much-publicised night club incident which left him facially scarred. He also underwent a cartilage operation. After leaving Liverpool he netted 17 goals in 73 games for Aston Villa, helping them reach the 1975 League Cup final, and then made over 100 appearances for Walsall, mainly in midfield. He later did well for himself in Australia.

EVANS, JOHN WILLIAM

Forward: 106 apps, 53 goals

Born: Tilbury, London, 28 August 1929 – *Died*: Essex, 6 January 2004

Career: Bata Sports FC (South Essex League), Ford's Juniors, Tilbury FC (London League), Watford (amateur, August 1948), Bata Sports (season 1948–49), Charlton Athletic (amateur, May 1949; professional, May 1950), LIVERPOOL (£12,500, with Frank Lock, December 1953), Colchester United (November 1957), Romford (July 1960), Ford United (November 1962), Grays Athletic (manager, season 1965–66)

Still regarded by many as the best header of a ball in Charlton Athletic's post-war history, John Evans had two excellent seasons at The Valley (1950–52) during which time he scored 26 goals in 66 games. He then lost his way somewhat before joining struggling Liverpool in December 1953, signed by manager Don Welsh. He made his debut (with Frank Lock) against high-flying West Bromwich Albion at The Hawthorns on Christmas Day (lost 5–2). Things didn't really improve after and the Reds were subsequently relegated but Evans, although disillusioned to slip back into the Second Division, responded magnificently by bagging 33 goals in 42 League and Cup games to set a new club record. He also became the first Liverpool player since Andy McGuigan in January 1902 to score five times in a match, doing so v. Bristol Rovers in September 1954. Unfortunately Evans was also the first Liverpool player to get sent off after WW2 – dismissed in an FA Cup tie v. Lincoln City in January 1955 – after scoring an extra-time goal that took the Reds into the fourth round. During his career Evans netted over 125 goals in more than 260 senior games, 109 of which were scored in 243 League appearances. He also represented the RAF and the Football League v. the Scottish League in March 1955, scoring in a 3–2 defeat at Hampden Park.

EVANS, ROY QUINTIN ECHLIN

Left-back: 11 apps

Born: Bootle, 4 October 1948

Career: Bootle Schools, LIVERPOOL (apprentice, April 1963; professional, October 1965, retired, injured, August 1974; appointed reserve team trainer; later assistant manager-coach, then caretaker-manager and manager from January 1994–July 1998; joint manager, with Gerard Houllier, during season 1998–99); later Swindon Town (Director of Football with manager Neil Ruddock, August 2001, resigned, December 2001); later assistant to manager John Toshack with the Welsh national squad (2005)

Skilful left-back Roy Evans looked destined for soccer oblivion when, in August 1974, two months before his 26th birthday, he was asked by Liverpool chief Bob Paisley if he would like to take over as manager of the reserve team at Anfield. Having hung on as a reliable reserve for four years, he considered a playing career elsewhere, perhaps at a lower level, but felt, deep down, that the boss was being realistic. It worked out very well for Evans who guided the club's second string to a series of Central League championship triumphs, including three in his first three seasons and a four on the trot from 1978, plus another two in the early 1980s.

An England schoolboy international, Evans did well in reserve team football before making his League debut in March 1970, at home to Sheffield Wednesday, partnering Chris Lawler in a 3-0 win. He had hoped to take over from Geoff Strong but Alec Lindsay was installed instead with Evans his able deputy.

As manager of the first XI (following in the footsteps of Graeme Souness) Evans broke the club's outgoing and incoming transfer fee records by recruiting Stan Collymore for £8.5m from Nottingham Forest in 1995 and then selling him to Aston Villa for £7m two years later. On the field of play, the only prize captured by the Reds with Evans in charge was the League Cup in 1995. Evans was employed at Anfield for 26 years and his obvious passion for the club was encapsulated in the wonderful quote he came out with in 1994: 'Anfield without European football is like a banquet without wine.'

FAGAN, CHRISTOPHER JAMES
Right-back: 1 app.
Born: Manchester, 5 June 1950
Career: Newton Heath Boys' Club, LIVERPOOL (apprentice, August 1966; professional, July 1970), Tranmere Rovers (July 1971), Bangor City (free, May 1975)

A 6ft tall, slim-lined full-back, Chris Fagan's only League appearance for Liverpool was against his boyhood heroes, Manchester City, at Maine Road in April 1971 when he deputised for Chris Lawler ahead of the FA Cup final with Arsenal. He made 84 League appearances in four seasons with Tranmere Rovers, mostly under the managership of former Reds centre-half Ron Yeats.

FAGAN, WILLIAM
Centre-forward/inside-left: 185 apps, 57 goals
Born: Musselburgh, Edinburgh, 20 February 1917 – *Died*: Wellingborough, 29 February 1992
Career: Balgonia Scotia FC, Wellesley Juniors (Edinburgh, 1934), Celtic (professional, March 1934), Preston North End (£6,850, October 1936), LIVERPOOL (£8,000, October 1937); joined the RAF (1939) and was a guest for Aldershot, Celtic, Chelsea, Crystal Palace, Leicester City, Millwall, Newcastle United, Northampton Town and Reading during WW2; Distillery (free, January 1952), Weymouth (player-manager, July 1952–May 1955); later worked in a Borstal hostel in Northamptonshire

Willie Fagan played in two FA Cup finals 13 years apart – for Preston in 1937 and Liverpool in 1950 – collecting a runners-up medal each time. He did, however, gain compensation by helping the Reds win the League championship in 1947 when he contributed 7 goals in 18 League appearances, 2 coming in a wonderful 7–4 win over Chelsea and 2 more when Grimsby Town were defeated 5–0. Unfortunately a spate of niggling and sometimes tedious injuries interrupted his progress from 1950 onwards. A strong, hard-running, hard-working forward with a powerful shot in both feet, Fagan made his debut for Celtic at the age of 17 and for Liverpool when he was 20, the latter against

Leicester City in October 1937, when he took over from Jack Balmer at inside-left. He scored the first of his 57 goals for the club in his next game, a 4–3 home win over Brentford. In 1938–39 he was Liverpool's joint top League scorer with 14 goals and then, during the hostilities, netted a further 68 times in 110 regional matches, including 20 in 36 League (N) fixtures in 1945–46. In fact he enjoyed a lot of representative football between 1940 and 1946, playing for Scotland v. the RAF in 1943 and 1944 and against England in 1945, appearing in two games for the Army versus an England XI and a Scottish XI in 1940, twice assisting the British Army v. the French Army and Army (Scotland), both in 1940, starring for the Army (Scotland) v. the Army (England) in 1942 and 1944, playing for the FA XI against a Yorkshire XI in 1940, for the British XI v. the Football League in 1941, for the Football League v. Western Command in 1942 and then twice for Scottish Services v. Belgium and Flanders, for South East Command v. AA Command and for the Berkshire and Bucks XI against the RAF, all in 1945. Fagan's uncle, 'Jean' McFarlane, played for Celtic and Middlesbrough.

FAIRCLOUGH, DAVID

Forward: 89+62 apps, 52 goals
Born: Liverpool, 5 January 1957
Career: LIVERPOOL (associate schoolboy forms, 1972; apprentice, July 1973; professional, January 1974), Toronto Blizzard/Canada (£150,000, April 1982), FC Lucerne/Switzerland (July 1983), Norwich City (March 1985), Oldham Athletic (August 1985), SK Beveren/Belgium (August 1986), Tranmere Rovers (August 1989), Wigan Athletic (August 1990–January 1991); later a soccer pundit on local and national radio and TV

Known as 'Super Sub' around Anfield because of his tremendous knack of scoring or setting up vital goals after coming off the bench, the tall, ginger-haired David Fairclough possessed electrifying pace, was direct with good control and always caused defenders problems. He would often linger near the touchline, seemingly uninterested in the game, before bursting into the danger zone with the ball at his feet and creating panic in the opposition ranks. He scored six goals in seven matches in 1975–76 to edge the Reds nearer the League title and the following season netted a crucial 84th minute goal against St Etienne in a third-round second-leg European Cup encounter to book a place in the semi-finals with a 3–2 aggregate victory. He made only 33 starts in 4 seasons from 1978 and became more of a squad member than an automatic choice. He left Anfield for a spell in Switzerland before returning to England to round off his career. He was capped by England once at under-21 level, won both UEFA Cup and European Cup winner's medals in 1976 and 1978 respectively and gained two runners-up prizes for League Cup final defeats in 1978 and 1983. Fairclough is a huge fan of Cassius Clay/Muhammad Ali.

FAIRFOUL, THOMAS

Right-half: 71 apps
Born: West Calder, Lothian, 16 January 1881 – *Died:* Scotland, 1952
Career: Edinburgh junior football, Kilmarnock (professional, August 1889), Third Lanark (June 1906), LIVERPOOL (August 1913–May 1915); did not play after WW1; later worked as a taxi driver in Liverpool

A Scottish League representative when he was associated with Third Lanark, the strong-tackling Tom Fairfoul made over 200 senior appearances north of the border before joining Liverpool at the age of 32. Making his debut against Derby County (away) on the opening day of the 1913–14 League programme, he proved to be an excellent signing and gave the Reds defence extra stability during the last two seasons prior to the Great War, collecting an FA Cup runners-up medal in 1914 when he was the only ever-present in the side. Along with seven other players, three from Liverpool, namely Jackie Sheldon, Tommy Miller and Bob Pursell (all q.v.), and four from Manchester United, he was suspended by the FA for his part in helping fix the result of a League game between the two clubs at Old Trafford on Good Friday, 1915. (Liverpool lost 2–0.)

FERGUSON, ROBERT

Half-back: 103 apps, 3 goals
Born: Cleland, Lanarkshire, June 1886 – *Died:* Philadelphia, USA, 1962
Career: Glasgow junior football, Third Lanark (professional, April 1906), LIVERPOOL (June 1912–May 1915); served in the Army during the war and later emigrated to the USA (1930s), choosing to live and work in Seranton, Philadelphia

Bob Ferguson played alongside Tom Fairfoul (q.v.) for six years at Third Lanark before joining Liverpool in 1912 and the following season he was joined at Anfield by his former colleague. Rated one of the best half-backs in Scotland when he arrived on Merseyside, Ferguson took over as pivot from Jimmy Harrop. He was an ever-present in his first season and after switching to left-half to accommodate Harry Lowe missed only two League games in 1913–14, before niggling injuries caught up with him. With Lowe sidelined for the 1914 FA Cup final he lined up at the heart of the defence, but despite his brave and noble efforts Liverpool missed out on glory, being beaten 1–0 by Burnley.

FERNS, PHILIP

Full-back/left-half: 28 apps, 1 goal
Born: Liverpool, 14 November 1937
Career: Merseyside junior football, LIVERPOOL (amateur, March 1956; professional, September 1957), Bournemouth and Boscombe Athletic (August 1965), Mansfield Town (August 1966), Rhyl (July 1968)

Phil Ferns spent nine years at Anfield, playing second-team football most of the time. In fact, he finally made his Football League debut at left-half against Manchester City in August 1962, at the age 24, competing well in a 4–1 win before a crowd of over 46,000. He had his best spell in the senior side between September and December 1963 when he deputised for both full-backs, Ronnie

Moran and Gerry Byrne, being rewarded with a First Division championship medal at the end of the season. He played in every game for Bournemouth in 1965–66 and was a steadying influence at Mansfield, for whom he made 63 appearances in two years.

FERRI, JEAN-MICHEL
Defender: 0+2 apps
Born: Lyon, France, 7 February 1969
Career: Nantes/France (professional, April 1988), Istanbulspor/Turkey (September 1998), LIVERPOOL (£1.5m, December 1998), Sochaux/France (July 1999)
Tall, stylish defender Jean-Michel Ferri had to bide his time at Anfield before making his Premiership debut as a second-half substitute for Paul Ince in a 2–1 defeat at Chelsea in February 1999. He made only one more appearance for the first team (at Sheffield Wednesday in May) before returning to his homeland when manager Gerard Houllier trimmed his squad at the end of the season. A French international capped five times at senior level, Ferri scored 21 goals in 290 League appearances for Nantes.

FINNAN, STEPHEN JOHN
Right-back: 122+12 apps, 1 goal
Born: Limerick, Ireland, 20 April 1976
Career: Wimbledon (associated schoolboy forms, 1992), Welling United (July 1993), Birmingham City (£100,000, June 1996), Notts County (loan, March–May 1996, signed for £300,000, October 1996), Fulham (£600,000, November 1998), LIVERPOOL (£3.5m, June 2003)
A Republic of Ireland international, capped at three different levels, 'B' (1), under-21 (8) and full (40), right-back Steve Finnan passed the milestone of 450 club appearances at senior level in 2005–06, having made his first with Birmingham City as a 20 year old in 1996. A competent right-back who loves to get forward at every opportunity, he is fast in recovery and possesses exceptional positional sense, often covering for his co-defenders. A Third Division championship winner with Notts County in 1998, he helped Fulham win the same title 12 months later and in 2001 gained a First Division winner's medal as the Cottagers climbed into the Premiership. Since then he has won the European Champions League trophy with Liverpool (2005) and his only goal for the club so far was struck home with venom against West Bromwich Albion at Anfield in September 2004. Gained an FA Cup winner's medal after Liverpool's victory over West Ham in 2006.

FINNERHAN, PATRICK
Inside-right/centre-forward: 8 apps, 1 goal
Born: Northwich, Cheshire, March 1872 – *Died*: Sale, Cheshire, *circa* 1941
Career: Northwich Victoria (professional, April 1891), Manchester City (June 1894), LIVERPOOL (£150, May 1897), Bristol City (August 1898–May 1899)

A Football League representative v. the Irish League in 1895, Pat Finnerhan played in the same forward-line as the great Welsh winger-wizard Billy Meredith at both Northwich Victoria and Manchester City. He scored 27 goals in 89 League and FA Cup games in his three seasons with City, being an ever-present in 1894–95 and 1895–96, before joining Liverpool. Unfortunately he never looked right in a red strip and after just eight outings was released back into Southern League football with Bristol City, for whom he netted 13 goals in 33 outings.

FINNEY, FRANK
Right-half: 2 apps
Born: Liverpool, *circa* 1922
Career: LIVERPOOL (amateur, season 1945–46)
Frank Finney was a registered player at Anfield for one season only, making his senior debut for Liverpool against Chester in the first-leg third-round FA Cup tie against Chester in January 1946, his second outing following against the same opposition four days later. Details of this player's career are very vague.

FITZPATRICK, HAROLD JAMES
Inside-left: 4 apps, 2 goals
Born: Ayr, Scotland, February 1880 – *Died:* Glasgow, *circa* 1953
Career: Vale of Garnock Strollers (Ayrshire), Luton Town (August 1905), LIVERPOOL (£75, July 1907), Chesterfield Town (£50, August 1908–May 1909); returned to Scotland
Signed after scoring 7 times in 20 Southern League games for Luton Town, Harry Fitzpatrick netted the winning goal on his debut for Liverpool against Sunderland in October 1907 (1–0) and a fortnight later opened the scoring in a 3–0 home victory over Sheffield Wednesday. After that he fell from favour and with Billy McPherson, Jack Parkinson and then Ronnie Orr all seemingly ahead of him for the inside-left berth, he was transferred to Chesterfield for whom he scored once in 17 League games.

FITZSIMMONS, MATTHEW JOHN
Centre-half: 1 app.
Born: Toxteth Park, Liverpool, 10 December 1913 – *Deceased*
Career: Mather United (Liverpool), LIVERPOOL (professional, October 1936), Ipswich Town (June 1938); served in Army during WW2; guest for York City (1943, retired, May 1944)
Initially a full-back with Mather United, Matt Fitzsimmons became a reserve centre-half at Anfield and made his only senior appearance for the club in that position against Bolton Wanderers at Burnden Park in September 1938 when he deputised for Fred Rogers in a 3–1 defeat. He failed to make Ipswich's first team and played twice for York during the war.

FLEMING, GEORGE

Half-back/inside-left: 83 apps, 6 goals

Born: Bannockburn, Stirlingshire, 20 May 1869 – *Died*: Liverpool, *circa* 1934

Career: East Stirlingshire (August 1890), Wolverhampton Wanderers (professional, July 1894), LIVERPOOL (with George Bowen, May 1901–May 1906; later appointed assistant trainer at Anfield)

A strong-tackling half-back who also played at inside-left, George Fleming made 187 senior appearances for Wolves but had the ill luck to miss the Midland club's 1896 FA Cup final triumph over Sheffield Wednesday. He missed only one game in his last four seasons at Molineux and when he joined Liverpool he left Wolves without a single Scotsman on their books (there were six at the club twelve months earlier). Making his debut for the Reds against Sunderland in September 1901, he became a firm favourite with the Liverpool supporters and gained a Second Division championship winner's medal in 1905. Fleming received a benefit match in December 1899 when Wolves entertained the famous amateur side the Corinthians.

FORSHAW, RICHARD

Inside-right/centre-forward: 288 apps, 124 goals

Born: Preston, Lancashire, 20 August 1895 – *Died*: Llandudno, *circa* 1963

Career: Gateshead schoolboy football, St George's Church Lads' Brigade (Gateshead), Gateshead St Vincent's FC, Army football (1914–18); guest for Nottingham Forest and Middlesbrough during WW1; LIVERPOOL (amateur, April 1919; professional, June 1919), Everton (March 1927), Wolverhampton Wanderers (August 1929), Hednesford Town (August 1930), Rhyl Athletic (October 1930, retired May 1931)

Dick Forshaw was the first player to win a League championship medal with both Merseyside clubs: Liverpool in 1922 and 1923 (being an ever-present on both occasions) and Everton in 1928. A fine, versatile forward with an eye for goal, he was one of the most consistent performers of his day and certainly deserved international recognition which unfortunately eluded him, mainly due to knee and ankle injuries which plagued him for several years. After playing against his future club Everton (in front of almost 37,000 fans) and Stockport County in the Lancashire Section Supplementary Tournament in April 1919, Forshaw made his Football League debut for the Reds against Arsenal in September 1919. Eight years later he caused something of a sensation by transferring from Anfield across to neighbours Everton in 1927, but quickly bedded down and scored in his first game for the Blues in a 7–3 defeat at Newcastle. He netted 136 times in a career total of 335 senior games.

FOWLER, ROBERT BERNARD

Striker: 289+47 apps, 175 goals
Born: Toxteth, Liverpool, 9 April 1975
Career: LIVERPOOL (apprentice, May 1991; professional April 1992), Leeds
    United (£12.5m, November 2001), Manchester City (£3m, January 2003),
    LIVERPOOL (free, January 2006)

Sold for a then club record fee by Liverpool to rivals Leeds United in
November 2001, Robbie Fowler proved to be one of the great marksmen of his
era, scoring a goal every two games for Liverpool whom he served admirably
for ten years during his first spell with the club, gaining five winner's medals
for triumphs in the finals of the League Cup in 1995 and the FA Cup, UEFA
Cup, European Super Cup and League Cup (again) in 2001. He was also
capped 22 times by England at senior level (later upping his tally to 26) and
also represented his country in one 'B', eight under-21 and seven under-18
internationals. Positive in his actions and blessed with speed, skill, vision,
subtlety, strength, courage and willpower, he simply has the wonderful and
gifted knack of putting the ball into the net from all angles with sweet aplomb
(using his head and both feet) and at times he has certainly cracked home some
superb efforts from well outside the penalty area. He scored on his debut for
Liverpool in a League Cup win over Fulham in September 1993 and followed
up with his first Premiership goal at Chelsea shortly afterwards. After
recovering from a hairline fracture of the right leg, he went on to form
wonderful strike partnerships with Ian Rush, Stan Collymore and then
Michael Owen, and finished up as the Reds' top scorer in 1994–95 (31 goals),
1995–96 (36) and 1996–97 (31). Having battled against tedious injuries as well
as being involved in off-the-field incidents, it still came as a shock to a lot of
fans when he left Anfield for Elland Road. He headed the scoring charts at
Leeds in his first season and actually figured in the 2002 World Cup, making
his last international appearance as a substitute against Denmark in round two.
He quickly moved to Maine Road on a £40,000-a-week contract, and after a
slow start he got back on the goal trail when playing alongside his former
Liverpool colleague Nicolas Anelka. His 12 goals in 2004–05 made him City's
leading striker but a rare penalty miss on the last day of the season v.
Middlesbrough denied City a place in the UEFA Cup. His 16th goal for City
(a penalty against Newcastle United in October 2004) was the 200th goal of
his career at club level. When Fowler returned to Anfield to a hero's reception
in January 2006, he was the first player re-signed by Liverpool on a permanent
basis since Steve Staunton in 1998. He made his 'second' Reds debut when
coming on as a substitute for Peter Crouch at home to Birmingham City on 1
February. His return almost had a fairytale ending, but unfortunately what
would have been an injury-time winner was ruled out for offside.

FOXALL, ABRAHAM

Centre-forward: 1 app.
Born: Sheffield, June 1874 – *Died*: Sheffield, *circa* 1930
Career: Tinsley FC (Sheffield), Gainsborough Trinity (August 1897),

LIVERPOOL (July 1899), Queens Park Rangers (May 1900), Woolwich Arsenal (May 1901), Gainsborough Trinity (August 1903–April 1906)

Abe Foxall's favoured position was outside-left and he was a regular in the first team for each of his other three major clubs, making 128 League appearances in his two spells with Gainsborough. His only outing for Liverpool came against Derby County in October 1899 when he deputised at centre-forward for 'Sailor' Hunter in a 2–0 defeat.

FRIEDEL, BRADLEY HOWARD

Goalkeeper: 30+1 apps

Born: Lakewood, USA, 18 May 1971

Career: University football in USA, Columbus Crew/USA (professional, February 1996), LIVERPOOL (£1m, December 1997), Blackburn Rovers (free, November 2000)

At 6ft 3in. tall and weighing 14st., Brad Friedel is now one of the biggest goalkeepers in the Premiership – and rated one of the best. He was a giveaway by Liverpool after making just 31 appearances for the Reds in almost three years, the first against Aston Villa (away) in February 1998 when he took over from David James. He improved ten-fold at Ewood Park and as well as being Blackburn Rovers' first choice he also starred for his country in the 2002 World Cup and was selected for the 2006 tournament in Germany. He has now gained almost 90 senior caps while also appearing in more than 250 competitive matches for Blackburn, with whom he won the League Cup in 2002. He kept 15 clean sheets in 38 Premiership matches in 2004–05.

FURNELL, JAMES

Goalkeeper: 28 apps

Born: Clitheroe, Lancashire, 23 November 1937

Career: Lancashire schoolboy football, Burnley (amateur, April 1954; professional, November 1954), LIVERPOOL (£18,000, February 1962), Arsenal (£15,000, November 1963), Rotherham United (£9,000, September 1968), Plymouth Argyle (£2,500, December 1970, retired, May 1976, appointed Argyle's assistant manager), Exeter City (scout, season 1977–78), Plymouth Argyle (administration staff, January 1979), Blackburn Rovers (assistant manager, June 1981–May 1983)

Jim Furnell made only three appearances in eight years with Burnley – due to the form of international goalkeepers Colin McDonald and Adam Blacklaw. Transferred to Anfield, he made his debut for Liverpool in a 1–1 draw at Walsall in March 1962, when he took over from Bert Slater, and collected a Second Division championship medal three months later after making 13 appearances. His 28-match unbroken run in the first team ended when Tommy Lawrence took over between the posts in October 1962. Strongly built and decisive in his actions, Furnell remained at the club for another 13 months and after leaving Liverpool he spent five excellent years at Highbury, going on to amass a career appearance total of 486 (430 in the Football League) before retiring in 1976.

GARCIA, LUIS JAVIER

Forward: 27+21 apps, 10 goals

Born: Badalona, Spain, 24 June 1978

Career: CF Barcelona/Spain (amateur June 1994; professional June 1996), Valladolid/Spain (August 1999), Toledo/Spain (loan, November 2000–March 2001), Tenerife/Spain (2000–01), Valladolid/Spain (season 2001–02), Atletico Madrid/Spain (season 2002–03), CF Barcelona/Spain (July 2003), LIVERPOOL (£6m, August 2004)

Joint top scorer for Liverpool in his first season at Anfield with 13 goals, including 5 in the European Champions League which the team ultimately won, Luis Garcia can occupy the right wing position or that of a more central attacker. A positive footballer when on song, he admitted that he was not at his best in 2004–05 yet still did the Reds proud. The Spanish international came on as a substitute in each of his first five outings for his country before netting a hat-trick when making his first start in a World Cup qualifier play-off clash against Slovakia in November 2005. Prior to moving to Anfield he struck home 64 goals in 215 La Liga games, including 29 in 97 outings for Barcelona. Missed Liverpool's 2006 FA Cup final win over West Ham due to suspension, but was in Spain's World Cup squad in Germany a month later.

GARDNER, THOMAS

Wing-half: 5 apps

Born: Huyton, Lancashire, 28 May 1909 – *Died*: Chester, 8 February 1970

Career: Orrell (May 1926), LIVERPOOL (amateur, July 1928; professional, April 1929), Grimsby Town (June 1931), Hull City (May 1932), Aston Villa (£4,500, February 1934), Burnley (April 1938); guest for Preston North End (1941–42), Blackpool (March–April 1943), Southport (1943–44), Manchester United (April 1944), Blackburn Rovers (May 1945), Wrexham (December 1945), Wellington Town (August 1947), Oswestry Town (player-manager, June 1950, reverting to player-coach, January 1952), Saltney FC (August 1952), Chester (assistant trainer/groundsman, July 1954–May 1967; later steward at club for 12 months); then a hotelier in Wrexham until his death

An enthusiastic sportsman, the fair-haired Tom Gardner (nicknamed 'Gandhi') had a fine career that spanned 40 years. A constructive wing-half, always wanting the ball at his feet, he suffered his fair share of injuries but always battled back. He possessed a decidedly long throw and won the *Daily Mail* competition in 1932 for propelling the ball 40 yards into the goalmouth from the touchline, albeit wind-assisted. Capped twice by England, in 1934 v. Czechoslovakia and 1935 v. Holland, he also played in an international trial (1935), gained a Third Division (N) championship medal with Hull City (1933) and a Wartime League (N) Cup winners medal as a guest with Blackpool (1943). He also played for a Football League XI (against a British XI) and for the Army (versus the Football League) in 1939–40. His first game for Liverpool was in place of Tom Morrison at home to Manchester United (won 1–0) in January 1930 and he left Anfield after failing to establish himself in the side. He went on to amass almost 250 pre-

and post-war senior club appearances: 5 for the Reds, 13 for Grimsby, 73 for Hull, 79 for Aston Villa, 40 for Burnley and 38 for Wrexham, whom he also served at outside-right.

GARNER, JAMES ALBERT
Full-back: 5 apps
Born: Pendlebury, Manchester, 18 January 1895 – *Died*: Liverpool, 9 April 1975
Career: Army football (from 1915), LIVERPOOL (professional, April 1922), Southport (July 1926), New Brighton (August 1927–May 1928)

Able to play in both full-back positions, Jim Garner was a capable reserve to Eph Longworth, Tom Lucas and Don McKinlay during his four years at Anfield. He made the first of his five senior appearances for the club against Cardiff City (away) in December 1924 when he deputised for Lucas in a 3–1 win. He did not play a senior game for New Brighton, a knee injury seeing to that!

GARSIDE, JAMES ARTHUR
Centre-forward /outside-left: 5 apps
Born: Manchester, 1885 – *Died*: Devon, *circa* 1939
Career: Manchester junior football, Preston North End (1900), Accrington Stanley (September 1903), LIVERPOOL (August 1904), Accrington Stanley (May 1906), Exeter City (August 1909, retired, May 1913)

A Southern League representative player when registered with Exeter City later in his career, Jim Garside had, prior to that, understudied England international Jack Cox at Anfield for a couple of years, during which time he appeared in just five senior matches, the first against Lincoln City (home) in January 1905 when, in fact, he lined up at centre-forward. He scored 22 goals (including a hat-trick against Stoke in November 1911) in 110 games for Exeter City.

GAYLE, HOWARD ANTHONY
Forward: 3+2 apps, 1 goal
Born: Liverpool, 18 May 1958
Career: Bedford FC (Merseyside Sunday League, 1973), LIVERPOOL (apprentice, June 1974; professional, November 1977), Fulham (loan, January–March 1980), Newcastle United (loan, November 1982–January 1983), Birmingham City (loan, late January 1983), Sunderland (£70,000, August 1984), Birmingham City (£75,000, June 1985), Dallas Sidekicks/USA Indoor League (May 1986), Stoke City (trial, February 1987, signed for £125,000, March 1987), Blackburn Rovers (£5,000, August 1987), Carlisle United (trial, January–February 1992), Wrexham (on trial, March–April 1992), Halifax Town (free, July 1992), Accrington Stanley (free, September 1993–May 1994)

An aggressive and potential match-winner when at his best, Howard Gayle had far too many off-days to become a quality footballer. Nevertheless he had a useful career, making over 200 League appearances before joining Accrington in 1993. He was a registered player with Liverpool for nine years, having just five senior outings, the first against Manchester City in October 1980 when he substituted for David Fairclough in a 3–0 win. An England under-21 international (capped as a Birmingham player), he also came off the subs bench for Sunderland in their 1985 League Cup final defeat by Norwich City.

GEARY, FREDERICK
Centre-forward: 45 apps, 14 goals
Born: Hyson Green, Nottingham, 23 January 1868 – *Died*: Liverpool, 9 January 1955
Career: Nottingham schoolboy football, Balmoral FC (Nottingham), Notts Rangers (April 1886), Grimsby Town (professional, June 1887), Notts Rangers (August 1888), Notts County (briefly), Notts Rangers (March 1889), Everton (July 1889), LIVERPOOL (£60, May 1895, retired, injured, May 1899); was a Liverpool licensee from 1919 to 1946

Fred Geary had the pleasure of scoring Everton's first competitive match hat-trick, in an FA Cup tie against Derby County in January 1890 (Alec Brady and Alf Milward also hit trebles in that same game). An ever-present and leading marksman with 20 goals when the Blues won the League title in 1891, he also topped the club's scoring charts in 1888–89 and 1892–93 and in all claimed 86 goals in 98 games for Liverpool's arch-rivals. Quick and tricky, with a lightning shot, Geary also won two full caps for England, lining up against Ireland in 1890 and Scotland in 1891. He also represented the Football League before joining Liverpool in 1895, adding a Second Division championship medal to his collection a year later. He made his debut for the Reds against his former club, Notts County, in September 1895 and struck 11 League goals in that season before struggling thereafter with a series of injuries which forced him to retire at the age of 31. A teetotaller since 1925, besides his football activities Geary also played for Lancashire at bowls.

GERHARDI, HUGH
Utility: 6 apps
Born: Johannesburg, South Africa, 5 May 1933
Career: Thistle FC/Johannesburg/South Africa (1950), LIVERPOOL (professional, August 1952, released May 1953); returned to South Africa

A versatile performer, able to play as a full-back, central defender, forward and even in goal (he did the latter for Thistle FC in South Africa), Hugh Gerhardi occupied three different positions for Liverpool, making his League debut at inside-right against Middlesbrough at Ayresome Park in February 1953 when he deputised for Kevin Baron in a 3–2 win. He became homesick and returned to South Africa after spending just one season in England.

GERRARD, STEVEN GEORGE
Midfield: 306+11 apps, 64 goals
Born: Huyton, Liverpool, 30 May 1980
Career: LIVERPOOL (apprentice, May 1996; professional, February 1998)
Known to certain people as 'Mr Motivator' and 'Captain Fantastic', Steven Gerrard has certainly played his part in Liverpool's success over the last six years,

helping the team win the European Champions League trophy (2005), the League Cup twice (2001, 2003) and the FA Cup twice (2001, 2006, scoring two stunning goals in the latter victory over West Ham United, plus a penalty in the deciding shoot-out), UEFA Cup (2001) and the European Super Cup (2001). A strong, forceful driving sort of player with a powerful right-foot shot, he is always on the go, battling gamely and manfully in centre field, never shirking a tackle and always looking to get into the opposing danger zone. Capped almost 40 times by England at senior level, having previously played in five youth and four under-21 internationals, he had his disagreements with the club at the end of the 2004–05 campaign but eventually sorted things out with manager Rafael Benitez and is now a major part of the Anfield set up . . . hoping to gain a lot more success and fame in the years ahead. Gerrard made his Premiership debut as a substitute against Blackburn Rovers in November 1998 and scored his first goal for the Reds against Sheffield Wednesday in December 1999 (won 4–1). Voted PFA 'Footballer of the Year' in 2006, he then played his part in the World Cup in Germany.

GILHESPY, THOMAS WILLIAM CYRIL

Outside-right: 19 apps, 3 goals
Born: Fence Houses, County Durham, 18 February 1898 – *Died*: 1985
Career: Chester-le-Street (1919), Sunderland (professional, August 1920), LIVERPOOL (August 1921), Bristol City (July 1925), Blackburn Rovers (June 1929), Reading (June 1930), Mansfield Town (August 1931), Crewe Alexandra (July 1932, retired, May 1933)

Cyril Gilhespy was a professional for 13 years during which time he served with seven different clubs, amassing a total of 199 League appearances and scoring 37 goals. A speedy winger in his younger days, he had to work hard to get into Liverpool's first team, eventually making his debut against his future employers, Blackburn Rovers, in March 1922 when he deputised for Bill Lacey at outside-right in a 0–0 draw at Ewood Park. He just missed out on a League championship medal in 1922 (insufficient appearances) but five years after leaving Anfield he helped Bristol City win the Third Division (S) title, missing only two matches.

GILLESPIE, GARY THOMPSON

Defender: 206+9 apps, 16 goals
Born: Bonnybridge, Stirling, Scotland, 6 July 1960
Career: Falkirk (amateur, July 1975; professional, August 1977), Coventry City (£75,000, March 1978), LIVERPOOL (£325,000, July 1983), Celtic (£925,000, August 1991), Coventry City (free, as player-coach, August 1994, retired as a player, February 1995, continued as youth team coach)

A Scottish international who won 3 youth, 8 under-21 and 13 full caps, the latter between 1987 and 1990, versatile defender Gary Gillespie also gained three League championship winning medals with Liverpool in 1986, 1988 and 1990 while occupying mainly the right-back position but occasionally lining up on the left flank and at centre-half. He came on as a second-half substitute for Mark

Lawrenson in the 1985 European Cup final defeat by Juventus in Brussels and was in Liverpool's team that won the Screen Sport Super Cup the following year. He made 25 appearances for Falkirk and 201 for Coventry City before bringing his poise and ability to read the game to Anfield. He certainly gave the Reds excellent service during his eight-year spell before transferring to Celtic, adding 82 more appearances to his tally (and playing in 3 domestic Cup semi-finals) prior to making his last 4 at competitive level with his former club Coventry. He came off the bench for the first of his 215 appearances for Liverpool against Tottenham Hotspur (away) in October 1984.

GILLIGAN, SAMUEL ALEXANDER

Inside-/centre-forward: 41 apps, 16 goals
Born: Dundee, Scotland, June 1882 – *Died*: Vancouver, Canada, *circa* 1973
Career: Dalry FC/Ayrshire (from 1898), Belmont Athletic (1901), Dundee (professional, August 1902), Celtic (January 1903), Bristol City (July 1904), LIVERPOOL (August 1910), Gillingham (player-manager, May 1913–May 1915); did not feature in football after WW1; later emigrated to Vancouver, Canada

A lively attacker who enjoyed taking on defenders, Sam Gilligan, with his trademark centre parting, had a wonderful career, scoring 127 goals in more than 350 club appearances spread over some 13 years. He certainly played his best football with Bristol City, for whom he struck home 92 goals in 217 games, and was considered to be the best forward the club had ever had up to that point. Earlier he spent 18 months with Dundee, during which time they finished runners-up in the Scottish First Division and reached the semi-final of the Scottish Cup. Celtic won the domestic Cup when he was at Parkhead (1904) and five years later Gilligan played for Bristol City in their FA Cup final defeat by Manchester United, having in between netted 20 goals in 37 League games to help City clinch the Second Division title in 1906. He scored on his senior debut for Liverpool in a 2–1 League win at Manchester City in September 1910 and later that season netted two beauties in a 3–0 victory over FA Cup finalists Newcastle United.

GIVENS, JAMES

Centre-forward/inside-left: 10 apps, 3 goals
Born: Glasgow, Scotland, January 1870 – *Died*: Edinburgh, 1940
Career: Paisley Boys' Club, Dalry FC (August 1890), LIVERPOOL (professional, February 1894), Abercorn (May 1895)

A versatile forward who in later years switched to being a half-back (with Abercorn), Jock Givens scored on his debut for Liverpool against Leicester Fosse in March 1894 when he took over the inside-left position, normally occupied by Jimmy Stott, who was sidelined through injury. He moved once Harry Bradshaw and new signing David Hannah had developed an ongoing partnership in the centre of the Reds' attack.

GLASSEY, ROBERT JOHN

Inside-left: 9 apps, 4 goals

Born: Chester-le-Street, 13 August 1914 – *Died*: Durham, 10 July 1984

Career: Horden Colliery (County Durham), LIVERPOOL (August 1933), Stoke City (May 1937), Mansfield Town (July 1939); guest for Hartlepools United, Newcastle United and Third Lanark during WW2; did not play competitive football after 1946

Bob Glassey showed plenty of aggression and commitment during his four years at Anfield which were spent mainly in the reserves, likewise when he was at Stoke. He scored on his League debut for the Reds against Preston North End in December 1935 when he came into the side (for a run of four games) in a reshuffled forward-line.

GLOVER, JOHN WILLIAM

Right-/left-back: 60 apps

Born: West Bromwich, 22 October 1876 – *Died*: Dudley, 20 April 1955

Career: Christ Church School (West Bromwich), West Bromwich Unity (1981), Great Bridge Unity (1892), Halesowen (1894), Rudge Whitworth FC (1895), West Bromwich Albion (reserves, season 1896–97), Blackburn Rovers (May 1897), New Brompton (£100, July 1899), LIVERPOOL (£350, October 1900), Small Heath/Birmingham (£250, January 1904), Brierley Hill Alliance (August 1898, retired May 1910); became a licensee in Brierley Hill

Rather on the small side for a full-back, John Glover was often brushed aside by taller and stronger opponents during his early days but he stuck to the task and developed into a fine, studious player, strong in the tackle with excellent positional sense and awareness. An England junior international on trial and later a Football League representative, he made 26 appearances for Blackburn and over 50 for New Brompton before joining Liverpool for whom he made his debut against Notts County in October 1900, deputising for Billy Dunlop at left-back. He later switched over to the right and become Dunlop's partner, winning a League championship medal in his first season with the club. After leaving Anfield, Glover made 124 appearances for Small Heath. Besides his duties as a footballer, he also represented Shropshire in county bowls championships.

GODDARD, ARTHUR MILTON

Outside-right/-left: 415 apps, 80 goals

Born: Heaton Norris, Stockport, 1876 – *Died*: Liverpool, *circa* 1960

Career: Heaton Norris Albion (1895), Stockport County (semi-professional, August 1897), Glossop North End (£250 as a professional, November 1899), LIVERPOOL (£1,000, March 1902), Cardiff City (£200, July 1914, served in WW1, retired September 1919); later ran his own business in Liverpool

The recipient of both Second Division and First Division championship winning medals with Liverpool in successive seasons, 1905 and 1906, Artie Goddard made well over 400 senior appearances for the Reds and also represented the Football League on three occasions between 1910 and 1913 during his 12 years at Anfield. A sterling performer, durable and totally dependable, he played mainly on the right wing, skippered the side on several occasions and was known generally as 'Graceful Arthur' (by his teammates) and 'Graceful Artie' (by the fans) . . . because of the stylish way he played the game.

He scored 11 goals in 28 League and Cup games for Stockport and 20 goals in 77 League games for Glossop before transferring his allegiance to Liverpool, for whom he made his senior debut against Wolves in March 1902 in place of Jack Cox on the right flank. He scored twice at the end of his first season to earn 1–1 draws at Grimsby and Nottingham Forest, missed only one game in each of the next two campaigns, was an ever-present in 1905–06 and played in 23 consecutive FA Cup matches between 1903 and 1912, being rewarded with a £250 benefit cheque for his efforts. He never made the first XI with Cardiff.

GOLDIE, ARCHIBALD
Right-back: 150 apps, 1 goal
Born: Hurlford, Ayrshire, 5 January 1874 – *Died*: Bordesley Green, Birmingham, 7 April 1953
Career: Clyde (professional, April 1892), LIVERPOOL (£50, June 1895), Bootle (briefly, July 1900), New Brighton Tower (September 1900), Small Heath/Birmingham (April 1901), Crewe Alexandra (September 1904, retired, May 1905); later returned to Birmingham to work in the BSA factory
Unusually for Edwardian full-backs, Archie Goldie was a footballing defender rather than a player who simply hoofed the ball downfield. He tried to find a colleague with a ground pass and often succeeded. A Second Division championship winner with Liverpool in 1896, he was a regular in the side for five seasons, making exactly 150 first-team appearances, many as partner to first Tom Wilkie and then Billy Dunlop. He made his debut for Liverpool at home to Burslem Port Vale in September 1895 and on leaving Anfield he succeeded John Glover (q.v.) who was soon to become a 'Red'. Goldie was the elder brother of William Glover Goldie (below) and brother to John Wylie Goldie who played for Fulham, Glossop, Bury, Kilmarnock, Dundee and Clyde either side of WW1, and his son, John Goldie (born in 1902), played for Preston North End and Accrington Stanley in 1921–22.

GOLDIE, WILLIAM GLOVER
Left-half: 174 apps, 6 goals
Born: Hurlford, Ayrshire, 22 January 1878 – *Died*: Leicester, *circa* 1924
Career: Hurlford Thistle (1895), Clyde (professional, May 1897), LIVERPOOL (March 1898), Fulham (December 1903), Leicester Fosse (August 1908, retired, April 1911); later ran a pub in Leicester and turned out occasionally for Leicester Imperial
A dour, tough-tackling left-half with a slide-rule pass, Bill Goldie followed his brother (see entry above) to Anfield and, in fact, the pair played together in four League games at the end of the 1897–98 season (the first against Notts County in the April) and regularly over the next two campaigns. An ever-present in the Reds' League championship winning side of 1901, Goldie gave the club five-

and-a-half excellent years' service before joining Fulham, whom he helped rise from non-League football to the Second Division in double-quick time, gaining two successive Southern League championship medals in the process (1906 and 1907). He made almost 500 club appearances during his career. Blessed with a near-impenetrable Scottish accent, Goldie once faced an FA disciplinary committee as a Leicester player and the presiding chairman simply couldn't understand him, so he called for an interpreter.

GOODE, BERTRAM JOHN
Inside-forward: 7 apps, 1 goal
Born: Chester, 11 August 1886 – *Died*: Wrexham, 30 April 1955
Career: Old St Mary's, Hoole FC, Broughton Combination, Saltney FC (Chester), Chester (trial, 1906; signed as a professional, December 1907), LIVERPOOL (£100, May 1908), Wrexham (June 1910), Aston Villa (£250, April 1911), Wrexham (1911), Hull City (£300, May 1912), Wrexham (£225, May 1913); guest for Millwall (October 1917), Southampton (season 1918–19); Rhos Athletic (August 1922), Chester (September 1922), Wrexham (August 1923, retired, May 1926)

Unable to make his mark at Anfield (scoring once in his 7 senior games), following his transfer from Wrexham, Bert Goode immediately netted 46 goals for Aston Villa's reserve side, leading them to the Birmingham and District League title in 1911–12. A terrific opportunist, with plenty of craft, he unfortunately failed to make an impact when presented with first-team football at a higher level and went back to Wrexham with whom he later enjoyed a third spell as a schemer, before retiring three months short of his 40th birthday. A Welsh Cup winner on six occasions – once with Chester in 1908 and five times with Wrexham in 1911, 1914, 1915, 1921 and 1925 – he also gained a runners-up medal in the same competition in 1920. Goode also starred in Wrexham's first-ever League game v. Hartlepools United in August 1921 and despite missing the whole of the 1923–24 and 1925–26 campaigns, he established a record for the Welsh side by scoring a total of 136 goals in 276 games. Regarded as one of that club's greatest-ever players, his benefit match versus a strong Liverpool XI in 1920 realised over £300.

GORDON, PATRICK
Outside-right: 30 apps, 8 goals
Born: Glasgow, Scotland, *circa* 1865 – *Died*: *circa* 1940
Career: Renton (1887), Everton (September 1890), LIVERPOOL (July 1893), Blackburn Rovers (October 1894–May 1895); returned to play in Scotland

Speedy Patrick Gordon was equally effective at outside-right and inside-right, occupying the latter position for Everton when they lost the 1893 FA Cup final to Wolves. Regarded mainly as a reserve at Goodison Park (23 appearances and 5 goals in 3 years) he spent 15 months at Anfield where, at times, he performed positively. He made his debut for Liverpool at Middlesbrough in September 1893 and gained a Second Division championship medal for his efforts that season.

GORMAN, JAMES

Centre-half: 23 apps, 1 goal
Born: Middlesbrough, 1882 – *Died*: *circa* 1957
Career: St Mary's FC (Middlesbrough), Newport Celtic (South Bank and District League), South Bank FC (Northern League), Darlington St Augustine's, LIVERPOOL (March 1906), Leicester Fosse (May 1908–April 1910)

A well-proportioned and adequate defender whose Anfield role was to understudy Alec Raisbeck, Jim Gorman made his League debut in an unusual position, lining up as an emergency inside-left against Sheffield United on the last day of the 1905–06 campaign. The following season he made 12 appearances at centre-half and 10 more in 1907–08 before joining Leicester. Unfortunately he suffered a serious knee injury on his debut, was out of action for quite some time and then, in the second match of his comeback Leicester lost 12–0 to Nottingham Forest. He never played again after that.

GRACIE, THOMAS

Centre-/inside-forward: 33 apps, 5 goals
Born: Glasgow, 12 June 1889 – *Died*: Glasgow, 23 October 1915
Career: Glasgow junior football, Greenock Morton (1909), Everton (March 1911), LIVERPOOL (with Billy Lacey, in exchange for Harold Uren, February 1912), Heart of Midlothian (April 1914 until his death)

Tommy Gracie represented the Scottish League as a Morton player and was highly rated north of the border. He was signed by Everton towards the end of the 1910–11 season and scored once in 13 games for the Blues before moving across Stanley Park to Liverpool in a transfer deal involving two other players. He scored on his debut for the Reds in a 2–2 draw with Bury in February 1912 and he switched to Hearts after losing his place to Jimmy Nicholl. Gracie was serving with the Royal Scots Guards when he was killed in action in 1915, aged just 26.

GRAHAM, ROBERT

Inside-forward: 124+8 apps, 42 goals
Born: Motherwell, 22 November 1944
Career: Scottish schoolboy and intermediate football, LIVERPOOL (apprentice, April 1960; professional November 1961), Coventry City (£70,000, March 1972), Tranmere Rovers (loan, January–March 1973), Motherwell (£20,000, September 1973), Hamilton Academical (£18,000, August 1977–May 1981)

Bobby Graham, whose idol was Ian St John, could play in any forward position and did so with confidence and no mean skill. However, he enjoyed the inside-left berth best and certainly produced some exciting performances in the number 10 shirt. At the age of 19 he had the pleasure, and honour, of scoring a hat-trick on his League debut in September 1964 against Aston Villa – four and a half years after joining the Reds – and made 14 appearances in the First Division that season but then, as the big signings moved in, he had only one outing in

1965–66, three the following term and four (two as a substitute) in 1967–68. Undaunted, he battled on and became a more regular performer after that. In fact, Graham was an ever-present in 1969–70 when he played at centre-forward for 21 matches and then on the left wing, top-scoring with 21 goals. But with John Toshack and Kevin Keegan in command of the two central scoring positions, he moved to pastures new and ironically in 1973 was loaned out by Coventry to Tranmere as a deputy for the injured Ian St John. Graham went on to do superbly well in Scottish football. In 1973–74 he top-scored for Motherwell, became a record signing for Hamilton in 1977 and was 'Accies' leading marksman in 1978–79 with 18 goals. When he quit top-class football in 1981, Graham's career record had realised 460 club appearances of which almost 300 came north of the border. He also netted 146 goals, 93 in Scotland . . . and it was a pleasure to see how well he performed after leaving the English scene.

GRAY, WILLIAM JAMES
Left-back: 1 app.
Born: Glasgow, 16 September 1900 – *Died*: 10 May 1978
Career: Glasgow Boys' Club, Transvaal FC/South Africa (from August 1921), LIVERPOOL (1926), Exeter City (£75, January 1930, retired, August 1936)
Jimmy Gray was the third member of the successful 1924 South African touring party to join Liverpool, the other two being goalkeeper Arthur Riley and forward Gordon Hodgson. Unlike his colleagues, however, he failed to make his mark at Anfield and his only senior appearance was against Sheffield United in September 1928 when he partnered the Reverend Jimmy Jackson at full-back in a 2–1 defeat. Fearless in the tackle, quick in recovery, he made 221 appearances for Exeter City (many alongside Charlie Miller) and is regarded as one of the Devon club's best-ever signings. A huge favourite with the supporters, his benefit match against Liverpool in May 1935 drew a crowd of 5,000 to St James Park. Gray played in 12 internationals for South Africa (after claiming citizenship) . . . and one reference book lists his Christian name as Alfred.

GRAYER, FRANK
Right-back: 1 app.
Born: Brighton, 13 February 1890 – *Died*: Southampton, 21 January 1961
Career: St Deny's School (Brighton), Fazeley St Mary's Athletic (Southampton), Southampton (trial, June–July 1908; professional, August 1908), LIVERPOOL (£100, June 1912); served in the Army from 1914 and was badly wounded at Ypres. Did not play after WW1 and later worked for a furniture company, Shepherd and Hedges in Southampton, until 1955
A solid and reliable defender, Frank Grayer made only six Southern League appearances for Southampton and just one in the First Division for Liverpool v. Manchester United, at Anfield in April 1914 when he deputised at right-back for Eph Longworth. Grayer was a big buddy of Reds goalkeeper Elisha Scott.

GREEN, THOMAS
Forward: 7 apps, 1 goal
Born: Rock Ferry, Cheshire, 25 November 1881 – *Died*: Lancaster, *circa* 1954
Career: Saltney FC (1889), LIVERPOOL (professional, August 1901), Swindon
   Town (May 1903), Stockport County (1904), Middlesbrough (£300,
   February 1905), Queens Park Rangers (June 1906), Stockport County
   (August 1907), Exeter City (May 1909), Preston North End (July 1910–May
   1912); returned to guest for LIVERPOOL during 1917–18 season

Able to play in most forward positions, Tommy Green preferred to lead the
attack or line up on the right wing. Fast and clever, he just wasn't good enough
in truth to make a name for himself in top-flight football but after leaving
Anfield he did well in lower divisions, being a regular with every club until
signing for Preston. He made the first of his seven appearances for Liverpool
against Bury in February 1902 when he deputised at outside-right for Jack Cox.
He scored 28 goals in 88 first-team outings for Stockport, whom he helped win
the Lancashire Combination in 1905.

GRIFFIN, MICHAEL RICHARD
Forward: 4 apps
Born: Middlesbrough, April 1887 – *Died*: Yorkshire, *circa* 1951
Career: Darlington St Augustine's (from 1904), LIVERPOOL (professional,
   July 1907), Crystal Palace (May 1909), Hartlepools United (April 1910),
   Barnsley (June 1912–May 1915, retired during WW2)

Mick Griffin played in the same St Augustine's team as James Gorman (q.v.)
and joined Liverpool at the age of 20, making his League debut in February
1908 against Arsenal at Anfield, starring in a 4–1 win. Unfortunately, with so
many other talented footballers at the club he struggled to get into the first XI
and after two seasons moved to Crystal Palace, for whom he made 34
appearances in the old Southern League. He followed up with 50 outings for
Hartlepools and 69 for Barnsley. Some reference books spell this player's
surname as Griffen.

GRIFFITHS, HAROLD
Full-back: 6 apps
Born: Middlesbrough, 2 January 1886 – *Died*: Glasgow, *circa* 1933
Career: Middlesbrough junior football, LIVERPOOL (professional, December
   1903), Chesterfield Town (August 1908), Partick Thistle (May 1909–May
   1912)

After an easing-in period at Anfield, Harry Griffiths finally made the first of his
six League appearances for Liverpool against Sheffield Wednesday (away) in
October 1905 when he deputised at right-back for Alf West in a 3–1 defeat. He
had 22 League outings with Chesterfield and played in over 40 first-team
matches for Partick.

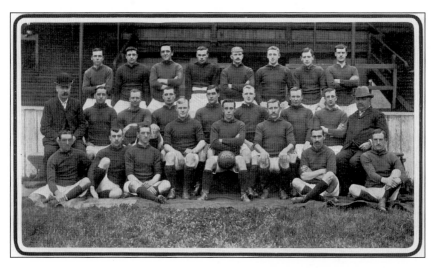
Liverpool team line-up (First Division champions 1905–06)

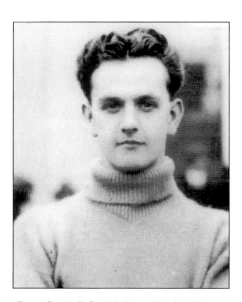
Kenny Campbell, Scottish international goalkeeper who kept Elisha Scott out of the side for a time

Jimmy Case, tough-tackling midfielder who helped Liverpool win six different trophies

Ray Clemence, England international goalkeeper who made well over 660 appearances for Liverpool

Willie Fagan, Scottish wartime international who was registered with Liverpool for 15 years (1937–52)

Gary Gillespie, Scottish international at three different levels who made almost 140 appearances for Liverpool (Ashton Sports Agency Ltd)

Extrovert goalkeeper Bruce Grobbelaar, who served Liverpool for 12 years (1981–93) during which time he made 621 senior appearances

Pre-WW2 outside-left Adolf Hanson scored 52 goals in 177 League and Cup games for Liverpool

Centre-forward Fred Howe netted 36 goals in 94 outings for Liverpool during the mid-1930s

FRED HOWE
Liverpool F.C.   Topical Times.

Republic of Ireland midfield Ray Houghton cost Liverpool £825,000 when signed from Oxford United in 1987

David Johnson played for both Everton and Liverpool, helping the Reds win three League titles and the European Cup — as well as playing for England

Phil Neal scored 60 goals in 650 games for Liverpool from the full-back position

Manager Bob Paisley's record of trophy wins for Liverpool has only been bettered in British football by Manchester United boss Sir Alex Ferguson and Celtic's Jock Stein

Bill Shankly, manager at Anfield from 1959 to 1974, during his time at Preston North End

Goalkeeper Cyril Sidlow, who won a League championship medal with Liverpool in 1947 and an FA Cup runners-up medal in 1950

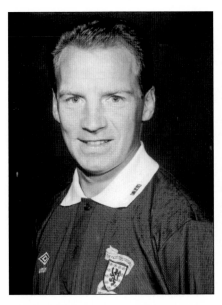
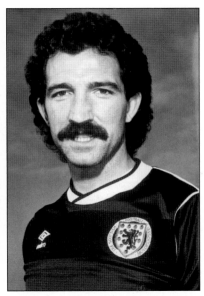

David Speedie, nomadic Scottish international striker who served with 11 different League clubs in an adventurous career

Scottish international midfielder Graeme Souness played for and managed both Liverpool and Glasgow Rangers (Sportapics Ltd)

Before joining Liverpool, Sammy Smyth scored one of the finest goals ever seen in a Wembley FA Cup final for Wolves against Leicester City in 1949

'Big' John Toshack, aide and accomplish to Kevin Keegan in Liverpool's attack for many years

Nick Barmby, versatile forward who cost Liverpool £6m when signed from Everton in 2000 — this being the first transfer between the 2 clubs for 41 years

David Burrows, Black Country-born defender who also played for Everton, made almost 200 appearances for Liverpool

Striker Stan Collymore cost Liverpool £8.5m when signed from Nottingham Forest in 1995

South African outside-right Berry Nieuwenhuys played for Liverpool before, during and after WW2. After retiring he became a professional golfer

Geoff Twentyman played centre-
half for Liverpool during the
1950s and worked as a scout
for the club

Alan A'Court, a fast-raiding winger
who played for England

Emlyn Hughes, known as 'Crazy Horse',
made over 650 appearances for
the Reds

Johnny Evans signed for Liverpool
in 1953 and went on to represent
the Football League

Billy Liddell, one of the great names in Liverpool's history and scorer of 229 goals

Scottish international Ian St John was a masterful signing by Bill Shankly in 1961

Ron Yeats, brilliant centre-half who gained two caps for Scotland

Craig Johnston, hard-working midfielder born in South Africa and brought up in Australia, who also played for Middlesbrough

GROBBELAAR, BRUCE DAVID

Goalkeeper: 621 apps

Born: Durban, South Africa, 6 October 1957

Career: Served in South Africa with, in turn, the Inyarura Police team, Salisbury Callies, Matabeleland Highlanders, Hamilton High School, Bulawayo Boys, Chibuka Shumba, Salisbury Callies (again), Durban City and Amazula (guest); then West Bromwich Albion (trial, July–September 1978), AFC Bournemouth (trial, September 1978), Vancouver Whitecaps/NASL (October 1978), Crewe Alexandra (trial/loan, December 1979–May 1980), LIVERPOOL (£250,000, March 1981), Stoke City (loan, March–April 1993), Southampton (free, August 1994), Plymouth Argyle (free, August 1996), Oxford United (free, early September 1997), Sheffield Wednesday (free, late September 1997), Oldham Athletic (free, December 1997–January 1998), Chesham (free, July 1998), Bury (free, September 1998), Lincoln City (free, December 1998, released, January 1999), Manning Rangers/South Africa (coach, from 2000)

Of Bruce Grobbelaar's 621 senior appearances for Liverpool, 440 came in the Football League (all in the First Division), 70 in the League Cup, 62 in the FA Cup and 30 in the European Cup. In a playing career that spanned 24 years, his overall appearance tally topped the 800 mark and that included 20 international outings for Rhodesia/Zimbabwe, and he also represented the Football League. During his time at Anfield he won six League championships (1982–83–84–86–88–90), three League Cup finals (1982–83–84), three FA Cup finals (1986–89–92), the European Cup (1984), three FA Charity Shields (1982–88–89) and the Screen Sport Super Cup (1986). Certainly an eccentric, often doing unbelievable things between the posts, sometimes acting as a sweeper, Grobbelaar, nevertheless, was an outstanding goalkeeper, brave, a brilliant shot-stopper and a great motivator, despite his antics. He was terrific in the 1984 European Cup final and if you are a Liverpool supporter you'll know that his wobbly legs routine was well worth the effort in the penalty shoot-out. And then there was that superb save that denied Everton's Graeme Sharp a goal in the 1986 FA Cup final – which proved to be the turning point and set the Reds up for a famous victory. Taking over from Ray Clemence, he was given his Liverpool baptism against Wolves in August 1981, keeping a clean sheet in a 0–0 draw and, in fact, he was an ever-present from that day until 3 May 1986 while making a total of 213 consecutive appearances at competitive level. He had a bout of meningitis during the 1988–89 season but recovered and regained his place. He kept well over 250 clean sheets for the Reds. His last League game in England came some 18 years after his first, for Lincoln City against Wycombe Wanderers in December 1999 (lost 4–1). He scored one goal at competitive level – a penalty in his last game for Crewe Alexandra versus York City in May 1980 (clinching a 2–0 win). It was never dull when Bruce Grobbelaar was keeping goal – believe me. Incidentally, in Dutch, Grobbelaar means clumsy!

GUNSON, JOSEPH GORDON
Outside-left: 87 apps, 26 goals
Born: Chester, 1 July 1904 – *Died*: Broughton, Flintshire, 8 September 1991
Career: Chester schoolboy football, Brickfields FC (Chester), Nelson (amateur, April 1923; professional, August 1923), Wrexham (May 1926), Sunderland (£1,500, June 1929), LIVERPOOL (March 1930), Swindon Town (June 1935), Wrexham (May 1935), Bangor City (player-manager, from August 1936), Crewe Alexandra (trainer, seasons 1945–50), Flint Town (manager, 1950–55), Welshpool (manager, 1956–62), Dolgellau FC (manager, during the 1964–65 season); also employed as a scout by Blackpool, Coventry City, Derby County and Wrexham

During his career in League football Joe Gunson scored 69 goals in 272 matches, playing his best football for Wrexham (for whom he netted 45 goals in 149 games in 2 spells) and Liverpool, for whom he was an ever-present in 1931–32, registering 19 goals. A clever winger, able to occupy both flanks but preferring the right, he could cross a ball inch-perfect and set up several chances for the likes of Gordon Hodgson, Archie McPherson, Jimmy Smith and Dave Wright. He made the first of his 87 appearances for Liverpool against Bolton Wanderers in March 1930 and his last against Blackburn Rovers in March 1933. After two seasons in the reserves, he moved to Swindon when Alf Hanson and Berry Nieuwenhuys were regarded as the first-choice wingers at Anfield. Gunson died in a nursing home at the age of 87.

HAFECOST, CHARLES HENRY
Right-half: 1 app.
Born: Sunderland, 22 March 1890 – *Died*: 1967
Career: Sunderland Royal Rovers, Gillingham (professional, July 1912), LIVERPOOL (August 1914); did not play after WW1

Charlie Hafecost joined Liverpool after topping Gillingham's scoring charts in 1913–14. He made 50 appearances in total for the Kent club (14 goals) but failed to impress at Anfield, having just one senior outing for the Reds against Middlesbrough (home) in November 1914 when he deputised for Tom Fairfoul in a 1–1 draw.

HAIGH, JOHN
Inside-forward: 11 apps, 3 goals
Born: Rotherham, 10 September 1928
Career: Gainsborough Trinity (1945), LIVERPOOL (October 1949), Scunthorpe United (£3,900, August 1952), Doncaster Rovers (£5,000, July 1960–May 1962)

Hard-working inside-forward Jack Haigh had to battle for a place in the first XI at Anfield and in three years made only 11 first-team appearances, the first against Blackpool in December 1950 when over 54,000 fans saw the Reds win 1–0. He did superbly well with Scunthorpe after leaving Liverpool and gained a Third Division (N) championship medal in 1958 when he formed a wonderfully exciting left wing partnership with another ex-Liverpool player,

Mervyn Jones. Haigh scored 65 goals in 329 League appearances in 8 seasons with Scunthorpe.

HALL, BRIAN WILLIAM, BSc
Forward: 198+24 apps, 21 goals
Born: Glasgow, 22 January 1946
Career: Preston Grammar School, Lancashire Grammar Schools; trials with Blackburn Rovers, Bolton Wanderers and Preston North End during season 1961–62; Liverpool University (graduated 1968); LIVERPOOL (professional, July 1968), Plymouth Argyle (£35,000, July 1976), Burnley (£25,000, November 1977); played non-League football between August 1980 and May 1985; later became a schoolteacher; now runs the ex-Liverpool Players' Association (from Anfield)

An aggressive, busy little player with a heart of gold, Brian Hall had to wait until April 1969 (when he was 23) before making his League debut for Liverpool as a substitute in a 0–0 draw at Stoke, the game in which another university student, Steve Heighway, also made his first appearance for the club. The pair were nicknamed 'Little Bamber' and 'Big Bamber'. Hall became a key member of the side in 1970–71 and made almost 225 first-class appearances before moving to Plymouth in 1976, having lost his place earlier to Peter Cormack, regained it and then lost it again to Jimmy Case. Hall won the UEFA Cup and League title with the Reds in 1973 and the FA Cup a year later, having gained a runners-up medal in this competition v. Arsenal in 1971. His career realised 328 appearances and 40 goals. Hall says he would have liked to have been an astronaut if he hadn't made it in football.

HAMANN, DIETMAR
Midfield: 252+29 apps, 11 goals
Born: Waldasson, Bavaria, Germany, 27 August 1973
Career: Wacker Munich/Germany (1990) Bayern Munich/Germany (April 1993), Newcastle United (£4.5m, August 1998), LIVERPOOL (£8m, July 1999)

Regarded as the 'metronome' at the heart of the Liverpool midfield, Didi Hamann's role in the Liverpool side seems to be unspectacular but his presence has, over the years, proved vitally important to the team. The anchorman in midfield and unusually tall at 6ft 3in. for a player in this position, he is a fine passer of the ball and packs a ferocious shot . . . one of his rockets scored for his country against England in a World Cup qualifier was, in fact, the last major competitive goal seen at the old Wembley Stadium in October 2000 and it decided the contest (1–0). A member of Liverpool's UEFA Cup, FA Cup, League Cup and Charity Shield winning sides in 2001, he added a Champions League winner's medal to his collection in 2005 and a second FA Cup winner's medal in 2006. He has 60 full caps under his belt plus others at both youth and under-21 levels. He made 105 appearances for Bayern Munich in the Bundesliga and only 23 in the Premiership for Newcastle, appearing in their 1999 FA Cup final defeat by Manchester United.

HANCOCK, EDMUND

Forward: 9 apps, 2 goals

Born: Rotherham, 29 March 1907 – *Deceased*

Career: Denaby United (1926), Gainsborough Trinity (1929), LIVERPOOL (January 1931), Burnley (February 1933), Luton Town (November 1936), Northwich Victoria (briefly, June 1938), Lincoln City (July 1938), Frickley Colliery (May 1939); did not play after WW2

A former miner, Ted Hancock appeared mostly as an inside-forward during a varied career. A forceful player with plenty of skill, he made his League debut for Liverpool against Huddersfield Town (home) in March 1932 and scored his first goal in the 88th minute of his third game to earn a 2–1 win over Chelsea. After leaving Anfield, Hancock netted 30 times in 123 outings for Burnley (in three and a half years) and gained a Third Division (S) championship winner's medal with Luton Town (1937).

HANNAH, ANDREW BOYD

Right-back: 70 apps, 2 goals

Born: Renton, Dunbartonshire, 17 September 1864 – *Died*: Scotland, 17 June 1940

Career: Renton (August 1883), West Bromwich Albion (September–October 1888), Renton (November 1888), Everton, (August 1889), Renton (July 1891), LIVERPOOL (July 1892), Rob Roy FC (October 1895, retired May 1897)

A noted Victorian footballer, Andrew Hannah was the first player to captain both Everton and Liverpool. Before he moved to Goodison Park, he appeared in three Scottish Cup finals with Renton, gaining winner's medals in 1885 and 1888, the same year he won his only cap for Scotland (against Wales). A formidable opponent, he was physically strong, possessed a biting tackle, kicked hard and true and above all was a very consistent performer, hardly ever out injured and utterly reliable. He partnered Dan Doyle at full-back for Everton and collected a League championship winner's medal in 1891, adding a Second Division prize to his awards with Liverpool in 1893. The first of his 70 games for the Reds was in fact the club's initial League game, a Second Division fixture against Middlesbrough (away) in September 1893. The first of his two goals came right at the end of that season in a 2–1 victory over Burslem Port Vale. Hannah was also a superb athlete and won prizes at four Highland Games competitions.

HANNAH, DAVID

Inside-left: 33 apps, 13 goals

Born: Raffrey, County Down, 28 April 1867 – *Died*: Glasgow, Scotland, 1940

Career: Renton (part time, August 1882), Sunderland (professional, July 1889), LIVERPOOL (November 1894), Dundee (July 1897), Woolwich Arsenal (October 1897–May 1899)

Davy and Andrew Hannah (above) were cousins. Irish-born Davy moved to Renton as a young boy and worked in a local dye factory from the age of 13,

100

eventually joining Renton in 1882 as a promising reserve. Equally at home in both inside-forward berths, he could also play on either wing (doing so admirably at times) and although he wasn't a Liverpool player all that long, he certainly gave the club good service, scoring almost a goal every three games. He made his debut for the Reds against Stoke in November 1894 and secured his first goal for the club in the Merseyside derby with Everton a week later in a 2–2 draw. He scored 24 goals in 88 games for Sunderland and 17 in 50 games for Arsenal.

HANSEN, ALAN DAVID

Defender: 618+2 apps, 13 goals
Born: Sauchie, Clackmannanshire, Scotland, 13 June 1955
Career: Sauchie Juniors (1970), Partick Thistle (amateur on non-contract forms, July 1973; professional, December 1973), LIVERPOOL (£100,000, May 1977, retired, May 1990); now a respected TV soccer pundit who also features in various adverts

Alan Hansen played in 104 League and Cup games for Partick Thistle, helping them win the Scottish First Division title in 1976. Then, after his club had turned down a £70,000 bid for his signature from Bolton Wanderers, he moved to Anfield shortly before his 22nd birthday – a snip of a signing by manager Bob Paisley – and gave Liverpool 13 years' excellent service, accumulating 620 first-team appearances while starring in eight First Division championship winning sides (1979–80–82–83–84–86–88–90), three League Cup winning teams (1981–83–84) and three triumphant European Cup sides (1978–81–84) as well as tasting victory in the Screen Sport Super Cup (1986) and FA Charity Shield (1979, 1980, 1982 and 1989, sharing the glory in 1986). After captaining the 1985–86 double-winning side he was surprisingly omitted from his country's World Cup finals squad that summer. However, during a wonderfully successful career he played in three under-23 and 26 full internationals for Scotland and also represented the Football League while at the same time earning the reputation as one of the best defenders in European (perhaps world) football. Cool and composed under pressure, he looked comfortable on the ball and in fact may well have become a midfield schemer had he not settled in defence where he produced many outstanding performances for club and country. He suffered a serious eye injury on the eve of the 1988–89 season which left him badly scarred – noticeable these days when he appears on TV – and at the time his career was threatened. But he recovered and continued playing for another year or so, dismissing rumours that he was about to join the club's coaching staff. He made his debut for Liverpool against Derby County in September 1977, partnering Emlyn Hughes at the heart of the defence and in later years his co-central defenders included Mark Lawrenson and Phil Thompson. Besides being a footballer, Hansen was also adept at basketball (being a Scottish international in this sport) and on the volleyball and squash courts, and he is also a very competent golfer.

His elder brother, John Angus McDonald Hansen, born in 1950, also played for Partick Thistle (1967–78) and won two full caps for Scotland.

HANSON, ADOLPH JONATHAN

Outside-left: 177 apps, 52 goals

Born: Bootle, 27 February 1912 – *Deceased*

Career: Bootle Schoolboys, Bootle JOC, Everton (trial, 'A' team, 1930), LIVERPOOL (professional, November 1931), Chelsea (£7,500, July 1938); guest for Bolton Wanderers, Chester, Crewe Alexandra, LIVERPOOL, Manchester City, New Brighton, Rochdale, Southport, Tranmere Rovers and Wrexham, during WW2; South Liverpool (player-manager, August 1946), Shelbourne United/Ireland (player-manager, July 1948), Ellesmere Port Town (player-manager, February 1949–May 1950)

'Alf' Hanson, a plumber by trade, and his brother, Stan Hanson, who went on to make 423 senior appearances for Bolton Wanderers (1936–56), were both at Anfield together during the early 1930s. A danger to all defences with his thrusting and intriguing wing-play, Alf loved to swing the ball from on or near the left hand touchline right over to the far post where either Gordon Hodgson or Dave Wright, then Sam English or 'Nivvy' Nieuwenhuys and later Fred Howe or Jack Balmer, were seemingly always on hand to nod them in. He made his debut in a Liverpool shirt against Aston Villa in January 1933, replacing Joe Gunson on the left wing in a 5–2 defeat. He remained at Anfield until 1938 when, just as Liverpool let his brother join Bolton, so they sold Alf to Chelsea for a substantial fee. Ironically he made his debut for the Londoners against Liverpool and played for England against Scotland in a wartime international in 1941 – his only representative honour – but the war surely robbed him of some plum seasons. However he did make over 130 appearances during the hostilities while starring as a guest for 10 different clubs, having his best spell with New Brighton (49 games). He had made just five outings with the Reds, scoring one goal. Also a very capable baseball player, Hanson was a pitcher for the Everton baseball team in the Merseyside and District League, playing mostly at Goodison Park.

HARDY, SAMUEL

Goalkeeper: 239 apps

Born: Newbold Verdom, Derbyshire, 26 August 1883 – *Died*: Chesterfield, 24 October 1966

Career: Newbold Church School (1898), Newbold White Star (July 1900), Chesterfield (professional, April 1903), LIVERPOOL (£500, October 1905), Aston Villa (£600, with Jimmy Harrop, May 1912); guest for Plymouth Argyle, Nottingham Forest and The Royal Naval Barracks FC/Plymouth during WW1; Nottingham Forest (£1,000, August 1921, retired, May 1925); later a hotelier in Chesterfield; also ran his own billiard/snooker hall in Alfreton, Derbyshire

'Sam "Chuffer" Hardy was one of the greatest goalkeepers I ever saw play,' said Jesse Pennington, the former West Bromwich Albion and England left-back who was in the game for 19 years (1903–22). Indeed, Hardy was quite a player and during a wonderful career he amassed more than 600 appearances for clubs and country. He made goalkeeping look easy and would have been considered a world-class player in any era. Commanding the number one spot in the England team either side of WW1, ahead of such greats as Burnley's Jerry Dawson and Tim Williamson of Middlesbrough, he won 21 caps between 1907 and 1921, played in three Victory internationals, twice represented the Football League against the Scottish League and starred for Birmingham against London, for England against the South of England in 1913 and against the North in 1914. He won a First Division championship medal with Liverpool in 1906, collected a Second Division winner's medal with Nottingham Forest in 1922 and also received two FA Cup winner's medals with Aston Villa in 1913 and 1920 as well as helping Nottingham Forest win the WW1 Championship play-off final against Everton. He was signed by Liverpool despite having conceded plenty of goals when keeping for Chesterfield, including six against the Reds in a Cup tie. Also known as 'Safe and Steady Sam', he made his debut for the club against his future employers Nottingham Forest in October 1905, taking over from Ted Doig, and remained first choice between the posts until 1912 when he handed over the duties to Scotsman Kenny Campbell. Hardy's last League outing was for Forest in October 1924, aged 41. His nephew, Ted Worrell, played for Aberdare, Fulham, New Brighton, Southport, Sheffield Wednesday and Watford between 1910 and 1929.

HARKNESS, STEPHEN
Utility: 119+20 apps
Born: Carlisle, 27 August 1971
Career: Carlisle United (apprentice, August 1987; professional, March 1989), LIVERPOOL (£75,000, July 1989), Huddersfield Town (loan, September–October 1993), Southend United (loan, February–May 1995), Benfica/Portugal (£750,000, March 1999), Blackburn Rovers (£400,000, September 1999), Sheffield Wednesday (£200,000, September 2000), Chester City (May 2002)

Former England youth international team captain who also represented his country as a schoolboy, Steve Harkness played in just 13 League games for Carlisle before joining Liverpool at the age of 17. With so much talent available at Anfield, he bided his time in the reserves and finally made his debut for the club against QPR in August 1991 when there was a minor injury crisis within the camp. Able to play at full-back (wing-back), in central defence or midfield, he was a fierce tackler and worked tirelessly whenever called into the first XI. 'Harkie' battled on gamely and eventually became a valuable member of the squad, going on to appear in almost 140 senior matches for the Reds, but sadly never collecting a winner's medal in a major competition. He suffered a badly broken leg in April 1996, shattered by an uncharacteristically wild tackle from Coventry City's John Salako, but came back strongly and went on to serve Liverpool (and two other English clubs) for another three years before moving to Portugal (signed by Graeme Souness). He was never the same player after returning from Portugal (he had a torrid time with injuries at Hillsborough) and entered non-League football with Chester City in 2002.

HARLEY, JAMES
Full-back: 133 apps
Born: Methil, Fife, Scotland, 21 February 1917 – *Died*: Liverpool, 1989
Career: Hearts o' Beath (amateur, April 1932), LIVERPOOL (professional, April 1934, retired, injured, February 1949); served in the Royal Navy during WW2

A Scottish wartime international, capped against England at Villa Park in February 1945 when fellow Anfield colleagues Billy Liddell and Matt Busby also starred, and against the same opponents at Hampden Park two months later in front of 133,000 spectators, Jim Harley helped Liverpool win the First Division championship in 1947 before injury ended his career at the age of 30. A powerful tackler, quick over the ground (he took part in the famous Powderhall sprint at the age of 18 using the pseudonym of A B Mitchell), he certainly enjoyed his football, always playing with a smile on his face (unless he was injured). He made the first of his 133 appearances for Liverpool in a 5–0 home League win over West Bromwich Albion in September 1935 when he partnered Ernie Blenkinsop in the absence of Tommy Cooper. Powerful in the tackle, with superb positional sense, he seemed at ease with all types of wingers. He was sent off in the last League game before WW2 versus Chelsea, but the case was never heard and he survived a suspension. Harley scored 3 times in 45 WW2 appearances for the Reds, and during the hostilities, besides his international outings, he played for his country against the RAF (1944) and for Scottish Services v. Belgium and the Royal Navy v. the Army (1945).

HARRINGTON, JAMES CHRISTOPHER
Outside-right/-left: 4 apps
Born: Edghill, Liverpool, 25 December 1896 – *Died*: 6 May 1978
Career: South Liverpool (August 1919), LIVERPOOL (professional, May 1920), Wigan Borough (September 1921), Southport (January 1923), Crewe Alexandra (May 1923), Mold FC (during season 1924–25); later with New York Giants/USA

Tall for a winger, Chris Harrington split his senior outings with Liverpool to two on either flank, making his debut on the left in February 1921 in place of Bert Pearson in a 1–1 draw with Manchester United at Old Trafford. He moved on when Fred Hopkin and Billy Lacey took over as the club's first-choice wingers at the start of the 1921–22 season. After leaving Anfield, Harrington made only 48 more League appearances prior to emigrating to the States.

HARROP, JAMES
Half-back: 139 apps, 4 goals
Born: Heeley, Sheffield, 1884 – *Died*: 1958
Career: St Wilfred's and Heeley County Schools, Kent Road Mission (1898), Ronmoor Wesleyans (1900), Sheffield Wednesday (trial, then amateur 1903; professional, August 1904), Denaby United (1906), Rotherham Town (1907), LIVERPOOL (January 1908), Aston Villa (£600 with Sam Hardy, June 1912); WW1 guest for Sheffield Wednesday (1915–19); Sheffield United

(£500, March 1921), Burton All Saints (August 1922, retired, April 1924)
The son of a Yorkshire farmer, Jimmy Harrop failed to make Sheffield Wednesday's first team and also struggled at Rotherham before finally making a start with Liverpool, who handed him his League debut against Bolton Wanderers in January 1908. Able to play in all three half-back positions, but preferring the pivotal role, Harrop was among the brainiest of defenders, a player who brought intelligence to bear when tackling and then feeding passes through to his forwards. He gave the Reds four years' excellent service before transferring to Villa Park – a month after goalkeeper Sam Hardy had taken the same road. He won the FA Cup with Villa in 1913 and then after WW1 (during which he worked in the manufacture of agricultural implements) he became captain, but missed the 1920 final through injury. He twice represented the Football League, played in two international trials, and starred for Birmingham against London in 1913, while acting as reserve for England v. Wales in the same year. Known as 'Head Up Harrop' he made 171 appearances for Villa, scoring 4 goals.

HARROWER, JAMES
Inside-forward: 105 apps, 22 goals
Born: Alva near Stirling, Clackmannanshire, 18 August 1935
Career: Sauchie Juveniles, Kilsyth Rangers, Sauchie Juveniles (again), Bo'ness United, Hibernian (amateur, September 1954; professional, August 1955), LIVERPOOL (£11,000, January 1958), Newcastle United (£15,000, March 1961), Falkirk (£3,115, January 1962), St Johnstone (July 1963), Albion Rovers (season 1965–66)
Jimmy Harrower enjoyed a good rapport with the Anfield crowd and gave the club excellent service for three years before moving to Newcastle United. A Scottish youth and under-23 international, he made his debut for the Reds against Fulham in January 1958 when he deputised at inside-right for fellow Scot Bobby Murdoch in a 2–1 win. He scored the first of his 22 goals for the club two months later against Ipswich Town and had his best run in the team in 1959–60 when partnering left-winger Alan A'Court, his 5 goals in 26 outings helping the Reds finish third in the Second Division. Harrower had the extraordinary ability to beat the goalkeeper with his eyes – glancing left (or right) and then slotting the ball towards the goal in the opposite direction. He struggled at St James' Park, making only six appearances, and following his release by manager Charlie Mitten he returned to Scotland, where his talents were always appreciated. His father and grandfather both played for St Mirren.

HARSTON, EDWIN
Centre-forward: 5 apps, 3 goals
Born: Monk Bretton near Barnsley, 27 February 1907 – *Deceased*
Career: Cudworth Village, Sheffield Wednesday (July 1928), Barnsley (May 1930), Reading (May 1931), Bristol City (June 1934), Mansfield Town (£250, October 1935), LIVERPOOL (£3,000, June 1937), Ramsgate Town (player-manager, June 1939); did not figure in football after WW2
Failing to make a serious impact with any of his first four major clubs, although he

did net a double hat-trick (six goals) for Barnsley against his future employers Mansfield Town in a Yorkshire Mid-week League game in April 1931, as well as netting 17 times in 28 League games for Bristol City, Ted Harston developed into a superb marksman as he got older and wiser. Rated by many as the best centre-forward Mansfield have ever had, he scored 85 goals in only 75 appearances for the Stags in two seasons before joining Liverpool. In fact, he holds in perpetuity the record for most strikes in a Third Division (N) campaign – 55 in 1936–37 – the same number that hot-shot Joe Payne fired home for Luton Town in that very same season. Quick yet unskilled and never a creator of chances, Harston was simply a snatch and grab marksman of the highest calibre, often sneaking up unnoticed to poke the ball home off the toe of a defender or move across his marker to flick home a free-kick or a corner with the deftest of touches. He possessed a powerful right-foot shot and often used it to good effect when given space, and he was no mean header of the ball either. After moving to Liverpool, he scored three times in five games for the Reds, the first on his debut in a 6–1 drubbing at Chelsea in August 1937, before a broken leg ended his progress. He returned with the reserves but was unable to regain his first-team place and eventually moved into non-League football with Ramsgate at the age of 32.

HARTILL, WILLIAM JOHN
Inside-/centre-forward: 5 apps
Born: Wolverhampton, 18 July 1905 – *Died*: Walsall, 12 August 1980
Career: Wolverhampton Schools; served in the Army (Royal Horse Artillery), Wolverhampton Wanderers (professional, August 1928), Everton (July 1935), LIVERPOOL (January 1936), Bristol Rovers (March 1936, retired, May 1938); became a Wolverhampton-based licensee
Nicknamed 'Artillery Billy', Hartill was rated as one of the best marksmen in the Football League during his time at Molineux. Indeed, he fired home 170 goals in 234 appearances for Wolves, with whom he gained a Second Division championship medal in 1932. Prior to that, he had netted 70 times in two seasons while playing for his Army unit in the RHA and for the British Army Select XI. He scored on his debut for Everton but never settled at Goodison Park or Anfield, appearing in exactly the same number of games for both Merseyside clubs (five). His first outing for Liverpool was against Grimsby Town (away) in January 1936 when he deputised at centre-forward for Fred Howe in a 0–0 draw. Hartill represented the Football League against a Midlands XI in 1935 – his only major representative honour.

HARTLEY, ABRAHAM
Forward: 12 apps, 1 goal
Born: Dumbarton, 8 February 1872 – *Died*: Southampton, 9 October 1909
Career: Artizan Thistle (Dumbarton), Dumbarton FC (professional, May 1890), Everton (December 1892), LIVERPOOL (December 1897), Southampton (May 1898), Woolwich Arsenal (July 1899), Burnley (December 1899, retired, May 1900); later employed by the South West Railway, he collapsed and died outside the pay office on the dockside at Southampton, aged 37

The son of a tailor and one of three brothers who all played for Dumbarton, Abraham Hartley was regarded as a 'useful' centre-forward, able also to occupy both inside berths and that of right-back (in an emergency). He did well north of the border and after moving south, scored on his debut for Everton in a 4–2 win at Wolves in March 1893. Never a regular in the Blues' side, he nevertheless gained an FA Cup runners-up medal in 1897 before joining Liverpool at the age of 25. His initial outing for the Reds was against Bolton Wanderers on Christmas Day 1897 and his only goal for the club proved to be the winner against Sheffield United four days later (2–1). He went on to net 16 goals in 24 games for Southampton, hit one in 5 for the Gunners and 5 in 13 for Burnley.

HATELEY, ANTHONY

Striker: 56 apps, 28 goals
Born: Derby, 13 June 1941
Career: Derby schoolboy football, Normanton Sports Club (Derby), Derby County (associated schoolboy forms, July 1955), Notts County (amateur, May 1956; professional, June 1958), Aston Villa (£20,000, July 1963), Chelsea (£100,000, October 1966), LIVERPOOL (£100,000, July 1967), Coventry City (£80,000, September 1968), Birmingham City (£72,000, August 1969), Notts County (£20,000, November 1970), Oldham Athletic (£5,000, July 1972), Bromsgrove Rovers (May 1974), Prescot Town (July 1976), Keyworth United (December 1978, retired August 1979); later worked in Everton's lottery office, then employed by Thwaites Brewery, Nottingham, before working for a well-known soft drinks company
Soccer nomad Tony Hateley's career realised 211 goals in a total of 434 senior appearances made over a period of 16 years. An out-and-out striker, tall and muscular and exceptionally strong in the air, he helped Notts County win the Fourth Division championship in 1971 and was an FA Cup runner-up with Chelsea in 1967. Aston Villa's leading scorer three seasons running, 1963–66, he is one of only two players to net four goals for the Birmingham-based club in the League Cup and when he joined Chelsea in 1966 he became only the second footballer in Britain to demand a six-figure fee (following Alan Ball). He did well at Anfield – scoring a goal every two games – including a hat-trick in his third game v. Newcastle United in August 1967, seven days after he had made his debut away to Manchester City. He formed an excellent partnership up front with Roger Hunt but lost his place to teenager Alun Evans. Hateley, who was once dubbed the 'wealthy wanderer', admitted that he loved it at Anfield and was sorry to leave Liverpool. His son, Mark Hateley, also a striker, played for Coventry City, Portsmouth, QPR, Glasgow Rangers, Leeds United, Hull City and England between 1978 and 1997.

HEGGEM, VEGARD
Right-back/midfield: 46+19 apps, 3 goals
Born: Trondheim, Norway, 13 July 1975
Career: Orkdal FC/Norway, Rosenborg/Norway, LIVERPOOL (£3.5m, July
    1998–May 2001); returned to Norway where he took over his father's farm
A Norwegian international at under-21 level, Vegard Heggem went on to gain
21 full caps for his country, half of them as a Liverpool player. Blessed with pace,
skill and consistency, he had a fine first season at Anfield, adding quality to the
Liverpool defence when making 36 senior appearances. His debut was against
Southampton at The Dell on the opening day of the Premiership programme
(16 August) when he took over from Rob Jones to partner Steve Staunton at
full-back in a 2–1 victory. He was later moved forward to play on the right side
of midfield and, with Rigobert Song behind him, the Reds looked pretty strong
down that right flank. Heggem scored on his debut for Norway v. France but
injury unfortunately ruled him out of the 1998 World Cup finals, although he
did participate in the European Championships two years later when he
performed exceedingly well. He struggled with a hamstring injury during the
2000–01 campaign. He never regained full fitness and eventually left the club
after making 65 appearances. In the autumn of 2005, Heggem received
confirmation from UEFA that he was an official winner of the 2001 UEFA Cup
– even though he never received a medal . . . because he played in two earlier
rounds and was listed in the 25-strong squad by Liverpool FC. The club received
25 medals for that victory but most of the spare ones were given to club officials
and backroom staff. Heggem retired from the game to take over his father's farm,
through which runs the River Orkla, famous for its salmon – with the farm
having exclusive fishing rights.

HEIGHWAY, STEPHEN DEREK, BA
Forward: 447+23 apps, 76 goals
Born: Dublin, 25 November 1947
Career: Cheshire and England Grammar Schools, Manchester City (amateur
    forms, 1962), Warwick University (from 1963), Universities Athletic Union,
    Skelmersdale United (amateur, 1966), LIVERPOOL (amateur, January
    1970; professional, May 1970), Minnesota Kicks/NASL (guest, summer
    1981, retired 1983); returned to LIVERPOOL (as coach, later director of the
    club's Youth Academy at Kirkby, Merseyside)
One of the key members of Liverpool's side during the 1970s, Steve Heighway
was a fast-raiding winger who loved to hug the touchline (mainly the left) before
cutting inside where he was able to glide a pass to a colleague or shoot at goal
himself. High-stepping with a long stride, he loved to run with the ball and
when in full flight was difficult to contain. In contrast, he couldn't defend for his
life . . . 'He was hopeless,' said his manager Bill Shankly. The recipient of four
League championship-winning medals in 1973–76–77–79, he also helped
Liverpool win the European Cup in 1977 and 1978 and the UEFA Cup in 1973
and 1976, while also being a victor in the 1974 FA Cup final and collecting
runners-up prizes in the same competition in 1971 and 1977, and in the 1978

League Cup. He made his senior debut for Liverpool as a 22 year old in September 1970, helping the Reds beat Mansfield Town 3–2 in a League Cup replay when he joined forces with Brian Hall, the pair being affectionately dubbed 'Big Bamber' and 'Little Bamber' owing to their university connections. The very next day he won the first of his 34 full caps for the Republic of Ireland v. Poland in Dublin, appearing in his last international while registered with Minnesota Kicks in 1982. Heighway, whose final game for Liverpool was against Arsenal at Highbury in March 1981, gained a BA in Economics at Warwick University. It is interesting to know that in 1969 Heighway played in the Cheshire League, in 1970 in the League Cup and First Division, in 1971 in an FA Cup final and the following season in the European Cup-Winners' Cup competition – what may be termed a rapid rise!

HENCHOZ, STEPHANE
Defender: 201+4 apps
Born: Billens, Switzerland, 7 September 1974
Career: FC Bulle/Switzerland, Neuchatel Xamax/Switzerland, SV Hamburg/ Germany, Blackburn Rovers (£3m, July 1997), LIVERPOOL (£3.7m, July 1999), Celtic (loan, January–February 2005), Wigan Athletic (free, June 2005)

Honoured by his country, Switzerland, at both youth and under-21 levels, blond central defender Stephane Henchoz went on to gain 72 full caps, 32 as a Liverpool player. Strong in all aspects of defensive play, he made over 100 competitive appearances in Swiss football and 49 in the German Bundesliga before joining Blackburn in 1997. He had two excellent seasons at Ewood Park, playing in 82 games before switching his allegiance to Anfield where he formed a splendid partnership at the heart of the Reds' defence with Finnish star Sami Hyypia, the pair playing together for virtually four full seasons before Henchoz eventually slipped out of contention. Also competent enough to play at right-back, he had a loan spell with Celtic before joining newly promoted Wigan Athletic for the start of the 2005–06 Premiership campaign, helping them to reach the League Cup final that season.

HENDERSON, ALASTAIR
Wing-half: 5 apps
Born: Shettlestone, Glasgow, 1910 – *Died*: Scotland, *circa* 1979
Career: Yoker Athletic, LIVERPOOL (professional, July 1931), Clapton Orient (July 1933–May 1935)

Ally Henderson played with Sam English at Yoker Athletic before joining Liverpool – and ironically when he left Anfield in 1933, the Reds signed English from Celtic. Able to occupy both wing-half positions with confidence, Henderson made his First Division debut against West Ham United in October 1931, deputising for Tom Morrison in a 2–2 draw. After a season in the second XI he was transferred to Clapton Orient, for whom he appeared in 21 competitive matches in two years.

HENDERSON, DAVID
Wing-half or utility forward: 24 apps, 12 goals
Born: Stirling, November 1868 – *Died*: Glasgow, 1933
Career: King's Park (Stirlingshire), LIVERPOOL (professional, September 1893), Partick Thistle (November 1894)
Davy Henderson was at right-half in Liverpool's first-ever League game v. Middlesbrough (away) in September 1893. As the season progressed, he occupied three other positions (left-half, centre-forward and inside-left) and scored a goal every two games, his first against Small Heath in his fourth game (won 4–1). However, the Reds couldn't hold on to him and after just one season with the club (and after collecting his Second Division championship winner's medal) he returned home to Scotland. He was not related to James Henderson (below).

HENDERSON, JAMES
Outside-right: 3 apps
Born: Scotland, 1870 – *Died*: Hamilton, Scotland, 1940
Career: Annbank (1888), LIVERPOOL (professional, March 1894, released May 1894), Broxburn (August 1894); later with Edinburgh Thistle
Signed as cover for outside-right Pat Gordon who had been struggling with injury, Jimmy Henderson played in three successive Second Division games on the right wing for Liverpool at the end of the 1893–94 season, the first in a 3–2 win at Northwich Victoria. Prior to his move to Merseyside, he won the coveted Ayrshire Cup with Annbank in 1892 and 1893. He returned to Scotland after spending just two months at Anfield. It should be noted that there is a possibility that James Henderson was signed earlier by Liverpool, although this is unconfirmed.

HESKEY, EMILE WILLIAM IVANHOE
Striker: 176+47 apps, 60 goals
Born: Leicester, 11 January 1978
Career: Leicester City (apprentice, April 1994; professional, October 1995), LIVERPOOL (£11m, March 2000), Birmingham City (£3.5m, July 2004)
Big, weighty and powerful, Emile Heskey possesses a strong right-foot shot and can be mighty dangerous in the air, given the chance. There's no doubt he is a talented footballer, full of enthusiasm and commitment, but he is missing the mean streak and unfortunately he lacks consistency. Yet, having said that, he has certainly produced the goods for each of his three League clubs and at times he's done likewise for England. He scored 46 goals in 197 games for Leicester, helping them twice win the League Cup (1997 and 2000). He then spent over four years at Anfield, partnering several strikers including Robbie Fowler and Michael Owen, and gaining two more League Cup winner's prizes (2001 and 2003), plus medals for triumphs in the 2001 FA Cup and UEFA Cup finals and also in the Charity Shield and European Super Cup. Initially capped by his country at youth team level, Heskey proceeded to add 16 under-21, one 'B' and 43 senior caps to his tally, playing and scoring in that memorable 5–1 win over Germany in a World Cup qualifying game in Munich in September 2001 when

110

of course, five other players with Liverpool connections – Michael Owen, Steven Gerrard, Nick Barmby, Jamie Carragher and Steve McManaman, the latter duo as substitutes – also starred. He became unsettled at Anfield and moved to Birmingham City where he finished as top scorer with 11 goals and was voted 'Player of the Season' and 'Players' Player of the Year' in 2005–06, becoming a huge hit with the St Andrews' fans in the process.

HEWITT, CHARLES WILLIAM

Inside-forward: 16 apps, 6 goals

Born: Greatham near Hartlepool, County Durham, 10 April 1884 – *Died*: Darlington, 31 December 1966

Career: Greatham, West Hartlepools and Billingham Schools, Middlesbrough (professional, August 1904), Tottenham Hotspur (£100, May 1906), LIVERPOOL (£75, August 1907), West Bromwich Albion (£75, April 1908), Spennymoor United (free, May 1910), Crystal Palace (£125, October 1910), Hartlepools United (May 1919, retired as a player, May 1923), Mold FC (manager, August 1923–May 1924), Wrexham (manager, November 1924–December 1926), Flint Town (manager, August 1927), Connah's Quay (manager, May 1928), Chester (manager, 1930), Millwall (manager, April 1936–April 1940), Leyton Orient (manager, January 1946–April 1948), Millwall (manager, August 1948–January 1956)

After scoring 14 goals in 38 games for Middlesbrough, inside-forward Charlie Hewitt joined Spurs but within a fortnight and without having played a game, he wanted to leave White Hart Lane – because he had heard that Liverpool had wanted to sign him before he had left 'Boro! The FA, however, decided he must honour his one-year contract with Spurs and he went on to net 15 goals in 49 outings before eventually transferring to Anfield. He had just one season with Liverpool, scoring on his debut v. Nottingham Forest, but was a regular in the side only until the November, after which his appearances were somewhat spasmodic. A well-built footballer, always looking for an opening, he did much better at The Hawthorns (28 goals in 64 games) and followed up with an even better record with Palace: 42 goals in 155 starts. He was a veteran at 39 when he played his last game for Hartlepools. As a manager, he was twice a Welsh Cup winner, with Wrexham in 1925 and Chester in 1933, and he then guided Millwall to the Third Division (S) championship in 1938. Hewitt, who was almost 72 years of age when he quit football, received £4,500 in damages in July 1956 after a great deal of publicity following his sacking as Millwall manager six months earlier.

HEWITT, JOSEPH

Centre-forward/inside-left: 164 apps, 69 goals

Born: Chester, 3 May 1881 – *Died*: Liverpool, 12 November 1971

Career: Chester works team, Sunderland (professional, 1901), LIVERPOOL (£150, January 1904), Bolton Wanderers (August 1910, retired May 1911), LIVERPOOL (coach, season 1911–12, later worked on the ground, was a club steward and finally press box attendant, to 1965)

Initially an inside-forward, Joe Hewitt was at his best leading the Liverpool attack which he did splendidly for six and half years. In the club's 1905–06 League championship-winning season, he netted 23 goals in 37 appearances but was injured the following term, only to bounce back in 1907–08 with 21 more goals and another 15 after that before moving to Bolton. Hewitt served Liverpool, in various positions, for some 60 years – a loyal and dedicated servant who was 90 when he died in 1971.

HEYDON, JOHN

Half-back: 67 apps
Born: Birkenhead, 19 October 1928
Career: Birkenhead junior football, Everton (amateur, 1946), LIVERPOOL (professional, December 1948), Millwall (£3,250, May 1953), Tranmere Rovers (June 1956–May 1961)

Able to play in both the right-half and centre-half positions, John Heydon preferred the latter. He was strong in the air and positive on the ground and had his best spell in Liverpool's first team between November 1951 and January 1953, playing in the centre of the defence most of the time. He made his debut for the Reds v. Stoke City in October 1950 and eventually took over from Lawrie Hughes as pivot. He added a further 164 senior appearances to his tally after leaving Anfield.

HICKSON, DAVID

Centre-forward: 67 apps, 38 goals
Born: Ellesmere Port, Cheshire, 30 October 1929
Career: Ellesmere Port (1944), Everton (amateur, August 1947; professional May 1949), Aston Villa (£17,500, September 1955), Huddersfield Town (£16,000, November 1955), Everton (£6,500, July 1957), LIVERPOOL (£10,500, November 1959), Cambridge City (free with Alan Banks, July 1961), Bury (£1,000 paid to Liverpool, January 1962), Tranmere Rovers (July 1962, two-month trial, signed permanently, September 1962), Ballymena United (player-manager, July 1964), Ellesmere Port (February 1965, player-manager from March 1965), Northwich Victoria (1966), Winsford United (September 1967), Fleetwood Town (1969), Ellesmere Port Town (manager, season 1973–74); later employed as a Liverpool bookmaker; also worked as Everton's stadium guide and match-day host

Dave Hickson was a colourful, dashing centre-forward, brilliant in the air and pretty useful on the ground too. Often hitting the headlines (more so due to brushes with the football authorities) he was a quiet, unassuming man off the field, even shy, but a lion on it! He scored 71 goals for Everton before moving to Villa Park as a replacement for Irish international Dave Walsh but failed to settle in the Midlands and was transferred to Huddersfield, returning for a second spell at Goodison Park in 1957. He took his goal-tally with the Blues to 111 in 243 appearances and then moved across Stanley Park to Anfield where he continued to bulge the net, averaging more than a goal every two games, netting a brace on his debut when he partnered Roger Hunt up front in a 2–1 home win over his former club, Aston Villa in November 1959. He ended his career (in

1964) with some 200 competitive goals under his belt, 182 of them coming in 404 Football League appearances. As a teenager Hickson, who had the great Bill Shankly as his manager at Huddersfield and Liverpool, was nurtured along by two superb international goalscorers from the past – at Ellesmere Port by Tom 'Pongo' Waring (ex Aston Villa) and with the Army cadet team by Ralph 'Dixie' Dean, the ex-Everton hero.

HIGNETT, ALAN JAMES
Right-half: 1 app.
Born: Liverpool, 1 November 1946
Career: Liverpool Schools, LIVERPOOL (apprentice, April 1962; professional, November 1963), Chester (three-month trial, August–October 1966)
An England schoolboy international, capped in 1961, Alan Hignett's only League game for Liverpool was against Wolverhampton Wanderers (away) in April 1965 when he deputised for Willie Stevenson ahead of the FA Cup final with Leeds United, Geoff Strong switching from right- to left-half to accommodate him. He made six appearances for Chester.

HIGNETT, SAMUEL
Right-half: 1 app.
Born: Liverpool, September 1885 – *Died*: Liverpool, *circa* 1933
Career: Liverpool junior football, LIVERPOOL (semi-professional, July 1906–May 1908)
Sam Hignett's only League appearance of his career was at right-half for Liverpool against Sunderland in October 1907 when he helped his side record a 2–1 win at Anfield.

HOARE, JOSEPH HENRY
Full-back: 7 apps
Born: Southampton, 11 November 1881 – *Died*: West End, Southampton, 24 March 1947
Career: Southampton Oxford FC (1897), Southampton (professional, May 1902), LIVERPOOL (£75, May 1903), Southampton (July 1904), Bitterne Guild (May 1905), Southampton (guest, April 1907), Salisbury City (August 1908), Bitterne Guild (August 1909), Woolston FC (June 1912–14); did not play after WW1; ran a tobacconist's shop in Woolston (Southampton) for many years
A carpenter and joiner by trade, Joe Hoare was understudy to Southampton's international full-back George Molyneux during the 1902–03 season before joining Liverpool. Only 10st. 8lb in weight, Hoare more than compensated for this handicap with his pluck and endurance on the field of play. He made the first of his seven appearances for the Reds against Derby County (home) in October 1903 when he partnered George Fleming in a 3–1 win. He returned to The Dell after one season on Merseyside and later played in the 1907 Southern Charity Cup final for Saints as a guest.

HOBBS, JACK
Defender: yet to make his senior debut for Liverpool
Born: Portsmouth, 18 August 1988
Career: Lincoln City (apprentice, August 2004), LIVERPOOL (£750,000, June 2005)
Highly rated teenage defender Jack Hobbs made only one substitute appearance for Lincoln City before his big-money transfer to Liverpool.

HOBSON, ALFRED
Goalkeeper: 28 apps
Born: County Durham, 9 September 1913 – *Died*: 21 February 2004
Career: Shildon Colliery, LIVERPOOL (April 1936), Chester (October 1938); guest for Burnley, LIVERPOOL and Southport during WW2; South Liverpool (August 1946–May 1947)
Alf Hodson was believed to have been the oldest surviving ex-Liverpool player at the time of his death, aged 90. Number one choice between the posts for the Reds for the first 25 League games of the 1936–37 season, he lost his place to Arthur Riley and with Kemp in reserve was transferred to Chester two months into the 1938–39 campaign. He returned to Anfield as a guest during WW2 and made 172 appearances in regional competitions, helping the team win the League (N) Cup at the expense of Bolton Wanderers. However, when peacetime football resumed after the hostilities, Hobson drifted into a lower grade of soccer with South Liverpool.

HODGSON, DAVID JAMES
Forward: 33+16 apps, 10 goals
Born: Gateshead, 1 November 1960
Career: Redheugh Boys' Club (Gateshead), Bolton Wanderers (trial), Ipswich Town (trial), Middlesbrough (professional, August 1978), LIVERPOOL (£450,000, August 1982), Sunderland (£125,000, August 1984), Norwich City (July 1986), Xerez Club Deportivo/Spain (July 1987), Sheffield Wednesday (July 1988), Mazda of Hiroshima/Japan (from July 1989), Metz/France (March 1990), Swansea City (non-contract, March–May 1992); then a player's agent (briefly); Darlington (manager, three spells)
Capped seven times by England at under-21 level and the recipient of a First Division championship winning medal with Liverpool in 1983, David Hodgson had an excellent career that spanned 16 years. After scoring 20 goals in 140 games for Middlesbrough, he followed Graeme Souness and Craig Johnston to Anfield. He maintained his form on Merseyside and added a further 49 appearances (10 goals) to his tally before joining Sunderland for whom he played over 60 times. After that his form dipped slightly and following a spell with Norwich City and an unhappy sojourn in Spain, he played in 12 competitive games for Sheffield Wednesday. His debut for Liverpool was against West Bromwich Albion at Anfield in August 1982, starring alongside Ian Rush in a 2–0 win. He had three spells as manager of Darlington, taking them to fourth place in the Third Division in 2000.

HODGSON, GORDON

Inside-/centre-forward: 378 apps, 240 goals

Born: Johannesburg, South Africa, 16 April 1904 – *Died*: Stoke-on-Trent, 14 June 1951

Career: Played in South Africa with Benoni FC (1919), Rustenberg FC (1921), Pretoria (from 1922), Transvaal (season 1924–25), LIVERPOOL (December 1925), Aston Villa (£3,000, January 1936), Leeds United (£1,500, March 1937; player/youth team coach, August 1942); guest for Hartlepools United (WW2); Port Vale (manager, October 1946 until his death in 1951); played cricket for Spen Victoria and Transvaal (South Africa), for Lancashire CCC (56 matches between 1928 and 1932) and Forfarshire (1934–36); he also excelled at baseball

Born of English parents, Gordon Hodgson was 21 years of age when he joined Liverpool, having already played in international (Test) matches for his native South Africa. He went on to win three full caps for England, twice represented the Football League and is the only player so far to have scored five goals in a game for Leeds United, doing so against Leicester City in October 1938. A tall, strong-looking forward, Hodgson first caught the eye of Liverpool when on tour with the South African party in 1924 and after some impressive displays he signed for the Reds as a full-time professional, making his debut in English League football against Manchester City (away) in February 1926 (1–1) and netting the first goal for the club against Manchester United at Old Trafford a fortnight later (3–3). When he left Anfield for Aston Villa in 1936, he had set a new club record for the aggregate number of goals (240), a figure later bettered by Roger Hunt whose tally was then surpassed by Ian Rush. During his time with Villa he partnered Eric Houghton on the left wing between tedious injury problems and during a wonderful career Hodgson scored no less than 304 goals in competitive football. He was in charge of Port Vale when they moved to their present ground in 1950 and his death at the age of 47 came as a great shock to a lot of people, especially the staff at Vale Park. For Lancashire CCC, his batting average was just 6.97 and his bowling average 27.75, with a best wicket haul of 6–77. He took 37 catches.

HOLDEN, RALPH

Half-back: 2 apps

Born: Blundellsands near Liverpool, 1890 – *Died*: Birkenhead, *circa* 1942

Career: St Helens Recreationalists (1909), LIVERPOOL (professional, June 1911), Tranmere Rovers (May 1914); did not play after WW1

A reliable reserve at Anfield for three seasons, Ralph Holden's two senior outings for the Reds were against Manchester City (at Hyde Road) in January 1913 (when he deputised for Ernie Peake at left-half) and at home to West Bromwich Albion in September 1913 when he occupied the centre-half position in the absence of Harry Lowe.

HOLMES, JOHN
Half-back: 44 apps
Born: Preston, Lancashire, 1869 – *Died*: *circa* 1945
Career: Preston junior football, Preston North End (professional, May 1889), LIVERPOOL (May 1895), Burton Swifts (July 1898), New Brighton Town (August 1899–May 1901 when the club folded)
Jack Holmes' career realised almost 160 senior appearances (147 in the Football League). Able to play in all three half-back positions, he did well at Deepdale without ever being brilliant, and was signed by Liverpool following the club's relegation to the Second Division. Two-footed, he made his debut in a red shirt in a 5–1 home League win over Newcastle United in September 1895 when he deputised for Joe McQue as pivot. Later in the season he moved to left-half and performed admirably, collecting a First Division winner's medal for his efforts before moving to Burton Swifts. His elder brother, Bob Holmes, born in 1867, was one of the Preston North End 'Invincibles' between 1884 and 1901, and made 300 League appearances for the club, as well as gaining seven caps for England.

HOOD, WILLIAM JOHN
Right-back: 3 apps
Born: Belfast, Northern Ireland, 3 November 1914 – *Died*: Belfast, 1992
Career: Cliftonville (1932), LIVERPOOL (March 1937), Derry City (August 1938, retired, injured, 1945)
Capped by Northern Ireland as an amateur when with Cliftonville, Billy Hood deputised at right-back for Tommy Cooper in three successive League games in November/December 1937, the first against Huddersfield Town. Just prior to leaving Anfield for Derry City, he starred in Northern Ireland's famous 5–1 win over England in an amateur international.

HOOPER, MICHAEL DUDLEY, BA
Goalkeeper: 72+2 apps
Born: Bristol, 10 February 1964
Career: Mangotsfield FC (Bristol), Swansea City (briefly as an amateur, 1981), Bristol City (professional, November 1983), Wrexham (free, February 1985), LIVERPOOL (£40,000, October 1985), Leicester City (loan, September–December 1990), Newcastle United (£550,000, September 1993), Sunderland (loan, October 1995); released by Newcastle United (May 1996)
A Screen Sport Super Cup and FA Charity Shield winner with Liverpool in 1986, goalkeeper Mick Hooper was 6ft 3in. tall and tipped the scales at 13st. He made only one League appearance for Bristol City and 34 for Wrexham before moving to Anfield where he replaced Bob Bolder as understudy to Bruce Grobbelaar, having his best unbroken spell in the first team during the 1988–89 season. He made his debut for the Reds in a 2–0 win over his future club Newcastle United (away) in August 1986 and played in the first leg of the Screen Sport Super Cup final v. Everton the following month, collecting a winner's medal after a 7–2 aggregate victory. However, he was disappointed at being left

out of the Reds' 1992 FA Cup final side, having played in four successive games following the semi-final victory over Portsmouth. A keen bird watcher and fell walker, Hooper holds a degree in English, taken at Swansea University.

HOPKIN, FREDERICK

Outside-left: 360 apps, 11 goals

Born: Dewsbury, Yorkshire, 23 September 1895 – *Died*: Darlington, 5 March 1970

Career: Darlington (professional, September 1912); guest for Tottenham Hotspur and Manchester United during WW1; Manchester United (£500, May 1919), LIVERPOOL (£2,800, May 1921), Darlington (August 1931–May 1932), Redcar Borough (trainer, season 1933–34), Leeds United (assistant trainer, 1935–39)

Fred Hopkin played for Manchester United against Liverpool in March 1919 and two years later moved to Anfield, where he won consecutive League championship medals in 1922 and 1923, forming a lethal partnership with Harry Chambers. Incidentally, while at Manchester United, the Red Devils were fined £350 by the Football League for paying Hopkin more than the minimum wage and promising him an illegal percentage of any transfer fee received. He made 360 senior appearances for the Reds over a period of ten years yet managed only 11 goals – an amazingly low return for the number of matches. He made his debut for the club against Sunderland at Roker Park in August 1921 and was an ever-present in his first season, missing only two games the following term when he claimed his first League goal, in a 3–0 home win over Bolton Wanderers. To celebrate this goal, delighted fans set off flares and a fire broke out in the Kemlyn Road stand. Nicknamed 'Kneeler' because of his peculiarity of going down on his right knee when crossing the ball from the wing, the prematurely balding Hopkin was a class player, a nimble left-winger with dash and penetration . . . the only thing missing from his game were goals. He failed to score in four successive seasons. An England international trialist in February 1923, he sadly never gained a full cap which his overall performances certainly deserved. Outside football, he enjoyed success on the athletics track as a hurdler, winning several prizes.

HOUGHTON, RAYMOND JAMES

Midfield: 195+1 apps, 38 goals

Born: Glasgow, 9 January 1962

Career: London junior football, West Ham United (apprentice; professional, July 1979), Fulham (free, July 1982), Oxford United (£147,000, September 1985), LIVERPOOL (£825,000, October 1987), Aston Villa (£900,000, July 1992), Crystal Palace (£300,000, March 1995), Reading (free, July 1997, retired, June 1999); later soccer summariser on Sky Sport

An industrious midfielder who spent 20 years in the game, Ray Houghton scored 99 goals in a career total of 789 appearances at club and international level, 68 of his goals coming in 576 League games. He failed to make an impact at Upton Park but he certainly made a name for himself with Fulham, whom he served for three years before joining the then newly promoted First Division side Oxford United. He gained the first of two League Cup winning medals with the 'Us' in 1985 – the second followed with Aston Villa in 1994 – and as a Liverpool player he received two League championship winning medals, in 1988 and 1990, collected two FA Cup winner's prizes in 1989 and 1992, and also triumphed in the 1988 FA Charity Shield. He made the first of his 196 competitive appearances for Liverpool in a 1–0 League win at Luton Town in October 1987 and was generally regarded as a vital cog in the Reds' midfield mechanism. He played superbly well for Eire in both the European Championships of 1988 and the World Cup finals of 1994 for manager Jack Charlton, scoring the seventh-minute winner against England in a group match in Stuttgart in Euro '88. He joined Crystal Palace too late to save them from demotion from the Premiership, but was then instrumental in helping the Eagles reach the First Division play-off final in 1996, where they were beaten by Leicester City. However, that disappointment was quickly forgotten when, a year later, Palace beat Sheffield United in their second successive play-off final to regain top-flight status.

HOWE, FREDERICK
Inside-/centre-forward: 94 apps, 36 goals
Born: Bredbury, Cheshire, 24 September 1912 – *Died*: 1984
Career: Wilmslow FC (1929), Stockport County (amateur, May 1931; professional, September 1931), Hyde United (free, June 1933), LIVERPOOL (£2,000, March 1935), Manchester City (June 1938), Grimsby Town (October, 1938); guest for Stockport County and Watford during WW2; Oldham Athletic (July 1946, retired, May 1947)
Fred Howe, a natural opportunist, was recommended to Liverpool by former player 'Tosh' Johnson – and after signing, the 22 year old quickly made a name for himself at Anfield. He made his debut against Derby County (home) and scored 3 times in his first 9 League games at the end of the 1934–35 season before finishing up as top marksman with 17 the following term. A plumber by trade, Howe played as an outside-left for both Stockport County (two appearances) and Hyde. However, he never enjoyed occupying the wing position and was used through the middle by the Reds, for whom he scored some important goals. After leaving Anfield he didn't achieve much with either Manchester City or Grimsby and after the war spent his last season in League soccer with Oldham Athletic, scoring another 20 goals in 31 games for the Latics who surprisingly released him at the age of 34 when he had at least another season left in him.

HOWELL, RABBI
Half-back: 68 apps
Born: Wincoback, Sheffield, 12 October 1869 – *Died*: Yorkshire, 1937
Career: Ecclesfield FC (Sheffield), Rotherham Swifts (1888), Sheffield United (£250; professional, June 1890), LIVERPOOL (£200, April 1898), Preston North End (June 1901, retired, injured, September 1903)
Rab Howell was the first full-blooded gypsy to play in the Football League and

represent England in a full international. Born in a caravan, the son of a tinker, and although on the small side (he was a fraction under 5ft 6in. tall) he was very effective, had loads of stamina and was quick over short distances. He helped Sheffield United win the League championship in 1898 and made 240 first-class appearances for the Blades (11 goals scored) before being transferred to Liverpool for disciplinary reasons. He made the first of his 68 appearances for the Reds against Aston Villa (home) on the last day of the 1897–98 League programme, taking over at right-half from John McCartney. He missed only four games the following season and eight in 1899–1900 before suffering a knee injury. He was forced to retire prematurely after breaking his leg playing for Preston against Burnley in September 1903. When he was being carried off the pitch at Deepdale, so upset were his colleagues and supporters that a collection was made there and then, raising £29. His two England caps were won against Ireland in March 1895 (when he scored in a 9–0 win) and Scotland in April 1899.

HUGHES, ABEL
Right-back: 1 app.
Born: Rhosllanerchrugog near Wrexham, July 1869 – *Died*: Cheadle Hulme, Cheshire, 12 August 1946
Career: Rhosllanerchrugog FC (semi-professional, June 1892), LIVERPOOL (January 1894), Rhosllanerchrugog (April 1895), Rhosllanerchrugog Rangers (season 1907–08); subsequently became a successful landlord of the Grapes Inn and then the Moreton Inn, both in Johnstown, and later the Nags Head in Rhosllanerchrugog
A gas fitter by trade, working many years for the Johnstown Gas Company, Wrexham, Abe Hughes was reputedly one of the founder members of the Rhos club, arch-rivals to Wrexham. A very capable footballer, he gained a Welsh Cup winner's medal in 1893 and the following year made his international debut for Wales at right-half against England. He did well and was rewarded with a second cap in the next game against Scotland. A strong kicker and fierce tackler, Hughes joined newly promoted Liverpool as defensive cover and appeared at right-back in his only outing for the Reds against Northwich Victoria in February 1894 when he deputised for Andrew Hannah in a 4–0 win. Hughes also served on the local council as a ratepayer representative.

HUGHES, EMLYN WALTER, OBE
Left-back or wing-half: 665 apps, 49 goals
Born: Barrow-in-Furness, 28 August 1947 – *Died*: Sheffield, 9 November 2004
Career: North Lancashire Schools, Roose FC (Blackpool), Blackpool (professional, September 1964), LIVERPOOL (£65,000, February 1967), Wolverhampton Wanderers (£90,000, August 1979), Rotherham United (player-manager, July 1981), Hull City (March 1983), Mansfield Town (August 1983), Swansea City (September–October 1983; retired at this point through injury)
Emlyn Hughes, nicknamed 'Crazy Horse', was a terrific competitor, a footballer

who played for the game, never shirking a tackle, giving 110 per cent effort out on the field, for club and country. After breaking into League football with Blackpool, Hughes joined Liverpool as a 19 year old and made the first of his 665 appearances for the club in March 1967 against Stoke City at Anfield wearing the unfamiliar number 10 shirt. After that he played at left-back, left-half, occasionally in midfield and also as an emergency central defender. He scored some spectacular goals, many from distance, and helped the Reds win two European Cup finals (1977 and 1978), the UEFA Cup (1973 and 1976), the European Super Cup (1977), four League championships (1973, 1976, 1977 and 1979), the FA Cup (1974) and the FA Charity Shield twice (1974 and 1976, while sharing the prize with Manchester United in 1977). He was a runner-up in the FA Cup in 1971 and 1977 and the League Cup in 1978 and was voted FWA 'Player of the Year', also in 1977. After leaving Anfield, he skippered Wolves to another League Cup triumph at Wembley in his first season at Molineux (v. Nottingham Forest). Capped 62 times by England at senior level (over a period of ten years: 1970–80), he also played in eight under-21 internationals and represented the Football League. After retiring Hughes became a TV personality, captaining one of the teams in *A Question of Sport*, where HRH Princess Anne once sat alongside him as a celebrity. His father was a Rugby League international who played for the Barrow club, his brother and uncle also played rugby, while his aunt represented England at women's hockey. Hughes sadly died of cancer at the age of 57.

HUGHES, JAMES
Wing-half: 15 apps
Born: Bootle, December 1885 – *Died*: Maidstone, Kent, 1948
Career: Merseyside junior football, LIVERPOOL (professional, August 1904), Crystal Palace (May 1909), Chatham (August 1920–May 1922)
A reserve during his five years at Anfield, Jimmy Hughes made the first of his 15 League appearances against Burton United in September 1904 after taking over from his namesake. He then lost his place after four games and after that played second fiddle to first George Fleming and then James Bradley. After leaving Liverpool, Hughes became one of the best wing-halves in the south of England. He scored 15 goals in 209 appearances for Crystal Palace and represented the Southern League before WW1. Please note that there were two players by the name of J. Hughes registered with Liverpool from August 1904 to May 1906 and some reference books have their appearance records mixed up.

HUGHES, JOHN
Half-back: 32 apps, 2 goals
Born: Flint, April 1877 – *Died*: Wallasey, 5 July 1950
Career: Wallasey Juniors, Seacombe FC (season 1898–99), Aberdare (from August 1902), LIVERPOOL (June 1903), Plymouth Argyle (May 1906, retired, injured, December 1906); later Harrowby FC (trainer, seasons 1908–27)
John 'Geezer' Hughes – a former lightweight boxer – made all of his 32 senior

appearances for Liverpool in his first season with the club. He made his debut at centre-half against Sunderland (away) in September 1903 and scored his two goals against Notts County in the November and at West Bromwich Albion in the January. A report prior to this game at The Hawthorns stated: 'Hughes is about the hardest working player at present figuring in League football. He never tires and is seldom beaten. One thing he lacks, however, is judgement and just a little more of this and Hughes could be classed among the best middies in the country.' He spent two years in Liverpool's second XI and was playing so well that he gained three full caps for Wales, lining up against Scotland, England and Ireland during the 1904–05 campaign. In fact, there was a dispute prior to the game with Ireland in Belfast as to whether or not he was eligible to play for Wales as some reports stated that he had an Irish connection. He duly produced his birth certificate and the matter was quickly sorted out. The game ended all square at 2–2. Hughes injured his knee when making his debut for Plymouth in a Western League fixture against Southampton. He never recovered and retired at the end of the year, aged 29.

HUGHES, LAWRENCE

Centre-half: 326 apps, 1 goal
Born: Waterloo, Liverpool, 2 March 1924
Career: Merseyside Schools and Liverpool junior football, Tranmere Rovers (amateur, 1942), LIVERPOOL (professional, February 1943, retired, May 1960)

Centre-half Lawrie 'Big Lol' Hughes was a shrewd tactician whose positional sense was of the highest calibre. Strong in the air, durable and courageous, he was also stylish, brainy and quick-thinking and maintained a high level of consistency throughout his career. A player who preferred the ground pass aimed with constructive intent rather than hoofing his clearances downfield, he made the first of his 326 senior appearances for Liverpool against Chester (away) in a third-round first-leg FA Cup encounter in January 1946. His League bow followed seven months later at Sheffield United, and he also played in 111 regional games for the Reds during WW2, gaining a League (N) Cup winner's medal in 1944 (after Bolton Wanderers had been eclipsed 6–3 on aggregate in the two-legged final). Unfortunately sidelined for the bulk of the 1948–49 and 1952–53 seasons (Bill Jones deputising) Hughes played in three full internationals for England, all in the 1950 World Cup finals, including that humiliating 1–0 defeat at the hands of the USA in Belo Horizonte – this after he had taken over from his Liverpool teammate Jones! He also played in one 'B' international. A League championship winner with the Reds in 1947, he was also a member of the 1950 FA Cup final side beaten by Arsenal.

HUNT, ROGER

Inside-forward: 487+5 apps, 286 goals
Born: Goldborne, Lancashire, 20 July 1938
Career: Lancashire schoolboy and junior football, Croft Youth Club, Devizes Town (briefly), Stockton Heath (1957), LIVERPOOL (amateur, August

1958; professional, July 1959), Bolton Wanderers (£31,000, December 1969, retired, May 1972); went into the family haulage business

Roger Hunt actually arrived at Anfield by sheer chance ... ex-Liverpool star and scout Bill Jones went to watch a non-League game between Knutsford and Stockton Heath along with another 1930s Liverpool player, Tom Bush. They got together and recommended the 20-year-old striker to the club. Unobtrusive yet so effective, Hunt was not a tall player but he certainly made defenders hop around a bit with his alertness and goal-poaching technique. Nicknamed 'Sir Roger' by the 'Kopites' he possessed many fine qualities including those of alertness, a capacity for hard work and shooting power – and he was no mean header of the ball either. He scored some memorable and vitally important goals for Liverpool during his time at Anfield. Indeed, he held the club scoring record of 286 goals for 23 years before Ian Rush took over the mantle. A Second Division championship winner with the Reds in 1962, Hunt later added two First Division winner's medals to his collection (1964 and 1966), gained an FA Cup winner's medal in 1965 and followed up in 1966 by helping England win the World Cup, whilst also gaining a runners-up prize when Liverpool lost in the final of the European Cup-Winners' Cup. He gained a total of 34 full caps for his country (17 goals scored), played for the Football League side and represented the British Army during his national service when he also assisted non-League side Devizes Town. After retiring in 1972, following a testimonial match at Anfield which attracted a crowd of 56,214 and raised over £25,000, Hunt chose to work in the family haulage business. His former manager, Bill Shankly, said that Hunt was 'a born player, a born competitor who must rate alongside all the great Liverpool goalscorers'.

HUNTER, JOHN BRYSON

Centre-forward: 44 apps, 13 goals

Born: Paisley, Renfrewshire, 6 April 1878 – *Died*: Motherwell, 12 January 1966

Career: Westmarch XI (Paisley), Abercorn FC, LIVERPOOL (professional, May 1899), Heart of Midlothian (£300 plus Tom Robertson, May 1902), Woolwich Arsenal (May 1904), Portsmouth (May 1905), Dundee (May 1907), Clyde (September 1910, retired injured, February 1911), Motherwell (manager, April 1911, secretary-manager, February 1913, relinquished manager's job, May 1946, remained as club secretary until August 1959)

John 'Sailor' Hunter was a strong, incisive and forceful centre-forward who could also play inside-left. He was a competent rather than a great footballer, although he did win a cap for Scotland against Wales in 1909. In fact, his playing career was eventually overshadowed by greatness as a manager at Motherwell, the club he served for a total of 48 years. He was a Scottish Cup runner-up with Hearts in 1903 and seven years later won the same trophy with Dundee. Signed to replace Jack Allan, he scored on his League debut for Liverpool against Stoke in September 1899. He later made 43 League appearances for Hearts (scoring 14 goals), 22 for Arsenal (4 goals), 37 for Portsmouth (11 goals) and 61 for Dundee (46 goals) but failed to make Clyde's first team. His nickname came from a rolling gait and not through any maritime connection.

HUNTER, THOMAS
Centre-half: 5 apps
Born: Liverpool, 1877 – *Died*: Liverpool, *circa* 1935
Career: LIVERPOOL (August 1899, released April 1902)
Primarily a reserve centre-half during his time at Anfield, Tom Hunter was asked, at times, to play as a forward (certainly in the second XI) and, in fact, he lined up at outside-right when he made his League debut for Liverpool against Wolves at Anfield in November 1899, when he stood in for Jack Cox. His four other outings were at centre-half in place of Alex Raisbeck.

HUNTER, WILLIAM
Inside-right: 1 app.
Born: Sunderland, 1888 – *Died*: *circa* 1940
Career: Sunderland West End (1908), LIVERPOOL (professional, August 1908), Sunderland (May 1909), Lincoln City (November 1909), Wingate Albion (May 1911), Airdrieonians (November 1911), South Shields (March 1912), Barnsley (July 1912), Manchester United (April 1913), Clapton Orient (August 1913), Exeter City (August 1914); did not play after WW1
Despite a long career in the game, Bill Hunter scored just 15 goals in only 55 League games. He was injured during his time at Anfield and Lincoln, and had his best years with the latter club, for whom he netted 8 times in 32 outings. His only game for Liverpool was against Preston North End, away, in March 1909, when he deputised for Bob Robinson in a 2–0 defeat.

HUTCHISON, DONALD
Midfield: 45+16 apps, 10 goals
Born: Gateshead, 9 May 1971
Career: Hartlepool United (apprentice, May 1987; professional, March 1990), LIVERPOOL (£175,000, November 1990), West Ham United (£1.5m, August 1994), Sheffield United (£1.2m, January 1996), Everton (£1m, February 1998), Sunderland (£2.5m, July 2000), West Ham United (£5m, August 2001, released, May 2005), Millwall (briefly 2005), Coventry City (loan, January 2006)
An all-round, attack-minded midfielder, tall and confident with a powerful right-foot shot, Don Hutchison won 2 'B' and 26 full caps for Scotland while also making 418 club appearances and scoring 57 goals up to 2005, when he was released by West Ham. Surprisingly he never won a major club prize – not for the want of trying. He always gave 100 per cent on the field of play, despite suffering niggling and sometimes tedious injury problems. Hutchison was brought to Liverpool's attention in an unconventional way. After Hartlepool's brilliant display against Spurs in a two-legged League Cup tie in 1990, their Chairman Garry Gibson arranged for 50 videos (costing £1,000) to be made and sent to all the First and Second Division clubs, hoping one or more would be interested in buying some of his players – Liverpool were very interested in what they saw and signed Hutchison, a former warehouseman and fork-lift truck driver, for £175,000 . . . good business!

He made the first of his 61 appearances in a Liverpool shirt as a substitute against Notts County in March 1992 – 16 months after joining the club.

HYSEN, GLENN
Defender: 93+2 apps, 2 goals
Born: Gothenburg, Sweden, 30 October 1959
Career: Warta FC/Sweden (semi-professional, 1977), IFK Gothenburg/Sweden (1979), PSV Eindhoven/Holland (1982), IFK Gothenburg/Sweden (1984), Fiorentina/Italy (1986), LIVERPOOL (£650,000, August 1989), GAIS Gothenburg/Sweden (May 1992)

Cool, dominating at times and very effective, Glenn Hysen turned down a move to Manchester United in favour of Anfield. He gave Liverpool sound and committed service for certainly two of his three years at the club before losing his way, his form and his appetite for the game, being stripped of the captaincy and then dropped from the first team under the new Graeme Souness regime. Making his debut for the Reds against Manchester City (home) in August 1989, he gained a League championship winner's medal that season after performing superbly well in defence with the likes of Alan Hansen, David Burrows, Barry Venison and others. The silver-haired Hysen, a Swedish international who captained his country many times, also represented the Football League during his Anfield days.

HYYPIA, SAMI
Defender: 370+1 apps, 26 goals
Born: Porvoo, Finland, 7 October 1973
Career: Pallo-Peikot/Finland (1989), KuMu/Finland (professional, October 1990), MyPa 47 Anjalankoski/Finland (April 1992), Willem II/Holland (August 1995), LIVERPOOL (£2.6m, July 1999)

An authoritative centre-back, strong in the air (most of the time) and competent on the ground, blond-haired Sami Hyypia is not the heftiest of defenders but he has a big heart and is a tenacious tackler. Honoured by Finland at youth team level, Hyypia progressed to the full national side and has now won over 70 senior caps, having also represented his country in 27 under-21 internationals. He formed a wonderful central defensive partnership at Anfield with Stephane Henchoz and later with Jamie Carragher. In fact, he missed very few games during his first five seasons at Anfield and was part of the Reds' famous five-trophy winning campaign of 2001 when the FA Cup, League Cup, UEFA Cup, European Super Cup and Charity Shield all ended up in the club's boardroom, later adding a second FA Cup winner's medal to his tally in 2006 (despite missing the spot in the penalty shoot-out v. West Ham). Captaining the side on several occasions, Hyypia also collected a Champions League winner's medal in 2005. Prior to joining Liverpool he made 63 League appearances for MyPa and 100 for Willem II.

IDRIZAJ, BESIAN
Midfield: yet to make his senior debut for Liverpool
Born: Austria, 12 October 1987
Career: Linzer ASK/Austria (professional, October 2004), LIVERPOOL (July 2005)

Promising young left-sided midfielder, 6ft 2in. tall and 12st. 5lb in weight, Besian Idrizaj, a boyhood Liverpool fan, was voted Austria's 'Young Player of the Year' for 2005. He moved to Anfield on a two-year contract. He is an Austrian under-21 international.

INCE, PAUL EMERSON CARLYLE
Midfield: 81 apps, 17 goals
Born: Ilford, Essex, 21 October 1967
Career: West Ham United (apprentice, October 1983; professional, July 1985), Manchester United (£2.4m, September 1989), Inter Milan/Italy (£8m, July 1995), LIVERPOOL (£4.2m, July 1997), Middlesbrough (£1m, August 1999), Wolverhampton Wanderers (free, August 2002)

An aggressive midfielder with courage, determination and a powerful shot (when he chose to deliver) Paul Ince was, at times, the ideal general in the centre of the park. Very talented but with a bit of a temper, he nevertheless was a fully committed footballer who loved a challenge, no matter what the circumstances. He made 95 appearances for West Ham, 281 for Manchester United and 60 for Inter Milan before joining Liverpool three months before his 30th birthday. Placed straight into the engine-room alongside Steve McManaman and Michael Thomas, he made his debut for the Reds against Wimbledon (away) in August 1997 and scored his first goal for the club on his home debut four days later v. Leicester City. After exactly two seasons at Anfield he switched across country to Middlesbrough for whom he added a further 106 senior appearances to his tally before dropping out of the Premiership to sign for Wolves, with whom he pushed his overall appearance total past the 650 mark. Unfortunately he failed to win a medal with Liverpool, but he certainly bagged his fair share during his six years at Old Trafford, helping United clinch two Premiership titles (1993 and 1994), win the European Cup-Winners' Cup (1991), the League Cup (1992), the FA Cup twice (1990 and 1994), the European Super Cup (1991), and two FA Charity Shields (1993, 1994). He then helped Wolves gain promotion to the Premiership in 2003 (via the play-offs). Capped 53 times by England at senior level, Ince also represented his country in four youth, one 'B' and two under-21 internationals. Runner-up to Aston Villa's Paul McGrath in the PFA 'Player of the Year' poll in 1993, he is the cousin of former champion boxer Nigel Benn.

IRELAND, ROBERT JOHNSTONE
Half-back: 1 app.
Born: Darvel, Ayrshire, 22 July 1900 – *Died*: 12 July 1962
Career: Scottish junior football, Glasgow Rangers (professional, April 1922), LIVERPOOL (November 1929), St Johnstone (August 1931–May 1934)

Bob Ireland's only League appearance for Liverpool was against Grimsby Town on Boxing Day 1930 when he deputised at right-half for Tom Morrison in the 1–1 draw. Prior to his move to Anfield, Ireland, who preferred the centre-half position, had been reserve to the famous Scottish international Davie Meiklejohn at Ibrox Park and made only 19 first-team appearances during his seven years at Ibrox Park. He never got a look-in with the Reds, especially when 'Tiny' Bradshaw arrived to accompany Morrison and McDougall in Liverpool's middle-line.

IRVINE, ALAN JAMES
Forward: 0+2 apps
Born: Broxburn, West Lothian, Scotland, 20 November 1962
Career: Hibernian (professional, March 1980), Falkirk (August 1983), LIVERPOOL (£75,000, November 1986), Dundee United (£100,000, August 1987), Shrewsbury Town (£40,000, February 1988)
Alan Irvine never got into Hibernian's first XI but after leaving Easter Road he made 118 League appearances in three years with Falkirk. With so much talent on show he never settled at Anfield, having just two outings for Liverpool – both as a substitute – at Charlton Athletic in December 1986 and at home to Southampton two months later. He had 8 outings for Dundee United and scored 6 goals in 37 League games for Shrewsbury.

IRWIN, COLIN THOMAS
Defender: 40+4 apps, 3 goals
Born: Liverpool, 9 February 1957
Career: Liverpool and District junior football, LIVERPOOL (professional, December 1974), Swansea City (£350,000, August 1981, retired, injured, May 1984)
Injury brought Colin Irwin's career to an abrupt end at the age of 27. Prior to that he had done extremely well in his seven years at Anfield where he played mainly in the second XI. He never let the senior side down when called into action and made the first of his 44 major appearances for the Reds against West Bromwich Albion (home) in August 1979 when he deputised at left-half for Alan Hansen in a 3–1 win. He captained Swansea in the top flight and made a return visit to Anfield in October 1981 when his side earned a 2–2 draw. Irwin, a strong competitor, played in the European Cup-Winners' Cup and in the Welsh Cup final in his first season at The Vetch Field, and the following year he was in the Swans team that beat Sliema Wanderers 12–0 in an ECWC encounter – the club's biggest-ever win.

JACKSON, BRIAN HARVIL
Outside-right: 131 apps, 12 goals
Born: Walton-on-Thames, Surrey, 1 April 1933
Career: Weybridge Schools, Chase of Chertsey (Arsenal nursery club), Arsenal (amateur forms, August 1949), Leyton Orient (professional, October 1950), LIVERPOOL (£6,500 plus Donald Woan, November 1951), Port Vale (£1,700, June 1958), Peterborough United (£2,000, July 1962), Lincoln City

(May 1964), Burton Albion (December 1964), Boston United (August 1965–May 1966)

An England schoolboy international, fast and clever, Brian Jackson was described by a soccer pundit as being 'one of the outstanding discoveries of 1950–51'. He certainly did well in Orient's League side that term, scoring twice in 21 games as a 17 year old. He quickly made his mark at Anfield, netting on his debut at home to Bolton Wanderers but was injured the following season. He came back strongly in 1953–54, although his efforts couldn't prevent the team from losing their First Division status. He continued to perform well after that despite being in and out of the side. He certainly had a great game when Everton were thumped 4–0 in an FA Cup tie in 1955, scoring once and setting up another for Johnny Evans. He helped Port Vale win the Fourth Division title in 1959 and claimed 34 goals in 178 League and Cup games for the Potteries club. He later played at right-half with Peterborough and Lincoln, skippering the latter club. His career realised a total of 378 League appearances (48 goals).

JACKSON, REVEREND JAMES
Full-back or half-back: 224 apps, 2 goals
Born: Newcastle-upon-Tyne, 4 December 1899 – *Died*: *circa* 1976
Career: Queen's Park (Glasgow), Motherwell (amateur, May 1919), Aberdeen (semi-professional, August 1923), LIVERPOOL (registered as semi-professional, May 1925); whilst with the club he invested his earnings in a scholarship at first Liverpool University and then Cambridge University, studying Philosophy and Greek; in June 1933 he was ordained as a Presbyterian minister at which time he quit playing football. He later worked in several churches in both Liverpool and Bournemouth

Known as Jim 'Parson' Jackson and a former shipyard worker on the Clyde, he represented both the Scottish and Football Leagues and was a very popular player north and south of the border. A fine defender, commanding, steady, strong and inspirational, always full of grim determination, he was also a brainy footballer who possessed good ball skills and above all, had a big heart. Versatile enough to occupy several positions, he made his debut for Liverpool in November 1925 against West Bromwich Albion (home) when he took the place of right-half Jock McNab in a 2–0 win. He later drew up a fine understanding in defence with first Tom Bromilow in 1926–27 and then Don McKinlay the following season before having an excellent spell at right-back as partner to Robert Done in 1928–29 when he was an ever-present. He captained the Reds for a time in 1928 and also represented the Football League against the Irish League . . . his only honour as a Liverpool player.

In August 1947, as the Reverend Jackson, he officiated at the funeral of the former Liverpool chairman W.H. McConnell. His father, Jimmy Jackson (born in Scotland in 1875), played left-back for Hamilton Academical, Glasgow Rangers (two spells), Newcastle United, Woolwich Arsenal, Leyton, West Ham United and Greenock Morton. His brother, Archie, starred for Sunderland, Southend United, Chester, Tranmere Rovers and Accrington Stanley between the two World Wars, while his cousin, also named Archie Jackson, played Test cricket for Australia.

JAMES, DAVID BENJAMIN
Goalkeeper: 276+1 apps
Born: Welwyn Garden City, Hertfordshire, 1 August 1970
Career: Tottenham Hotspur (on associated schoolboy forms, 1985), Watford
  (apprentice, August 1986; professional, July 1988), LIVERPOOL (£1m, July
  1992), Aston Villa (£1.8m, June 1999), West Ham United (£3.5m, July
  2001), Manchester City (£1.3m, January 2004)
On his day David James, 6ft 5in. tall and 14st. 5lb in weight, was one of the best
keepers in the game, pulling off some breathtaking saves. However, at times he
somehow lost concentration and let in a soft goal, even goals, for both club and
country. He can and does make the most difficult shot look easy but then bows
his head in shame after a crucial handling mistake or error of judgement that
costs his team dear. He made almost 100 appearances for Watford with whom
he won the FA Youth Cup (1989) before joining Liverpool, making his debut for
the Reds against Nottingham Forest (away) in August 1992, after taking over
between the posts from Bruce Grobbelaar. He spent seven years at Anfield,
gaining a League Cup winner's medal in 1995 while adding to his collection of
full England caps, eventually gaining 32 and being named in the national squad
for the 2006 World Cup in Germany. He also represented his country in one 'B',
ten under-21 and three youth internationals. He replaced David Seaman in the
Manchester City goal, signed by ex-Liverpool star Kevin Keegan. James reached
the milestone of 700 competitive appearances at club and international level in
2006.

JAMES, NORMAN LESLIE
Centre-half: 8 apps
Born: Liverpool, 25 March 1908 – *Died*: 12 October 1985
Career: Bootle St James' FC, Braby's Athletic (Liverpool), LIVERPOOL
  (professional, April 1929), Bradford City (May 1933), Queens Park Rangers
  (October 1936–May 1939); did not play after WW2
Reserve and adequate cover for 'Tiny' Bradshaw, Norman James spent four years
at Anfield during which time he made only eight League appearances, the first
against Blackpool in February 1931. He was also on standby at Bradford but did
much better with QPR for whom he made 73 appearances.

JENKINSON, WILLIAM
Full-back: 13 apps
Born: Golborne, Lancashire, 2 March 1892 – *Died*: Merseyside, 3 April 1967
Career: Golborne United, LIVERPOOL (amateur, November 1916;
  professional, August 1919), Wigan Borough (June 1921), Wallasey United
  (July 1923–April 1925)
After making 59 appearances for Liverpool during WW1, Bill Jenkinson was
never able to hold down a regular place in the side after the hostilities owing to
the presence and form of Eph Longworth and Tom Lucas. He made the first of
his 13 senior appearances for the Reds as Don McKinlay's partner against
Bradford City (away) in August 1919 and after leaving Anfield played 10 games

for Wigan in their first season in the Football League. He was also a very useful club cricketer with Bootle CC.

JOHNSON, DAVID EDWARD
Forward: 177+33 apps, 78 goals
Born: Liverpool, 23 October 1951
Career: Everton (apprentice, April 1967; professional, April 1969), Ipswich Town (November 1972), LIVERPOOL (£200,000, August 1976), Everton (August 1982), Barnsley (loan, February–March 1984), Manchester City (March 1984), Tulsa Roughnecks/NASL (June–September 1984), Preston North End (non-contract, October 1984–March 1985)

David Johnson was an exciting forward at the peak of his career. He was able to shoot, head, dribble, challenge for possession and create chances for his colleagues and gave Liverpool excellent service for six years, averaging a goal every three games. He made his first start for the club against Norwich City in August 1976 and secured his initial goal in his third game versus Birmingham City. Prior to joining the Reds, Johnson had netted on his FA Youth Cup, Central League, Football League, FA Cup, League Cup and European debuts for Everton, and he also hit the target in his first Merseyside derby, doing so at Goodison Park in November 1971. He then scored on his debuts for both Ipswich Town and England, for whom he appeared in eight full internationals plus nine at under-23 level. He did very well in his first spell with Everton and also at Portman Road before Liverpool boss Bob Paisley recruited him to take over from John Toshack. He helped the Reds win three League titles (1977, 1979 and 1980), the European Cup (1981) and reach the FA Cup final (1977), beaten by Manchester United. Eyebrows were raised when Johnson rejoined Everton at the age of 30 and it proved to be a disastrous return as he struck only 5 goals in 50 outings, bringing his total to 20 in 103 games for the Blues. During his career Johnson scored 156 goals in 540 club games, including 110 in 409 League matches spread over a period of 14 years. In Johnson's own words: 'Once I had signed for Liverpool I hated Everton . . . In exactly the same way as I'd hated Liverpool when I joined Everton.'

JOHNSON, RICHARD KEMP
Centre-forward: 83 apps, 30 goals
Born: Gateshead, June 1895 – *Died*: West Derby, Liverpool, 3 January 1933
Career: Redheugh Boys' Club (Gateshead), Felling Colliery (County Durham); WW1 guest for Sunderland (season 1918–19); LIVERPOOL (professional, January 1920), Stoke (£1,200, February 1925), New Brighton (September 1929), Connah's Quay (August 1931, retired, May 1933)

Unfortunately Dick Johnson's career at Anfield was marred by a knee injury which forced him to miss the whole of the 1921–22 championship-winning season. However, he came back strongly and collected his overdue medal when the Reds won the title again the following year, featuring in attack with Dick Forshaw and Harry Chambers, the trio scoring 55 League goals between them. A lively performer who loved to swing the ball across the field from wing to

WHO'S WHO OF LIVERPOOL 1892—2006

wing, he had speed, good close control and was strong in the air, once scoring with a 20-yard header. The *Athletic News* described him as 'The crafty one' and a local newspaper said 'he was a forward who used his brains as well as his feet'. He made his debut for Liverpool against Oldham Athletic in April 1920 and after leaving Anfield helped Stoke win the Third Division (N) championship in 1927. When he left the Potters for New Brighton he received a fee as his accrued share of a small benefit.

JOHNSON, THOMAS CLARK FISHER
Inside-/centre-forward: 39 apps, 8 goals
Born: Dalton-in-Furness near Barrow, 19 August 1901 – *Died*: 29 January 1973
Career: Dalton Athletic, Dalton Casuals, Manchester City (amateur, May 1918; professional, February 1919), Everton (£6,000, March 1930), LIVERPOOL (£2,500, March 1934), Darwen (August 1936, retired, May 1937)
Tommy 'Tosh' Johnson, one-time apprentice riveter in a Cumbrian shipyard, scored 238 goals in a total of 552 competitive games for his three major clubs (Darwen were out of the League at that time). He netted 22 times and missed only one game when Everton won the League title in 1932. Forming a lethal partnership with Dixie Dean at Goodison Park, between them the duo netted over 200 goals in more than 300 games, including 180 in three seasons, 1931–34. Johnson also helped the Blues win the Second Division championship in 1931, the FA Cup in 1933 (against his former club Manchester City) and between 1926 and 1932, he scored five goals in five internationals for England while also representing the Football League. Prior to joining Everton he netted 166 goals in 364 outings for Manchester City, with whom he reached the FA Cup final in 1926 and won the Second Division title (1928). He hit a five-timer for City v. Everton in September 1928 and still holds the record for most goals scored by a Manchester City player. He was approaching his 33rd birthday when he joined Liverpool and although well past his best, he still gave the Reds good service, starring on his debut in a 6–2 home win over Middlesbrough in March 1934, having a hand in three of the goals.

JOHNSTON, CRAIG PETER
Midfield: 232+37 apps, 40 goals
Born: Johannesburg, South Africa, 8 December 1960
Career: Lake McQuarrie FC/Australia (junior, 1976), Sydney City/Australia (amateur, April 1977), Middlesbrough (apprentice, August 1977; professional, February 1978), LIVERPOOL (£575,000, April 1981, retired, May 1988); returned to Australia where he became a full-time photographer; also designed the famous 'Predator' football boot manufactured by Adidas
Born in South Africa, Craig Johnston had a Scottish grandfather and Irish grandmother, and graduated from Australian State football to become a British citizen. He made his name in the Football League with Middlesbrough for whom he scored 16 goals in 77 appearances before transferring to Anfield. A long-haired ball-winning midfielder with a terrific engine, he covered acres of ground every game and cracked home some stunning goals for the Reds. An

England under-21 international, he helped Liverpool win five First Division titles in 1982, 1983, 1984, 1986 and 1988, lift the European Cup in 1984 and finish second a year later, carry off the FA Cup in 1986 and collect a runners-up medal in 1988 and twice win the League Cup in 1983 and 1984, finishing second in 1987. His debut for Liverpool came in August 1981 when he came on as a second-half substitute for Ray Kennedy in a 1–0 defeat at Wolves. Johnston created a minor sensation when, in 1988, he announced his retirement from competitive football at the age of 27 . . . this after an American specialist saved his leg from amputation after he had suffered a rare bone disease as a boy. Johnston is the only footballer ever to take the FA Cup out of the British Isles – he took it to Australia after Liverpool's victory in 1986. Newcastle United as a team took the trophy to South Africa in 1952.

JONES, ALLAN POWELL
Right-back: 5 apps
Born: Flint, North Wales, 6 January 1940
Career: Flint Schools, LIVERPOOL (amateur, April 1955; professional, April 1957), Brentford (£6,500, August 1963, released, May 1970)
A Welsh schoolboy international centre-half at the age of 15, Allan Jones made only five League appearances for Liverpool before enjoying a seven-year spell at Brentford, for whom he played in well over 250 senior games in seven seasons. He was unable to gain a regular place at Anfield owing to the form of right-back John Molyneux, who he deputised for when making his debut against Cardiff City a week before Christmas, 1959.

JONES, HAROLD
Inside-left: 1 app.
Born: Liverpool, 22 May 1933 – *Died*: 6 September 2003
Career: Merseyside Schools and Liverpool junior football, LIVERPOOL (professional, January 1952), Rhyl (free, June 1954–May 1957)
Harry Jones's only League game in his entire career was for Liverpool against Newcastle United in September 1953 when he deputised for Irish international Sammy Smyth in a 4–0 defeat in front of 47,000 fans at St James' Park.

JONES, JOHN HUBERT
Goalkeeper: 4 apps
Born: Holyhead, 1900 – *Died*: North Wales, *circa* 1970
Career: Holyhead FC, LIVERPOOL (amateur, September 1924–April 1925), Llandudno Town (free, seasons 1925–27)
Welsh amateur international goalkeeper John Jones was capped against England in March 1924 when his club Holyhead were one of the strongest sides in the Welsh League (Northern Section). Registered with Liverpool as extra cover for Elisha Scott, he made his League debut against Preston North End in November 1924 (won 3–1) but was not retained for the following season.

JONES, JOHN MERVYN

Inside-left: 4 apps

Born: Bangor, Caernarfonshire, 30 April 1931

Career: Bangor City, LIVERPOOL (professional, November 1951), Scunthorpe United (£2,000, July 1953), Crewe Alexandra (£3,000, June 1959), Chester (free, August 1961), Lincoln City (trial, October 1963), Gainsborough Trinity (free, May 1964, released, May 1965)

During his career the sprightly Mervyn Jones, who played mainly on the left wing after leaving Anfield, made over 400 League and Cup appearances, around 250 with Scunthorpe whom he helped win the Third Division (N) championship in 1958. His colleague at The Old Show Ground was another ex-Liverpudlian, Jack Haigh. The first of his four outings for the Reds was against Fulham in March 1952 when he played at inside-left in a reshuffled forward-line.

JONES, JOSEPH PATRICK

Full-back: 100 apps, 3 goals

Born: Llandudno, North Wales, 4 March 1955

Career: Mostyn Secondary Modern School, Llandudno Estates FC, Llandudno Swifts, Clwyd and Conwy under-15s, Caernarfonshire under-15s, Wrexham (apprentice, April 1971; professional, January 1973), LIVERPOOL (£110,000, July 1975), Wrexham (£210,000, October 1978), Chelsea (£34,500, October 1982), Huddersfield Town (£35,000, October 1985), Wrexham (£7,000, August, 1987; later player-coach, November 1989, retired as a player in May 1992, being appointed senior coach)

Welshman Joey Jones had a wonderful career, amassing over 700 club and international appearances (35 goals scored) and winning 70 full caps, a record at the time (1986) but bettered later by Everton goalkeeper Neville Southall. He also represented his country in four under-23 internationals. The dressing room comedian, he proved to be a resilient defender, playing mainly as a full-back but occasionally doing a splendid job in the centre of defence. Jones helped Liverpool win successive League titles in 1976 and 1977, lift the European Cup, also in 1977, triumph in two FA Charity Shield encounters at Wembley and was an FA Cup runner-up, also in 1977. He made the first of his 99 appearances for the Reds against QPR (away) in August 1975 when he partnered Phil Neal and he retired as a player 17 years later, having had three excellent spells with Wrexham, with whom he won the Welsh Cup in 1975 and gained runners-up prizes in 1988 and 1991. In fact, when he rejoined the Welsh club in 1978 it was for a club record fee. He was also a Second Division championship winner with Chelsea in 1984 . . . his last club honour.

JONES, PHILIP LEE

Forward: 0+4 apps

Born: Wrexham, 29 May 1973

Career: Wrexham (apprentice, May 1989; professional, July 1991), LIVERPOOL (March 1992), Crewe Alexandra (loan, September–October

1993), Wrexham (loan, January–May 1996 and again, January–February 1997), Tranmere Rovers (free, March 1997), Barnsley (free, July 2000), Oswestry Town (free, March 2002), Wrexham (free, March 2002), Caernarfon Town (April 2004)

Lee Jones played for Wales at youth team level before going on to represent his country in one 'B', 14 under-21 and 2 full internationals. Unfortunately he failed to make the grade at Liverpool, having spent three years with Wrexham, the club he eventually served in four separate spells. He did very well with Tranmere for whom he scored 18 goals in 97 games and when he was released by Wrexham in 2004 his career record stood at 70 goals in 289 club appearances. His debut for Liverpool came as a substitute against Burnley in a League Cup tie in October 1994.

JONES, ROBERT MARC
Right-back: 241+2 apps
Born: Wrexham, 5 November 1971
Career: Ellesmere Port Youth Centre, Holton Boys, Crewe Alexandra (apprentice, May 1988; professional, December 1988), LIVERPOOL (October 1991, retired, injured, July 1999)

Attacking right-back Rob Jones was plagued by a series of injuries during the last three years or so at Anfield (causing him to miss the European Championships with England in 1996) and in the end was forced to retire from competitive football at the age of 27. Prior to that he had performed splendidly for the Reds, gaining FA Cup and League Cup winner's medals in 1992 and 1995 respectively while also representing England in eight full, two under-21 and two youth internationals, having been capped by Wales as a schoolboy. Decisive in the tackle, a clean passer of the ball with good pace, he was in effect classed as a traditional winger at times when scampering down the right flank. He made his debut for Liverpool in the live televised game against Manchester United in front of almost 45,000 fans at Old Trafford in October 1991 and partnered David Burrows for the remainder of that season. After that he had several full-back partners but always gave a good account of himself, even when asked to play out of position. He appeared in 90 games for Crewe under manager Dario Gradi's tuition, and in fact was the youngest outfield player to appear for the Railwaymen when he made his League debut in 1988. Jones' grandfather, Bill Jones (q.v.), played for Liverpool between 1938 and 1954.

JONES, RONALD
Outside-/inside-right: 5 apps, 1 goal
Born: Mold, Flintshire, June 1914 – *Died*: Wrexham, *circa* 1981
Career: Mold junior football, Wrexham (professional, August 1935), LIVERPOOL (March 1938); guest for Wrexham during the war; did not play after 1946

A short, compact forward, Ron Jones netted 23 goals in 86 games for Wrexham before joining Liverpool. He failed to make the same sort of impression at Anfield, although WW2 certainly disrupted his progress. He scored on his debut for the Reds in a 2–0 home League win over Manchester City in March 1938 when he deputised for Phil Taylor at inside-right.

JONES, WILLIAM HENRY
Inside-forward/right-back/half-back: 278 apps, 17 goals
Born: Whaley Bridge, Derbyshire, 13 May 1921
Career: Hayfield St Matthews' FC (Derbyshire), LIVERPOOL (professional, September 1938); guest for Leeds United, Reading and York City during WW2; Ellesmere Port (player-manager, May 1954), LIVERPOOL (scout during the 1960s and '70s)

Bill Jones joined Liverpool as a 17-year-old inside- or centre-forward but after the war he gave the club splendid service as a versatile performer, deservedly claiming the 'play anywhere' tag when occupying both full-back and all three half-back positions. Best as a pivot (centre-half), he was stylish and showed an innate positional sense and was never found wanting. After scoring twice in 14 WW2 appearances for the Reds he finally made his League debut in August 1946 (some eight years after joining the club) against Sheffield United at Bramall Lane and then netted twice in a 4–0 win over Chelsea in his third game. Jones gained a League championship medal in 1947 and also played in the losing FA Cup final three years later. He starred in two internationals for England, against Portugal and Belgium in 1950, both of which ended in wins, 5–3 and 4–1 respectively.

(JOSEMI) GONZALES JOSE MIGUEL
Defender: 28+8 apps
Born: Malaga, Spain, 15 November 1979
Career: Malaga/Spain (professional, November 1997), LIVERPOOL (£2m, July 2004), Villarreal/Spain (player-exchange deal with Jan Kronkamp, January 2006)

Principally a right-back, Josemi, of average height but strong in body and mind, had mixed fortunes at Anfield, although he did receive a European Champions League winner's medal in 2005 (as a squad member). Signed to strengthen the defence by manager Rafael Benitez, he has looked a little out of his depth at times, having started off reasonably well before Steve Finnan regained the right-back position. Josemi made his Premiership debut against Tottenham Hotspur in August 2004. Not guaranteed first-team football, he moved back to Spain early in 2006 in a deal that brought Jan Kronkamp to Anfield.

JOWITT, CHARLES HENRY
Goalkeeper: 1 app.
Born: Liverpool, *circa* 1872 – *Died*: *circa* 1940
Career: LIVERPOOL (season 1896–97)

An unknown goalkeeper, signed during the 1896–97 season, Charlie Jowitt's only first-team game for Liverpool was against Sheffield Wednesday (home) in April 1897 when he deputised for Harry Storer in a 2–2 draw. Some reference books give this player's surname as Jowett.

KANE, STANLEY
Goalkeeper: 6 apps
Born: Workington, 17 April 1912 – *Died:* 13 February 1976
Career: Junior football, Birmingham (professional, August 1934), LIVERPOOL
   (January 1935–May 1937)
Reserve to England international Harry Hibbs at Birmingham, Stan Kane was
also on standby at Anfield, deputising for Arthur Riley. He played in just half a
dozen senior matches for Liverpool, the first in the Merseyside derby against
Everton in March 1935 before slipping back into the second XI. He was released
following the arrival of Alf Hobson.

KAYE, GEORGE HENRY
Right-half: 2 apps
Born: Liverpool, 19 April 1919 – *Died:* Swindon, 1992
Career: LIVERPOOL (signed initially in 1940, turned professional, April 1941);
   guest for Bradford City during WW2, also served in the Army; Swindon
   Town (May 1947–May 1953)
George Kaye made the first of his two senior appearances for Liverpool in an FA
Cup game against Bolton Wanderers in January 1946. His other outing was in a
home League match v. Blackpool 15 months later when he deputised for Phil
Taylor at right-half. A strong player, he scored twice in 170 regional games for
the Reds during the hostilities and after leaving Anfield he gave Swindon Town
excellent service for 6 years, making a further 175 senior appearances.

KEECH, WILLIAM
Half-back: 6 apps
Born: Irthlingborough, Northants, 22 February 1872 – *Died:* London, 1934
Career: Wellingborough (1890), Barnsley (September 1894), LIVERPOOL
   (October 1895), Blackpool (May 1897), Leicester Fosse (February 1898),
   Loughborough (February 1899), Queens Park Rangers (June 1899),
   Brentford (July 1902), Kensal Rise United (May 1904)
A footballing nomad, the versatile Bill Keech, who could occupy all 3 half-back
positions, served 8 different clubs in 12 years before entering non-League soccer
in 1904. He had his best spells at Blackpool, Leicester Fosse and Loughborough
and actually scored a hat-trick on his debut for the Fosse in a friendly against his
next club, Loughborough, in 1898. During his two seasons at Anfield he played
second fiddle to the more accomplished players like John Holmes, John
McCartney, Duncan McLean, Joe McQue and Tom Cleghorn. He made his
League debut for Liverpool against Notts County in October 1895 in place of
Holmes. A member of Queens Park Rangers' first professional side, his brother,
Ben Keech, also played for the same London club.

KEEGAN, JOSEPH KEVIN, OBE
Forward: 323 apps, 100 goals
Born: Armthorpe near Doncaster, 14 February 1951
Career: St Peter's Grammar School (Doncaster), Enfield House Youth Club,

Peglars Brass Works, Lonsdale Hotel FC (Doncaster Sunday League), Coventry City (trialist), Scunthorpe United (apprentice, December 1967; professional, December 1968), LIVERPOOL (£33,000, May 1971), SV Hamburg/Germany (£500,000, June 1977), Southampton (£400,000, July 1980), Newcastle United (£100,000, August 1982, retired as a player, May 1984); then out of the game for eight years; Newcastle United (manager, February 1992–January 1997), Fulham (as manager/Chief Operating Officer, September 1997–June 1999), England (manager, appointed initially in February 1999 when still Fulham manager, resigned, October 2000), Manchester City (manager, May 2001, resigned March 2005)

Kevin Keegan was an incisive forward who, if required, would play in any front-line position. He was quick, had great skill, was a smart header of the ball and could shoot with both feet. He and John Toshack worked superbly well together, the smaller figure of Keegan feeding off the tall but so effective Welsh international – and between them they gave several world-class defenders plenty of nightmares . . . before and during a game! A snip-of-a-signing by Bill Shankly at £33,000, Keegan paid that money back ten times over with some superb performances in a red shirt. He was a leading light during the 1970s, helping Liverpool win three Football League championships in 1973, 1976 and 1977, the UEFA Cup twice in 1973 and 1976, the FA Cup in 1974 when he scored twice against his future club Newcastle United, the European Cup in 1977 and two Charity Shield matches in 1974 and 1977, getting himself sent off with Billy Bremner of Leeds in one of those Shield clashes at Wembley. He was also an FA Cup runner-up in 1977.

He captained England and won 32 of his 63 caps as a Liverpool player (scoring 21 goals in total). He also represented his country in five under-23 internationals and played in one unofficial England game in 1976. He made the first of his 323 appearances for the Reds in August 1971, scoring after just 12 minutes to set up a 3–1 win over Nottingham Forest at Anfield. He was voted FWA 'Player of the Year' in 1976 and after moving from Merseyside, was twice named 'European Footballer of the Year' in 1978 and 1979 as well as receiving the German 'Player of the Year' in 1978. Twelve months later he won the Bundesliga title with Hamburg and in 1982, after returning to his homeland, he was voted PFA 'Footballer of the Year' while also receiving the OBE (for services to football). He did wonders at Newcastle, helping them regain top flight status in 1984 and then as manager he guided the Magpies into the Premiership in 1993, Fulham into the First Division in 1999 and Manchester City back into the Premiership in 2002, but unfortunately he didn't have much success as the England boss, quitting after Liverpool star Didi Hamann's goal had given Germany a 1–0 win in a World Cup qualifier, the last international played at the 'old' Wembley. That said Kevin Keegan, without doubt, has been one of Liverpool's greatest-ever players.

KEETLEY, JOSEPH FREDERICK

Inside-forward: 9 apps, 3 goals
Born: Derby, 28 June 1897 – *Died*: Allerton near Derby, 30 March 1958
Career: Victoria Ironworks/Derby (from 1914), Bolton Wanderers (August 1920), Accrington Stanley (free, June 1923), LIVERPOOL (£1,200, November 1923), Wolverhampton Wanderers (May 1925), Wrexham (November 1925), Doncaster Rovers (January 1926), Horwich Railway Mechanics Institute (August 1926, retired, May 1933)

Joe Keetley was an artistic sort of player, clever on the ball and smart at beating his opponent – and he could shoot as well. He had not really impressed at Bolton but did well in his short spell at Accrington. He made his debut for Liverpool at Cardiff in December 1923 (lost 2–0) and scored the first of his three goals for the club, to no avail, against Newcastle United four days later (lost 2–1). In his senior career he played in just 42 League games. Keetley had one sister and ten brothers, these being Albert, Arthur, Bill, Charlie (the youngest, born in 1906), Frank, Harry, Jack, Lawrence, Sidney and Tom, five of whom played League football. Only Lawrence and Sidney did not enjoy the game and, in fact, three of the brothers (Tom, Harold and Joe) played together for Doncaster Rovers in February 1926 and when Joe left, Frank was signed to replace him. For one match prior to WW1, there were seven Keetley brothers in the same Victoria Ironworks side, Frank, Harry, Tom, Joe and Jack forming the forward-line. Between the five Keetleys who played at the top level and were all forwards, they accumulated a total of 902 League appearances and notched 516 goals, of which Tom netted 284 (including 180 for Doncaster and 6 in one game v. Ashington in February 1929), Charlie 117 (108 for Leeds United), Frank 71, Harry 25 and Joe 19.

KELLY, JAMES

Inside-/outside-left: 3 apps
Born: Glasgow, Scotland, 1870 – *Died*: Scotland, *circa* 1931
Career: Shettleston FC (Glasgow), Lincoln City (£22, with Bob Cameron, September 1892), LIVERPOOL (November 1892, released, April 1893)

A reserve with Liverpool during their Lancashire League campaign of 1892–93, Jim Kelly's debut for the club was against Rossendale United (away) in November when he played on the left wing in a 2–0 win. His other two outings were at inside-left v. Fairfield and Southport.

KELSO, ROBERT ROBINSON

Right-half: 1 app.
Born: Renton, Dunbartonshire, 1 October 1865 – *Died*: Scotland, 10 August 1942
Career: Renton FC (1886), Newcastle West End (July 1888), Preston North End (September 1889), Everton (January 1889), Preston North End (May 1889), Everton (May 1891), LIVERPOOL (guest, September 1892), Dundee (May 1896), Bedminster (season 1897–98)

Bob Kelso's only game for Liverpool was as a guest (from Everton) against Bury at home in the second Lancashire League fixture of the 1892–93 season. Nicknamed the 'Renton Ruffian' and a player with sure judgement and a gritty style, he made 103 appearances during his time at Goodison Park. He also gained eight full caps for Scotland between 1885 and 1898 and was twice a Scottish Cup winner with Renton (1885 and 1888) and a League Championship winner with Preston (1890).

His uncle, Tom, also a Scottish international (born in 1882), played for Third Lanark, Manchester City, Glasgow Rangers, Dundee and Aberdare Athletic.

KELVIN, ARTHUR GEORGE
Outside-left: 8 apps, 1 goal
Born: Liverpool, 1871 – *Died*: *circa* 1930
Career: LIVERPOOL (September 1892, released, April 1893)
Arthur Kelvin served the club during the 1892–93 season. He made his debut in the opening Lancashire League fixture against Higher Walton (home), creating two of the goals in an 8–0 win, and then secured his only goal in a Lancashire Cup qualifying-round tie against West Manchester.

KEMP, RICHARD JAMES
Goalkeeper: 33 apps
Born: Cape Town, South Africa, 15 October 1913 – *Died*: South Africa, *circa* 1983
Career: Sea Point Boys Club/South Africa (1929), Arcadia FC/South Africa (1931), Transvaal/South Africa (1934), LIVERPOOL (December 1936); guest for Brighton and Hove Albion, Southport and York City during WW2; returned to South Africa in 1945
'Dirk' Kemp was one of several South African footballers who came to England between the two World Wars. He made his League debut for Liverpool against Manchester United (home) three months after arriving at Anfield when he took over from fellow countryman Arthur Riley in a 2–0 win. He remained second choice at the club until 1939, playing in seven WW2 games for the Reds and keeping goal for the Army against the Football League at Anfield in February 1940, before returning to his home country.

KENNEDY, ALAN PHILIP
Left-back: 355+2 apps, 21 goals
Born: Sunderland, 31 August 1954
Career: Wearside junior football, Newcastle United (apprentice, July 1971; professional, September 1972), LIVERPOOL (£330,000, August 1978), Sunderland (£100,000, September 1985), Husqvarna/Sweden (September 1987), Beerschot/Belgium (October 1987), Hartlepool United (non-contract, November 1987), Grantham Town (briefly, 1987), Wigan Athletic (December 1987 after a trial), Sunderland (March 1988), Colne Dynamos (August 1988), Wrexham (March 1990–December 1990), Morecambe (March 1991), Netherfield (player-manager, July 1991–August 1992), Northwich Victoria (October 1992), Radcliffe Borough (December 1992),

Netherfield (player-manager, November 1993), Barrow (player-coach, August 1994, retired March 1996); is now an occasional after-dinner speaker

In a long and varied career that spanned 25 years (1971–96) left-back Alan Kennedy played in more than 700 club matches including 506 in the Football League. A self-developed footballer, he quickly became a firm favourite with the Newcastle supporters once they had seen his 50-50 challenges. He played in 199 senior games for Newcastle, including the 1974 FA Cup final against Liverpool and the 1976 League Cup final against Manchester City, before moving to Anfield following the Geordies' demotion to the Second Division. His first outing for Liverpool was against QPR in August 1978 when he partnered Phil Neal in a 2–1 win. Impressing every game with his thrusts down the left and strong tackling, Kennedy went on to score some vital goals for the Reds, none more so than in the 1981 European Cup final against Real Madrid when, with nine minutes left, he collected his namesake Ray Kennedy's throw-in, charged forward and smacked the ball home for the winner – great stuff. A second European Cup final triumph came his way in 1984 when he also found the net, firing in the winning penalty in the shoot-out against AS Roma. This was followed by a loser's medal in the same competition a year later. He also gained five League championship winner's medals, in 1979, 1980, 1982, 1983 and 1984, four League Cup winner's prizes, in 1981, 1982, 1983 and 1984, and earned himself eight 'B' and two full caps for England, the latter coming in 1984, some nine years after he had first been chosen to represent his country when injury forced him to pull out at the last minute. Earlier he was awarded six under-23 outings as a Newcastle player during 1974–75. He lost his place in the Liverpool line-up to Jim Beglin and after that became something of a soccer nomad, serving several non-League clubs as his playing career slowly wound down.

Kennedy is now an accomplished after-dinner speaker living in Ormskirk. His younger brother, Keith, also played for Newcastle United (1968–72), as well as Bury, Mansfield Town and Barrow.

KENNEDY, MARK
Midfield: 5+16 apps
Born: Dublin, 15 May 1976
Career: Millwall (apprentice, May 1992; professional, May 1994), LIVERPOOL (£1.5m, March 1995), Queens Park Rangers (loan, January–March 1998), Wimbledon (£1.75m, March 1998), Manchester City (£1m, July 1999), Wolverhampton Wanderers (£1.8m, July 2001)

A Republic of Ireland international, capped 34 times at senior level, on seven occasions by the under-21s and also at schoolboy and youth team levels, Mark Kennedy, besides his main role as a midfielder, has also played left-back and on the left wing, performing well in all three positions. He made 54 appearances for Millwall before his big-money transfer to Anfield where he never quite fitted into manager Roy Evans' plans following his debut as a substitute against Leeds United in April 1995. The Reds made a profit when he moved to Wimbledon but his stay there was tentative. He finally produced the goods with Manchester City, for whom he netted 11 goals in 77 games. He then switched his allegiance to Molineux and helped Wolves gain Premiership status in 2003. Two years later he reached the career milestone of 400 club and international appearances.

KENNEDY, RAYMOND

Forward/midfield: 389+3 apps, 72 goals

Born: Seaton Delaval, Northumberland, 28 July 1951

Career: South Northumberland Schools, New Hartley Juniors (Seaton Delaval), Port Vale (apprentice, August 1967, released January 1968), New Hartley Juniors (February 1968), Arsenal (apprentice, May 1968; professional, November 1968), LIVERPOOL (£180,000, July 1974), Swansea City (£160,000, January 1982–October 1983), Hartlepool United (November 1983–May 1985); later Sunderland (part-time coach, February 1987, first-team coach April 1987–May 1991); was also a licensee in Hartlepool until Parkinson's disease forced him into retirement

Scorer of some superb goals for both Arsenal and Liverpool, Ray Kennedy was leading marksman for the Gunners in their double-winning season of 1970–71 when, of course, they beat Liverpool in the FA Cup final, and it was he who grabbed the crucial goal that beat rivals Spurs in the last League game to clinch the title. Used as an attacker at Highbury, Kennedy was Bill Shankly's last signing as manager before his retirement in 1974. New manager Bob Paisley astutely switched him into midfield where he became a vital cog in the Anfield power machine of the 1970s. He scored on his debut for the Reds against Chelsea in August 1974 (won 3–0) and after that things went from strength to strength. Described by his boss as 'some player' he won five more League championship winner's medals in 1976, 1977, 1979, 1980 and 1982, gained a League Cup winner's prize in 1981, was rewarded with three European Cup winner's medals in 1977, 1978 and 1981 (after his brilliant away strike had knocked Bayern Munich out in the semi-final) and tasted glory again in the 1976 UEFA Cup final when his exquisite volley had turned the tide in the final against the Belgium club Bruges. A couple of runners-up medals also came his way. Capped 17 times by England at senior level, Kennedy appeared in six under-23 internationals and after leaving Anfield he added two Welsh Cup winner's medals to his collection in 1983 and 1984 when teaming up with fellow Liverpudlians John Toshack and Colin Irwin at Swansea. He battled on gamely when struck down with Parkinson's disease but that was the essence of Ray Kennedy – a fighter to the last.

KERR, NEIL

Outside-right: 12 apps, 3 goals

Born: Bowling, Dunbartonshire, 13 April 1871 – *Died*: Scotland, 5 December 1901

Career: Cowlairs FC (August 1887), Glasgow Rangers (professional, May 1889), LIVERPOOL (June 1894), Falkirk (August 1895, retired, ill heath, June 1899)

Playing with some of the game's greatest players north of the border, outside-right Neil Kerr created and scored goals aplenty for Rangers, netting 28 times himself in 69 appearances during his 4 years at Ibrox Park. As an ever-present, he was the recipient of a Scottish League championship winner's medal in 1891 when for the only time the title was shared, Dumbarton being declared joint champions. He was certainly unlucky not to gain international recognition. Surprisingly, when he joined Liverpool, he made his debut at centre-forward against Bolton Wanderers at Anfield and netted his first goal for the Reds against Sheffield United two matches later after switching back to his normal right wing position. He never really bedded down on Merseyside and returned to Scotland after just one season. He was only 30 years of age when he died.

KETTLE, BRIAN
Left-back: 4 apps
Born: Prescot, Lancashire, 22 April 1956
Career: Local junior football, LIVERPOOL (apprentice, May 1972; professional, May 1973), Houston Hurricane/NASL (on loan, 1978–79), Wigan Athletic (£25,000, September 1980, contract cancelled by mutual consent, October 1981)
England youth international left-back Brian Kettle spent eight years with Liverpool, being a key member of a very strong second team. He made only four senior appearances in that time, the first against Real Sociedad in a UEFA Cup clash at Anfield in November 1975 when he partnered Phil Neal in the absence of Joey Jones and Alec Lindsay. His League debut followed soon afterwards, in a 2–2 draw with Arsenal. He had just 14 outings with Wigan before his release.

KEWELL, HAROLD
Forward: 100+21 apps, 15 goals
Born: Sydney, Australia, 22 September 1978
Career: Australian Academy of Sport (September 1993), Leeds United (professional, December 1995), LIVERPOOL (£5m, July 2003)
A player who enjoys playing out wide on either flank, Harry Kewell has deceptive speed, can dribble and shoot and his crosses are precise and dangerous. He did superbly well during his eight years with Leeds United, for whom he scored 63 goals in 242 competitive games, gaining an FA Youth Cup winner's medal in 1997. He also performed admirably for his country and at 2006 had won almost 20 full caps (5 goals), having earlier starred in several youth internationals. Making his Liverpool debut against Chelsea in August 2003, he went on to have an excellent first season at Anfield, netting 11 goals in 49 games, including a strike in the 3–0 Merseyside derby win over Everton. However, he struggled with injuries in 2004–05 and manager Rafael Benitez gambled on his fitness by including him in the team to contest the European Champions League final. The gamble backfired, Kewell being substituted in the first half, but he did go up and collect his winner's medal after the Reds' nail-biting penalty shoot-out win over AC Milan. Injuries still affected his performances, though, and he was in and out of the side during the first half of 2005–06, playing well after Christmas and ending up by gaining an FA Cup winner's medal after Liverpool's win over West Ham. He was also named in Australia's World Cup

squad for Germany in 2006. Kewell is married to *Emmerdale* and *I'm a Celebrity, Get Me Out of Here* star Sheree Murphy.

KEWLEY, JOHN KEVIN
Midfield: 0+1 app.
Born: Liverpool, 2 March 1955
Career: Liverpool junior football, LIVERPOOL (apprentice, May 1971; professional, March 1972, contract cancelled, February 1978)

Kevin Kewley was a reserve forward at Anfield for almost seven years, figuring in League action for only ten minutes as a second-half substitute for Terry McDermott against Middlesbrough (home) in January 1978 when the crowd topped 49,000. He left the club the following month and never played senior football again.

KINGHORN, WILLIAM JOHN DARROCH
Outside-left: 19 apps, 4 goals
Born: Strathblane, Scotland, 27 February 1912 – *Deceased*
Career: Queen's Park (amateur, from 1929), LIVERPOOL (professional, April 1938); guest for Blackburn Rovers, Brighton and Hove Albion, Burnley, Leeds United, Leicester City, Manchester City and Newcastle United during WW2; did not play competitive football after 1946

A Scottish amateur international with over 20 caps to his credit, Bill Kinghorn joined Liverpool at the age of 26 with war clouds hovering over England. Prior to his transfer to Anfield he had been a registered player for nine years with the famous Glasgow club Queen's Park, but owing to various commitments and niggling injuries he only managed 51 League games, scoring 12 goals. He made his debut for Liverpool against Chelsea a week after joining and played his last game for the club in May 1945, scoring in a 7–0 win at Oldham in a Football League (North) second phase game, having netted 3 times in 12 WW2 games. He also played for Western Command v. the RAF in 1944. In later years he lived and worked in his native Scotland.

KIPPAX, FREDERICK PETER
Outside-left: 1 app.
Born: Burnley, 17 July 1922 – *Died*: 1987
Career: Burnley schoolboy and junior football, Burnley (amateur, April 1939); guest for Charlton Athletic, Fulham, Grimsby Town, Heart of Midlothian, Hibernian, LIVERPOOL, Manchester United during WW2; rejoined Burnley (August 1945), Yorkshire Amateurs (July 1948), LIVERPOOL (amateur, February 1949), Preston North End (March 1950), Yorkshire Amateurs (May 1950, retired 1956)

A leading amateur player during the 1940s, Peter Kippax gained a 1947 FA Cup runners-up medal with Burnley, also helping the Clarets win promotion from the Second Division that same season when he appeared in 26 League games. An England amateur international, with over 20 caps to his credit, he represented Great Britain in the 1948 Olympic Games and also played for the

Football League. Fast and clever, he appeared in plenty of regional games during the war, including once for Liverpool when he scored in a 2–2 home draw with Bolton Wanderers in August 1945. His only League game for the Reds followed in March 1949.

KIPPE, FRODE
Defender: 0+2 apps
Born: Oslo, Norway, 17 January 1978
Career: FC Kolbotn/Norway (1996), Lillestroem/Norway (professional, May 1997), LIVERPOOL (January 1999), Stoke City (loan, December 1999–March 2000 and again, October 2000–May 2001), Lillestroem/Norway (March 2002)

A competent defender, 6ft 4in. tall, who won one 'B' and 27 under-21 caps for Norway, Frode Kippe spent more than three years as a registered player with Liverpool during which time he made only two substitute appearances for the first team, both in the League Cup. However, he was plagued by injuries at Anfield and when the opportunity arose he returned to his previous club, Lillestroem. His debut for the Reds was against Grimsby Town in October 2001.

KIRKLAND, CHRISTOPHER
Goalkeeper: 45 apps
Born: Leicester, 2 May 1981
Career: Coventry City (apprentice, June 1997; professional May 1998), LIVERPOOL (£6 million, August 2001), West Bromwich Albion (season-long loan from June 2005)

An England youth international, 6ft 6in. tall goalkeeper Chris Kirkland gained eight under-21 caps as a Coventry City player before his big-money move to Liverpool. He started out as an outfield player but after being told he wasn't good enough, decided to go in goal as a last resort! Recruited as cover for the Polish star Jerzy Dudek, he suffered finger, wrist and leg injuries at Anfield but did make the subs bench for England's full international v. Poland in February 2004 and has figured in the squad ever since. A brave, confident keeper, he was signed by Albion boss Bryan Robson at the start of the 2005–06 season, having made 45 senior appearances for the Reds – the first in a humiliating 2–1 defeat by Grimsby Town in a League Cup tie at Anfield in October 2001 and his second in the 1–1 Premiership home draw with rivals Everton in February 2002.

KOZMA, ISTVAN
Midfield: 3+5 apps
Born: Paszto, Hungary, 3 December 1964
Career: Pecs/Hungary (junior, April 1980), Ujpest Dosza/Hungary (professional, March 1982), Bordeaux/France (August 1987), Dunfermline Athletic (£600,000, July 1989), LIVERPOOL (£300,000, February 1992, released, May 1993); returned to play in Hungary

Experienced Hungarian international Istvan Kozma never really made much headway at Anfield following his transfer from Dunfermline for whom he appeared in almost 100 competitive matches, 87 in the Scottish League. His League debut for Liverpool was against Norwich City (away) in February 1992 when he lined up in midfield with Ray Houghton, Jamie Redknapp and Steve McManaman in a 3–0 defeat.

KRONKAMP, JAN
Defender: 7+10 apps
Born: Makkinga, Holland, 17 August 1980
Career: Go Ahead Eagles/Holland (amateur March 1997; professional, August 1998), AZ Alkmaar/Holland (August 2000), Villarreal/Spain (August 2005), LIVERPOOL (player-exchange deal involving Josemi, January 2006)
Dutch international Jan Kronkamp was never a regular in Villarreal's La Liga side, although he proved to be a vital member of the Spanish club's Champions League squad. When approached by Rafael Benitez, he quickly agreed terms with Liverpool and moved to Anfield early in 2006, making his debut for the Reds when he came off the bench to replace Peter Crouch in the thrilling 5–3 FA Cup third-round win at Luton Town. A competent right-back who loves to overlap, he made the first of 61 appearances for Go Ahead Eagles in the Dutch Eerste Division (the equivalent to the English Championship). He went on to play in over 100 games for Alkmaar, with whom he won his first full cap as a substitute against Sweden in August 2004, then going on to play in the next seven internationals. Kronkamp is the fourth Dutchman to join Liverpool, following Westerveld, Meijer and Zenden. In 2006, he gained an FA Cup winner's medal (v. West Ham) and was also named in Holland's World Cup squad for Germany.

KVARME, BJORN TORE
Defender: 48+6 apps
Born: Trondheim, Norway, 17 June 1972
Career: Rosenborg/Norway, LIVERPOOL (free, January 1997), St Etienne/France (August 1999); later with Rosenborg Ballklub/Norway (from 2003)
A 6ft 2in. tall Norwegian international defender, able to play in any position across the back, Bjorn Kvarme had mixed fortunes during his two and a half years at Anfield. A powerful player who enjoyed driving forward, he played in 16 out of the last 20 games in his first half-season and certainly looked the part with some outstanding performances. Resembling a young-looking Mark Lawrenson, he made an impressive Premiership debut against Aston Villa at Anfield soon after joining but was sorely missed in the latter stages of the European Cup-Winners' Cup, having already played in the competition for Rosenborg. Injuries interrupted his game in 1998–99 when he made only eight appearances. He moved to St Etienne once Sami Hyypia and Stephane Henchoz had arrived on the scene.

KYLE, PETER
Inside-right: 5 apps
Born: Glasgow, Scotland, 21 December 1878 – *Died*: Glasgow, 19 January 1957
Career: Glasgow Schools, Glasgow Parkhead (June 1896), Partick Thistle, Clyde (trial, October 1898), LIVERPOOL (May 1899), Leicester Fosse (May 1900), Wellingborough (August 1901), West Ham United (November 1901), Kettering Town (December 1901), Wellingborough (April 1902), Aberdeen (September 1902), Cowdenbeath (January 1903), Heart of Midlothian (August 1903), Leicester Fosse (October 1903), Port Glasgow Athletic (April 1904), Royal Albert/Scotland (June 1904), Partick Thistle (April 1905), Royal Albert (May 1905), Watford (November 1909), Royal Albert (season 1910–11)

Peter Kyle was a useful inside-forward but not an out-and-out goalscorer as such. He loved to dribble with the ball, sometimes to the annoyance of his colleagues, and had a varied career in the game. A Scottish international trialist, he appeared in over 200 matches overall, the first of his five for Liverpool coming against Stoke (away) in September 1899. He never got a look in at Anfield after John Walker had joined Sam Hunter and Hugh Morgan as the Reds' three main inside players. Another member of the Kyle family, Archie, born in 1887, played for Glasgow Rangers, Blackburn Rovers, Clyde, St Mirren and Hamilton Academical between 1905 and 1915. There is a strong possibility (unconfirmed but listed in various other football books) that this same Peter Kyle may well have assisted four other clubs between 1905 and 1908, namely Tottenham Hotspur (season 1905–06), Woolwich Arsenal (from April 1906), Aston Villa (March 1908) and Sheffield United (October, 1908).

LACEY, WILLIAM
Right-half/utility forward: 258 apps, 29 goals
Born: Wexford, 12 December 1889 – *Died*: Ireland, 30 May 1969
Career: Shelbourne (1906), Everton (January 1909), LIVERPOOL (with Tom Gracie for Harold Uren as part of the deal, February 1912), New Brighton (June 1924), Shelbourne (May 1925), Cork Bohemians (September 1927, retired April 1931)

Bill Lacey was a great footballing character and, as someone once wrote: '. . . a round, lovable personality whose jutting chin was the delight of the cartoonists'. His career covered almost 25 years during which time he appeared in more than 350 senior matches, the majority with Liverpool. The first player to be honoured at full international level with both Merseyside clubs, he won 23 caps in all between 1909 and 1925, gaining the first 10 with Everton, the next 12 with Liverpool and his last with New Brighton. Able to play on either wing (preferring the left) as well as centre-forward and right-half, he made his initial appearance for the Reds against Middlesbrough in March 1912 as a left-winger, scored his first goal v. Tottenham Hotspur a fortnight later and after that went from strength to strength, although WW1 certainly disrupted his progress. An FA Cup finalist in 1914 when Liverpool lost to Burnley, Lacey was twice a League championship winner after the war (in 1922 and 1923) and besides his full caps he also represented the League of Ireland. He was the subject of probably one of the best 'swap deals' in early football history, when in 1912 he moved to Anfield from Goodison Park in a three-player transaction.

LAMBERT, RAYMOND
Full-back: 341 apps, 2 goals
Born: Baglitt, Flintshire, 18 July 1922
Career: Flint Schools, LIVERPOOL (amateur, January 1936; professional, July 1939); served in the Army; guest for New Brighton and Reading during WW2; retired May 1956; became a newsagent in Queensferry (until 1989)

Besides his 341 senior appearances for Liverpool, Ray Lambert also starred in 113 regional games for the Reds during WW2. He was handed his senior debut for the club against Chester in the first leg third round of the FA Cup in January 1946 and played in his first League game a fortnight or so into the 1946–47 season against Bolton Wanderers when he took over from Jim Harley. A Welsh schoolboy international who served in the RAF, he went on to win five caps at senior level after collecting three during the war, all against England, in 1943 (lost 8–0), and twice in 1944, at Cardiff and Anfield. He also played for a Wales XI v. Western Command in 1942 and v. the RAF in 1944 as well as representing the Football League v. British XI in 1941 at Anfield. His first full cap was awarded against Scotland in 1947 and his last versus Switzerland in 1949. He also represented the Army against Portugal. Initially a centre-half, he developed into a very fine full-back, able to play in both positions. He joined the staff at Anfield six months before his 14th birthday and played in his first wartime game at the age of 17 in November 1939 v. Wrexham. He had the ideal temperament, never suffered with nerves, was solidly built, cool and unruffled and his forté was his positional play. Able to nod off at the drop of a hat, he was always wide awake on the field of play. He gained a League championship medal in 1947 and three years later was in Liverpool's beaten FA Cup final side. His son, Wayne Lambert, was registered with Manchester City for a time in the late 1940s and also played for several Welsh non-League clubs.

LANE, FRANK
Goalkeeper: 2 apps
Born: Wallasey, 20 July 1948
Career: Stanley Arms FC (Wallasey), Tranmere Rovers (professional, August 1968), LIVERPOOL (£15,000, September 1971), Notts County (July 1975), Kettering Town (1977); later worked as a self-employed kitchen and bathroom fitter in the Nottingham area

After three seasons and 76 appearances for Tranmere Rovers, former Wallasey train driver Frank Lane made an upward move to First Division neighbours Liverpool as cover for Ray Clemence. Unfortunately his chances were restricted to just two outings in four years at Anfield, the first against Derby County (away) in September 1972 (lost 2–1), having his second outing three days later in a League Cup draw at Carlisle. He played second fiddle to Eric McManus at Meadow Lane.

LATHAM, CAPTAIN GEORGE

Half-back: 19 apps

Born: Newtown, Montgomeryshire, 1 January 1881 – *Died*: Newtown, 9 July 1939

Career: New Road School (Newtown), Newtown FC (August 1897); served in the Boer War in South Africa; Everton (trial, 1900), LIVERPOOL (amateur, August 1902; professional, May 1903), Southport Central (June 1909), Cardiff City (trainer, appointed, March 1911); served in the Welch Fusiliers during WW1; returned as trainer at Ninian Park (August 1919), Chester (trainer, August 1932–May 1934), Cardiff City (trainer, June 1934–May 1937); also trainer of the Welsh national side during the 1930s

One of the great characters of Welsh football for many years (both as a player and trainer) George Latham was a popular individual who had to work long and hard during his first six seasons at Anfield, getting very little opportunity in the League side. He made his debut against Burslem Port Vale in April 1905 (when the Reds won 8–1) and he had his best spell in the senior side in December and January 1906–07 when he made seven consecutive appearances at right-half in place of fellow Welsh international Maurice Parry. Nevertheless, he was considered good enough to win eight full caps for Wales, later adding two more to his tally with Southport Central and Cardiff City, also receiving a Welsh Cup winner's medal with the latter club (1912). He came out of retirement to play in a League game for Cardiff in April 1922 at Blackburn, aged 41. During WW1, Latham served as a captain in the 7th Battalion, Royal Welch Fusiliers on the Turkish front, winning the Military Cross. In the first battle of Gaza in March 1917, Latham's party of 40 men were successful in overcoming the Turkish line, only to learn that HQ had, the previous midnight, ordered a withdrawal on the basis of reports that 7,000 Turkish reinforcements were on their way! The line was abandoned and re-occupied by the Turkish troops only for Latham's fusiliers to be ordered to retake the position again.

Throughout the 1920s, Latham enjoyed a reputation as a trainer of rare skill; he acted as manager of the Great Britain Olympic team in 1924 and played an important part in Cardiff City's preparation for their historic 1927 FA Cup final win over Arsenal. In 1932 he left Ninian Park for Chester but returned to Cardiff two years later to resume his old position. Latham was badly injured in a cycling accident in 1936 and ill health later forced him to retire to his beloved Newtown, where he died a few months before the outbreak of WW2. Outside football Latham did a lot of excellent work for charity, regularly raising money for the Newtown Hospital where his mother was matron. It was said that during his many years with Cardiff, 'Gentleman George' (as he was known) never failed to send a telegram to his beloved mother after every match, telling her the score. Latham's trial game with Everton was abandoned due to snow and he returned to South Africa. His name is now associated with Latham Park, home of the present day Newtown FC (members of the Welsh League), although some reference books spell his surname as Lathom.

LAWLER, CHRISTOPHER
Right-back: 549 apps, 61 goals
Born: Liverpool, 20 October 1943
Career: Liverpool and District Schools, LIVERPOOL (amateur, May 1959; professional, October 1960), Portsmouth (free, October 1975), Stockport County (free, August 1977), Bangor City (free, July 1978–May 1980); coached in Norway (from October 1980), Wigan Athletic (assistant manager, October 1981); LIVERPOOL (reserve team coach, 1983–June 1985)

Strongly built, resourceful, confident and fast enough to catch and even dispossess the quickest wingers in the game, Chris Lawler was, without doubt, a wonderfully consistent full-back, a master at clearing his lines, positive in his methods with superb positional sense and covering ability. He assembled a splendid scoring record with the Reds – notching 61 goals, none from the penalty-spot – with 10 coming in 1969–70. Honoured by England at schoolboy level, he went on to gain four full and four under-23 caps for his country and helped Liverpool win two League championships (1966 and 1973) and the FA Cup (1965) while receiving runners-up prizes for defeats in the finals of the European Cup-Winners' Cup (1966) and FA Cup (1971). Nicknamed the 'Silent Knight' by the Anfield fans, Lawler's first League game for Liverpool was against West Bromwich Albion in March 1963 when he partnered Gerry Byrne in a 2–2 draw before a near-44,000 crowd. A former Liverpool teammate and then manager at Fratton Park, Ian St John, signed Lawler for Portsmouth in 1975. During his career Lawler amassed a total of 629 club appearances (League and Cup).

LAWRENCE, THOMAS JOHNSTONE
Goalkeeper: 390 apps
Born: Dailly, Ayrshire, 14 May 1940
Career: Warrington FC, LIVERPOOL (amateur, April 1947; professional, September 1957), Tranmere Rovers (trial, August 1971, signed, free, September 1971), Chorley (trial, August 1974, retired, May 1975)

Stocky and well-built, courageous, confident in his own ability, a safe handler, certainly spectacular at times, Tommy Lawrence often made difficult shots look easy and he certainly did a thoroughly honest job between the posts for Liverpool whom he served for more than 24 years, making close on 400 senior appearances. Referred to by the 'Kopites' at Anfield as the 'Flying Pig' (he weighed close to 14 stone at one time), Lawrence had to wait until claiming a regular place in the Liverpool side, eventually establishing himself as the club's number one during the 1962–63 season, having made his League debut in the October against West Bromwich Albion (away) when he took over from Jim Furnell. A League championship winner in 1964 and 1966 and the recipient of an FA Cup winner's medal in between times, he also played in the final of the European Cup-Winners' Cup of 1966. A Scottish international brought up in Lancashire with no sign of a Scots' accent, he gained three full caps over a period of six years, 1963–69, lining up against Eire, Wales and West Germany while also playing in one under-23 international. Somewhat underrated, Lawrence made a further 80 League appearances for Tranmere, where he was joined later by another ex-Liverpool star, Ron Yeats. Lawrence was involved in a bizarre incident in the 2nd leg of the European Cup semi-final clash with Milan in May 1965 when Inter's Joaquin Peiro seemed to kick the ball out of his grasp and into the net. Liverpool lost the contest 4–3 in aggregate.

LAWRENSON, MARK THOMAS

Defender: 346+14 apps, 18 goals

Born: Preston, Lancashire, 2 June 1957

Career: Preston Schools, Preston North End (associated schoolboy forms, aged 14, apprentice, June 1973; professional, August 1974), Brighton and Hove Albion (£100,000, July 1977), LIVERPOOL (£900,000, August 1981, retired, injured, March 1988), Thame United FC (briefly, 1988), Oxford United (manager, April–October 1988); Barnet (briefly, during the 1988–89 season), Tampa Bay Rowdies/NASL (April–August 1989), Peterborough United (manager, September 1989–November 1990), Corby Town (player, season 1991–92), Chesham United (player, season, 1992–93), Newcastle United (coach, November 1996–May 1997); now a respected football analyst on BBC's *Match of the Day* programme with another ex-Liverpool star, Alan Hansen

Mark Lawrenson, the son of a former Preston and Southport player, was a footballing centre-half – not a player who simply tackled an opponent, gained possession and then banged the ball upfield in hope. He looked up, saw a colleague and aimed a pass towards him. Obviously in certain instances he had to clear his lines the best way he could – and occasionally the ball went into row 'Z' – but he was so calm, cool and collected most of the game that the whole team benefited from his presence out on the field. He qualified to play for the Republic of Ireland through his mother and won a total of 38 full caps. A record signing by Liverpool, he helped the Reds win the League championship on four occasions (in 1982, 1983, 1984 and 1986), lift the League Cup three times in succession (1982, 1983 and 1984), the European Cup (1984) and FA Cup (1986). He also collected winner's medals for victories in the FA Charity Shield (1982) and Screen Sport Super Cup (1986) while accepting a runners-up prize for defeat in the final of the European Cup in 1985.

An Achilles tendon injury, initially sustained in 1987, ended his major professional playing career shortly before his 30th birthday. As a manager, Lawrenson didn't do a great deal . . . he was sacked as Oxford boss following the transfer of Dean Saunders to Derby County without his knowledge, agreed by the Rams' chairman Robert Maxwell and his son, Kevin, who was the Oxford chairman. He was then surprisingly sacked by Peterborough, despite Posh making a decent start to the 1990–91 campaign.

LAWSON, HECTOR STEWART RAMSEY

Forward: 16 apps

Born: Shettleston, Glasgow, 21 May 1896 – *Died*: 1971

Career: Shettleston FC (Glasgow), Glasgow Rangers (professional, April 1916),

Vale of Leven (loan, 1918), Third Lanark (loan, 1919), Clyde (loan, 1922) LIVERPOOL (January 1924), Airdrieonians (March 1926), Aberdeen (July 1926), Brighton and Hove Albion (June 1928), Newport County (August 1929), Shamrock Rovers (August 1931, retired, May 1933)

The last four years of Hector Lawson's career with Glasgow Rangers saw him acting as reserve to the great Scottish international outside-left Alan Morton. Lawson, in fact, scored 4 goals in 47 appearances during his Ibrox Park career before joining Liverpool, where he found it tough to get into the first team. Indeed, he made his debut for the Reds against Manchester City (away) in January 1924 at outside-right and went on to occupy three different positions for the club before moving back to Scotland after Cyril Oxley and Fred Hopkin had firmly established themselves as the Reds' two main wingers. Lawson perhaps had his best years late on with Newport County, for whom he scored once in 55 League games.

LEAVEY, HERBERT JAMES
Forward: 5 apps
Born: Guildford, Surrey, November 1886 – *Died*: Dorset, *circa* 1933
Career: Woodland Villa (1904), Plymouth Argyle (professional, July 1907), Derby County (February 1909), Plymouth Argyle (May 1909), LIVERPOOL (August 1910), Barnsley (September 1911), Bradford Park Avenue (1913), Llanelli (player-manager, August 1919), Portsmouth (as a player, March 1921), Boscombe United/Bournemouth and Boscombe Athletic (player-coach, October 1921–May 1924)

Bert Leavey's playing career spanned some 20 years during which time he surprisingly made only 65 League appearances, 28 for Barnsley. He did reasonably well during his two spells with Plymouth Argyle in the old Southern League but failed to make a single first-team appearance for Derby. He then spent a season at Anfield, playing mainly in the second XI and appearing in just five first-team matches, making his debut against Aston Villa on Christmas Eve, 1910 when he deputised at centre-forward for Jack Parkinson. He was a key member of the Barnsley attack in 1911–12 before breaking his right leg in an FA Cup fourth-round third-replay victory over the holders Bradford City. Unfortunately Leavey missed the final which the Tykes won 1–0 against West Bromwich Albion. He was with Boscombe when, as Bournemouth and Boscombe Athletic, they gained entry into the Football League in 1923.

LEE, SAMUEL
Midfield: 288+7 apps, 19 goals
Born: Liverpool, 7 February 1959
Career: LIVERPOOL (apprentice, May 1972; professional, April 1976), QPR (£200,000, August 1986), Osasuna/Spain (£200,000, June 1987), Southampton (free, January 1990), Bolton Wanderers (free, October 1990, retired May 1991), LIVERPOOL (coach, July 1992), Bolton Wanderers (assistant manager and coach, from 2003); also coach to the England national team for several years

An energetic, all-action midfielder who darted here, there and everywhere in search of the ball while covering acres of ground every time he played, Sammy Lee was also aggressive when required and loved a challenge. He served Liverpool splendidly for 13 years, making almost 300 senior appearances, the first of which was as a substitute for David Johnson against Leicester City in April 1978 when he scored in a 3–2 win at Anfield in front of almost 43,000 fans. He gained winner's medals for two European Cup final victories (1981 and 1984), three League Championship triumphs in succession (1982, 1983 and 1984), four League Cup final wins in a row (1981, 1982, 1983 and 1984) and for beating Spurs 1–0 in the 1982 FA Charity Shield game at Wembley. Capped by England at youth team level, Lee went on to represent his country in 6 under-21 and 14 full internationals, scoring 2 goals in the latter category and playing a huge part in a thumping 9–0 win over Luxembourg in his second game. In later years, after returning from a sojourn in Spain where he performed creditably and following spells with Southampton (with another ex-Liverpool star, Jimmy Case) and Bolton, he became a very successful and respected coach at Anfield, recruited by manager Graeme Souness to take over the reserves from Phil Thompson. He has also acted as senior coach to the Reds and is now part of the England coaching staff.

LEISHMAN, THOMAS
Left-half: 119 apps, 7 goals
Born: Stenhousemuir, Stirlingshire, 3 September 1937
Career: Camelon Juniors (Stirling), St Mirren (amateur, August 1953; part-time professional, September 1954), LIVERPOOL (£9,000 as a full professional, November 1959), Hibernian (£10,000, January 1963), Linfield (player-manager, July 1965–February 1968)
Determined in style, the long-striding Tommy Leishman was a tough-tackling, hardened footballer whose crew-cut hairstyle made him look perhaps more rugged than he really was. Prior to joining Liverpool at the age of 22 (as a straight and seemingly reliable replacement for Geoff Twentyman) he had won the Scottish Cup with St Mirren (1959) and added a Second Division championship medal to his collection with the Reds in 1962 (when he missed only one League game) before gaining an Irish Cup runners-up prize with Linfield in 1966. He made his debut in the English First Division against Charlton Athletic at Anfield in December 1959 (won 2–0) but couldn't quite cope with life in the top flight and moved back to Scotland with Hibs during the arctic winter of 1963.

LEONHARDSEN, OYVIND
Midfield: 42+7 apps, 7 goals
Born: Kristiansund, Norway, 17 August 1970
Career: Clausenengen/Norway (August 1987), Molde Fotballklubb/Norway (June 1989), Rosenborg Ballklubb/Norway (August 1992), Wimbledon (£660,000, November 1994), LIVERPOOL (£3.5m, June 1997), Tottenham Hotspur (£3m, August 1999), Aston Villa (£500,000, August 2002, released, June 2003), Lyn Oslo/Norway (August 2003)
Scorer of 19 goals in 86 senior games for his country, right-sided midfielder

Oyvind Leonhardsen also represented Norway in 14 under-21 and 3 youth internationals and, in fact, he netted 29 goals in 107 Norwegian League games before joining Wimbledon in 1994. He continued to find the target with the Dons (16 strikes in 102 outings) and then, following his transfer to Liverpool, he made his debut for the Reds in a 2–0 League Cup win at West Bromwich Albion in mid-October 1997, before taking part in his first Merseyside derby against Everton a few days later (lost 2–0). After two years at Anfield this plucky, chunky footballer had three useful campaigns at White Hart Lane (making 72 appearances) but suffered with injuries late on. He recovered to give Aston Villa a season's work (23 games) before moving back to Norway.

LESTER, HUGH
Outside-left: 2 apps
Born: Lehigh, Iowa, USA, 1891 – *Died*: USA, *circa* 1955
Career: Merseyside junior football, LIVERPOOL (professional, December 1911), Oldham Athletic (May 1914); served in Army and was a guest for LIVERPOOL and Prescot during WW1; Reading (August 1919–April 1920)
American-born Hugh Lester was classed as an 'adequate reserve' at Anfield. He became surplus to requirements and was released after spending three seasons with the club. Able to play at right-back, as a wing-half or outside-left, he was handed just two League outings, the first at right-half (in place of Bob Robinson) against Bradford City (away) in April 1912. He appeared once in Oldham's senior side. A noted sprinter, he once ran the 100 yards in 10.5 seconds. It is believed he returned to his native USA *circa* 1925.

LE TALLEC, ANTHONY
Midfield: 13+19 apps, 1 goal
Born: Hennebont, France, 3 October 1984
Career: Le Havre/France, LIVERPOOL (July 2003), St Etienne/France (loan, August 2004–January 2005), Sunderland (loan, August 2005–May 2006)
An attack-minded midfielder who proved to be a very useful asset to the squad, Anthony Le Tallec made his Premiership debut for Liverpool as a substitute for Steven Gerrard in a 3–1 win at Blackburn in September 2003. He did reasonably well in his first season at Anfield but missed out on all the glory that followed in 2004–05.

LEWIS, HENRY
Inside-forward: 70 apps, 12 goals
Born: Birkenhead, 18 December 1893 – *Died*: 1976
Career: The Comets FC (Liverpool), LIVERPOOL (September 1916; professional, August 1919), Hull City (October 1923–May 1925); later with Mold FC/Wales (during season 1927–28)
Harry Lewis was a short, chunky inside-forward who displayed a touch of class during a war-interrupted career, and one wonders what he might have achieved had not the Germans invaded Belgium! He scored 56 goals in 99 regional games

for Liverpool between 1916 and 1919 and after the hostilities gained a League championship winner's medal in 1922, appearing in 19 matches, but missing out on a second medal a year later when he was unable to oust the main three forwards, Dick Forshaw, Tommy Johnston and Harry Chambers. Lewis's League debut for the Reds came in August 1919 against Bradford City (away) when he netted in the 10th minute to help set up a 3–1 win.

LEWIS, KEVIN
Outside-right/-left: 81 apps 44 goals
Born: Little Sutton near Ellesmere Port, Cheshire, 19 September 1940
Career: Ellesmere Port Boys' Club, Sheffield United (as a junior, April 1955; amateur, September 1955; professional, October 1957), LIVERPOOL (£13,000, June 1960), Huddersfield Town (£18,000, August 1963), Port Elizabeth City/South Africa (July 1965)

Kevin Lewis was a record signing by Liverpool when he joined the Reds from Sheffield United in 1960, having been initially spotted by former Everton wing-half Joe Mercer when he was manager of Sheffield United. He went on to average more than a goal every two games during his three seasons at Anfield before moving across the Pennines to sign for Huddersfield Town. An England youth international, he gained a Second Division championship winner's medal in 1962 when he formed an excellent right wing partnership with Roger Hunt during the first half of the campaign before being replaced in the team by Ian Callaghan. He played on the opposite flank in 1962–63. Quick over the ground and possessing a strong right-foot shot, he netted 15 times in 52 games for Huddersfield before emigrating to South Africa.

LIDDELL, WILLIAM BEVERIDGE, J.P.
Outside-left/centre-forward: 537 apps, 229 goals
Born: Townhill near Dunfermline, Scotland, 10 January 1922 – *Died*: 3 July 2001
Career: Dunfermline Combined Schools, Kingseat Juveniles, Lochgelly Violet (1938), LIVERPOOL (professional, April 1939); served in the RAF as a navigator in Pathfinders during WW2, played as a guest for Cambridge Town, Chelsea, Dunfermline Athletic, Heart of Midlothian (1943), Linfield and Toronto FC/Canada (retired May 1961)

As a teenager Billy Liddell was studying to become an accountant whilst playing football for the Scottish junior team Lochgelly Violet. With both Hamilton Academical and Partick Thistle keeping an eye on him, fellow Scot Matt Busby recommended him to his club, Liverpool. Liddell, though, was apprehensive at first as to whether to join the Reds but after serious negotiations a deal was struck which enabled him to continue his studies and work part time for a local accountancy firm. The club also had to meet certain moral standards as Liddell, himself, had been raised a strict Presbyterian. With these formalities agreed, Liddell duly signed a contract . . . and he never looked back after that!

He scored 83 goals in 149 wartime appearances and finally made his senior debut for Liverpool in a third-round first-leg FA Cup encounter against Chester in January 1946, netting the opener in a 2–0 win. In the first League season after the war (1946–47) Liddell played 35 games on the left wing and hit 7 goals as the title came to Anfield, Liverpool squeezing home ahead of Manchester United and Wolves. A strict teetotaller and non-smoker, Liddell refused to have a glass of champagne with his teammates once the title was won. Honoured five times by Scotland in wartime internationals during season 1945–46, lining up v. Wales, England twice, Switzerland and Ireland, Liddell went on to win 28 full caps for his country, the first against Wales in October 1946. He also represented Great Britain twice in fixtures against the Rest of Europe in 1947 and 1955 – confirming that he was the best left-winger in the British game at that time. He also played for his unit when serving as a flying officer in the RAF and other representative honours included two games for the Football League side against a British XI (at Anfield) in 1941 and Western Command in 1942, for Scotland v. the RAF in 1944 and for the Scottish Services XI v. Belgium and Flanders in 1945.

At the end of the 1949–50 season he played in the FA Cup final against Arsenal and was bitterly disappointed to end up a loser. A very quick, direct player with strength and a powerful shot, Liddell occupied the centre-forward berth during his last few seasons at Anfield, playing on until the end of the 1960–61 campaign when Liverpool were a run-of-the-mill Second Division side. He retired having amassed well over 500 competitive appearances (a record at the time but later beaten by Ian Callaghan) and having scored 229 goals for the Reds – with another (a beauty) being disallowed. This came right at the end of a fifth-round FA Cup replay against Manchester City at Anfield in 1956. With seconds remaining and City leading 2–1, Liddell raced away from the halfway line, cut inside and cracked a left-footed rocket past German keeper Bert Trautmann . . . but the referee had blown for full-time before the ball crossed the line and Liverpool were out of the competition. After his footballing days were over Liddell devoted his time to being a Justice of the Peace (appointed in 1958), lay preaching, being a Sunday school teacher, doing general accountancy work for the Students' Union at Liverpool University (when he became assistant bursar) and also acting as chairman of the East Wavertree tennis club. A crowd of 38,789 (producing receipts of £6,340) attended Liddell's testimonial match at Anfield in September 1960 when Liverpool beat a star-studded International XI 4–2.

Jimmy Hill wrote this about Liddell in his book *Great Soccer Stars*, published in 1978: 'He would chase any lost cause and no defender could settle while he was around . . . stronger than most wingers, he was able to ride tackles well . . . and what most of his fellow professionals envied was his acceleration . . . a model player he was booked only once in 20 years, including wartime.' Teammate Kevin Baron said: 'Billy could get goals out of nothing . . . and if he did not get one he always looked as though he could. He used to scare defenders rigid.'

LINDSAY, ALEC
Left–back: 246+2 apps, 18 goals
Born: Bury, Lancashire, 27 February 1948
Career: Bury junior football, Bury Schoolboys, Bury (apprentice, April 1963;

professional, March 1965), LIVERPOOL (£67,000, March 1969), Stoke City (loan, August 1977, signed for £25,000, September 1977), Oakland Stompers/USA (£7,000, March 1978), Toronto Blizzard/NASL (May 1980), Newton FC (North West Counties League, October 1982, retired, May 1983); later employed as a scrap metal merchant, a licensee and fish and chip shop proprietor

Sandy-haired Alec Lindsay played as a wing-half and inside-forward for Bury before establishing himself as a rugged and robust yet fine overlapping left-back with Liverpool for whom he appeared in almost 250 first-class matches, gaining UEFA Cup and League First Division medals in 1973 and then an FA Cup winner's medal in 1974, while also receiving a runners-up prize for the 1971 FA Cup final. An England international at youth team level, he went on to play in four full internationals, all in 1974, and wasn't on the losing side once. He made his League debut for the Reds as a substitute against Ipswich Town (away) in October 1969 (drew 2–2) . . . this after making over 130 senior appearances for Bury and adding a further 22 to his tally with Stoke City.

LINDSAY, JOHN

Utility: 16 apps, 3 goals
Born: Fife, Scotland, 1900 – *Deceased*
Career: Partick Thistle (semi-professional, 1922), Rhyl Athletic (briefly, from late 1927), LIVERPOOL (professional, April 1928), Swansea Town (January 1930), Lochgelly Amateurs (May 1931–April 1932)

Able to play anywhere but preferring a half-back and inside-forward berth, Jack Lindsay actually occupied six different positions in his first season at Anfield. His League debut for Liverpool came in a 3–0 home win over Derby County in December 1928 when he deputised for Dave Davidson at centre-half. He drew up exactly the same set of statistics with Swansea – 3 goals in 16 games.

LIPSHAM, JOHN REGINALD

Outside-left: 3 apps
Born: Chester, 1881 – *Died*: 13 December 1959
Career: Chester and Cheshire junior football, Chester (1905), LIVERPOOL (professional, June 1906), Chester (August 1907–April 1914); did not play after WW1

Reserve to Jack Cox during his one season at Anfield, Jack Lipsham made his League debut on the left wing for Liverpool against Manchester United (away) on Christmas Day, featuring in a 0–0 draw. He spent eight years in total with Chester, gaining Welsh Cup winner's and runners-up medals in 1908 and 1910 respectively. He was awarded a benefit in 1913 for his loyal and excellent service to the then non-League club. Lipsham's elder brother, Herbert Lipsham, also an outside-left, played for Chester, Crewe Alexandra, Fulham, Millwall and Sheffield United and England (one cap).

LITMANEN, JARI OLAUI

Midfield: 19+24 apps, 9 goals

Born: Lahti, Finland, 20 February 1971

Career: Reipas FC/Finland (1987; professional, March 1988), HJK Helsinki/Finland (July 1991), MyPa/Finland (August 1992), Ajax Amsterdam/Holland (December 1992), CF Barcelona/Spain (August 1999), LIVERPOOL (free, January 2001), Ajax Amsterdam (August 2002)

Already an established Finnish international with over 350 club appearances under his belt (and 155 goals scored), attacking midfielder Jari Litmanen was almost 30 years of age when he joined Liverpool in 2001. He made his debut in a 3–0 win away to Aston Villa soon after arriving at the club and later in the year helped the Reds win the European Super Cup. He was troubled by injury in his first full season on Merseyside but he quickly made up for lost time in 2002–03 by producing some outstanding performances, appearing in 32 senior matches and upping his total of senior caps to 75. Playing in the hole behind the two main attackers (Michael Owen and Emile Heskey) he scored some cracking goals, including two wonderful long range efforts against Tottenham Hotspur in the Premiership and Dynamo Kiev in the Champions League in his final season at Anfield.

LIVERMORE, DOUGLAS ERNEST

Midfield: 14+3 apps

Born: Liverpool, 27 December 1947

Career: Liverpool and District junior football, Bolton Wanderers (amateur, August 1964), LIVERPOOL (apprentice, April 1965; professional, November 1965), Norwich City (£22,000, November 1970), AFC Bournemouth (loan, March–April 1975), Cardiff City (£15,000, August 1975), Chester (October 1977–May 1979); later coach with Cardiff City (season 1979–80) and Swansea City (seasons 1980–83), then reserve team manager of Tottenham Hotspur (from 1984, caretaker-manager, October 1987), LIVERPOOL (coach, from 1994, later assistant manager to Roy Evans and Gerard Houllier); was also part-time assistant manager of Wales (late 1980s)

Unable to gain a regular place in Liverpool's first team, Doug Livermore certainly made a name for himself after leaving Anfield. He appeared in 139 competitive games for Norwich City (collecting a Second Division championship winner's medal in 1972 and a runners-up prize in the League Cup final a year later), had 10 outings with Bournemouth, 88 for Cardiff City (whom he helped gain promotion from the Third Division in 1975, win the Welsh Cup in 1976 and finish runners-up 12 months later) and 80 for Chester. With his shrewd, technical and tactical knowledge he became a very successful coach and was in charge of Spurs for a short while, between the reigns of David Pleat and Terry Venables. He made the first of his 17 appearances for Liverpool as a substitute (for Tony Hateley) against West Ham United (away) in April 1968.

LIVINGSTONE, GEORGE TURNER
Inside-right: 32 apps, 4 goals
Born: Dumbarton, 5 May 1876 – *Died*: Helensburgh, Dumbarton, 15 January 1950
Career: Sinclair Swifts (Dumbarton), Artizan Thistle (Dumbarton), Parkhead FC (Glasgow), Dumbarton FC (August 1895), Heart of Midlothian (June 1896), Everton (briefly, 1899), Sunderland (£175, June 1900), Celtic (May 1901), LIVERPOOL (May 1902), Manchester City (May 1903), Glasgow Rangers (November 1906), Manchester United (January 1909, appointed reserve team player-manager, August 1911, retired as a player, 1918); Dumbarton (manager, January 1919), Clydebank (manager, August 1919), Glasgow Rangers (trainer, July 1920–December 1927), Bradford City (trainer, July 1928–May 1935); later ran a successful plumbing and gas-fitting business in Helensburgh

'Geordie' Livingstone was a fine, constructive footballer who could also play equally well in the right-half position. Strong and confident, he had already appeared in more than 100 first-class games when he joined Liverpool but he never really settled down on Merseyside and after a season at Anfield switched his allegiance to Manchester City with whom he gained an FA Cup winner's medal in 1904. He was suspended in 1906, following the FA inquiry into illegal payments and when his ban was lifted he returned to Scotland, spending just over two years with Rangers, returning to Manchester in 1909 and helping United win the First Division title in 1911. The recipient of two full caps for Scotland (the first in 1906), Livingstone also represented the Scottish League the following year. During an interesting career Livingstone scored 73 goals in 298 competitive matches north and south of the border, collecting a Scottish League runners-up medal with Celtic in 1902.

LLOYD, LAURENCE VALENTINE
Defender: 218 apps, 5 goals
Born: Bristol, 6 October 1948
Career: Bristol Rovers (apprentice, August 1965; professional, July 1967), LIVERPOOL (£60,000, April 1969), Coventry City (£240,000, August 1974), Nottingham Forest (£60,000, October 1976), Wigan Athletic (player-manager/coach March 1981, retired as a player, March 1983), Notts County (manager, July 1983–October 1984); later worked as a publican in Nottingham and as a soccer pundit on local radio (Nottingham)

The real 'sheet anchor' centre-half, solid, brave and reliable, Larry Lloyd inspired players around him and at times was regarded as one of the best defenders in the English game. He gave Liverpool wonderful service for more than five years, gaining winner's medals for triumphs in both the UEFA Cup and League First Division competitions in 1973 while receiving three full caps for his country, against Wales, Switzerland and Northern Ireland in 1971. He later added a fourth to his tally in 1980, having previously played at youth team level as a teenager and in eight under-23 internationals. He made the first of his 218 senior appearances for Liverpool against West Bromwich Albion (home) in

September 1969 when he deputised for Ron Yeats in a 2–2 draw, establishing himself at the heart of the Reds' defence towards the end of that season. He left Anfield after Phil Thompson and Emlyn Hughes had formed a fine partnership in defence, and as a Forest player he was twice a European Cup winner (1979 and 1980) and also helped Brian Clough's team complete the League championship and League Cup double in 1978 while adding a second League Cup winner's prize to his collection in 1979. In 1977, he had played in Forest's Anglo-Scottish Cup-winning side. As manager at Wigan, he helped the Latics gain promotion to the Third Division in 1982. Incidentally, Lloyd was the first player to appear before an independent disciplinary tribunal, on 9 November 1982.

LOCK, FRANK WILLIAM
Full-back: 42 apps
Born: Whitechapel, London, 12 March 1922 – *Died*: Clacton, Essex, 17 March 1985
Career: Middlesex Boys, London FA, Finchley, military service (1942–45), Charlton Athletic (professional, December 1945), LIVERPOOL (£12,500, with John Evans, December 1953), Watford (June 1955), Cambridge United (July 1957), Clacton Town (July 1959, later two spells as manager); still playing football aged 59 for Clacton's Golden Oldies (the Coach and Horses reserves) competing in the Clacton Sunday League while also working as a 'rep' for a Clacton-based soft drinks company
A corporal in the Royal Artillery, serving in Africa, Italy and Greece during WW2, Frank Lock represented the Army team managed by Arthur Rowe and was recommended to Charlton by his commanding officer, Colonel Dowlman, who had been an amateur at The Valley in the early 1930s. He made his League debut for the London club against Manchester United at Maine Road in January 1947 and went on to appear in 230 first-class matches for Athletic before transferring to Liverpool at the age of 31 in a deal that took Johnny Evans to The Valley. A classy and most astute full-back, Lock faced, and invariably matched, some of the finest wingers in the game. Two-footed, he partnered first Jack Lambert and then Tom McNulty at full-back at Anfield before losing his place in the side to Ronnie Moran. Earlier, in 1951–52, he was honoured by England 'B' against the Great Britain 'Possibles' Olympic team and toured Australia, but was injured playing in the first Test match.

LONGWORTH, EPHRAIM
Full-back: 371 apps
Born: Halliwell, Bolton, 2 October 1887 – *Died*: Lancashire, 7 January 1968
Career: Bolton and District Schools, Bolton St Luke's (August 1901), Chorley Road Congregationalists (July 1904), Bolton St Luke's (August 1906), Halliwell Rovers (September 1906), Hyde (professional, April 1907), Bolton Wanderers (June 1907), Leyton (October 1908), LIVERPOOL (May 1910, retired, May 1928, remained at Anfield on coaching staff)
As well as his 371 peacetime appearances, Eph Longworth played 120 times for

the Reds during WW1. A highly talented, distinctively bow-legged full-back with tremendous on-the-ball ability, his positional play was first class and he remained in the game until he was 40 years of age. He made his League debut for Liverpool against Sheffield United in September 1910 when he was introduced to the team in place of Bob Crawford, who later returned to the side and became Longworth's partner. His last outing came in April 1928. An FA Cup runner-up with the Reds in 1914, Longworth was a key member of two championship-winning sides in successive seasons (1922 and 1923) and gained five full caps for England (1920–23), becoming the first Liverpool player to skipper the national team. He also played in one Victory international, represented the Football League on six occasions and toured South Africa with the FA party in 1920.

LOW, NORMAN HARVEY
Centre-half: 13 apps
Born: Aberdeen, 23 March 1914 – *Died*: Toronto, Canada, 21 May 1994
Career: Newcastle Schools, Rosehill FC (Newcastle), Newcastle United (amateur, 1931), LIVERPOOL (professional, October 1933), Newport County (£2,000, November 1936); guest for Bristol City, Everton, LIVERPOOL, Lovells Athletic and Swindon Town during WW2; Norwich City (October 1946; retired as a player when appointed manager, May 1950; sacked, April 1955), Workington Town (manager, January 1956), Port Vale (manager, February 1957; resigned October 1962), Stoke City (scout, 1962–65), LIVERPOOL (chief scout, July 1965–May 1967), Witton Albion (manager, during season 1967–68); emigrated to North America (late 1968); became coach of Cleveland Stokers/USA; briefly back to Liverpool as a licensee before returning to the USA (1975)
A granite-like centre-half, tall and commanding with a crunching tackle, Norman Low found it hard to get into the first team at Anfield, making only 13 senior appearances in three years, the first against Manchester City in September 1934 when he deputised for 'Tiny' Bradshaw in a 2–1 win. He made 115 League appearances either side of WW2 for Newport County, helping the Welsh club win the Third Division (S) championship in 1939 before having 163 games for Norwich City. In 1959 he steered Port Vale to the Fourth Division championship. His father Wilf Low, who was tragically killed in a road accident in 1933, was a Scottish international centre-half who played for Montrose, Aberdeen and Newcastle United either side of WW1 while his uncle, Harold Low, played for Aberdeen and Sunderland before the Great War, lining up for the Wearsiders in the 1913 FA Cup final against Aston Villa. Low was a brother-in-law of boxers Nel Tarleton and Ernie Roderick.

LOWE, HENRY CHARLES
Half-back: 135 apps, 2 goals
Born: Whitwell, Derbyshire, 20 March 1886 – *Died*: Worksop, 25 October 1958
Career: Whitwell St Lawrence FC, Gainsborough Trinity (professional, June 1907), LIVERPOOL (April 1911); guest for Nottingham Forest during

WW1; signed permanently by Forest (March 1920; released, May 1921), Mansfield Town (May 1923), Newark Town (seasons 1925–30)

A very consistent performer, able to play as a wing-half or centre-half, Harry Lowe skippered Liverpool on several occasions but was unlucky to miss the 1914 FA Cup final through injury. He made his debut for the Reds against Bolton Wanderers (away) in September 1911 and soon afterwards gained a permanent place in the side. Described as having 'admirable powers of imparting steadiness', he fed his wingers exceedingly well and as a guest he helped Forest win the Wartime Victory Shield in 1919.

LOWRY, THOMAS
Full-back: 1 app.
Born: Liverpool, 26 August 1945
Career: Merseyside junior football, LIVERPOOL (apprentice, August 1961; professional, April 1963), Crewe Alexandra (June 1966, retired May 1978)

Tom Lowry simply couldn't make any headway whatsoever at Anfield owing to the presence of Gerry Byrne, Chris Lawler and Ronnie Moran. His only League game for the Reds was against Wolverhampton Wanderers (away) in April 1965 when he deputised for Lawler ahead of the FA Cup final showdown with Leeds United. He certainly made up for lost time at Gresty Road, appearing in 475 competitive games for Crewe, with 436 coming in the Football League – a club record that still stands today.

LUCAS, THOMAS
Full-back: 366 apps, 3 goals
Born: St Helens, Lancashire, 20 September 1895 – *Died*: Buckinghamshire, 11 December 1953
Career: Sherdley Villa, Sutton Commercial FC, Heywood United, Peasley Cross, Eccles Borough, Manchester United (trial, during season 1914–15), LIVERPOOL (semi-professional, August 1916; professional, August 1919), Clapton Orient (July 1933, retired May 1934), Ashford Town (manager, season 1934–35); then a pub licensee in Stoke Mandeville, Bucks (for 18 years until his death in 1953)

Slight of frame, Tom Lucas scored 4 goals in 41 games for Liverpool during WW1 before going on to become one of the club's finest full-backs. Able to play on the right or left, he made his League debut against Aston Villa (home) in September 1919 and remained a vital and valuable member of the first-team squad until 1932. An England international, capped against Ireland, France and Belgium over a period of five years (1921–26), he also represented the Football League and gained a League championship winning medal with Liverpool in 1922 when he appeared in 27 games. Unfortunately he missed out on a second medal a year later when the preferred full-back partnership comprised Eph Longworth and Don McKinlay. On leaving Anfield Lucas played in 21 Division Three (S) games for Orient at the age of 38.

LUMSDEN, JOSEPH
Forward: 8 apps, 2 goals
Born: Derby, *circa* 1875 – *Died*: Burton-on-Trent, 1923
Career: Burton Wanderers (May 1895), LIVERPOOL (August 1897), Glossop
  North End (June 1898, released, May 1900)
After a very good last season with Burton Wanderers when he scored 5 goals in
33 League games, Joe Lumsden joined Liverpool, initially as cover for Harry
Bradshaw, making the first of his eight appearances for the Reds against
Nottingham Forest in November 1897, scoring twice in a 3–2 win. Able to play
in any forward position, he lined up at inside-right, centre-forward and inside-
left for Liverpool and likewise for Glossop whom he also served as a left-winger,
helping that club gain promotion to the First Division as runners-up to
Manchester City in 1899 when he was an ever-present. He was only 25 when he
pulled out of League football.

MacDONALD, KEVIN DUNCAN
Midfield: 49+15 apps, 5 goals
Born: Inverness, 27 December 1960
Career: Inverness Caledonian Thistle (1976; professional, January 1978),
  Leicester City (£40,000, May 1980), LIVERPOOL (£400,000, November
  1984), Leicester City (loan, December 1987), Glasgow Rangers (loan,
  November–December 1986), Coventry City (free, July 1989), Cardiff City
  (loan, March–April 1991), Walsall (free, July 1991–May 1993), Aston Villa
  (coach, mid 1990s; later reserve team coach, also assistant manager), Republic
  of Ireland (assistant manager/coach, January 2006)
During his varied career, Kevin MacDonald made well over 300 club
appearances, having his best spell at Leicester for whom he played in a total of
155 games. He did very well in his second season at Anfield, helping Liverpool
win the League and Cup double and then added a Charity Shield medal to his
collection at the start of the next campaign, followed by a Screen Sport Super
Cup winner's medal when Liverpool beat Everton over two legs in the final
(September 1986). A tall, powerful footballer, he created a big impression with
Inverness Caley and in his first spell at Filbert Street he helped Leicester gain
promotion to the top flight. He had the misfortune to break his leg in September
1986. That injury required two operations and although he did continue to play
on for a further six years, he was never the same player he had been before the
accident. His debut for the Reds was against Luton Town (home) in December
1984 when he played alongside John Wark and Ronnie Whelan in midfield. He
teamed up with another ex-Liverpool star, Steve Staunton, as his assistant
manager to the Republic of Ireland national team in 2006.

McALLISTER, GARY
Midfield: 52+35 apps, 9 goals
Born: Motherwell, 25 December 1964
Career: Fir Park Boys' Club (from 1979), Motherwell (professional, September
  1981), Leicester City (£125,000, August 1985), Leeds United (£1m, July

1990), Coventry City (£3m, July 1996), LIVERPOOL (free, July 2000), Coventry City (free, July 2002, player-manager, April 2002, retired December 2003)

Scottish international midfielder Gary McAllister had gained one under-21, 2 'B' and 57 full caps for his country and had also appeared in 730 club games and scored 130 goals when he joined Liverpool at the age of 35. A wonderfully balanced player who packed a powerful shot, he was adept at taking on and beating defenders and then creating a chance (or two) for his colleagues. Playing predominantly down the left, he was also an expert at dead-ball situations and scored some stunning goals from free-kicks as well as firing home several vital penalties. He made the first of his 87 appearances for Liverpool as a substitute against Bradford City at Anfield in August 2000 and scored his first League goal for the club three months later when his former employers, Coventry City, were defeated 4–1. The winner of a Scottish First Division medal in 1985, he went on to gain a League championship medal and FA Charity Shield prize with Leeds in 1992, won the League Cup, FA Cup, UEFA Cup and Super Cup with Liverpool in 2001 and then added a second Charity Shield medal to his collection in 2002. He reluctantly quit as player-manager at Highfield Road in 2003 (to spend more time with his family), having amassed 877 club appearances and netted 151 goals.

McATEER, JASON WYNN
Utility: 119+20 apps, 6 goals
Born: Birkenhead, 18 June 1971
Career: Marine (1988), Bolton Wanderers (professional, January 1992), LIVERPOOL (£450,000, September 1995), Blackburn Rovers (£4m, November 1999), Sunderland (£1m, October 2001), Tranmere Rovers (free, July 2004)

An aggressive, hard-working, versatile performer, Jason McAteer made 145 senior appearances for Bolton and was impressive against Liverpool in the 1995 League Cup final before moving to Anfield. He made his Premiership debut for the Reds as a substitute against his future club, Blackburn Rovers, in September 1995 and thereafter was deployed as an attacking right-wing back, due to his ability to drive forward, take on and beat defenders and deliver a telling cross for his strikers. He was very effective and had an excellent first season with the club, starring in 40 games. He followed up with 51 appearances in 1996–97 but injuries started to affect his performances after that and he eventually moved to Ewood Park, Liverpool making a substantial profit from the deal. McAteer went on to win 52 full caps (plus one at 'B' team level) for the Republic of Ireland but for all his efforts, he surprisingly never figured in a trophy-winning side. He was appointed captain of Tranmere immediately on signing for the club. Moved by the news footage from Asia, McAteer organised a successful Tsunami benefit game at Anfield in March 2005 which featured many former Liverpool legends and colleagues. McAteer comes from a boxing family – his uncles Pat and Les were both British champions.

McAVOY, DOUGLAS HAIG
Inside-left: 2 apps
Born: Kilmarnock, 29 November 1918 – *Deceased*
Career: Cummock Juniors, Kilmarnock (professional, August 1936), LIVERPOOL (£7,000, December 1947), Queen of the South (September 1949–May 1950)

A Scottish Cup winner with Kilmarnock in 1938, Doug McAvoy was a splendid ball-player whose career was severely hampered by WW2. He joined Liverpool with a glowing reputation but he struggled at Anfield and made only two senior appearances for the Reds, the first against Stoke City (home) in January 1948 when he partnered Billy Liddell on the left wing in a 0–0 draw.

McBAIN, NEIL
Right-back/left-half: 12 apps
Born: Campbeltown, Argyll, 15 November 1895 – *Died*: Scotland, 13 May 1974
Career: Campbeltown Academical, Hamilton Academical (trial, 1913), Ayr United (July 1914); guest for Portsmouth and Southampton during WW1; Manchester United (£5,000, November 1921), Everton (£4,000, January 1923), St Johnstone (£1,000, July 1926), LIVERPOOL (March 1928), Watford (player-manager, November 1928, retired as a player, May 1931, remained as manager until August 1937), Ayr United (manager, season 1937–38), Luton Town (manager, June 1938–June 1939), New Brighton (secretary-manager, June 1946), Leyton Orient (assistant manager, February 1948, manager April 1948–May 1949), Estudiantes de la Plata FC/Argentina (coach, from August 1949), Ayr United (manager, season 1955–56), Watford (manager, August 1956–February 1959); then scout for Watford, Mansfield Town, Chelsea and Everton (1959–62), Ayr United (manager January 1963–May 1964)

A superb header of the ball, Neil McBain had toured Canada and the USA with Scotland in 1921 and had appeared in 43 games for Manchester United with whom he won the first of his three full caps for his country before joining Everton. Strong in all aspects of defensive play, he enjoyed a challenge and added a further 103 appearances to his tally during his three years at Goodison Park. He returned to Merseyside in 1928 after a sojourn with St Johnstone but found it tough going at Anfield where he remained for just six months. On 15 March 1947, as New Brighton's secretary-manager, McBain was forced to come out of retirement and make up the team against Hartlepools United in a Third Division (N) game at the age of 51 years, 4 months – thus beating the feat of Halifax Town's trainer Bob Suter, who played in a game at the age of 48 years, 10 months in April 1929. McBain's is a Football League record that still stands today. He had made his League debut 32 years earlier with Ayr United. Besides being a fine footballer, McBain was also excellent on the billiard table and achieved a personal break of 157.

McBRIDE, JAMES

Left-half: 55 apps, 7 goals

Born: Renton, Dunbartonshire, 30 December 1873 – *Died*: Scotland, *circa* 1950

Career: Renton Wanderers (1889), Renton FC (July 1890), LIVERPOOL (professional, August 1892), Ardwick/Manchester City (December 1894), Ashton North End (September 1897–May 1898); later worked as a ship-builder in Glasgow

Jim McBride was only 18 when he was named as a reserve for the Scottish League representative side against the Football League at Bolton in 1892. He had been playing splendidly north of the border and it was no surprise when Liverpool pipped several other leading clubs for his signature. He was outstanding on his debut, scoring in an 8–0 home win over Higher Walton in a Lancashire League fixture in September 1892, being one of four 'Macs' in the team. He made 26 appearances in each of his first two seasons at Anfield, helping the Reds win the Second Division title in 1894. He eventually lost his place in the side to another ex-Renton player, Duncan McLean. During the 1890–91 campaign, McBride was caught up in the litigation surrounding Renton FC, who had been expelled by the SFA for professionalism.

McCALLUM, DONALD

Right-back: 2 apps

Born: Glasgow, Scotland, June 1880 – *Died*: Scotland, 1959

Career: Glasgow junior football, Queen's Park (amateur, August 1896), LIVERPOOL (professional, August 1901), Greenock Morton (May 1903), Sunderland (April 1904), Middlesbrough (December 1904), Port Glasgow Athletic (January 1906), Kilmarnock (1907), Renton (1908), Lochgelly United (1910), East Fife (1912), Mid-Rhondda (1913), East Fife (1914, retired during WW1)

A sturdy full-back, Don McCallum spent his first season with Liverpool in the reserves, eventually making his debut for the Reds in October 1902 against West Bromwich Albion at The Hawthorns when he deputised for John Glover in a 2–1 win. McAllum's career spanned at least 15 years and during that time he appeared in well over 250 competitive matches, the majority north of the border.

McCANN, WILLIAM

Goalkeeper: 17 apps

Born: Renfrewshire, 1871 – *Died*: Paisley, Scotland, 1924

Career: Renfrew Juniors, Abercorn (June 1902), LIVERPOOL (professional, July 1894, released March 1895), Paisley Celtic (from August 1895)

Unfortunately Billy McCann conceded 39 goals in his 15 League outings for Liverpool and was replaced between the posts by the versatile Matt McQueen. He made his debut in a 1–1 draw at Blackburn on the opening day of the 1894–95 relegation season and left Anfield after an eight-month stay.

McCARTHY

Right-back: 1 app.
Born: Liverpool 1870 – *Died*: *circa* 1950
Career: LIVERPOOL (season 1893–94)
There are conflicting references surrounding this player. Some record books show him as playing at right-back for Liverpool against Rotherham (away) in January 1894 while others (including local and national newspapers) do not list him at all in this game, or even having ever played for the Reds. However, there are no references anywhere as to his Christian name!

McCARTNEY, JOHN

Right-half: 164 apps, 5 goals
Born: Newmilns, Ayrshire, 1870 – *Died*: *circa* 1942
Career: Newmilns FC, St Mirren, LIVERPOOL (October 1892), New Brighton Tower (July 1898–May 1900)
A stalwart in the Liverpool defence during the early-to-mid 1890s, rugged John McCartney was a regular in the side for five seasons. A strong tackler, he distributed the ball well and always gave encouragement to his teammates. Twice a Second Division championship winner (1894 and 1896), he made the first of his 164 appearances for the Reds against Higher Walton (away) in the Lancashire League in October 1892 and played his first League game almost a year later against Lincoln City (Second Division). McCartney joined Liverpool during a cotton strike (in Scotland) and may have been employed by a Paisley cotton firm.

McCONNELL, JOHN MORRISON

Half-back: 53 apps, 1 goal
Born: Cambusnethan, Lanarkshire, 9 December 1890 – *Died*: *circa* 1937
Career: Lanarkshire junior football, Motherwell (amateur, June 1907), Airdrieonians (professional, May 1908), LIVERPOOL (£80, April 1909), Aberdeen (August 1912–May 1915); did not play after WW1
Jock McConnell made his League debut for Motherwell as a 16 year old before making rapid headway with Airdrie, for whom he played in all half-back positions. He had to wait until mid-December 1909 before Liverpool handed him his first game, away to Aston Villa. However, due to a crisis (Sam Hardy and Gus Beeby were both sidelined) he was asked to keep goal in his next game on Christmas Day against Bolton. Thankfully a resolute defence kept the opposition at bay and the Reds won 3–0. After leaving Anfield, McConnell made 20 appearances for Aberdeen.

McCOWIE, ALEXANDER ANDREW

Inside-forward: 35 apps, 11 goals
Born: Scotland, 1872 – *Died*: Scotland, *circa* 1940
Career: Garthside FC (Glasgow), LIVERPOOL (professional, January 1897), Woolwich Arsenal (May 1899), Middlesbrough (October 1900), Chesterfield (May 1901–April 1902)
A canny forward, able to play in most positions, Andrew McCowie found it

tough going at Anfield where he had to battle for first-team football with internationals Frank Becton and fellow Scots Hugh Morgan and John Walker. He persevered, nevertheless and played in 35 games, the first against Sheffield Wednesday in April 1897. After leaving Anfield, McCowie made 33 appearances for Arsenal, 20 for Middlesbrough and 18 for Chesterfield.

McDERMOTT, TERENCE
Midfield: 317+12 apps, 81 goals
Born: Kirkby, Liverpool, 8 December 1951
Career: Liverpool schoolboy football, Bury (apprentice, April 1967; professional, October 1969), Newcastle United (£22,000, February 1973), LIVERPOOL (£170,000, November 1974), Newcastle United (£100,000, September 1982–September 1984); later with Cork City (January–March 1985), Apoel FC/Cyprus (July 1985–April 1987), Newcastle United (assistant manager/coach, from February 1992)

A workaholic in midfield, Terry McDermott covered acres of ground every game he played in, a real box-to-box grafter who also scored some stunning goals, many from distance. Initially an orthodox wing-half and thought to be an expensive misfit at Anfield, he proved the critics wrong with some brilliant displays in midfield where he played alongside Graeme Souness, Jimmy Case and Ray Kennedy and also with Sammy Lee and Ronnie Whelan, amongst others. He made the first of his 329 competitive appearances for the Reds in the Merseyside derby against Everton in November 1974 but surprisingly he did not consolidate himself in the team until 1977–78. He then became a key figure and collected medals galore during his eight years at Anfield – helping the Reds win the European Cup in 1977, 1978 and 1981, the League title in 1977, 1979, 1980 and 1982, the League Cup in 1981 and 1982 and the European Super Cup in 1977 as well as gaining winner's medals for FA Charity Shield victories in 1979 and 1980. He was also an FA Cup runner-up in 1977, having received a similar award when playing for Newcastle against Liverpool in the 1974 final, and collected another runners-up medal in the 1978 League Cup final. He helped Newcastle gain promotion to the top flight in 1984 and two years later with Apoel he won the Cypriot League but lost in their domestic Cup final. Coached into being one of the best 'linkmen' in European football, in 1980 he became the first man to be voted the PFA and Football Writers' Association 'Player of the Year'. McDermott gained one 'B', one under-21 and 25 full caps for England and during his career amassed 452 Football League appearances, scoring 80 goals – none better than his tremendous effort in a 7–0 win over Spurs in 1978 which manager Bob Paisley described as the best he'd ever seen at Anfield. McDermott has been assistant manager to three former Liverpool players at Newcastle – Kevin Keegan, Kenny Dalglish and Graeme Souness.

McDEVITT, WILLIAM
Centre-half: 4 apps
Born: Belfast, 5 January 1898 – *Died*: Belfast, 10 January 1966
Career: Belfast junior football, Swansea Town (professional, August 1920),

Belfast United/Celtic (August 1922), LIVERPOOL (June 1923), Exeter City (May 1925, appointed player-manager, April 1929, retired as a player, May 1931, remained as manager until September 1935), Belfast Celtic (manager, October 1935), Distillery (manager, season 1936–37)

A reliable reserve during his two seasons at Anfield, tall, shrewd Ulsterman Billy McDevitt made his debut for Liverpool at centre-half against Aston Villa (away) in November 1923 when he deputised for Walter Wadsworth in a 0–0 draw. He switched to inside-right on joining Exeter City and then, as the Grecians' manager, steered them into the sixth round of the FA Cup in 1931 (where they were defeated 4–2 by Sunderland after a replay) and twice into runners-up spot in the Third Division (S). He made 139 senior appearances for the Devon club and has been arguably the best manager the club has ever had. In 1933 he turned down an offer to become boss of QPR.

McDONALD, JOHN
Outside-left: 78 apps, 4 goals
Born: Kirkcaldy, Fife, June 1886 – *Died*: Scotland, 1943
Career: Wemyss Harp FC, Vale of Wemyss, Raith Rovers (August 1902), Glasgow Rangers (£100 plus proceeds from a match, January 1907), LIVERPOOL (May 1909), Newcastle United (£650, May 1912), Raith Rovers (August 1914); served in Army during WW1; Raith Rovers (returned, briefly during season 1919–20)

A noted and respected player in Liverpool's ranks for three seasons, John McDonald had good pace and delivered a high-quality cross, sometimes on the run. The first of his 78 senior outings for the Reds was against Chelsea (away) in September 1909 and his first goal was scored against Blackburn Rovers a week later in a 3–1 win. McDonald, who could be temperamental at times, was fined a week's wages by Newcastle after failing to turn up for a League game against Derby in 1913. Four years earlier he had played for Rangers against Celtic in the 1909 Scottish Cup final when the notorious Hampden Park riots disrupted the replay and as a result the trophy was withheld. He made 48 appearances for the Ibrox Park club (10 goals), was a Scotland international trialist in 1910 and a Scottish Qualifying Cup winner in 1907.

McDOUGALL, JAMES
Left-half/inside-left: 357 apps, 12 goals
Born: Port Glasgow, 23 January 1904 – *Died*: Allerton, Liverpool, July 1984
Career: Port Glasgow Athletic, Partick Athletic (August 1925), LIVERPOOL (April 1928), South Liverpool (player/youth team coach, July 1938, retired, May 1939); not involved in football after WW2; later ran a successful chandlery business in Liverpool

A Scottish international who skippered his country in his two games, both in 1931 against Austria and Italy (the latter in Rome when he was handed a bouquet by the Italian dictator Mussolini), Jimmy McDougall was a skilful, cultured and sportsmanlike player who with Matt Busby and 'Tiny' Bradshaw formed an all-Scottish half-back line at Anfield. He averaged 35 appearances per season in his decade with Liverpool – a tribute to his consistency. The first of his 357 games for the Reds was at inside-left against Bury in August 1928, when he starred in a 3–0 win. His older brother, John McDougall, born in 1901, played for Airdrieonians, Sunderland, Leeds United and Scotland between 1921 and 1937.

McDOUGALL, ROBERT
Forward: 8 apps, 1 goal
Born: Glasgow, 1894 – *Died*: Glasgow, *circa* 1965
Career: Glasgow junior football, LIVERPOOL (professional, 1913); served in
  Army during WW1; Falkirk (July 1919), Ayr United (season 1921–22)
A promising young forward who could occupy any position in the front-line, like so many other footballers of his generation Bob McDougall's career was ruined by WW1. After the hostilities he did very well in Scotland, appearing in 73 League games for Falkirk and 35 for Ayr, scoring a total of 14 goals. He scored the winning goal from the inside-right berth on his debut for Liverpool at West Bromwich Albion in January 1914.

McFARLANE, JOHN
Centre-forward: 2 apps
Born: Shettleston, Glasgow, 1906 – *Died*: Glasgow, *circa* 1977
Career: Shawfield Juniors (Glasgow), Aberdeen (professional, August 1924),
  LIVERPOOL (November 1928), Halifax Town (July 1930), Northampton
  Town (July 1932), Kidderminster Harriers (April 1934), Darlington (August
  1935), Kidderminster Harriers (August 1938–September 1939); did not
  figure after WW2
A reserve with Aberdeen for over four years, Jock McFarlane made only seven senior appearances for the Dons before trying his luck with Liverpool. He never bedded in at Anfield and after just two outings, the first against Everton in the Merseyside derby in February 1929, he moved over to Yorkshire to play for Halifax Town.

McGUIGAN, ANDREW
Inside-left: 35 apps, 14 goals
Born: Newton Stewart, Scotland, 24 February 1878 – *Died*: Liverpool, 1948
Career: Newton Stewart (1893), Hibernian (professional, May 1898),
  LIVERPOOL (May 1900), Middlesbrough (April 1904), Southport Central
  (August 1904), Accrington Stanley (1905), Burslem Port Vale (1906), Bristol
  City (May 1907), Barrow (March 1908), Exeter City (August 1908, retired,
  injured, May 1910); LIVERPOOL (scout, late 1920s); also did much charity
  work on behalf of the Liverpool and Merseyside pensioners
A soccer nomad who served with nine professional clubs and basically played all over England, Andy McGuigan hardly did a thing after leaving Anfield in 1904, being a reserve with most of his future employers. He was outstanding with Hibernian where he was rated as one of the best players in his position since the great Scottish international Willie Groves. The first player to score five goals in

a League game for the Reds (doing so against Stoke in January 1902), McGuigan's debut for Liverpool came in a 3–2 win at Derby in October 1900, when he had a hand in two of his side's goals.

McINNES, JAMES SLOAN, BSc
Left-half: 51 apps, 2 goals
Born: Ayr, Scotland, August 1912 – *Died:* Liverpool, 5 May 1965
Career: Third Lanark (professional, August 1932), LIVERPOOL (£5,500, March 1938; guest for Brighton and Hove Albion, Fulham, Leeds United, Luton Town, Manchester United, Millwall, Newcastle United, Queens Park Rangers and York City during WW2; retired August 1946), joined the administration staff at Anfield, later appointed assistant secretary and then club secretary from August 1955 until his death
Besides his first-class record with Liverpool, Jimmy McInnes also scored once in 15 WW2 games for the Reds. He found the net on his League debut in England when Brentford were defeated 3–1 at Griffin Park in March 1938 when he was brought into the side to replace John Browning at left-half. A positive footballer with a big heart, he was a Scottish Cup runner-up with Third Lanark in 1936 and made over 100 senior appearances north of the border before his big-money transfer to Merseyside. In September 1944, McInnes twice represented the Northern Command in 1942 and played for the Cumberland Services v. Western Command and for the Western Command v. the RAF two years later. He gained his BSc degree at Edinburgh University.

McKENNA, JOHN
Outside-right: 1 app.
Born: Liverpool, 1882 – *Died:* Liverpool, *circa* 1956
Career: Merseyside schoolboy football, Old Xaverians (Liverpool), LIVERPOOL (August 1906–May 1908)
John McKenna spent two seasons at Anfield where he was a regular member of the reserve team. His only League game was against Birmingham (home) at the end of January 1907 when he deputised for Arthur Goddard in a 2–0 win.

McKINLAY, DONALD
Left-back/left-half: 434 apps, 34 goals
Born: Newton Mearns near Glasgow, 25 July 1891 – *Died:* Liverpool, 16 September 1959
Career: Newton Swifts (Glasgow), Newton Villa (Glasgow), LIVERPOOL (professional, January 1910), Prescot Cables (July 1929, retired, May 1931); later became a licensee in Liverpool
A Scottish international (capped twice in 1922 v. Wales and Northern Ireland), Don McKinlay gave Liverpool 19 years' supreme service – one of the longest spells by a Scotsman with an English club – and during that time he appeared in 568 first-team games, 134 coming in WW1. A celebrated name in Anfield history, he was a wonderfully consistent defender who gained back-to-back League championship winner's medals in 1922 and 1923, having earlier

collected a runners-up prize when Liverpool lost in the 1914 FA Cup final. He skippered the side for many years and, in fact, occupied seven different positions during his lengthy career. A powerful player who could hit a dead ball as hard as anyone, he loved to venture forward into the opposition's penalty area and drew up an excellent goal return for a defender, weighing in with 6 in each of 3 seasons – 1912–13, 1922–23 and 1923–24 – within his overall tally of 34. Unfortunately, a bad injury, suffered in a 3–1 League defeat at Villa Park in September 1928, effectively ended McKinlay's career with Liverpool.

McKINNEY, PETER
Forward: 3 apps, 1 goal
Born: Consett, County Durham, 16 December 1897 – *Died*: New York, USA, 23 December 1979
Career: Consett FC, LIVERPOOL (professional, August 1920), New York Giants/USA (September 1923, retired May 1928)
Peter McKinney's three outings for Liverpool were in different forward positions during the 1920–21 season and his only goal was scored on his debut in a 2–2 draw with Sheffield United in the October when he deputised for Dick Forshaw at inside-right. A reserve for three years at Anfield, he later did well in America where he died at the age of 82.

McLAUGHLIN, JOHN THOMAS
Midfield: 53+2 apps, 3 goals
Born: Liverpool, 25 February 1952
Career: Kirkby Schools (Liverpool), LIVERPOOL (apprentice, April 1967; professional, February 1969), Portsmouth (loan, October 1975); remained a registered player at Anfield until May 1976; later played non-League football
One of Ian St John's pals, John McLaughlin spent nine years with Liverpool, having his best spell in the first XI during the 1970–71 season when he made 33 League appearances. His debut came in April 1970 against FA Cup finalists Chelsea when he replaced Emlyn Hughes. He was only 24 when he moved into a lower grade of football.

McLEAN, DUNCAN
Left-back: 84 apps, 6 goals
Born: Dumbarton, Scotland, 12 September 1869 – *Died*: Scotland, *circa* 1950
Career: Renton Union, Renton FC, Everton (October 1890), LIVERPOOL (August 1892), Edinburgh St Bernard's (October 1895–May 1899)
A Scottish international left-back, capped twice against Wales in 1896 and Ireland a year later, Duncan McLean was a key man in Liverpool's 1894 Second Division championship and promotion-winning side that conceded only 18 goals and never lost a game. Utterly reliable, solid and a steadying influence on his defensive colleagues, he tipped the scales at 13st. 8lb to complement a handy height of almost 5ft 11in. He partnered Andrew Hannah in his early years at Anfield and made the first of his 84 senior appearances for the club against Higher Walton in a Lancashire League fixture in September 1892 (won 8–0),

170

following up with his Football League baptism against Middlesbrough 12 months later. He made 26 appearances for Everton and later captained St Bernard's for several years.

McLEAN, JAMES
Right-back: 4 apps
Born: Edinburgh, 1880 – *Died*: Scotland, 1947
Career: Edinburgh Thistle, Vale of Leven, LIVERPOOL (September 1903–May 1904)
Jimmy McLean arrived at Anfield with the highest possible credentials, having performed exceedingly well north of the border. Unfortunately, after a decent start with Liverpool, when he played in four of the opening six League games, the first against Sunderland at Roker Park, he slipped into the second team following the arrival of Alf West from Notts County.

McLEAN, JOHN CAMERON
Centre-/left-half: 29 apps
Born: Port Glasgow, 22 May 1872 – *Died*: *circa* 1932
Career: Greenock Volunteers (May 1890), LIVERPOOL (professional, September 1894), Grimsby Town (June 1897), Bristol City (£40, May 1898), Bristol Rovers (July 1902), Millwall Athletic (April 1904), Queens Park Rangers (May 1906, retired, injured, April 1908)
Well built, fearless in the tackle, hard and resilient yet a shade on the small side, Jock McLean relished a tough battle and he never produced less than 100 per cent on the field of play. As good as any defender in the game when at his peak (1890s), he had the first of his 29 outings for Liverpool against Stoke (away) in November 1894 and during his career accumulated well over 400 club appearances, having his best spell (158 games in 4 years) with Bristol City. He gained a Southern League championship medal with QPR in 1908. McLean also represented Renfrewshire and Scotland in a junior international against Northern Ireland in 1893.

McLEOD, THOMAS
Centre-forward/inside-left: 7 apps
Born: Musselburgh, Edinburgh, 26 December 1920
Career: Edinburgh Royal; served in the Army/BAOR (during WW2); LIVERPOOL (professional, October 1945), Chesterfield (July 1951), Wisbech Town (August 1952–April 1954)
Spotted playing services football in Germany, Tommy McLeod was quickly recruited to Anfield and taken on the professional staff at the age of 24, making the first of his seven senior appearances against Preston North End (away) in April 1947 when he deputised for Albert Stubbins at centre-forward in a 0–0 draw. Possessing a strong right-foot shot, he did much better with Chesterfield for whom he scored 3 goals in 25 Third Division (N) games before joining non-League side Wisbech Town.

McMAHON, STEPHEN
Midfield: 286+2 apps, 51 goals
Born: Liverpool, 20 August 1961
Career: Everton (apprentice, June 1977; professional, August 1979), Aston Villa (£300,000, May 1983), LIVERPOOL (£350,000, September 1985), Manchester City (£900,000, December 1991), Swindon Town (player-manager, November 1994–October 1999), Blackpool (manager, January 2000–May 2004)

An aggressive, hard-tackling, totally committed central midfielder, Steve McMahon made 120 appearances for Everton and 91 for Aston Villa for whom he played against his former club in the 1984 League Cup semi-final, before joining Liverpool at the age of 24. After making his debut against Oxford United (away) in September 1985, when he linked up with Jan Molby and Ronnie Whelan in the engine-room, he went on to gain medals galore – three League championships (1986, 1988 and 1990), successive FA Cup final wins (1988 and 1989), a European Super Cup success (1989), three FA Charity Shield victories (1986, 1988 and 1989) and glory in the Screen Sport Super Cup final of 1986 against his former club Everton. During a wonderful career he also won 17 full, 6 under-21 and 2 'B' caps for England and was in his country's 1990 World Cup squad. After leaving the Reds he added a further 90 appearances to his tally with Manchester City and 51 with Swindon. One of only a handful of players to have skippered both Everton and Liverpool, McMahon had no real luck as a manager. He and his brother John (now coach at Tranmere Rovers) were at Goodison Park together while Steve's son, Stephen junior, joined Blackpool in 2002.

McMANAMAN, STEPHEN
Midfield/wing-forward: 348+16 apps, 66 goals
Born: Bootle, 11 February 1972
Career: LIVERPOOL (apprentice, April 1988; professional, February 1990), Real Madrid (free, July 1999), Manchester City (free, August 2003, out of contract, May 2005)

Steve McManaman's League career (in England and Spain) realised 399 appearances (272 for Liverpool, 92 for Real Madrid and 35 for Manchester City, where he was beset by injuries during his second season). He scored just 54 goals – it should have been more. After representing his country at youth team level, he went on to win 7 under-21 and 37 senior caps (3 goals scored) while gaining winner's medals for team victories in the FA Cup final of 1992, the League Cup final of 1995, the European Cup finals of 2000 (when he scored for Real in a 3–0 win over Valencia) and 2002 (v. Bayer 04 Leverkusen) and as champions of Spain's La Liga in 2001 and 2003. There is no doubt that on his day McManaman ('Stevie Wonder' to the fans) was one of the finest attacking midfielders in the game. Week after week he used to tease and torment defenders, at Anfield and elsewhere, and the 'Kopites' loved him. With his floppy hair, he enjoyed showing the ball to a defender, weaving one way and then the other, before darting past him (and sometimes them) into the danger zone, often

172

setting up a scoring chance for a colleague or, failing that, having a shot at goal himself. Perhaps he gave the ball away far too easily at times, yet there is no doubting that McManaman was a terrific footballer – one of the very best Liverpool have had since WW2. He made the first of his 364 appearances for the club against Sheffield United in December 1990 (as a second-half substitute for Peter Beardsley) and he netted his first goal against his future club, Manchester City, at Maine Road in August 1991. His last outing for the Reds, before his move to the Bernabeu Stadium in Madrid, was against Wimbledon at Anfield in May 1999 when almost 42,000 fans said 'farewell' to one of Liverpool's superstars.

McMULLAN, DAVID
Right-half: 35 apps
Born: Belfast, 1901 – *Died*: Belfast, *circa* 1977
Career: Distillery (August 1921), LIVERPOOL (£400, October 1925), New York Giants/USA (July 1928), Distillery (November 1928), Exeter City (May 1929, retired, April 1930); later a part-time coach with Belfast Celtic

An Irish League representative, Dave McMullan won the Irish Cup with Distillery in 1925, just before joining Liverpool. A versatile performer, able to occupy both wing-half positions and most in the forward line (he was on the left wing in the Irish Cup final), he also played in goal for Exeter in their 4–0 home League defeat by Newport County in April 1930 when the club's two main keepers were injured. McMullan's debut for Liverpool was against Manchester City in October 1925 when he lined up at outside-right in a 2–1 win. He added three Northern Ireland caps to his collection during his time at Anfield.

McNAB, JOHN SEYMOUR
Right-half: 222 apps, 6 goals
Born: Cleland, Lanarkshire, 17 April 1894 – *Died*: Bootle, 2 January 1949
Career: Army football, Bellshill Athletic, LIVERPOOL (professional, November 1919), Queens Park Rangers (June 1928, retired, April 1930); returned to Merseyside where he became licensee of the Jawbone Inn, Bootle

Scottish international half-back Jock McNab was invariably and accurately described as raw-boned. Tall, long-legged and strong in defence, his tackling had a cogency that enabled him to win most 50-50 situations. He certainly never held back and some of the players who came up against him took quite some time to regain their composure. After helping Bellshill win the Glasgow Junior League championship in 1919, he played reserve team football for practically two years before establishing himself in the first team at Anfield. He made his debut at left-back against Manchester United on New Year's Day 1920 and played at left-half in his second game 48 hours later. He eventually took over at right-half from Jack Bamber in October 1921. Capped against Wales in March 1923, McNab gained successive League championship winning medals with Liverpool (1922 and 1923), missing only three games in the initial triumph. He was suspended for six weeks during the 1924–25 season after being sent off against Newcastle United. He made 59 appearances for QPR before retiring at the age of 36.

McNAMARA, ANTHONY

Outside-right: 11 apps, 3 goals
Born: Liverpool, 3 October 1929
Career: Merseyside Schools, Liverpool amateur and junior football, Everton (amateur, July 1947; professional, May 1950), LIVERPOOL (£4,000, December 1957), Crewe Alexandra (July 1958), Bury (September 1958–April 1959), Runcorn (season 1959–60)

The principal part of Tony McNamara's career was the seven and a half years he spent at Goodison Park where he scored 22 goals in 113 senior appearances for the Blues. Heavily built but described as an elegant footballer, who seemed to smooth his way over the turf, he played in four games when Everton gained promotion to the First Division in 1954. Unfortunately he failed to do himself justice at Anfield, making only 11 appearances for the Reds, the first against Bristol City (home) in December 1957 when he scored in a 4–3 win. His place on the right wing was eventually taken by Fred Morris. McNamara, in fact, played in all four Divisions of the Football League in the space of 12 months (1957 and 1958).

McNAUGHTON, HAROLD

Goalkeeper: 1 app.
Born: Edinburgh, 1896 – *Died*: Edinburgh, *circa* 1966
Career: Edinburgh St Bernard's (1914), LIVERPOOL (August 1920–May 1921), later with Peterlee FC

Signed as cover for the great Elisha Scott, Harry McNaughton's only League outing for Liverpool was against arch-rivals Everton in October 1920 when he did extremely well in a 1–0 win before 50,000 fans at Anfield. Prior to moving to Merseyside, McNaughton, who was said to be 'a rather cool customer', had played in over 150 games for St Bernard's and was on the brink of gaining international honours.

McNULTY, THOMAS

Full-back: 36 apps
Born: Salford near Manchester, 30 December 1929
Career: Salford Boys' Club, Manchester United (amateur, May 1945; professional, June 1947), LIVERPOOL (£7,000, February 1954–June 1958); later with Hyde United (season 1963–64)

An outstanding junior footballer, Tom McNulty appeared at Wembley Stadium in youth representative matches. Unfortunately he was unable to emulate his achievement after turning professional, although he did help Manchester United win the League title in 1952, playing in 23 matches. He eventually moved to Anfield (after Billy Foulkes had been installed as Roger Byrne's full-back partner at Old Trafford) but was unable to check Liverpool's descent into the Second Division. He made only 36 appearances in four seasons with the Reds (the first against Sheffield Wednesday at Hillsborough in February 1954) and after leaving the club little was heard of him until he reappeared with Hyde United in 1963.

McOWEN, WILLIAM ARTHUR

Goalkeeper: 28 apps
Born: Blackburn, March 1871 – *Died*: Blackburn, 27 December 1950
Career: Cherry Tree FC, Blackburn Olympic (amateur), Blackburn Rovers (amateur, March 1886; professional August 1888), Darwen (March 1890), LIVERPOOL (August 1892), Blackpool (May 1894), Nelson (season 1895–96)

Billy McOwen was the only Englishman in the first-team squad at Anfield during the early 1890s . . . the other players were all Scots, eight of them 'Macs'. He was a brilliant goalkeeper on his day and conceded only 16 goals when the Reds won the Second Division championship in 1894, having made his debut against his previous club, Darwen, in a Lancashire Cup tie in January 1893. His League debut followed at Middlesbrough eight months later, after he had taken over the goalkeeping duties from Jack Ross. As a 15 year old with Blackburn Rovers, McOwen was in line to play in the 1886 FA Cup final v. West Bromwich Albion but was overlooked as Rovers won 2–0.

McPHERSON, ARCHIBALD

Inside-left: 133 apps, 19 goals
Born: Alva near Alloa, Clackmannanshire, 10 February 1910 – *Died*: Scotland, 1969
Career: Tillicoultry and Alloa Boys' Club, Bathgate (1926), Glasgow Rangers (professional, March 1928), LIVERPOOL (£2,000, November 1929), Sheffield United (£1,895, December 1934), Falkirk (June 1937, retired, May 1938), Alloa Athletic (manager, seasons 1945–47)

A teenager with Rangers for whom he made six senior appearances, dour little Scot Archie McPherson was quickly into his stride at Anfield, scoring 5 goals in 25 League games in his first half-season. He made his debut for the Reds against Leeds United 48 hours after joining and struck his first goal (the winner) versus Arsenal the following month. Taking over from Harry Race, he formed an excellent left wing partnership with Fred Hopkin and one reporter wrote in 1930 that he was . . . 'An accurate purveyor, he is also a fine manipulator and excellent controller of the ball.' He spent five splendid years at Anfield and after leaving the club he was converted into a wing-half by Sheffield United, for whom he appeared in the 1936 FA Cup final (beaten 1–0 by Arsenal).

McPHERSON, WILLIAM

Inside-left: 55 apps, 17 goals
Born: Beith, Ayrshire, 1880 – *Died*: Scotland, *circa* 1950
Career: Beith FC (August 1902), St Mirren (professional, October 1904), LIVERPOOL (£200, August 1906), Glasgow Rangers (£300, July 1908), Heart of Midlothian (seasons 1911–13)

Billy McPherson enjoyed two seasons at Anfield, scoring 11 goals in 28 League games in his first (1906–07) when he joined Jack Cox on the left wing. He netted on his debut for the Reds against Arsenal shortly after joining the club and hit two crackers in a 6–1 home win over Preston North End a month later.

A player who always had his wits about him, on his return to Scotland he did very well with Rangers (27 goals in 60 outings), helping the Ibrox Park side win the Scottish Cup in 1909. He was the nephew of John 'Kitey' McPherson, ex-Rangers and Scotland.

McQUE, JOSEPH

Centre-half: 134 apps, 14 goals
Born: Glasgow, Scotland, February, 1870 – *Died*: Glasgow, Scotland, 1934
Career: Govan Boys, Pollockshields, Celtic (professional, August 1890),
    LIVERPOOL (August 1892–April 1898); later with Third Lanark
Understudy to the great Scottish international centre-half James Kelly at Celtic, Joe McQue had no hesitation in joining Liverpool, knowing he had the ability and confidence to make a name for himself in English League football. He did just that and gave the Reds six years' commendable service, helping them twice win the Second Division title (1894 and 1896). He made 24 appearances in Lancashire League and Cup football before playing in Liverpool's first-ever League game v. Middlesbrough in September 1893. He and his co-defenders conceded only 12 League goals that season with McQue often attacking in the usual centre-half style of his day . . . and he was always eager to get in a shot, scoring 5 of his 14 goals for the Reds in 1895–96.

McQUEEN, HUGH

Outside-left: 62 apps, 18 goals
Born: Hartill, Lanarkshire, 1 October 1867 – *Died*: Norwich, 8 April 1944
Career: Leith Athletic (1890), LIVERPOOL (October 1892), Derby County
    (July 1895), Queens Park Rangers (May 1901), Gainsborough Trinity (July
    1902), Fulham (player/assistant trainer, August 1903, retired April 1904,
    appointed club's first-team trainer), Norwich City (assistant trainer, May
    1905–April 1907); later ran a tobacconist and confectioner's shop in Norwich
    up to WW1
Younger brother of Matthew (q.v.), Hugh McQueen was a forceful, speedy winger, an accurate crosser of the ball with a powerful shot. He had performed with gusto at Leith and immediately made his mark at Anfield, scoring 5 times in 19 Lancashire League and Cup games in 1892–93. He then netted 11 goals when the Second Division championship was won the following season before losing his place on the left flank to John Drummond. The scorer of 22 goals in 168 games for Derby County, McQueen was awarded a gold medal by a national football magazine after being voted the best player on view in the 1898 FA Cup final when the Rams lost 3–1 to Nottingham Forest. McQueen once had a narrow escape after jumping head first off a springboard at Southport baths where the Liverpool team was training. He had to be dragged out of the water, confessing he couldn't swim.

McQUEEN, MATTHEW
Utility: 105 apps, 6 goals
Born: Harthill, Lanarkshire, 18 May 1863 – *Died*: Liverpool, 28 September 1944
Career: Leith Athletic (1880), Heart of Midlothian (1887), Leith Athletic (1890), LIVERPOOL (professional, October 1892–April 1899); later qualified as a referee (intermediate level) and was also a Football League linesman (1904); LIVERPOOL (director, 1917, then team manager, February 1923, retired through ill health, February 1928)

The moustachioed Matt McQueen was the soul of versatility – able to play anywhere on a football pitch. He helped Liverpool win the Second Division championship twice in three years in 1894 and 1896, when he actually occupied 6 different positions, including 20 outings in goal, the majority in the latter campaign after taking over from Billy McCann. Capped twice at senior level by Scotland, against Wales in March 1890 (won 5–0) and March 1891 (won 4–3), his main and, indeed, favoured position was right-half, although he hardly ever played there!

He was astute as a manager, signing some fine players including the South African Gordon Hodgson (q.v.) and guided Liverpool to the First Division title in 1923, although the achievement was marred when he had to have a leg amputated following a serious road accident which occurred in the February when returning home from a scouting mission.

McRORIE, DANIEL
Outside-right: 35 apps, 6 goals
Born: Glasgow, 25 June 1906 – *Died*: Cheshire, 26 July 1963
Career: Queen's Park Strollers (Glasgow), Airdrieonians (August 1925), Stenhousemuir (July 1927), Greenock Morton (August 1928), LIVERPOOL (November 1930), Rochdale (October 1933), Greenock Morton (December 1933), Runcorn (August 1934–May 1936)

Danny McRorie was outstanding when Morton gained promotion to the top flight of Scottish football in 1929 and he continued to impress the following season before joining Liverpool. At his peak, his assertive and opportunist methods brought him plenty of goals, more so in Scotland although he did well enough at Anfield, making his debut for the Reds against Sheffield United in November 1930 when he created two goals in an emphatic 6–1 win. Capped by his country against Wales in 1931, he also represented the Scottish League.

McVEAN, MALCOLM
Utility forward: 127 apps, 38 goals
Born: Jamestown, Dunbartonshire, 7 March 1871 – *Died*: Glasgow, 6 June 1907
Career: Scottish junior football, Third Lanark (semi-professional, 1889), LIVERPOOL (May 1892), Burnley (March 1897), Dundee (August 1897), Bedminster (August 1898–May 1899); returned to Scotland to work as a labourer in a Glasgow shipyard

Malcolm McVean appeared in all five forward-line positions for Liverpool but preferred the inside- or outside-left berths where his blistering pace over 20–30

177

yards was a huge asset to the team. He had the pleasure of scoring the Reds' first-ever League goal in a 2–0 win at Middlesbrough in September 1893 – this after he had starred in 28 Lancashire League and Cup games the previous season, hitting the target on his debut in an 8–0 home win over Higher Walton. Twice a Second Division championship winner in 1894 and 1896, he failed to make headway with Burnley or Dundee and after retiring in 1899 he returned to the docks, where he had previously worked as a boiler man in a shipyard on the River Clyde.

MALONEY, JOSEPH JOHN
Inside-forward/wing-half: 12 apps
Born: Liverpool, 26 January 1934
Career: Liverpool schoolboy and junior football, LIVERPOOL (professional, January 1951), Shrewsbury Town (£1,500 with Russell Crossley, July 1954), Port Vale (July 1961), Crewe Alexandra (August 1961), Winsford United (May 1963–May 1965), Crewe Alexandra (trainer, seasons 1965–67)
After leaving Anfield where he had acted as a reliable reserve for three and a half years, Joe Maloney made over 250 senior appearances for Shrewsbury (237 in the Football League). Maloney made his debut for the Reds against Bolton Wanderers (home) in March 1953, deputising for Bob Paisley in a 0–0 draw.

MARSH, MICHAEL ANDREW
Right-back/midfield: 71+31 apps, 6 goals
Born: Liverpool, 21 July 1969
Career: Kirkby Town (amateur, August 1984), LIVERPOOL (free as a professional, August 1987), West Ham United (£2.5m exchange deal involving David Burrows for Julian Dicks, September 1993), Galatasaray/Turkey (£300,000, July 1995), Coventry City (£450,000, December 1994), Southend United (£500,000, September 1995), Barrow (February 1998), Kidderminster Harriers (season 1999–2000), Boston United (August 2001), Accrington Stanley (May 2002)
An FA Cup winner with Liverpool in 1992, midfielder Mike Marsh spent seven years at Anfield during which time he had to battle long and hard to get first-team football owing to the array of talent within the club. Nevertheless, he stuck in there and produced some exciting, all-action performances, having his best seasons in the early 1990s when he occupied a variety of positions. The first of his 102 outings for the Reds was in March 1989 when he came on as a substitute for Jan Molby in a 2–0 home League win over Charlton Athletic. When he moved into non-League football with Barrow in 1998, Marsh had chalked up a record at senior level of 282 appearances and 23 goals. He later gained a Conference winner's medal with Kidderminster (2000).

MARSHALL, ROBERT GRANT
Outside-right: 21 apps, 2 goals
Born: Edinburgh, Scotland, 1876 – *Died*: *circa* 1931
Career: Leith Athletic (May 1894), LIVERPOOL (August 1897), Portsmouth (August 1899), Brighton and Hove Albion (July 1904–May 1906)

After three seasons playing for Leith, Bobby Marshall was given the chance to prove his worth in the English First Division with Liverpool. He made his debut for the Reds against Stoke in September 1897 but after a 16-match run in the side he was replaced on the right wing by Fred Geary. With Jack Cox around as well, he eventually moved to Fratton Park. He helped Portsmouth win the Southern League title in 1902 when two more ex-Liverpool players, Tom Cleghorn and Tom Wilkie, were teammates. He went on to make 227 appearances for Pompey at competitive level, scoring 35 goals. His brother, John Marshall, who gained international honours for Scotland, won the Scottish Cup with Third Lanark in 1899.

MARSHALL, WILLIAM HENRY

Goalkeeper: 1 app.
Born: Liverpool, 1880 – *Deceased*
Career: LIVERPOOL (season 1902–03)
Relatively unknown local-born goalkeeper Bill Marshall spent just the one season with Liverpool, appearing in the League side once when he deputised for Bill Perkins. Unfortunately, it wasn't a happy occasion as Everton won the Merseyside derby 4–0 at Goodison Park.

MARTIN, DAVID EDWARD

Midfield: yet to make his debut for Liverpool
Born: Romford, Essex, 22 January 1986
Career: MK Dons (apprentice, April 2002; professional, January 2004),
    LIVERPOOL (January 2006)
Former England youth international, 6ft 1in. tall and weighing 13st. 7lb, David Martin was signed by Liverpool boss Rafael Benitez as a squad member shortly before the transfer window closed in January 2006, having made just over 50 senior appearances for MK Dons.

MATTEO, DOMINIC

Defender: 137+18 apps, 2 goals
Born: Dumfries, Scotland, 28 April 1974
Career: LIVERPOOL (apprentice, May 1990; professional, May 1992), Sunderland (loan, March 1995), Leeds United (£4.75m, August 2000), Blackburn Rovers (free, June 2004)
Dominic Matteo spent ten years at Anfield and although never quite establishing himself as a regular in the first team, often stepping in for and then giving way to the more senior professionals, he was totally reliable and would play anywhere to get a game. A very skilful, highly intelligent and composed defender or midfielder, he was born in Scotland of an Italian father and English mother and after serving his apprenticeship, made his debut for Liverpool in a Premiership game against Manchester City (away) in October 1993. He played in 12 more games that season but then had to wait another three years before having another decent run in the side. An England international, capped at youth, 'B' and under-21 levels, he then went on to play in six games for

179

Scotland's senior side. He made almost 150 appearances for Leeds before moving to Blackburn in 2004.

MATTHEWS, ROBERT WILLIAM
Centre-half/centre-forward: 9 apps, 4 goals
Born: Plas Bennion near Ruabon, North Wales, 14 April 1897 – *Died*: Wrexham, 18 December 1987
Career: Colwyn Bay FC (1916), LIVERPOOL (amateur, December 1918; professional, January 1919), Bristol City (£750, March 1922), Wrexham (£350, November 1923), Northwich Victoria (£200, June 1925), Barrow (£100, October 1925), Bradford Park Avenue (free, January 1926), Stockport County (free, May 1930), New Brighton (free, October 1930), Chester (free, January 1932), Oswestry Town (free, August 1932), Witton Albion (September 1932), Sandbach Ramblers (November 1932), Colwyn Bay (March 1933), Rossendale (August 1933, retired May 1936); Llangollen (manager, seasons 1936–39); served in WW2; Nottingham Forest (scout, 1940/50s), Blackpool (scout, 1960s)

Billy Matthews (sometimes called Bob) played football until he was 39 and during his adventurous career he served with no fewer than 14 different clubs, 8 in the Football League. He started out as a centre-half with Liverpool, quickly switched to the centre-forward position where he performed superbly well and then reverted back to being a defender. He went on to win three full caps for Wales, the first against Ireland in 1921 whilst at Anfield, followed by a second in 1923 and his last in 1926. A tall, cultured footballer who believed in positional play, ball control and intelligent distribution, Matthews scored eight goals in three WW1 games for the Reds before making his League debut against Derby County in April in 1920. Called into action only once more over the next 18 months, he was then named as leader of the attack in 7 games at the start of the 1921–22 season, netting 4 times. After leaving Anfield he helped Bristol City win the Third Division (S) championship in 1923 and five years later gained a Third Division (N) winner's medal with Bradford, while in between he won the Welsh Cup with Wrexham (1924). He scored almost 20 goals in well over 300 senior games (281 in the Football League) and without doubt had his best spell with Bradford (117 games). He was candidate for the manager's job at Wrexham in 1936 but was overlooked. A fitness fanatic, Matthews was a keen cyclist and was seen out on the road regularly until he was 80. He was known as 'Billy White Hat' for his distinctive headgear which could be seen bobbing up and down over the hedgerows as he rode by.

MAXWELL, LAYTON JONATHAN
Midfield: 1 app., 1 goal
Born: Rhyl, 3 October 1979
Career: LIVERPOOL (apprentice, April 1996; professional, July 1997), Stockport County (loan, July 2000–February 2001), Cardiff City (free, August 2001), Swansea City (free, March 2004), Newport County (August 2004), Mansfield Town (free, December 2004)

A busy, bustling, all-action wide-midfielder, Layton Maxwell looked impressive as a teenager in Liverpool's Academy side, gaining Welsh youth honours and playing five times for the under-21s, later taking the tally in the latter category to 14. He was never able to push hard enough for a regular place in Liverpool's first team despite scoring in his only senior outing, in a League Cup tie against Hull City in September 1999.

MEIJER, ERIK
Striker: 10+17 apps, 2 goals
Born: Meerssen, Holland, 2 August 1969
Career: Meerssen FC/Holland (September 1985), Fortuna Sittard/Holland (professional, July 1987), Royal Antwerp/Belgium (May 1989), PSV Eindhoven/Holland (November 1989), Fortuna Sittard (August 1990), Maastricht/Holland (July 1991), PSV Eindhoven/Holland (August 1993), Uerdingen/Germany (May 1995), Bayer 04 Leverkusen/Germany (August 1996), LIVERPOOL (free, July 1999), Preston North End (loan, October–November 2000), SV Hamburg/Germany (December 2000)
Giant 6ft 2in. Dutch international striker Erik Meijer seemed to be a first-class signing from Bundesliga side Leverkusen after an impressive first season at Anfield. Strong in the air and certainly useful on the ground, he was a real trier, excited the crowd and certainly enjoyed his days with Liverpool. But a year later he found himself on the fringe of first-team football and after just 27 games for the Reds, plus a loan spell with Preston, he returned to Germany with SV Hamburg. Prior to joining Liverpool he had scored 85 goals in 271 League games in Dutch, Belgian and German football. He made his first appearance for the Reds as a substitute (for Titi Camara) against Sheffield Wednesday in August 1999.

MELIA, JAMES
Inside-forward: 287 apps, 78 goals
Born: Liverpool, 1 November 1937
Career: St Anthony's School (Liverpool), Liverpool Schools, Liverpool Boys, LIVERPOOL (groundstaff, April 1953, amateur, May 1954; professional, November 1954), Wolverhampton Wanderers (£55,000, March 1964), Southampton (£30,000, December 1964), Aldershot (£9,000, player-coach, November 1968, player-manager, April 1969, sacked January 1972), Crewe Alexandra (player-manager, May 1972, retired as a player, 1973, remained as manager until December 1974), Southport (manager, July 1975, resigned September 1975); coached in the Middle East (October 1975), California Lasers/USA (scout), Brighton and Hove Albion (scout, then manager, March–October 1983), Belenenses/Portugal (manager, October 1983–November 1985), Stockport County (manager, July–November 1986), Kuwait (coaching, 1987–90), Dallas, Texas/USA (indoor coaching School, 1991–93)
A very fine play-maker and excellent passer of the ball, Jimmy Melia was in the shadow of the late, great Johnny Haynes as far as England were concerned, although he did manage to play in two full internationals . . . but only after

Haynes had been involved in a car crash. He also represented his country at schoolboy and youth team levels and played for the Football League. After developing through the ranks at Anfield, Melia scored on his League debut against Nottingham Forest in December 1955 and gained a regular place in the first team the following season, later helping the Reds win both the Second and First Division titles (1962 and 1964 respectively). He had a brief sojourn at Molineux and gained promotion to the top flight with Southampton in 1966, following his record £30,000 transfer from Wolves. When he retired as a player in 1973, Melia's record looked impressive: 622 appearances at competitive level, 122 goals scored of which 105 came in 571 League games. He began his managerial career at Aldershot whom he guided to the fourth round of the FA Cup in 1970 but was sacked when the 'Shots started to drift alarmingly towards the relegation zone early in 1972. When he was in charge at Gresty Road, Crewe, he twice had to seek re-election. He lasted only three months at Southport and nine months at Brighton but he did step out at Wembley with the latter club when they lost to Manchester United in the 1983 FA Cup final after a replay. He then resigned when, against his wishes, Albion appointed Chris Cattlin as coach. Alex Young, the Everton forward of the 1960s, described Melia as being 'one of the best backside men in the game . . . he could turn his back on you magnificently and jockey for position holding the ball all the time'.

MELLOR, NEIL ANDREW
Forward: 15+7 apps, 6 goals
Born: Sheffield, 4 November 1982
Career: LIVERPOOL (apprentice, April 1999; professional, February 2002), West Ham United (loan, August 2003–January 2004), Wigan Athletic (loan, January–May 2006)

A prolific scorer in Liverpool's under-19 and reserve teams (netting 46 in competitive games and 56 overall in season 2001–02), Neil Mellor despaired of ever making the first XI. He eventually got a game with the seniors in October 2004, making an impressive debut in a League Cup tie against Millwall. Despite some enterprising displays for the first team, scoring the goal of his life against the reigning Premiership champions Arsenal and netting two more against Olympiakos of Greece in the European Champions League, he simply couldn't keep his place in the side – although in fairness, a knee problem which required a double operation in 2005 didn't help matters one iota. When he regained full fitness, he had a useful loan spell at West Ham (playing in 21 games under three different managers) before joining Paul Jewell's Wigan Athletic in January 2006, scoring a dramatic late winner in his first game for his new club at Middlesbrough. Mellor is on contract at Anfield until January 2007.

METCALF, ARTHUR
Forward: 63 apps, 28 goals
Born: Seaham near Sunderland, 8 April 1889 – *Died*: Liverpool, 9 February 1936
Career: St George's FC (Seaham), Herrington Swifts (1907), Hebburn Argyle (August 1908), North Shields Athletic (January 1909), Newcastle United

(£100; professional, April 1909), LIVERPOOL (£150, May 1912), Stockport County (August 1918), Swindon Town (June 1920), Accrington Stanley (June 1922), Aberdare Athletic (June 1923), Norwich City (July 1925, retired, May 1926)

Arthur Metcalf claimed a high profile on Tyneside for his positive play. Stockily built, he earned a professional contract with Newcastle at the age of 20 and acted as reserve for several star players during his three years at St James' Park, making only 12 first-team appearances. He went on to occupy all five forward-line positions with Liverpool, appearing in the 1914 FA Cup final defeat by Burnley. A forceful opportunist with an eye for goal, he made his debut for the Reds in September 1912 in a 2–1 defeat at West Bromwich Albion and netted the first of his 28 goals for the club against Sheffield United the following month, finishing up as leading marksman that season. Injury caused him to lose his place in the side for a while and although he came back strongly he didn't sign a new contract at Anfield after WW1, having netted 42 goals in 91 regional games during the hostilities. His career realised 76 goals in 235 peacetime League appearances. Metcalf's brother, George, played for Huddersfield Town, North Shields Athletic, Sunderland, Merthyr Town and Portsmouth before WW1.

MICHAEL, WILLIAM
Inside-forward: 23 apps, 4 goals
Born: Wishaw, Lanarkshire, 1874 – *Died*: Wishaw, 5 July 1938
Career: Wishaw Thistle (1890), Heart of Midlothian (May 1893), LIVERPOOL (July 1896), Heart of Midlothian (July 1897), Bristol City (May 1900–April 1901); later President of Wishaw Thistle FC (1920s)

Prior to moving to Anfield, Bill Michael had represented the Scottish League and won both League championship and Scottish Cup medals with Hearts in 1895 and 1896 respectively. A physically strong player who it was said 'could charge into a bull elephant and still come off best', he was known as the 'India Rubber Man' and certainly had a knack of scoring vital goals – although his record with Liverpool wasn't great. He found the net for Hearts in ten successive matches during the 1893–94 season to set a club record and after making his debut for the Reds on the left wing against Blackburn Rovers in September 1896, he struck his first goal for the club in his second game, a 3–0 home win over Nottingham Forest a month later. He later netted 15 times in 20 games for Bristol City and all told scored over 50 goals for Hearts in his two spells at Tynecastle.

MILLAR, WILLIAM THOMAS
Forward: 3 apps, 2 goals
Born: Ballymena, County Antrim, 21 June 1903 – *Died*: Northern Ireland, *circa* 1990
Career: Lochgelly United (August 1922), Linfield (professional, May 1926), LIVERPOOL (£1,500, August 1928), Barrow (£300, January 1930), Newport County (free, June 1933), Carlisle United (free, July 1934), Sligo

Rovers (free, April 1935), Cork City (free, May 1937), Drumcondra (free, August 1938); did not play after WW2

Initially a wing-half, Billy Millar became an attacker by chance, filling in at centre-forward in an emergency with Linfield. He never looked back and went on to have a useful career, although he never quite fitted the bill at Anfield, playing in only three games. Fast and decisive, he scored in the first minute of his debut against Bury (home) in August 1928 when he partnered Edmed on the right wing in a 3–0 win. After that he never really figured but after moving to pastures new he became a Northern Ireland international, capped twice in 1932 and 1933, set a club scoring record for Barrow in 1931–32 with 30 goals in 30 League games and, in fact, is still the only player ever to win full international honours for that club. Some reference books spell this player's name as Miller.

MILLER, JOHN

Centre-forward: 13 apps, 7 goals
Born: Dumbarton, 1868 – Died: Glasgow, 1933
Career: Dumbarton (1888), LIVERPOOL (August 1892), The Wednesday (£50, August 1893), Airdrieonians (£25, April 1894); became a steeplejack.

After gaining a Scottish League championship winner with Dumbarton in 1891 when they shared the title with Rangers, Miller top-scored for Liverpool in his only season at Anfield. He claimed two goals on his Lancashire League debut in a 4–0 win over Bury in September 1892, struck a five-timer in a 7–0 win over Fleetwood and grabbed hat-tricks in victories over Higher Walton (5–0) and Nantwich (4–0). His brother Jack and two sons, Arthur and Tom, all played football.

MILLER, JOHN

Outside-/inside-right: 8 apps
Born: Dalziel near Motherwell, 12 March 1897 – *Died*: before 1990
Career: Larkhall Thistle (junior, August 1913), Hamilton Academical (professional, August 1914), LIVERPOOL (December 1918), Aberdeen (£3,000, June 1921), Partick Thistle (December 1924), Aberdeen (August 1926), Clyde (£350, February 1927), Dunfermline Athletic (late 1927), Partick Thistle (1928), Prescot Cables (1929), Barrow (1930), Carlisle United (August 1931; retired, May 1932)

Jack Miller scored 9 goals in 19 games for Liverpool during WW1 but failed to find the net in his 8 peacetime League appearances, making his debut against Chelsea in October 1919 when he deputised for Fred Pagnam at inside-right. A record signing by Aberdeen, he claimed 61 goals in 123 outings during his two spells at Pittodrie Park, top-scoring in 1921–22 and 1923–24. He missed most of the 1922–23 campaign with a broken leg. His brother Tom Miller (q.v.) was at Anfield with him, while nephew John Govan played for Hibernian and Scotland.

MILLER, THOMAS
Inside-left/centre-forward: 146 apps, 58 goals
Born: Motherwell, 29 June 1890 – *Died*: 3 September 1958
Career: Larkhall Hearts (1905), Glenview FC (1906), Lanark United (1907), Third Lanark (professional, August 1908), Hamilton Academical (May 1910), LIVERPOOL (£400, February 1912), Manchester United (£2,000, September 1920), Heart of Midlothian (£550, plus Arthur Lochhead, valued at £2,300, July 1921), Torquay United (August 1922), Hamilton Academical (£100, June 1923), Raith Rovers (December 1926, retired, May 1927)

A Lanarkshire Cup winner with Larkhall United in 1908, Tom Miller also represented the Lanarkshire Junior League against The Irish Juniors and scored seven times in two games against Dalziel Rovers (a Motherwell team) before signing for Third Lanark. Despite being only 5ft 9in. tall, he was well equipped physically and his game improved as he gained speed and stamina, especially at Anfield. In his first full season with Liverpool (1912–13) he netted 10 goals and was leading marksman with 20 in 1913–14 as the Reds reached the FA Cup final when, surprisingly, he was completely off his game. He continued to produce the goods but hardly played at all during WW1. He netted twice on his international debut for Scotland in a 5–4 defeat by England in 1920 and after leaving Anfield added two more caps to his tally with Manchester United. He twice represented the Anglo-Scots against the Home Scots in 1920 and 1921. On Good Friday 1915, Miller was involved in a match-fixing scandal when Liverpool played his future club, Manchester United. Eight players were involved – three of his teammates, Bob Pursell, Tom Fairfoul and Jackie Sheldon (all q.v.), plus four from United. All eight players were suspended as a result of an enquiry, with the United defender Enoch West being banned *sine die* (later lifted).

MILNE, GORDON
Wing-half: 278+2 apps, 19 goals
Born: Preston, Lancashire, 29 March 1937
Career: Preston Amateurs, Morecambe, Preston North End (professional, January 1956), LIVERPOOL (£16,000, August 1960), Blackpool (£30,000, May 1967), Wigan Athletic (player-manager, January 1970–May 1972); was appointed England youth team manager (August 1971), Coventry City (manager, June 1972, executive manager, May 1981–August 1982), Leicester City (manager, August 1982, general manager, June 1986–May 1987), Besiktas/Turkey (manager, July 1987–1993), Everton (coach and youth development officer), Newcastle United (Director of Football, 2003)

A polished wing-half, son of the 1930s Dundee United and Preston star Jimmy Milne, Gordon Milne was an integral part of the Liverpool side which won the Second Division championship in 1962. He also starred in the two First Division title successes of 1964 and 1966, missed out on FA Cup glory in 1965 (through injury) and collected a runners-up medal when the Reds lost in the European Cup-Winners' Cup final of 1966 to the German outfit Borussia Dortmund. He won 14 full caps for England, represented the Football League on two occasions and was a member of Alf Ramsey's breakdown squad of 27 for the 1966 World Cup but missed out when the final 22 were selected. Milne enjoyed a long career as a player, amassing well over 400 senior appearances, 381 in the Football League (25 goals). As a coach he guided England's youngsters to victory in the 'Little World Cup' and then, as a manager, won the Northern Premier League title in 1971 with Wigan and guided Besiktas to successive Turkish League championships (1990, 1991 and 1992), achieving the double in 1990, this after his charges had finished second in the League in his first season there. He forged an excellent partnership with Coventry City, eventually taking over as boss at Highfield Road with Joe Mercer as general manager.

MINSHULL, RAYMOND
Goalkeeper: 31 apps
Born: Bolton, 15 July 1920 – *Died*: Southport, 15 February 2005
Career: Southport Schools and junior football, Southport (amateur, August 1939); served in and represented the Army during WW2; LIVERPOOL (professional, September 1946), Southport (June 1951), Bradford Park Avenue (£500, December 1957), Wigan Rovers (player-manager, July 1959, retired May 1960), Southport (assistant trainer, seasons 1960–62), coached in Austria and Gibraltar (1962–65), FA Regional Coach (North-West), Everton (youth development officer, late 1960s)

Ray Minshull moved from Bolton to Southport with his family at the age of 13. A very capable deputy to Welsh international Cyril Sidlow at Anfield, he made only 31 senior appearances for the Reds in 5 years before transferring to Southport for whom he played in 217 League games, twice representing the Third Division (N) against the South. He suffered his fair share of injuries but always looked confident between the posts.

MITCHELL, FRANK WILLIAM
Goalkeeper: 18 apps
Born: Elgin, Morayshire, Scotland, 25 May 1890 – *Died*: Scotland, *circa* 1970
Career: Elgin and district junior football, Milngarvie Alexander, Maryhill FC, Motherwell (1911), Everton (August 1913), LIVERPOOL (July 1920), Tranmere Rovers (June 1923–May 1925); assisted Blue Circle FC (season 1925–26)

At Motherwell, goalkeeper Frank Mitchell had to vie for a first-team place with the competent Colin Hampton; at Everton he had to battle for supremacy with Tommy Fern and at Anfield he had the great Elisha Scott barring his way. Nevertheless, he grafted away honestly and after making 50 senior appearances north of the border, he added 24 more to his tally, plus 99 in WW1 (gaining a Lancashire Principal Tournament winner's medal in 1919) with Everton and a further 18 with Liverpool before claiming a regular place in Tranmere's first XI, going on to play in 60 competitive matches (55 in the League North). He made his debut for the Reds against Manchester United in February 1921 (won 2–0) . . . this after Scott had been injured the previous week at Old Trafford.

186

MOLBY, JAN

Midfield: 261+32 apps, 61 goals

Born: Kolding, Jutland, Denmark, 4 July 1963

Career: Danish football, Kolding FC/Denmark (junior, September 1979), Ajax Amsterdam/Holland (£10,000 as a professional, March 1981), LIVERPOOL (£575,000, August 1984), Barnsley (loan, September–October 1995), Norwich City (loan, December 1995–January 1996), Swansea City (free, player-manager, February 1996, sacked October 1997), Kidderminster Harriers (manager, August 1999–May 2002), Hull City (manager July–October 2002), Kidderminster Harriers (manager, again, October 2003–November 2004); currently engaged as a commentator on the Danish TV2 channel

Blessed with an array of ball skills and powerful shooting, Jan Molby was also a brilliant cross-field passer who delivered some pretty beefy challenges in midfield during his association with Liverpool. Pitched straight into the first team by manager Joe Fagan – he was handed his debut in a 3–3 draw at Norwich City in August 1984 – the 'Great Dane' made an immediate impact, although he did struggle with his fitness (and form) halfway through the campaign before returning to play some splendid football over the next two years, and more so as timed passed by. Twice a League championship winner (1986 and 1990), he also gained two FA Cup winner's medals (1986 and 1992), a League Cup winning prize (1995) and triumphed in the Screen Sport Super Cup (1986). He was one of the few players to score a hat-trick of penalties, doing so in Liverpool's fourth-round League Cup victory over Coventry City in November 1986 (won 3–0). Molby won 21 youth, 6 under-21 and 67 full caps for Denmark and was a member of the Danish squad that reached the semi-finals of the European Championships in France in 1984. He retired as a player in 1999 with well over 450 senior appearances under his belt at club and international level, plus more than 80 goals. In his first season as manager he guided Kidderminster into the Football League as Conference champions but when he left Aggborough second time round, Harriers were on their way to losing their League status.

MOLYNEUX, JOHN ALAN

Right-back: 249 apps, 3 goals

Born: Warrington, 3 February 1931

Career: Orford Youth Club, Chester (amateur, May 1947; professional, February 1949), LIVERPOOL (£4,500, June 1955), Chester (£2,000, August 1962), New Brighton (August 1965–May 1967)

A former England youth international, John Molyneux became a very popular player during his seven years at Anfield during which time he made almost 250 first-class appearances. Strong and resilient, he proved to be a steadying influence on the Reds' defence and formed an excellent full-back partnership with first Ronnie Moran (for five seasons) and then Gerry Byrne. He made his debut in a red shirt against Blackburn Rovers (away) in September 1955 and scored his first goal for the club inside 50 seconds of a third-round FA Cup replay win at Southend in January 1958, this being his 98th appearance for the club. After leaving Anfield, Molyneux took his tally of senior outings with Chester past the 250-mark, having twice been a Welsh Cup finalist prior to joining Liverpool. His brother Geoff was also on Chester's books in 1962–63.

MOLYNEUX, WILLIAM STANLEY
Goalkeeper: 1 app.
Born: Ormskirk, 10 January 1944
Career: Earle FC (Liverpool Combination), LIVERPOOL (amateur, April 1961; professional, November 1963), Oldham Athletic (June 1967–May 1969)

A small, spring-heeled goalkeeper, Bill Molyneux was one of several reserves to Jim Furnell and Tommy Lawrence during his association with Liverpool. He made just one League appearance in six years, starring in a 3–1 win at Wolves in April 1965 when Lawrence was rested ahead of that season's FA Cup final. He was also in reserve at Oldham, for whom he made eight appearances.

MONEY, RICHARD
Defender/midfield: 15+2 apps
Born: Lowestoft, 13 October 1955
Career: Lowestoft Town (September 1971), Scunthorpe United (professional, July 1973), Fulham (£40,000, November 1977), LIVERPOOL (£333,333, May 1980), Derby County (loan, January–early March 1982), Luton Town (loan, late March 1982, signed for £100,000, April 1982), Portsmouth (£55,000, August 1983), Scunthorpe United (October 1985, player-coach, 1986, caretaker-manager March–April 1987, remained registered as a player until May 1989), Aston Villa (youth team coach, 1991), Scunthorpe United (manager, January 1993, sacked March 1994), Nottingham Forest (coach, June 1994), Manchester City (assistant manager/coach, January 1997), Coventry City (Academy head coach, May 1998–June 2002), AIK Stockholm/Sweden (coach, January 2003–April 2004), Vasteras SK/Sweden (coach, May 2004), Walsall (manager, May 2006)

During his 16-year professional career, Richard Money occupied six different outfield positions and made 527 senior appearances, 465 in the Football League and 279 in two spells with Scunthorpe United, where two other Liverpool players, Ray Clemence and Kevin Keegan, had commenced their footballing lives. Principally a full-back, Money played for England 'B' against New Zealand at Brisbane Road in October 1979 and after moving to Anfield made the first of his 17 outings for the Reds against West Bromwich Albion in September 1980, coming on as a second-half substitute for Alan Hansen in a 4–0 win. A Second Division championship winner with Luton in 1982, he didn't do too well as a manager but later excelled as a coach.

MOONEY, BRIAN JOHN
Forward: 0+1 app.
Born: Dublin, 2 February 1966
Career: Home Farm (Dublin), LIVERPOOL (professional, August 1983),

Wrexham (loan, December 1985), Preston North End (October 1987), Sunderland (February 1991), Burnley (loan, September 1992); returned to Ireland (May 1992)

Must be regarded as a player who escaped from the Anfield net, wing-forward Brian Mooney went on to appear in 170 first-class matches after leaving Anfield. A Republic of Ireland international at three different levels – youth, under-21 (four caps) and under-23 (two) – his only senior outing for Liverpool came as a substitute in a second-round second-leg League Cup encounter against Fulham at Craven Cottage in October 1986 when he replaced Jim Beglin in a 3–2 win – for a 13–2 aggregate victory.

MORAN, RONALD

Full-back: 380 apps, 16 goals

Born: Crosby, Liverpool, 28 February 1934

Career: Crosby and District Schoolboys, LIVERPOOL (amateur, April 1949; professional, January 1952, retired as a player, 1965, appointed youth team coach, March 1969, reserve team manager, 1972, first-team coach, 1976, chief coach from 1983 until 1999 when he retired from football at the age of 65); had two separate spells as caretaker-manager at Anfield in 1991 and 1994

Ronnie Moran joined Liverpool at the age of 15, recommended to the club by his local postman and later Anfield director and club President, Tom Williams. He turned professional in 1952 and went on the club's third tour of North America before making his League debut in November of that year against Derby County at the Baseball Ground when he deputised for Jack Lambert in a 3–2 defeat. He made a further ten appearances that season but only one in 1953–54 when the Reds were relegated to the Second Division. He established himself in the side in 1955 and became a permanent fixture at full-back, missing only six games in five seasons up to 1960. Unfortunately a spate of injuries sidelined him for two years before he became automatic choice again, helping the Reds regain their top-flight status in 1963 when he scored five times, including late penalty equalisers that earned draws at Old Trafford and at home to West Bromwich Albion, plus the clincher in a 2–1 home win over Arsenal. A year later he gained a League championship winner's medal, but he missed the 1965 FA Cup final triumph over Leeds United, having been replaced by Gerry Byrne. The burly, strong-tackling Moran, who topped 13st. at one stage in his career, was exquisite in his positioning and this saved him from getting too many roastings from speedy wingers, as he wasn't the fastest player in the team. After retiring with 380 appearances under his belt, he became a valuable member of the Anfield backroom staff, continuing to serve the club as a coach and manager (various levels) until 1999, serving Liverpool FC for 50 years. In fact, in his first season in charge of the second XI, the Central League title was won (1973). He acted as caretaker-boss when Kenny Dalglish left and again prior to Roy Evans' appointment. He served Liverpool FC under eight different managers – a terrific clubman, highly respected and admired.

MORGAN, HUGH

Centre-forward/inside-left: 69 apps, 18 goals

Born: Longriggend, Lanarkshire, 20 September 1869 – *Died*: Scotland, December 1930

Career: Lanarkshire junior football, St Mirren (professional, 1896), LIVERPOOL (March 1898), Blackburn Rovers (June 1900–May 1903)

A canny, dapper, cool-headed Scottish international forward (two caps won in 1898 and 1899), Hugh Morgan possessed wonderful ball skills, could thread a pass through the eye of a needle and was no mean goalscorer either. He gained sufficient experience with St Mirren before having a shade over two years at Anfield, making the first of his 69 appearances for Liverpool against Notts County (away) in April 1898, when he became the seventh player used in the centre-forward position by the Reds that season. Top marksman in 1898–99 with 13 goals when forming an excellent left wing partnership with Jack Robertson, Morgan moved to Blackburn Rovers following the emergence of Charlie Satterthwaite. He netted 18 goals in 79 games during his service at Ewood Park.

MORIENTES, FERNANDO

Striker: 46+14 apps, 12 goals

Born: Caceres, Spain, 5 April 1976

Career: Albacete/Spain (apprentice, May 1993; professional, April 1994), Real Zaragoza/Spain (August 1995), Real Madrid/Spain (June 1997), AS Monaco/France (loan, during season 2003–04), LIVERPOOL (£6.3m, January 2005)

Experienced Spanish international striker who first played for his country in 1998 and was still in the senior squad in 2006 with over 40 caps to his credit (26 goals), Fernando Morientes failed to set the Premiership alight following his move to Anfield early in 2005. Arriving with a massive reputation as a goalscorer (he netted 105 times in 266 La Liga games in 10 years) he struggled at times with the Reds but occasionally produced a touch of class which he had certainly shown when playing for Real Madrid (alongside Raul) and, indeed, with AS Monaco. Twice a Spanish La Liga championship winner in 2001 and 2003, he also gained three UEFA Champions League winner's medals in 1998 (v. Juventus), 2000 (v. Valencia) and 2002 (v. Bayer Leverkusen) and was a runner-up in the 2004 final when AS Monaco lost 3–0 to FC Porto – having scored in both legs of the semi-final against Chelsea. He netted 3 times in 15 matches for Liverpool during the second half of 2004–05 and claimed only 9 goals in 45 games the following season. Morientes and Luis Garcia played together and created havoc in the Slovakian defence when Spain won a World Cup qualifier 5–0 in November 2005. Garcia hit a hat-trick while Morientes scored once. He gained an FA Cup winner's medal in 2006 when Liverpool beat West Ham on penalties.

MORRIS, FREDERICK WILLIAM

Outside-right: 48 apps, 14 goals

Born: Pant near Oswestry, 15 June 1929 – *Died*: Oswestry, 1999

Career: Oswestry Town (semi-professional, 1946), Walsall (professional, £500, May 1950), Mansfield Town (£1,500, March 1957), LIVERPOOL (£7,000, March 1958), Crewe Alexandra (£4,000, June, 1960), Gillingham (£1,500, January 1961), Chester (free, July 1961), Altrincham (free, July 1962), Oswestry Town (player-manager, seasons 1963–65); launched his own building contractor's business in the early 1960s and later ran a garage in Oswestry

Strong-running outside-right Fred Morris spent eight years in the lower Divisions before joining Liverpool three months before his 29th birthday. He served Walsall for 7 of those years, scoring 49 goals in 230 games, including 151 in succession between 1953 and 1956. On Boxing Day 1954 he netted a hat-trick against Brighton but still finished up on the losing side. He then struck 17 goals in 56 outings for Mansfield before spending just over two seasons at Anfield, making his debut for the Reds in September 1958 at home to Brighton, when he was the fourth different player used on the right wing in successive League games (following Billy Liddell, Bobby Murdoch and Johnny Morrissey). He left Anfield after Kevin Lewis had claimed the right wing berth.

MORRIS, RICHARD

Forward: 39 apps, 5 goals

Born: Newtown, Montgomeryshire, April 1883 – *Died*: Newtown, *circa* 1950

Career: Druids (Ruabon), Newtown RWW (1900), Druids (February 1902), LIVERPOOL (professional, March 1902), Leeds City (July 1905), Grimsby Town (June 1906), Plymouth Argyle (August 1907), Reading (July 1908), Huddersfield Town (briefly, 1909)

A Welsh international, capped 11 times between 1902 and 1908, once partnering the immortal Billy Meredith, Dicky Morris was a member of the Welsh team that won their first-ever Home International championship in 1907. Two-footed and able to occupy three central forward positions, preferring the inside-left berth, he was a tireless runner, smart dribbler and adept at shooting. He possessed plenty of pluck but was a player who blew hot and cold – great one game, dire the next! He made his debut for Liverpool against Bury (home) in April 1902 and scored his first two goals in the Merseyside derby v. Everton in October 1903 which the Reds won 2–0. The first Plymouth Argyle player to win a full cap, Morris fought in the Boer War with George Latham (q.v.).

MORRISON, THOMAS

Right-half: 254 apps, 4 goals

Born: Coylton, Ayrshire, 1904 – *Died*: Ireland, *circa* 1973

Career: Troon Athletic (1921), St Mirren (professional, August 1923), LIVERPOOL (£4,000, November 1927), Sunderland (November 1935–May 1936); assisted a Cambridgeshire junior side in 1936–37 using the pseudonym of 'Anderson'; Ayr United (July 1937, retired May 1939), Drumcondra (coach, throughout WW2, from August 1939)

A wonderful servant to Liverpool, Tom Morrison joined the club a year after gaining a Scottish Cup winner's medal with St Mirren. A bold and noble defender with a crisp tackle, he was also a very creative player who enjoyed his excursions upfield. He made the first of his 254 senior appearances for the Reds against Portsmouth (away) in February 1928 when he took over at right-half from David McMullan and was an ever-present the following season, having a run of 82 consecutive League outings before taking a rest! He formed an excellent middle-line at Anfield with 'Tiny' Bradshaw and Jimmy McDougall. Morrison, who was capped by Scotland against England in 1927, played at full-back during a First Division championship winning spell at Sunderland.

MORRISSEY, JOHN JOSEPH

Outside-left: 37 apps, 6 goals
Born: Liverpool, 18 April 1940
Career: Merseyside Schools, LIVERPOOL (professional, April 1957), Everton (£10,000, August 1962), Oldham Athletic (May 1972, retired, injured, January 1973)

Mainly a left-winger, hard working with lots of pace and neat skills, Johnny Morrissey made his League debut for Liverpool as a 17 year old against Stoke City (away) in September 1957 when he deputised for Alan A'Court in a 2–1 win. He made only three more appearances during the next two seasons before having nine outings in 1959–60 when he scored his first goal, to no avail at Sheffield United (lost 2–1). Unable to oust A'Court, he moved to Goodison Park where he became a star performer, netting 50 goals in 314 appearances for the Blues in ten years, gaining two League championship winning medals (1963 and 1970) and an FA Cup winner's medal in 1966, while collecting a loser's prize in this same competition in 1968. A schoolboy international, Morrissey also played for the Football League. A spate of injuries ruined his career and he retired at the age of 32. His son, Johnny Morrissey junior, also a winger, played for Everton as well as for Wolves and Tranmere Rovers, making over 600 appearances in 14 years at Prenton Park (1985–99).

MUIR, ALEXANDER JOHNSTON

Outside-right: 4 apps
Born: Inverkeithing, Fife, Scotland, 10 December 1923 – *Died*: Birkenhead, 4 September 1995
Career: Lochgelly Violet, LIVERPOOL (professional, July 1947), South Liverpool (August 1949–April 1951); later Tranmere Rovers (coach, 1970–1975)

One of four players used on the right wing by Liverpool during the 1947–48 season, Alex Muir was small and compact but he never really stood a chance of making the grade at Anfield with so many other quality players at the club. The first of his four games was against Middlesbrough (home) in February 1948 when he partnered Kevin Baron in a 2–1 defeat. Muir kept himself supremely fit after retiring as a player and at the age of 58 turned out (in an emergency) for Tranmere's second XI, playing the full 90 minutes.

MURDOCH, WILLIAM ROBERT
Inside-right: 19 apps, 7 goals
Born: Garston, Liverpool, 25 January 1936
Career: South Liverpool (1952), Bolton Wanderers (amateur, 1953), LIVERPOOL (amateur, April 1954; professional, May 1957), Barrow (September 1959), Stockport County (£3,000, July 1960), Carlisle United (in exchange for George Whitelaw, January 1962), Southport (July 1962), Wigan Athletic (July 1963), South Liverpool (July 1965, later player-manager, then manager until 1976); football coach at the Ohio State University/USA (1976 and 1977)

After an impressive 15-match run during the 1957–58 season which included his debut on Boxing Day against Grimsby Town, Bobby Murdoch found it difficult to oust Jimmy Harrower from Liverpool's attack the following year and as a result moved to struggling Fourth Division side Barrow. He made over 150 senior appearances after leaving Anfield, 143 in the League.

MURPHY, DANIEL BENJAMIN
Midfield: 178+71 apps, 44 goals
Born: Whiston, 18 October 1976
Career: Crewe Alexandra (apprentice, October 1992; professional, March 1994), LIVERPOOL (£1.5m, July 1997), Crewe Alexandra (loan, February–May 1999), Charlton Athletic (£2.5m, August 2004), Tottenham Hotspur (£2m, January 2006)

Danny Murphy made 165 senior appearances for Crewe before joining Liverpool. He had a reasonably sound first season at Anfield but was restricted to just four outings in 1998–99 owing to the fierce competition for places. Nevertheless, the midfield dynamo stuck to his task and came back strongly with some all-action displays, helping the Reds win five trophies in 2001 (the FA Cup, League Cup, UEFA Cup, Super Cup and Charity Shield) while gaining a second League Cup triumph in 2003. An England international at schoolboy and youth team levels, he added five under-21 and nine full caps to his tally before joining Charlton Athletic in the summer of 2004, signed by Valiants' boss Alan Curbishley to add class to the London club's midfield. And he did just that, even getting himself back into the England reckoning with some brilliant performances. The first of his 259 outings for Liverpool was against Wimbledon on the opening day of the 1997–98 Premiership campaign when he came off the bench in a 1–1 draw. Only Vladimir Smicer (74) has made more substitute appearances for Liverpool than Murphy. When the transfer window opened in January 2006, Murphy switched across London from the Valley to White Hart Lane.

MURRAY, DAVID BOYD

Full-back: 15 apps
Born: Glasgow, 1882 – *Died*: Glasgow, August 1915
Career: Glasgow Rangers (junior, 1898; professional, 1900), Everton (September 1903), LIVERPOOL (May 1904), Hull City (November 1905), Leeds City (December 1905), Mexborough Town (August 1909), Burslem Port Vale (briefly, 1910)

A reserve team player with Rangers for whom he made just a handful of first-team appearances, Dave Murray also found it hard going to get into Everton's senior side (two games). He did somewhat better at Anfield, helping the Reds win the Second and then First Division titles in 1904 and 1905, although he didn't receive a medal for his efforts in the latter success, playing only three times. After leaving Hull he scored 7 goals in 85 starts for Leeds City. His first game for Liverpool was against Burton United (home) in September 1904 when he partnered Billy Dunlop at full-back. He moved when Alf West became first choice on the right flank.

MURRAY, WILLIAM THOMAS

Centre-half/centre-forward: 4 apps, 1 goal
Born: Alexandria, Dunbartonshire, 6 November 1904 – *Died*: 1940
Career: Bowhill Celtic (1920), Vale of Clyde (1922) Clydebank (semi-professional, April 1924), Preston North End (March 1926), New Brighton (October 1926), Clydebank (March 1927), LIVERPOOL (November 1927), Barrow (January 1930), Bristol Rovers (December 1933), Folkestone (seasons 1936–38)

The versatile Bill Murray played two games at centre-forward and two at centre-half during his time at Anfield. His debut came as leader of the attack against Tottenham Hotspur in April 1928 when he deputised for Tommy Reid, and his only goal was scored from a defensive position in a 3–2 win at Aston Villa in November 1929 after taking over from Bob McDougall. He later captained Barrow, for whom he made 137 League appearances in almost 4 years, and Bristol Rovers (40 outings).

NEAL, PHILIP GEORGE

Right-back: 648+2 apps, 60 goals
Born: Irchester near Northampton, 20 February 1951
Career: Irchester FC (August 1966), Northampton Town (apprentice, July 1967; professional, December 1968), LIVERPOOL (£66,000, October 1974), Bolton Wanderers (player-manager, December 1985, retired as a player, May 1989, continued as manager until May 1992), Coventry City (assistant manager, July 1992, manager, October 1993–February 1995), Cardiff City (manager, February 1996–July 1997), Manchester City (coach/caretaker-manager, briefly, 1999–2000); now works part time in the media

Phil Neal was a great servant to Liverpool, accumulating 650 senior appearances in 11 years – that's an amazing average of almost 60 games per season. A model of consistency, he was also very successful, missing only a handful of competitive matches between 1975 and 1984 when the Reds (and Neal himself) won 21 trophies (16 in major tournaments). He also shared another triumph and gained nine runners-up medals . . . what a record. The prizes won by Neal with Liverpool were as follows: the European Cup in 1977, 1978, 1981 and 1984 (runner-up in 1985); the UEFA Cup in 1976; the First Division in 1976, 1977, 1979, 1980, 1982, 1983 and 1984; the League Cup in 1981, 1982, 1983 and 1984 (runner-up in 1978); FA Cup (runner-up in 1977); FA Charity Shield in 1976, 1979, 1980 and 1982 (shared in 1977); the European Super Cup in 1977 and the World Club Championship (runner-up in 1981 and 1984). He was capped 50 times by England at senior level – winning his first against Wales in March 1976 and his last against Denmark in a European Championship qualifier in September 1983. After 234 outings for Northampton, he became one of the most important and beneficial signings in Liverpool's history (recruited by Bob Paisley). He made an impressive debut for the Reds in a 0–0 draw in the Merseyside derby at Goodison Park in November 1974 when he lined up in place of the injured Alec Lindsay at left-back as partner to Tommy Smith, switching over to the more favoured right flank at the start of the next season, although for 18 months or so he actually altered between both full-back positions before settling down in the number 2 shirt, first as partner to Joey Jones and then to Alan Kennedy. He never looked back after that, played wonderfully well week in, week out, and was an ever-present in the League side nine times in ten seasons, missing only one game, against Sunderland in October 1983, after being injured at Old Trafford seven days earlier. Blessed with exceptional positional sense, he loved to overlap but was quick enough to get back and thwart any possible danger. His tally of goals (remarkably high for a full-back) was mainly due to his expertise as a penalty-taker and he had his best bout of scoring in 1982–83 when he netted 11 times (6 off the spot). However, one mustn't forget that crucial 12-yard kick in the 1977 European Cup final against Borussia Moenchengladbach, Neal cooly slotting home late on to clinch a famous 3–1 victory.

During his career Neal played in 1,018 club and international matches and scored 68 goals – not bad for an orthodox and quite splendid right-back. As a manager Neal guided Bolton to promotion from the Third Division in 1988 and to Sherpa Van Trophy success at Wembley a year later.

NEIL, ROBERT SCOTT GIBSON
Centre-half. 27 apps, 3 goals
Born: Govan, Glasgow, 24 September 1875 – *Died*: Glasgow, 7 March 1913
Career: Glasgow Ashfield (1891), Hibernian (professional, June 1894), LIVERPOOL (May 1896), Glasgow Rangers (April 1897, retired, May 1904); went into business in Glasgow as a restaurateur

Surprisingly on the short side for a centre-half at 5ft 4in., Bobby Neil was only 10st. in weight but he certainly made up for the lack of height and physique with some excellent defensive displays for the three major clubs he served and also for Scotland, for whom he gained two full caps, while also making one appearance for the Scottish League and playing twice for Glasgow against Sheffield in the annual challenge match. Cool and thoughtful in his overall play, his methodical style made no concessions to frills yet it was so effective and he certainly was a player of the highest quality. A strong tackler, he also possessed a powerful right-foot shot and scored some important goals including the odd penalty. He made 40 appearances for Hibs before joining Liverpool who handed him his debut against Sunderland (away) in October 1896. He replaced McQue at the heart of the Reds' defence but left Anfield after just 11 months. He netted 28 goals in 109 senior appearances for Rangers, gaining a Scottish Cup winner's medal in 1898 and four successive League championship winning medals, 1899–1902. He was only 37 when he died.

NEWBY, JONATHAN PHILIP ROBERT

Forward: 0+4 apps
Born: Warrington, 28 November 1978
Career: LIVERPOOL (apprentice, April 1995; professional, May 1997), Crewe Alexandra (loan, March–May 2000), Sheffield United (loan, August–November 2000), Bury (£100,000, February 2001), Huddersfield Town (free, August 2003), York City (loan, March–May 2004), Bury (free, August 2004), Kidderminster Harriers (March 2006)

A positive forward, as keen as mustard, Jon Newby was a registered player at Anfield for almost six years during which time he tasted less than 90 minutes of action, coming on as a substitute for the Reds in four competitive matches. He was a member of Liverpool's FA Youth Cup-winning side of 1996 and came off the bench for his senior debut against Hull City in a second-round second-leg League Cup encounter at Anfield in September 1999, replacing Stephane Henchoz in a 4–2 (9–3 aggregate) win. After leaving Anfield he came good with Bury (first time round) for whom he scored 24 goals in 122 games, later increasing his goal tally to 27 in a total of 174 games after returning to Gigg Lane following spells with Huddersfield and York City.

NICHOLL, JAMES

Inside-/outside-left: 59 apps, 14 goals
Born: Port Glasgow, Scotland, 1890 – *Died*: Glasgow, *circa* 1955
Career: Glasgow junior football, Port Glasgow FC, Middlesbrough (professional, September 1910), LIVERPOOL (January 1914–May 1915); did not play after WW1

Jimmy Nicholl scored 13 goals in 56 games for Middlesbrough before acquiring a very similar record with Liverpool. Preferring the outside-left position, he actually made 13 of his first 14 appearances for the Reds in the inside berth, performing very well when making his debut in a 1–0 win at West Bromwich Albion in January 1914, where he partnered Billy Lacey. A bright, incisive footballer, he was on top of his game when WW1 ended his career in 1915.

NICHOLSON, JOHN PURCELL

Centre-half: 1 app.

Born: Liverpool, 2 September 1936 – *Died*: Doncaster, 3 September 1966

Career: Merseyside junior and intermediate football, LIVERPOOL (professional, January 1957), Port Vale (£2,000, August 1961), Doncaster Rovers (£5,600, September 1965 until his death)

John Nicholson, reserve to Dick White at Anfield, was a stocky and formidable centre-half who made only one senior appearance for Liverpool (against Brighton and Hove Albion in October 1959) before joining Port Vale for whom he starred in 208 competitive games, all in succession – a club record. An ever-present for three seasons at Vale Park, from August 1962, he lost his place in September 1963 and the Vale supporters were bitterly disappointed when he was sold to Doncaster that same month. Nicholson was tragically killed in a car crash a day after his 30th birthday. Port Vale FC donated 100 guineas (£110) to his widow.

NICKSON, HAROLD

Goalkeeper: 3 apps

Born: Liverpool, *circa* 1921

Career: LIVERPOOL (season 1945–46)

Local-born goalkeeper Harold Nickson appeared in ten regional and three FA Cup games for the Reds during the transitional wartime season of 1945–46. He made his debut against Chesterfield (away) in mid-December (FL North) and then played in both third-round FA encounters against Chester and had another Cup outing versus Bolton Wanderers in the next round. There is no record of him ever playing in the Football League.

NICOL, STEPHEN

Midfield/defender: 466+17 apps, 47 goals

Born: Irvine, Scotland, 11 December 1961

Career: Ayr Boys Club, Ayr United (amateur, April 1977; professional, December 1979), LIVERPOOL (£300,000, October 1981), Notts County (free, January 1995), Sheffield Wednesday (free, November 1995), West Bromwich Albion (loan, March–May 1998), Hull City (trial), Doncaster Rovers (free, June 1998), Boston Bulldogs/NASL (coach, April 1999); head coach, July 1999), New England Revolution/USA (from January 2002)

Steve Nicol was a reliable and dependable footballer who could play in both full-back positions, as a sweeper, orthodox centre-half and in midfield. A tireless worker, he was an attack-minded player who scored some splendid goals during his time at Anfield, being a huge favourite with the fans. He made the first of his senior appearances for the Reds against Birmingham City (away) in August 1982 and had his last outing some 12 years later in a League Cup tie against Burnley in October 1994. In between times he gained 27 full and 14 under-21 caps for Scotland and won four League championships (1984, 1986, 1988 and 1990), three FA Cup finals (1986, 1989 and 1992), the European Cup (1984), the FA Charity Shield (1989) and the Screen Sport Super Cup (1986). He was also voted FWA 'Player of the Year' in 1989 when he was Liverpool's only ever-present. Stocky, mobile and durable, he went on to win the American League title with New England Revolution in 2003. When he was registered with Notts County, Nicol did not escape the dressing-room banter – his specially designed size 13 boots were christened QEIIs by the players.

NIEUWENHUYS, BERRY
Outside-right: 260 apps, 79 goals
Born: Boksburg, Transvaal, South Africa, 5 November 1911 – *Died*: Johannesburg, South Africa, 12 June 1984
Career: Boksburg FC/South Africa, Germiston Callies/South Africa, LIVERPOOL (September 1933); served in the RAF and was a guest for Arsenal and West Ham United during WW2 (retired, May 1947); returned to South Africa in 1949 where he became the assistant professional to the famous golfer Bobby Locke in Johannesburg
A former engineer in his homeland, Berry Nieuwenhuys – nicknamed 'Nivvy' – was a tall, probing winger, deceptively fast, a terrific header of the ball with a powerful right-foot shot and dynamic personality. One of several South African-born footballers to grace the UK during the late 1920s/'30s, he spent 14 years at Anfield and during that time became a firm favourite with the supporters. He made his debut in English soccer for the Reds in a 3–0 League win at Tottenham in September 1933 when he took over on the right wing from Harry Taylor. He netted ten goals in his first season and, in fact, claimed double figures in the scoring stakes in each of his first six campaigns when forming a splendid understanding in the forward-line with fellow South African Gordon Hodgson and Vic Wright, as well as Harry Eastham, Fred Howe and others. He loved to move in from his wing position and get on the end of high crosses delivered from the left – and he certainly scored some wonderful headed goals in his time. In February 1939 he was awarded a benefit match against Everton which earned him £658 from a 13,000 crowd. He helped Liverpool beat Bolton Wanderers 6–3 on aggregate in the two-legged 1944 League (N) Cup final, scoring in the first game, and struck 61 goals in 161 appearances for the Reds during wartime football, going on to gain a League championship in 1947. He also represented Great Britain twice against England (at Sheffield and Anfield), played for the FA XI against the Army in Cardiff and in the 1940–41 wartime season starred for an All British XI against the Football League and for the RAF side versus the Army, later playing for the RAF against Western Command in 1944. A keen golfer, Nivvy was a big pal of the South African champion Bobby Locke and became assistant professional to him when he returned home. He also enjoyed driving classy sports cars.

NUNEZ, ANTONIO
Midfield: 13+14 apps, 1 goal
Born: Madrid, Spain, 15 January 1979
Career: Real Madrid/Spain (professional, April 1999), LIVERPOOL (in the deal involving Michael Owen, August 2004), Celta Vigo (season 2005–06)

Tall, right-sided midfielder Antonio Nunez was relatively new to first-class football when he moved to Anfield as make-weight in the Michael Owen transfer, having appeared in only a handful of senior games for Real Madrid as a substitute. After recovering from a tedious knee injury, he came off the bench for his Liverpool debut v. Arsenal in November 2004 and made 27 appearances for the Reds in his first season, scoring one goal, a consolation effort in the League Cup final defeat by Chelsea.

OGRIZOVIC, STEVEN

Goalkeeper: 5 apps
Born: Mansfield, 12 September 1957
Career: ONR Youth Club (1976), Chesterfield (apprentice, July 1977; professional, September 1977), LIVERPOOL (£75,000, November, 1977), Shrewsbury Town (£70,000 plus Bob Wardle, August 1982), Coventry City (£72,500, June 1984, retired, May 2000, immediately appointed Youth Academy coach at Highfield Road)

Unable to get into Liverpool's side owing to the form of Ray Clemence, giant goalkeeper Steve Ogrizovic, a confident handler of the ball with fine positioning, made just five senior appearances for the Reds in five years, four in the League, the first (his debut) against Derby County at the Baseball Ground in March 1978 when Clemence was rested for two matches ahead of the League Cup final.

After leaving Anfield, 'Oggy', who was awarded two European Cup winner's medals as a non-playing substitute in 1978 and 1981, appeared in 96 competitive games for Shrewsbury Town and a club record 601 for Coventry City, his last at the age of 42. He also became the first Sky Blues goalkeeper to score in a competitive match, his wind-assisted punt downfield earning his side a point from a 2–2 draw with Sheffield Wednesday at Hillsborough in October 1986. He gained an FA Cup winner's medal a year later and in October 1989 his club-record run of 241 consecutive appearances came to an end, when he missed the League fixture against Luton Town. The previous record set by another keeper, Alf Wood, had stood for 40 years. He represented the Football League against the Rest of the World in the League's Centenary game at Wembley in 1987. Ogrizovic was also an accomplished cricketer who played Minor Counties cricket for Shropshire and was a member of the Shropshire team that beat Yorkshire – who had Geoffrey Boycott in their team – in a NatWest Trophy match in 1984.

OGSTON, JOHN KESSACK

Goalkeeper: 1 app.
Born: Aberdeen, 15 January 1939
Career: Aberdeen Schools, Banks o' Dee, Aberdeen (professional, March 1957), LIVERPOOL (£10,000, September 1965), Doncaster Rovers (season loan, August 1968–May 1969, signed permanently for £2,500, July 1969, left May 1971)

A Scottish under-23 international (three caps won), John 'Tubby' Ogston (nicknamed so because of his huge frame) also represented the Army when completing his national service. He made 230 senior appearances for Aberdeen before moving to Anfield, signed as cover for Tommy Lawrence. His only senior game for Liverpool was against Newcastle United in April 1967, performing well in a 3–1 win. He won the Fourth Division championship in 1969 with Doncaster Rovers, for whom he played in over 70 competitive games.

ORR, RONALD
Inside-right/-left: 112 apps, 38 goals
Born: Bartonholm, Irving, Ayrshire, 6 August 1880 – *Died*: Scotland, *circa* 1949
Career: Kilwinning Eglinton FC (1896), St Mirren (professional, May 1898), Newcastle United (with Bob Bennie, May 1901), LIVERPOOL (£350, April 1908), Raith Rovers (January 1912), South Shields (March 1913); guest for Fulham (1916–19); did not play after WW1
Ron Orr netted 70 goals in 180 games for Newcastle United in his 7 years at St James' Park. He also gained two full caps for Scotland, played in four international trials, won two League championship medals (1905 and 1907) and collected an FA Cup runners-up prize in 1906. A rather chunky-looking forward, small in stature, quick over the ground and blessed with a powerful left foot shot, he continued to find the net on a regular basis with Liverpool, scoring on his debut in a 5–1 defeat at Aston Villa in April 1908. In fact, he found the target in each of his first three outings and went on to average a goal every three games during an admirable four-year spell at Anfield. He was top marksman in 1908–09 with 23 goals, including a hat-trick in a 5–1 Cup win over Lincoln City. His two second-half goals against his former club Newcastle, in December 1909, earned Liverpool an epic 6–5 victory after they had trailed 5–2 at half-time. He lost his place to Tom Miller and returned to his homeland early in 1912. Some reference books state that Orr also played for Glossop North End in 1897 but the player who served with this club was named William Orr.

OTSEMOBOR, JOHN
Defender: 6 apps
Born: Liverpool, 23 March 1983
Career: LIVERPOOL (apprentice, April 1999; professional, March 2000), Hull City (loan, March–May 2003), Bolton Wanderers (loan, February 2004)
An England youth international, John Otsemobor gained first-team experience as a loan player with Hull (nine games) and Bolton before making his debut for Liverpool at right-back against the latter club in a League Cup tie in December 2003.

OWEN, MICHAEL
Striker: 267+30 apps, 158 goals
Born: Chester, 14 December 1979
Career: LIVERPOOL (apprentice, April 1996; professional, December 1996), Real Madrid/Spain (£8m, deal also involving Antonio Nunez, August 2004), Newcastle United (August 2005)
One of the great Liverpool goalscorers of all time, Michael Owen's record speaks

for itself and he certainly revelled in the Anfield atmosphere after an impressive first full season as a professional, when he netted 18 times in 36 Premiership matches, following up with double-figure returns every term after that until his surprise transfer to the Spanish giants Real Madrid in 2004. Sharp and decisive in and around the penalty area, he wanders into the right place at just the right time, getting on the end of knock-downs, flick-ons, defensive errors and dead-ball situations. Certainly he scores a lot of goals from short distances but over the course of time he's also netted some brilliant individual efforts for both club and country, including a terrific strike against Argentina in the 1998 World Cup finals in France when only a teenager and a hat-trick in a 5–1 win in a World Cup qualifier over Germany in Munich in September 2001. Regarded as 'The Boy Genius' at the age of 20, Owen is a tireless worker who keeps defenders on their guard for the whole 90 minutes (and more) of a game. He made the first of his senior appearances for the Reds as a substitute against Wimbledon in May 1997, scoring in a 2–1 defeat, and he also netted in his last outing, against his future club, Newcastle United, at Anfield in May 2004 (a 1–1 draw). He teamed up with his international colleague David Beckham in Spain but was never an automatic choice in Real's senior side, regularly coming off the bench to score some important goals. When the opportunity presented itself, he had no second thoughts about returning to England with Newcastle (under Graeme Souness's management) in August 2005. Honoured by his country at schoolboy and youth team levels, Owen added one under-21 cap to his collection while also totting up his senior appearances, and just prior to the 2006 World Cup finals in Germany, his record for England was impressive, 35 goals in 75 full internationals, placing him fourth in his country's all-time scoring charts behind Bobby Charlton (49), Gary Lineker (48) and Jimmy Greaves (44). He gained winner's medals as a Liverpool player for an FA Youth Cup final victory (1996), two League Cup triumphs (2001 and 2003) and successes in the FA Cup, UEFA Cup, European Super Cup and Charity Shield (all in 2001). In his only season in Spain's La Liga, he collected a runners-up medal as Real qualified once more for the Champions League. Unfortunately Owen was booed on his return to Anfield in December 2005 as a Newcastle player . . . but that's commonplace in football these days!

OXLEY, CYRIL

Outside-right: 34 apps, 6 goals

Born: Worksop, Nottinghamshire, 2 May 1904 – *Died*: 20 December 1984

Career: Whitwell Colliery (Derbyshire), Chesterfield (professional, January 1924), LIVERPOOL (£2,100, October 1925), Southend United (September 1928), Kettering Town (August 1929), Morecambe (June 1930), Southend United (August 1931–May 1932)

As a youngster Cyril Oxley produced some exciting performances for Chesterfield in the Third Division (N). Capable of using both feet, he played on both wings but preferred the right where he made the majority of his appearances for Liverpool, the first in place of Archie Rawlings against Sunderland (home) just 48 hours after arriving at Anfield. Finding it hard going to retain his place in the side, with Dick Edmed taking priority, he didn't do much after leaving Merseyside. His brother, Bernard Oxley, played for Chesterfield, Sheffield United, Sheffield Wednesday, Plymouth Argyle and Stockport County between 1925 and 1938.

PAGNAM, FREDERICK
Inside-right/centre-forward: 39 apps, 30 goals
Born: Poulton-le-Fylde near Blackpool, 4 September 1891 – *Died*: Hertfordshire, 7 March 1962
Career: Poulton Grammar School (Lytham), Blackpool Wednesday (1909), Huddersfield (professional, August 1910), Southport Central (July 1912), Blackpool (February 1913), LIVERPOOL (September 1914), Arsenal (£1,500, October 1919), Cardiff City (£3,000, March 1921), Watford (£1,000, December 1921, team manager August 1926–April 1929); also licensee in Rickmansworth from 1924; later Turkey's national team coach (for eight years from 1932); also coached in Holland; continued as a licensee after returning to England

Initially an outside-right, Fred Pagnam scored 43 goals in 49 WW1 appearances for the Reds as well as amassing an impressive senior record of 30 strikes in only 39 outings for the Reds. A robust, stocky player, the son of a Blackpool bank manager, he was as keen as mustard inside the 18-yard box and was both brave and dangerous with considerable shooting power. He scored on his Liverpool debut against Chelsea (away) in October 1914 and finished up as leading marksman that campaign . . . before heading off to war. He returned to hit 27 goals in 53 games for Arsenal, netted 6 times in 27 outings for Cardiff and claimed 72 goals in 144 appearances during five seasons with Watford.

PAISLEY, ROBERT, OBE, MSc (HON.)
Left-half: 278 apps, 13 goals
Born: Hetton-le-Hole, County Durham, 23 January 1919 – *Died*: Liverpool, 14 February 1996
Career: Bishop Auckland (amateur, July 1935), LIVERPOOL (professional, May 1939); guest for Bristol City during WW2; retired as a player, July 1954; LIVERPOOL (assistant trainer/physiotherapist, then chief trainer, 1957, assistant manager, manager from July 1974 to June 1983; also appointed a director and adviser of the club, a position he held until February 1992)

Bob Paisley, one-club man as a professional, scored 11 times in 60 WW2 games for the Reds and made his senior debut against Chester in a third-round first-leg FA Cup encounter in January 1946. He was a registered player at Anfield for more than 15 years, making 338 first-team appearances, 253 in the Football League. Prior to moving to Anfield he had won the FA Amateur Cup with Bishop Auckland in a 1938 final replay at Sunderland, and eight years later gained a League championship winner's medal. A dour tackling left-half, determined and pugnacious, he was blessed with an indefatigable spirit and scored a vital goal in the FA Cup semi-final clash with Everton in 1950 but was then left out of the final team against Arsenal. He was also a long-throw expert and many goals were scored from his deliveries which dropped deep into the danger zone. On retiring he joined the famous 'boot room' at Anfield and became one of the most successful managers in British football after taking over the duties of team leadership from the great Bill Shankly in 1974. Unlike 'Shanks' he chose to keep a low profile, always saying that the team would do the talking for him – and it did as he saw the Reds win six League championships (1976, 1977, 1979, 1980, 1982 and 1983), three League Cup finals (1981, 1982 and 1983), three European Champions' Cup finals (1977, 1978 and 1981), the UEFA Cup (1973), European Super Cup (1977) and lift the annual FA Charity Shield on six occasions (one shared). A person with a deep understanding of football, one of his master-strokes was to convert forward Ray Kennedy into an attacking (and goalscoring) midfielder. He also signed two Scots, Kenny Dalglish (to replace Kevin Keegan) and Graeme Souness. His down-to-earth attitude and strong work ethic were summarised by a quote he made in 1982: 'There's so many clubs been ruined by people's ego. The day after we [Liverpool] won our first European Cup, we were back at the club at 9.45 in the morning, talking about how we would do it again, working from that moment, because nobody has the right to win anything they haven't earned.'

Voted 'Manager of the Year' a record six times between 1976 and 1983, Paisley was awarded the OBE in 1977. He stood down as manager in June 1983 but continued to serve the club as a director and adviser until he retired through ill health early in 1992. He had served Liverpool FC for almost 53 years and was aged 77 when he died.

PARKINSON, JOHN

Inside-/centre-forward: 222 apps, 128 goals
Born: Bootle, 13 September 1883 – *Died*: Liverpool, 13 September 1942
Career: Hertford Albion and Valkyrie FC (both Merseyside junior clubs),
    LIVERPOOL (amateur, September 1901; professional, April 1903), Bury
    (July 1914, retired during WW1); later ran two shops, a newsagents and
    tobacconists, in Liverpool

Jack Parkinson was a dashing, fearless forward whose effervescent style was laced with vigour and, at times, cunning. A sharp-shooter of the highest quality, he served Liverpool admirably for 13 years and made a scoring debut against Small Heath (away) in October 1903 (won 2–1). Although he struggled at times with injuries, he always bounced back and was leading marksman at Anfield three seasons running, hitting 30, 20 and 13 goals respectively in 1909–10, 1910–11 and 1911–12. A Second Division championship winner with the Reds in 1905, unfortunately he missed out on a First Division prize the following season owing to injury. He was capped twice by England, against Wales and Scotland in 1910, and also represented the Football League.

PARR, STEPHEN VALENTINE

Full-back: 20 apps
Born: Bamber Bridge near Preston, 22 December 1926
Career: Farrington Villa (Preston), LIVERPOOL (professional, May 1948), Exeter City (May 1955), Rochdale (December 1956, retired, May 1958)

Able to play in both full-back positions, Steve Parr made 16 of his 20 appearances for Liverpool on the left flank as partner to Bill Jones during the 1951–52 season, the first against Portsmouth on the opening Saturday of the League programme. After leaving Anfield he was converted into a centre-half at Exeter.

PARRY, EDWARD

Full-back: 13 apps
Born: Colwyn Bay, North Wales, 8 December 1892 – *Died*: Rhos-on-Sea, Denbighshire, 18 November 1976
Career: Colwyn Bay Celts (April 1910); served in the Army during WW1 (the 16th Battalion, the Royal Welch Fusiliers); Colwyn Bay United (amateur, August 1919), Bury (on trial, early 1920), Oldham Athletic (on trial, mid-1920), LIVERPOOL (professional, February 1921), Walsall (August 1926), Colwyn Bay United (July 1927–May 1928), Llandudno Town (seasons 1928–31), Colwyn Bay United (September 1931–May 1933), later Colwyn Bay FC (trainer, season 1948–49)

Said to have been the finest full-back on the North Wales coast in 1920, Ted Parry had unsuccessful trials at Gigg Lane and Boundary Park before captaining the Welsh amateur side to victory over England in 1921, a performance that led to a professional contract at Anfield worth £5 a week, at the age of 28. Unable to get a regular place in the Liverpool side (there were 10 other full-backs at the club, three of them internationals) he had offers to go elsewhere but remained loyal to the Reds and skippered the second XI while making only 13 appearances in the first team (in five years), the first at Derby County in April 1921 when he deputised for Eph Longworth in a 0–0 draw. He won five full caps for his country, all as a Liverpool player, between 1922 and 1926, collecting his last v. Ireland at the age of 35. He continued to play in the Welsh League until well into his forties. He and his two brothers both captained golf clubs in North Wales, Ted at Colwyn Bay with his brothers at Abergele and Rhos-on-Sea. Outside football, Parry enjoyed painting and decorating and started his own business with one of his brothers. He later turned his hand to crown green bowling and was also trainer to the North Wales Coast FA XI in 1948. He died a month short of his 84th birthday.

PARRY, MAURICE PRYCE

Half-back: 221 apps, 3 goals
Born: Trefonen near Oswestry, 7 November 1877 – *Died*: Bootle, 24 March 1935
Career: Newtown (1894), Long Eaton Rangers (1896), Oswestry United (1897), Leicester Fosse (semi-professional, August 1898), Loughborough (February 1899), Brighton United (May 1899), LIVERPOOL (professional, March

1900), Partick Thistle (June 1909); coached and played in South Africa (re-instated as an amateur, from 1911); Oswestry United (September 1913, retired May 1914), Rotherham County (manager, October 1921, resigned, April 1923); subsequently coached in Spain (Barcelona), Jersey and Germany (Dusseldorf, Frankfurt and Cologne); also LIVERPOOL (coach, 1930s)

After progressing via three intermediate clubs, Maurice Parry travelled to Leicester to seek work as an engineer. He asked for a trial with Fosse, was successful, signed professional forms at Filbert Street and went on to play League football until 1915. He did well with Brighton (in the Southern League) before joining Liverpool where he enjoyed nine excellent years. A big, strong ball-winning right-half, he gained both Second and First Division championship medals in 1905 and 1906 respectively and won 16 full caps for Wales. The first of his 221 senior appearances for the Reds was, in fact, at centre-half against Bolton Wanderers in October 1900 when he deputised for Alex Raisbeck in a 2–1 home League win. He later starred for Partick Thistle and was in their side for the first-ever game at Firhill Park. He quit as Rotherham manager after the Millermen had suffered relegation from the Second Division. An organ-playing advocate of teetotalism, he suffered long-term after-effects of wartime gassing but battled on to become a very successful coach. He died in 1935 of chronic bronchitis. His brother, Tom Parry, was a Welsh international who played with Oswestry for several years while his son, Frank, assisted Everton (1920s), Grimsby Town, Accrington Stanley and Nelson.

PARTRIDGE, RICHARD JOSEPH
Outside-left: 1+2 apps
Born: Dublin, 12 September 1980
Career: LIVERPOOL (apprentice, April 1996; professional, September 1997), Bristol Rovers (loan, March–May 2001), Coventry City (loan, September 2002–March 2003), Sheffield Wednesday (free, July 2005)

Richie Partridge made his debut in senior football in a fourth-round Worthington Cup tie away at Stoke City in November 2000, when Liverpool won 8–0! Three months later he was loaned to Bristol Rovers before appearing in 31 games for Coventry during another loan spell. He returned to Liverpool but failed to progress and was released by the Reds in July 2005, joining Sheffield Wednesday on a free transfer.

PATTERSON, GEORGE LONGMORE
Outside-left: 3 apps, 1 goal
Born: Aberdeen, 19 December 1916 – *Died*: Liverpool, 1996
Career: Hall Russell's FC (Aberdeen), LIVERPOOL (with Jock Penrose, May 1937); guest for Brighton and Hove Albion, Burnley, Leeds United, Queens Park Rangers, Reading and York City during WW2; Swindon Town (October 1946, retired May 1950); also worked as an assistant warden at a Swindon youth club; LIVERPOOL (coaching staff under Bill Shankly, seasons 1960–65)

A Scottish junior international who could also play at inside-right, George

Patterson made his League debut for Liverpool in December 1938 when he deputised for Bill Kinghorn in a 1–0 home win over Stoke City. His solitary goal for the Reds was scored against Luton Town in a third-round FA Cup tie in January 1939 (won 3–0). WW2 severely disrupted his career and after retiring as a player, having appeared in more then 50 League games for Swindon, he qualified as an FA coach and later returned to Anfield under manager Bill Shankly.

PAYNE, JAMES BOLCHERSON
Outside-/inside-right: 245 apps, 42 goals
Born: Bootle, 10 March 1926
Career: Bootle Schools, Bootle ATC, LIVERPOOL (amateur, May 1942; professional, September 1944), Everton (£5,000, April 1956; retired, injured, February 1957); went on to run newsagent and confectionery shops in the Liverpool area

England 'B' international Jimmy Payne was dubbed the 'Merseyside Matthews' by the Liverpool fans and played against Arsenal in the 1950 FA Cup final. Possessing excellent ball control and a deceptive body swerve, he loved to hug the right-hand touchline, often drawing his opponent close to him before attempting to beat him on the outside. Unfortunately, despite some excellent performances early in his career, he failed to win a full cap, owing to the form and presence of Blackpool's Stanley Matthews and Tom Finney of Preston. Payne, who was later switched to the inside-left position, generally did very well with Liverpool for whom he made almost 250 senior appearances before transferring to neighbours Everton in 1956. Taking over from Billy Watkinson, his first senior outing in a Red shirt was against Bolton Wanderers in September 1948 – six years after joining the club – although WW2 didn't help matters.

PEAKE, ERNEST
Centre-/left-half: 55 apps, 6 goals
Born: Aberystwyth, May 1888 – *Died*: Angleton, Bridgend, 19 November 1931
Career: Aberystwyth Barbarians, Aberystwyth FC (1904), Blackburn Rovers (reserves, April 1908), LIVERPOOL (professional, June 1908), Third Lanark (May 1914), Blyth Spartans (August 1919), Aberaman (secretary-manager, September 1920–February 1922), Caerphilly (secretary-manager, June 1922–May 1924); later worked as a fitter in Aberdare

Dark-haired and clever, Ernie Peake was a ball-playing defender who made one appearance for Blackburn's second team before joining Liverpool at the age of 20.

Capped by Wales at both amateur and full international levels, starring in 11 games in the latter category between 1908 and 1914, he once scored a brilliant goal from fully 40 yards against England at Bristol in 1913. Peake proved to be an excellent squad player at Anfield, serving the club for six years during which time he made only 55 first-class appearances, the first in a 5–0 League defeat at Arsenal in February 1909 when he was brought into the team in place of Jimmy Bradley. One felt he would have been a regular in any other club's senior side had he moved on – and he could have done easily, turning down several offers from First Division managers. Sadly his health started to break down in 1929 and he was only 43 when he died.

PEARSON, ALBERT VICTOR

Outside-left: 52 apps, 4 goals

Born: Tynemouth, 6 September 1892 – *Died*: Newcastle-under-Lyme, 24 January 1975

Career: Hebburn Argyle (April 1910), Sheffield United (professional, August 1912), Port Vale (July 1914 – although registration retained by Sheffield United); served in Army during WW1; LIVERPOOL (£500, January 1919), Port Vale (May 1921), Llanelli (June 1922), Rochdale (April 1923), Stockport County (1926), Ashton National (June 1929, retired 1930)

A 'traditional' winger, on his day Albert Pearson was fast and clever but not a prolific marksman, choosing to create chances for his colleagues rather than finding the net himself. The first of his 52 outings for Liverpool was in August 1919 when he scored in a 3–1 win at Bradford City. He had 34 League outings that term before eventually losing his place to Harry Wadsworth. Pearson made 114 first-team appearances in his two spells with Port Vale (only 19 in the Football League) and was a North Staffordshire Infirmary Cup winner in 1915. He also did well with Rochdale (12 goals in 53 games).

PEARSON, JOSEPH

Right-half: 1 app.

Born: Lancashire, 1868 – *Deceased*

Career: Bolton Wanderers (professional, August 1887), LIVERPOOL (August–December 1892)

Reserve half-back Joe Pearson played in Liverpool's first-ever competitive game against Higher Walton in the Lancashire League in September 1892, setting up three goals in an 8–0 win. He remained at Anfield for barely five months before moving to pastures new. He had earlier played in one League game for Bolton in a 6–3 defeat at West Bromwich Albion in November 1889.

PELLEGRINO, MAURICIO ANDRES

Defender: 12+1 apps

Born: Leones, Argentina, 5 October 1971

Career: Velez Sarsfield/Argentina (April 1992), CF Barcelona/Spain (loan December 1998–May 1999), Valencia/Spain (August 1999), LIVERPOOL (loan, January–May 2005); returned to Valencia for 2005–06 season

Experienced Argentinian international right-back or central defender Mauricio Pellegrino was 33 years of age when he joined Liverpool on loan from Valencia early in 2005. Standing 6ft 4in. tall and weighing 13st. 3lb, he was certainly a veteran in terms of signings made by the Reds and at times struggled for pace in the Premiership. Prior to his arrival at Anfield he had gained two Spanish La Liga championship medals, played in two losing Champions League finals and collected a UEFA Cup winner's medal (under Rafael Benitez in 2004) while amassing almost 400 club appearances in major competitions, including 175 in the League for Sarsfield, 23 for Barcelona and 139 for Valencia. He made his debut for Liverpool against Manchester United (home) shortly after arriving from manager Rafael Benitez's former club in Spain.

PENMAN, JAMES
Full-back: 1 app.
Born: Kelty, Fife, 26 May 1896 – *Died*: Scotland, 11 October 1976
Career: Glasgow Ashfield (from 1912), LIVERPOOL (professional, April 1919), Lochgelly United (May 1921–April 1923)
A Scottish Junior Cup winner with Glasgow Ashfield in 1914, Jim Penman played in a Lancashire Regional game at the end of WW1 before making his League debut for Liverpool against Bradford Park Avenue in November 1920 when he deputised for Don McKinlay at left-back in a 1–0 defeat. His son, Willie Penman, played for Raith Rovers in the 1949 Scottish Cup final.

PEPLOW, STEPHEN THOMAS
Inside-right: 3 apps
Born: Liverpool, 8 January 1949
Career: Liverpool and Merseyside Schools, LIVERPOOL (apprentice, June 1964; professional, September 1966), Swindon Town (loan, March 1970, signed permanently, May 1970), Nottingham Forest (free, July 1973), Mansfield Town (loan, December 1973–January 1974), Tranmere Rovers (£6,000, January 1974–May 1981)
During his first ten years as a professional, Steve Peplow played in fewer than 50 League games but following his transfer to Tranmere in 1974 he became an established member of the first XI at Prenton Park and amassed over 270 appearances for Rovers, 248 in the Football League, scoring 44 goals while helping the Birkenhead side gain promotion to the Third Division in 1976. A hard-working forward, he made his Liverpool debut in November 1969 against West Ham United, taking over from Roger Hunt at inside-right in a 2–0 win. He found it hard going to get into the side after that and enjoyed a useful spell with Swindon Town before joining Brian Clough's Nottingham Forest.

PERKINS, WILLIAM HENRY
Goalkeeper: 116 apps
Born: Wellingborough, Northamptonshire, 26 January 1876 – *Died*: Rushden, Northampton, *circa* 1940
Career: Wellingborough Trinity (1892), Kettering (August 1894), Luton Town (professional, July 1898), LIVERPOOL (March 1899), Northampton Town (July 1903–May 1906)
A sound and reliable goalkeeper, Bill Perkins took over from Harry Storer as Liverpool's last line of defence. He made his League debut against Newcastle United at Anfield in April 1899 (won 3–2) and was an ever-present in 1900–01 when he gained a First Division championship medal after conceding only 22 goals in 34 games. Replaced in the side by Peter Platt, he went on to appear in

100 out of a possible 102 Southern League games for Northampton Town in three seasons.

PERRY, FREDERICK NOEL
Right-back: 1 app.
Born: Cheltenham, 30 October 1933
Career: Worthing FC, LIVERPOOL (professional, July 1954), Sittingbourne (January 1957–May 1959)
Also a reliable right-half, Fred Perry failed to establish himself in the first team at Anfield, making only one League appearance against Blackburn Rovers (home) on New Year's Eve, 1955 when he deputised for John Molyneux at right-back in a 2–1 defeat. He played with Alan Arnell at Worthing.

PETERS, KEITH
Left-back: 1 app.
Born: Port Sunlight, Cheshire, 19 July 1915 – *Deceased*
Career: Cheshire junior football, LIVERPOOL (amateur, July 1936; professional, March 1937); served in the Army and was a guest for Brighton and Hove Albion during WW2 (retired, injured, 1944)
Along with Ben Dabbs and Barney Ramsden, solid defender Keith Peters was reserve at Anfield to Jim Harley and made just one League appearance for the Reds, taking over at left-back against Middlesbrough in January 1939 (lost 3–0). He was forced to retire prematurely after suffering injury during WW2.

PIECHNIK, TORBEN
Defender: 23+1 apps
Born: Copenhagen, 24 September 1972
Career: BK Copenhagen/Denmark (professional, September 1990), LIVERPOOL (£500,000, September 1992), AGF Aarhus/Denmark (May 1994)
Danish international defender Torben Piechnik was unable to settle on Merseyside, despite having a decent enough first season at Anfield when he appeared in 23 senior games. However, after that he struggled with his form and was given only one more outing before being released. Watched by manager Graeme Souness for quite some time before joining the Reds, he made his Premiership debut in a 4–2 defeat at Aston Villa in September 1992 when he partnered David Burrows at full-back. He was a European Championship winner with Denmark in Sweden in 1992.

PITHER, GEORGE BERTRAND
Outside-left: 12 apps, 1 goal
Born: Kew, Surrey, 24 June 1899 – *Died*: Tunbridge Wells, 3 June 1966
Career: Richmond Wednesday (1914), Isleworth Town (1915), Brentford (amateur, August 1921; professional, September 1921), Millwall Athletic (May 1922), Bristol Rovers (August 1924), Torquay United (August 1925), Merthyr Town (May 1926), LIVERPOOL (November 1926), Crewe

Alexandra (£100, May 1928), New Brighton (August 1929), Tunbridge Wells
Rangers (August 1931), Margate (September 1932, retired, May 1934)
Besides his dozen appearances for Liverpool in the top flight, the first against
Bolton Wanderers on New Year's Day 1927 when he stood in for Fred Hopkin,
George Pither spent the rest of his career playing in the Third Division of the
Football League. He had his best spells with Crewe (13 goals in 42 games) and
New Brighton (10 goals in 79 outings) being one of five outside-lefts used by the
latter club in 1931—32. His career realised a total of 172 League appearances (27
goals).

PLATT, PETER

Goalkeeper: 45 apps
Born: Oldham, February 1883 – *Died*: Nuneaton, Warwickshire, 1922
Career: Great Harwood (1898), Oswaldtwistle Rovers (1899), Blackburn Rovers
(professional, September 1900), LIVERPOOL (free, September 1902),
Nuneaton Town (free, August 1904); licensee of the White Swan pub,
Nuneaton, until his death

Peter Platt's first two League games of his career were on the same ground
against the same opposition, 17 months apart. He made his debut for Blackburn
Rovers against West Bromwich Albion at The Hawthorns in March 1901 at the
age of 18, and following his transfer to Liverpool, still young and inexperienced,
the first of his 45 starts for the Reds was also against the Baggies on their patch
in the Midlands. He was handed 22 League outings in each of his two seasons
at Anfield before entering minor football with Nuneaton in 1904
. . . this after Liverpool had signed the veteran Ted Doig from Sunderland. Platt
was only 39 when he died.

POLK, STANLEY

Inside-left: 13 apps
Born: Liverpool, 28 October 1921
Career: South Liverpool (1938), LIVERPOOL (August 1940; professional,
August 1945), Port Vale (£10,000 with Mick Hulligan, July 1948), Worcester
City (August 1952), Flint Town (1954), Oswestry Town (seasons 1956—58)

Stanley Polk helped Liverpool beat Bolton Wanderers 6—3 on aggregate in the
1944 League (N) Cup final. He scored 14 goals in 61 WW2 appearances for the
club before making 13 in peacetime football. An intelligent, hard-working and
creative inside-left, he made his senior debut for the Reds in a 5—0 home League
win over Grimsby Town in February 1947 but did not make sufficient
appearances that season to qualify for a championship winner's medal. He scored
14 goals in 169 competitive games during his four years with Port Vale, being an
ever-present two seasons running (1948—50). Believed to be still alive in 2006,
Polk is one of Liverpool's oldest former players.

POTTER, DARREN MICHAEL

Midfield: 10+7 apps
Born: Liverpool, 21 December 1984
Career: LIVERPOOL (apprentice, March 2001; professional, April 2002), Southampton (loan, January 2006–May 2006)

Darren Potter came on in leaps and bounds at Anfield, graduating through the club's Youth Academy to make his first-team debut as a substitute in the Champions League qualifying encounter away to Graz AK of Austria in August 2004. The tall midfielder, who was capped by the Republic of Ireland at youth team level, has now played in three under-21 matches and looks set for a bright and prosperous career in club and international football.

PRATT, DAVID

Half-back: 85 apps, 1 goal
Born: Lochore, Fife, 5 March 1896 – *Died*: Scotland, *circa* 1974
Career: Lochore Welfare (1912), Lochgelly United (1914), Hill o'Beath/Fife (1917), Celtic (professional, June 1919), Bradford City (November 1921), LIVERPOOL (January 1923), Bury (November 1927), Yeovil and Petters United (player-manager, June 1929), Clapton Orient (manager, May 1933–December 1934), Notts County (manager, April–June 1935), Heart of Midlothian (manager, July 1935–February 1937), Bangor City (manager, July–October 1937), Port Vale (manager, December 1944–July 1945); served in the RAF during WW2; he also worked as a sports commentator for the BBC

A highly efficient half-back who played 22 games for Celtic and 55 for Bradford before joining Liverpool, David Pratt had his best spell in Liverpool's senior side during the second half of the 1924–25 season when he made a quarter of his senior appearances for the club. Able to occupy both the centre-half and left-half positions, he made his debut for the Reds against Blackburn Rovers in February 1923 when he deputised for Tom Bromilow in a 3–0 win . . . on their way to the title. His career realised well over 250 senior appearances and as a manager he made some very positive and useful signings, especially for Hearts. Unfortunately he was unable to obtain his release from the RAF and therefore had to relinquish his position as Port Vale's manager after seven months in office, during which time he was hardly seen at the ground!

PRICE, JOHN GERAINT

Left-back: 1 app.
Born: Aberystwyth, 22 November 1936
Career: Fordhouse Youth Club (Wolverhampton), LIVERPOOL (signed as a professional, with reserve Graham Wood, October 1954), Aston Villa (free, March 1957), Walsall (£1,500, July 1957), Shrewsbury Town (free, July 1958–May 1959)

During his five years as a professional, left-back John Price made only ten League appearances, one for Liverpool (v. Leeds United, away, in November 1955 when he deputised for Ronnie Moran in a 4–2 defeat) and nine for

Shrewsbury. A squad member with Aston Villa, he was at Wembley when they won the FA Cup in 1957.

PRIDAY, ROBERT HERBERT

Outside-right/-left: 39 apps, 7 goals
Born: Cape Town, South Africa, 29 March 1925
Career: South African football (in Cape Town and Transvaal), LIVERPOOL (professional, April 1945), Blackburn Rovers (£10,000, March 1949), Clitheroe (June 1951), Northwich Victoria (August 1952), Accrington Stanley (December 1952), Rochdale (trial, August–October 1953); believed to have returned to South Africa

Bob Priday made his senior debut for Liverpool on the left wing against Chester in a third-round first-leg FA Cup encounter in January 1946, the same game in which Bob Paisley and Billy Liddell made their bows. Red-haired, quick, incisive with a powerful right-foot shot, he was able to play on both wings and proved a very capable deputy to Billy Liddell. He scored 11 goals in 44 League games for Blackburn and whilst at Ewood Park was involved in a serious car accident from which he escaped with shock and minor bruising. After three-and-a-half years out of top-line football he returned with Accrington Stanley in 1952 but failed to make an impact.

PURSELL, ROBERT RUSSELL

Left-back: 112 apps
Born: Campbeltown, Argyll, 18 March 1899 – *Died*: Hanley, Stoke-on-Trent, 24 May 1974
Career: Aberdeen University, Queen's Park/Glasgow (amateur, 1909), LIVERPOOL (professional, September 1911); served in the Army during WW1; Port Vale (May 1920, retired, injured, May 1922)

Described as being a 'cool and brainy full-back', Bob Pursell had a good innings at Anfield, playing in 99 League and 13 Cup games over a period of nine years after being 'poached' from Queen's Park – a move which cost Liverpool £250. He made his debut in a 2–1 win at Sunderland in September 1911 when he partnered Eph Longworth and continued on the left flank (injuries permitting) until Don McKinlay took over the role in 1919. Unfortunately he was one of the four Liverpool players involved in the match-fixing scandal v. Manchester United on Good Friday, 1915 . . . and was never selected again. After leaving Anfield, Pursell made 68 appearances for Port Vale before retiring after breaking his leg during a League game with Leicester City in April 1922. His brother, Peter Pursell, a Scottish international, also played for Port Vale, Queen's Park, Glasgow Rangers and Wigan Borough while his father, Robert Wilson Pursell, was also registered with Port Vale as well as Wolverhampton Wanderers.

RACE, HAROLD HENRY

Centre-forward/inside-left: 43 apps, 18 goals
Born: Evenwood, County Durham, 7 January 1906 – *Died*: killed in action, 1941
Career: Raby United (County Durham), LIVERPOOL (professional, October

1927), Manchester City (£3,000, July 1930), Nottingham Forest (June 1933), Shrewsbury Town (May 1937), Hartlepools United (August 1938 until his death)

A hard worker and very consistent performer, Harry Race was the brains and driving force of the Forest attack after doing well with Liverpool and Manchester City. In fact, he scored 30 goals in 124 appearances during his four years at The City Ground. Aged 21 when he moved to Anfield, he netted on his debut for the Reds in a 3–2 win at Derby in February 1928 and secured nine of his goals for the club the following season when he formed a very useful left wing partnership with Fred Hopkin. He won the Welsh Cup with Shrewsbury in 1938.

RAISBECK, ALEXANDER GALLOWAY

Centre-half: 340 apps, 21 goals

Born: Wallacestone near Polmont, Stirlingshire, 26 December 1878 – *Died*: Liverpool, 12 March 1949

Career: Blantyre Boys Brigade (1892), Larkhall Thistle (1893), Royal Albert (1895), Edinburgh Hibernian (professional, May 1896), Stoke (March 1898), LIVERPOOL (£350, May 1898), Partick Thistle (£500, June 1909), Hamilton Academical (secretary-manager, April 1914, club director, 1917, manager for a year, 1918), Bristol City (secretary-manager, December 1921–June 1929), Halifax Town (secretary-manager, July 1930–May 1936), Chester (secretary-manager, June 1936–April 1938), Bath City (manager, August 1938 to mid-1940s), LIVERPOOL (scout after WW2 until his death, aged 70)

One of the greatest ever Scottish international centre-halves, Alex Raisbeck was quick in recovery, smart in the tackle, brilliant in the air and a clean kicker of the ball – a commanding figure generally. Under six feet tall with fair hair (almost blond) he surprisingly gained only eight full caps for his country, seven v. England (1900–07) and made three appearances for the Scottish League, the last in 1913. His League record with Liverpool, however, was first-class; 340 games in 11 seasons. He made his debut for the Reds in a 4–0 home League win over Sheffield Wednesday in September 1898, scored his first goal in another 4–0 victory over Derby County in April 1899 and played his last game for the club at left-back at Newcastle United in April 1909. Twice a League championship winner in 1901 and 1906, he also helped Liverpool win the Second Division title in 1905 and skippered the side several times. As a manager he twice guided Bristol City to the Third Division (S) title in 1923 and 1927. Two of his six brothers also played football – Andrew for Liverpool reserves (1903) and Hull City and William for Hibernian, Clyde, Sunderland, Derby County, New Brompton and Reading. Two other relatives were also professional League players.

RAMSDEN, BERNARD

Left-back: 66 apps
Born: Sheffield, 8 November 1917 – *Died*: California, USA, *circa* 1990
Career: Hampton Sports (Sheffield), Sheffield Victoria, LIVERPOOL (professional, March 1935); guest for Brighton and Hove Albion, Leeds United and York City during WW2; Sunderland (March 1948), Hartlepools United (January 1950, retired, May 1950); emigrated to the USA

Besides his senior appearances for Liverpool, wavy-haired Barney Ramsden also played in 15 WW2 games for the Reds. He linked up superbly with Jim Harley to form a very efficient and, indeed, effective full-back partnership which spread over 12 years. The first of his League outings was against Chelsea (away) in August 1937 and the first time he teamed up with Harley was against Leeds United in February 1938. He had 13 outings with both Sunderland and Hartlepools. He returned for a nostalgic visit to Merseyside in 1972 and at Anfield he insisted on a few choruses of 'Ilkley Moor Baht 'at' which he and his teammates used to sing on away trips.

RAVEN, DAVID HAYDN

Defender: 3+1 apps
Born: Birkenhead, 10 March 1985
Career: LIVERPOOL (apprentice, April 2001; professional, May 2002)
A promising central defender who came through the Liverpool Adacemy with flying colours, David Raven, an England youth international, made his senior debut against Tottenham Hotspur in a League Cup tie in December 2004 when the Anfield youngsters went through via a penalty shoot-out. He then played in the FA Cup and Premiership before the end of the season.

RAWLINGS, ARCHIBALD

Outside-right: 67 apps, 10 goals
Born: Leicester, 2 October 1891 – *Died*: Lancashire, 1952
Career: Wombwell (1906), Shirebrook (1907), Northampton Town (May 1908), Barnsley (August 1911), Rochdale (July 1914), Dundee (September 1919), Preston North End (£1,500, June 1920), LIVERPOOL (March 1924), Walsall (June 1926), Bradford Park Avenue (February 1927), Southport (July 1928), Dick Kerr's FC/Preston (December 1928), Burton Town (August 1931, retired, May 1933), Preston North End (assistant trainer, seasons 1933–35)

Archie Rawlings was certainly on the tall side for a winger at close on six feet. He was not a great footballer by any means, often attempting the impossible, but when in the right frame of mind he proved very dangerous with his powerful shooting and terrific pace over 20–30 yards. He gained one cap for England and played for Preston in their 1922 FA Cup defeat by Huddersfield Town before joining Liverpool, making the first of his 67 appearances against Blackburn Rovers in March 1924 (0–0). He retained his position on the right flank until handing over the mantle to Cyril Oxley in October 1925. His son, Syd, also an outside-right, played for Preston, Huddersfield, West Bromwich Albion,

Northampton Town, Everton, Plymouth Argyle and Millwall, helping the latter club win the Third Division (S) title in 1938.

RAYBOULD, SAMUEL FREDERICK
Outside-right/centre-forward: 224 apps, 127 goals
Born: Chesterfield, January 1875 – *Died*: Chesterfield, 1949
Career: Ilkeston Town (1891), Chesterfield Town (May 1893), Derby County
   (£300, August 1894), Ilkeston Town (January 1895), Poolsbrook United
   (May 1897), Ilkeston Town (February 1898), Bolsover Colliery (August
   1899), New Brighton Tower (October 1899), LIVERPOOL (£250, January
   1900), Sunderland (May 1907), Woolwich Arsenal (May 1908), Chesterfield
   (September 1910), Sutton Town (August 1911), Barlborough United (July
   1913, retired, May 1915)
Former soccer journeyman Sam Raybould was 25 years of age when he joined Liverpool from New Brighton Tower, having failed to make much of an impact during his early travels. He made his debut for the Reds against West Bromwich Albion (home) 48 hours after signing and in 1902–03 set a new scoring record for a season of 32 goals, which was to stand for 29 years, when it was beaten by the South African Gordon Hodgson. Not very tall, he was alert and forever active inside the penalty area and actually found the net after just 30 seconds of his second League game against Everton. Unfortunately he was struck down with injuries during the 1903–04 campaign but came back strongly and went on to average more than a goal every two games for the club before joining Sunderland in 1907. The recipient of two First Division championship winning medals, in 1901 and 1906, he also helped the Reds clinch the Second Division title in 1905 and represented the Football League v. the Scottish League on three occasions as a Liverpool player. After leaving Anfield, Raybould scored 13 goals in 27 games for Sunderland and 7 in 30 for Arsenal.

REDKNAPP, JAMES FRANK
Midfield: 271+38 apps, 41 goals
Born: Barton-on-Sea, 25 June 1973
Career: Tottenham Hotspur (associated schoolboy forms), Bournemouth
   (apprentice, June 1989; professional, June 1990), LIVERPOOL (£350,000,
   January 1991), Tottenham Hotspur (free, April 2002), Southampton (free,
   January 2005, retired, injured, August 2005); now a TV soccer pundit
Son of Harry Redknapp (the former Bournemouth and West Ham United winger and ex-manager at Upton Park and Southampton, now in his second spell in charge of Portsmouth), Jamie Redknapp was a beautifully balanced yet aggressive midfielder who enjoyed the 50-50 challenges. During a wonderful career that spanned 16 years, having his best seasons at Anfield, he amassed over 400 club and international appearances, represented England at schoolboy and youth team levels and won one 'B', 19 under-21 and 17 full caps while playing with and against some of the greatest midfield players in the game. A League Cup and European Super Cup winner with Liverpool in 1995 and 2001 respectively, the first of his 309 outings for the Reds came as a substitute against

the French club Auxerre in the UEFA Cup in October 1991 before he made his League bow against his future employers, Southampton, two months later. Unfortunately niggling injuries began to affect his game in the early 2000s, and after 11 splendid years on Merseyside he joined Tottenham, the club with whom he had been registered as a 15-year-old schoolboy. He had one decent season at White Hart Lane and then, with his father in charge, he failed to save Southampton from losing their Premiership status in 2005. Redknapp is married to the pop star Louise.

REID, THOMAS JOSEPH

Centre-forward: 55 apps, 31 goals

Born: Motherwell, 15 August 1905 – *Died*: Prescot, Liverpool, 1972

Career: Blantyre Victoria (1923), Clydebank (August 1925), LIVERPOOL (£1,000, April 1926), Manchester United (January 1929), Oldham Athletic (loan, March–April 1933, signed permanently for £400, June 1933), Barrow (September 1935–May 1936); out of the game for two years; Rhyl (as a part-time player, May 1938–May 1939); did not feature after WW2

Tom Reid was a robust centre-forward, as tough as steel with a great sense of humour. Described in the Manchester United programme of February 1932 as being 'somewhat cumbersome in his methods but an opportunist of the highest water', he was certainly not a ball artist in any way or form – just simply a top-notch marksman whose career realised over 200 goals (165 in the English and Scottish Leagues). After leaving Anfield (reluctantly I might add) he netted 67 times in 101 outings for United, claimed a further 38 in 72 starts for Oldham and weighed in with 17 goals in 31 matches for Barrow – and he also secured a handful more while playing for Rhyl in the late 1930s. He made the first of his 55 appearances for Liverpool against Sheffield United in May 1926, scoring both his side's goals in a 2–2 draw. Members of Oldham Athletic's Supporters Club raised the £400 required to sign Reid from Manchester United.

REINA, JOSE MANUEL

Goalkeeper: 52 apps

Born: Madrid, Spain, 31 August 1982

Career: CF Barcelona/Spain (amateur, September 1998; professional, May 2000), Villarreal/Spain (July 2002), LIVERPOOL (£6m, July 2005)

Prior to his move to Liverpool, Jose 'Pepe' Reina – who looks far older than he really is – saved seven out of nine penalties while playing for Villarreal in Spain's La Liga in 2004–05. Signed by manager Rafael Benitez to replace the Polish international Jerzy Dudek, and rated the best goalkeeper in Spain at the time, Reina, who has been capped twice by his country at senior level, played at Anfield for Barcelona in the 2001 UEFA Cup semi-final, conceding a Gary McAllister penalty. He made his Liverpool debut in the Champions League qualifying match against Total Network Solutions of Wales before appearing in his first Premiership game, a 0–0 draw at Middlesbrough in August 2005. He had an excellent first season with the Reds and during one splendid spell, he kept a clean sheet for a total of 17 hours and 7 minutes. The run started right at the end of the Premiership game with Fulham on 22 October and ended in the 27th minute of the World Club Championship final against the Brazilian side Sao Paolo in Yokohama, Japan, on 18 December 2005, a game Liverpool lost 1–0. He gained an FA Cup winner's medal with Liverpool in 2006 after saving three penalties in the shoot-out with West Ham United (following a 3–3 draw). Prior to moving to Anfield, he had saved 35 spot kicks in Spain. He was in his country's squad for the World Cup in Germany in 2006.

RICHARDSON, WALTER
Wing-half: 1 app.
Born: Liverpool, *circa* 1870 – *Died*: *circa* 1960
Career: LIVERPOOL (season 1892–93)
Unknown reserve wing-half Wally Richardson was registered with Liverpool for one season, making his only first-team appearance against Rossendale in a Lancashire League game in March 1893.

RIEDLE, KARL-HEINZ
Forward: 42+34 apps, 15 goals
Born: Simmerberg-Weiler, Germany, 16 September 1965
Career: Augsburg/Germany (1984), Blau-Weiss 90 Berlin/Germany (professional, August 1986), Werder Bremen/Germany (July 1987), SC Lazio/Italy (August 1990), Borussia Dortmund/Germany (July 1993), LIVERPOOL (£1.6m, August 1997), Fulham (£250,000, September 1999, player/caretaker-manager, February 2001, retired, injured, June 2001)
The scorer of 15 goals in 42 internationals for Germany between 1988 and 1994, versatile forward Karl-Heinz Riedle, tall, strong in the air with good footwork and an appetite (at times) for scoring goals, was selected quite regularly to partner a youthful Michael Owen in Liverpool's attack between 1997 and 1999. Between them they certainly rattled a few defensive cages but Riedle sadly failed to produce the goods expected of him at Premiership level, being used a considerable number of times as a substitute during his two seasons at Anfield. His days were clearly numbered when Titi Camara and Erik Meijer arrived at the club. The first of Riedle's 76 appearances for the Reds came in the 1–1 draw at Wimbledon in August 1997 and he struck his first goal for the club against Leeds United at Elland Road three weeks later in a 2–0 win. During his career Riedle scored a total of 119 goals in 386 League games in West Germany, Italy and England, appearing in 467 matches in all competitions (for clubs and country). He had his best spell with Werder Bremen for whom he struck 38 goals in 86 outings while winning the Bundesliga title in 1988. He later gained two more Bundesliga championship medals in successive seasons with Dortmund, in 1995 and 1996.

RIISE, JOHN ARNE
Left-back/midfield: 220+35 apps, 26 goals
Born: Molde, Norway, 24 September 1980
Career: Aalesund/Norway (amateur, 1996; semi-professional, September 1997),

217

AS Monaco/France (professional, August 1998), LIVERPOOL (£3.77m, July 2001)

John Arne Riise's surging runs and powerful shooting have made him one of the best attacking left wing-backs in the game. The red-headed Norwegian international has scored some stunning goals for Liverpool and there are surely more to come. Signed after making only 44 appearances for AS Monaco in the French League, he quickly helped the Reds win the European Super Cup and Charity Shield (2001) and then played his part in the European Champions final success in 2005, despite missing from the spot in the nail-biting penalty shoot-out. Also a capable midfielder, he represented his country in 17 under-21 internationals before going on to make over 50 full international appearances, having been honoured at youth team level as a teenager. He made his debut for Liverpool in the 2001 Charity Shield showdown with Manchester United at Cardiff's Millennium Stadium. Gained an FA Cup winner's medal in the penalty shoot-out v. West Ham United.

RILEY, ARTHUR JACK

Goalkeeper: 338 apps

Born: Boksburg, Transvaal, South Africa, 26 December 1903 – *Died*: Cape Town, South Africa, *circa* 1978

Career: Boksburg FC/South Africa, LIVERPOOL (August 1925, retired, April 1940); returned to South Africa

Goalkeeper Arthur Riley joined Liverpool four months ahead of his fellow countryman Gordon Hodgson, both players having starred together in several amateur internationals in their homeland and on tour to England in 1924. Eventually taking over from the great Elisha Scott, Riley was a class act, ideally built with a safe pair of hands. He was reliable and had the knack of stopping shots with any part of his body – he simply got in the way of anything directed at his goal. He lost his form in 1931 when Scott returned, but he came back superbly well and took his tally of senior appearances for the club to a creditable 338 plus 11 more during the 1939–40 WW2 season when he also played for an All British XI against the Football League, a Football League XI and the French Army, as well as starring for the Army against an England XI, before returning to South Africa. A resident at Anfield for 15 years, Riley made his debut for Liverpool against Tottenham Hotspur (away) in October 1925 and when nearing the end of his career he gave way to compatriot Dirk Kemp. Riley was an engineer by trade and he reverted to that line of work until he was over 60 years of age. He also became an expert racing judge in Liverpool.

ROBERTS, JOHN EDGAR

Centre-forward: 1 app.

Born: Blundellsands, Liverpool, 15 March 1910 – *Died*: Cape Town, South Africa, 1 June 1985

Career: Marine FC, Orrell FC, Blundellsands FC, Northern Nomads, Southport (amateur, September 1931), LIVERPOOL (professional, May 1933), Wigan Athletic (£500, June 1934), Port Vale (£1,500, December 1935); guest for

Wrexham (1939, retired May 1940); enlisted in the forces and was captured by the enemy in Tunisia, escaping from a prisoner-of-war camp in 1944; later emigrated to South Africa where he died, aged 75

Centre-forward John 'Nipper' Roberts scored in the first minute of his amateur international debut for England. Reserve to Sam English and Tom Johnson at Anfield, he made only one senior appearance for Liverpool, in a 1–1 draw at Stoke City in September 1933. After leaving Anfield he netted 66 goals in 55 appearances during an 18-month spell with Wigan before going on to score 74 goals in 118 first-team matches for Port Vale – being the Football League's leading marksman in 1937–38 with 28 goals. As a youngster, Roberts captained England at baseball.

ROBERTS, SYDNEY
Inside-left: 61 apps, 13 goals
Born: Bootle, 3 March 1911 – *Deceased*
Career: Bootle Junior Ordnance Corps, LIVERPOOL (amateur July 1929; professional, February 1931), Shrewsbury Town (August 1937), Chester (January 1938), Northfleet (August 1939, retired during WW2)

After three years playing in Liverpool's 'A' and Central League teams, Syd Roberts finally made his senior debut for the Reds, lining up against Portsmouth (home) in April 1932 at the age of 21. The following season he formed a useful left wing partnership with Gordon Gunson and then did likewise on the right with Harold Barton before delivering the goods as outside-left Alf Hanson's aide in 1933–34. He played for Shrewsbury in the Birmingham and District League before returning to top-line football with Chester, for whom he netted 5 goals in 29 Third Division (N) games. Roberts was a decorator by trade and he continued in that line of work for many years after retiring from football.

ROBERTSON, JOHN THOMAS
Right-back: 46 apps, 1 goal
Born: Newton Mearns, Renfrewshire, 6 June 1877 – *Died*: Hove, Sussex, *circa* 1948
Career: Newton Thistle (1892), Edinburgh St Bernard's (1893), Edinburgh Hibernian (professional, May 1894), Stoke (£90, May 1897), LIVERPOOL (April 1900), Southampton (May 1902), Brighton and Hove Albion (June 1904, retired, May 1906); later became a licensee in Hove, Sussex

A member of Liverpool's League championship winning side of 1901, Tom Robertson was a reliable full-back, brave and daring, strong in the tackle with good positional awareness. Taking over from Archie Goldie, he made the first of his 46 senior appearances for the Reds against Blackburn Rovers (home) in September 1900 when he partnered Billy Dunlop in a 3–0 victory. He subsequently left Anfield for Southampton against the wishes of the Liverpool management team and their reluctance to release him was vindicated when he played his part in Saints' Southern League championship winning campaigns of 1903 and 1904. He made 113 appearances in his two spells with Stoke. Off the pitch Robertson was known as a retiring fellow and once had the 'holy horror' of being interviewed by the press, and thereafter was always elusive when a reporter was seeking a story!

ROBERTSON, THOMAS

Outside-left: 141 apps, 37 goals

Born: Renton, Lanarkshire, 1873 – *Died*: Scotland, *circa* 1939

Career: East Benhar Heatherbell, Motherwell, Fauldhouse FC, Heart of Midlothian (August 1896), LIVERPOOL (£350 with John Walker, March 1898), Heart of Midlothian (£300 plus John Hunter, May 1902), Dundee (£200, October 1902, retired April 1904)

A member of Hearts' championship winning side of 1897, Tom Robertson went on to gain a First Division winner's medal with Liverpool four years later. A very skilful and effective player, he netted on his international debut for Scotland against Ireland at the age of 25 in 1898, and was transferred for three fairly substantial fees in the space of six years. In fact, when he joined the Reds it is believed he was earning £4 a week – a considerably high wage in those days. Robertson scored in the first of his 141 senior appearances for Liverpool in a 4–0 home win over Sheffield Wednesday just 48 hours after his switch from Tynecastle Park and in April 1901 was involved in a remarkable incident whereby he and the Reds' right-winger Jack Cox both scored within 15 seconds of each other in the fifth minute of the match against Manchester City, which they won 3–1.

ROBINSON, MICHAEL JOHN

Forward: 46+6 apps, 13 goals

Born: Leicester, 12 July 1958

Career: Blackpool Schools, Coventry City (associated schoolboy forms), Waterloo Wanderers (Blackpool Sunday League side), Dolphinstone FC (Blackpool), Preston North End (apprentice, July 1974; professional, July 1976), Manchester City (£756,000, June 1979), Brighton and Hove Albion (£400,000, July 1980), LIVERPOOL (£200,000, August 1983), Queens Park Rangers (£100,000, December 1984), Osasuna/Spain (August 1987, retired, 1990); now living in Spain, working in the media

An aggressive, mobile forward, never found in the same position five minutes apart, he worked hard at his game and had impressive spells at Preston (15 goals in 48 League games) and Manchester City (8 in 30) before going on to score 37 times in 115 outings for Brighton, whom he helped reach the 1983 FA Cup final (beaten in a replay by Manchester United). After his transfer to Anfield, he gained a European Cup winner's medal at the end of his first season (1984) when he came off the bench to replace Kenny Dalglish against AS Roma. He followed up by receiving a runners-up prize with QPR in the 1985 League Cup final. A Republic of Ireland international (through his parentage) Robinson won 24 caps between 1981 and 1986 (five whilst with the Reds). He partnered Ian Rush in attack when making his debut for Liverpool against Wolves at Molineux in August 1983 (1–1 draw).

ROBINSON, ROBERT SMITH
Right-half/inside-right: 271 apps, 65 goals
Born: Sunderland, 10 October 1879 – *Died*: Birkenhead, *circa* 1951
Career: Sunderland Royal Rovers, Sunderland (professional, November 1902), LIVERPOOL (£500, February 1904), Tranmere Rovers (August 1912, retired, May 1915)
Robbie Robinson gave Liverpool supreme service for over eight years during which time he appeared in more than 270 first-class matches and gained both Second and First Division championship medals (1905 and 1906). He started out as an inside-forward, making his Liverpool debut against Stoke (home) in February 1904. He netted 5 times in 9 games that season and was top scorer in 1904–05 with a total of 23, 4 coming in the second half of the home match v. Leicester Fosse (won 4–0). Switched to the right-half berth in place of Maurice Perry at the start of the 1909–10 season, allowing Jimmy Stewart to come into the attack, he missed only nine games in his last three years with the club, being an ever-present in 1910–11.

ROGERS, FREDERICK
Half-back: 75 apps
Born: Frodsham, Cheshire, 17 April 1910 – *Died*: 1 April 1967
Career: Helsby Athletic (1930), LIVERPOOL (professional, March 1933–August 1940); served in WW2; did not resume playing after 1945
'Franny' Rogers, one of the 'pets of the Kop', could play in both the right-half and centre-half positions and did so with pride and commitment. Besides his senior appearances for the Reds he also made six more during the first season of WW2 before going off to serve his country. Nicknamed 'Bullet' by the Anfield fans because of his crew-cut hair-style, he made his League debut in a 2–2 draw at Preston in October 1934 but had to wait three years before gaining a regular place in the side at centre-half, performing the 'policeman' role very effectively.

ROGERS, THOMAS
Left-back: 40 apps
Born: Prescot, Lancashire, 1885 – *Died*: *circa* 1952
Career: Rossendale United, LIVERPOOL (professional, April 1907, released, May 1912)
Never an automatic choice during his five years at Anfield, Tom Rogers was, nonetheless, a very capable and worthy full-back who made the first of his 40 senior appearances against Sheffield United (home) in April 1907 when he deputised for Billy Dunlop in a 2–2 draw.

ROSENTHAL, RONNY
Forward: 42+57 apps, 22 goals
Born: Haifa, Israel, 11 October 1963
Career: Maccabi Tel Aviv/Israel (professional, October 1980), FC Brugge/Belgium (1984), Standard Liege/Belgium (1988), Luton Town (loan, 1989), Hibernian (loan, 1989), LIVERPOOL (loan, March 1990, signed

permanently for £1m, June 1990), Tottenham Hotspur (£250,000, January 1994), Watford (free, August 1997, retired, injured, May 1999)

Ronny Rosenthal, one of the quickest players ever to don a Liverpool shirt, loved to run at defenders, his pace and willingness causing plenty of problems for the opposition. He made a great start to his Anfield career, scoring seven goals in his first eight games when on loan. He made his debut as a 'sub' in a 3–2 home win over Southampton in March 1990 and then rattled in a hat-trick on his first start against Charlton (away) eleven days later. However, after signing full time for the club, he was never really able to deliver the goods at that sort of pace and, in fact, was used quite effectively as a second-half substitute on many occasions. Indeed, he came off the bench far more times than he actually started games for Liverpool. He went on to score 11 goals in exactly 100 games for Spurs and spent two seasons at Watford before retiring just as the Hornets had earned a place in the Premiership. Rosenthal was capped 60 times at full international level by Israel. Only two players, Vladimir Smicer (74) and Danny Murphy (71) have made more substitute appearances for Liverpool than Rosenthal.

ROSS, IAN

Midfield/defender: 59+9 apps, 4 goals
Born: Glasgow, 26 November 1947
Career: Glasgow and District Schools, LIVERPOOL (apprentice, June 1963; professional, August 1965), Aston Villa (£70,000, February 1972), Notts County (loan, October 1976), Northampton Town (loan, November 1976), Peterborough United (December 1976), Santa Barbara FC/USA (May 1978), Wolverhampton Wanderers (player-coach, August 1979), Hereford United (non-contract, player-coach, October 1982), Wolverhampton Wanderers (coach, early 1983), Oman (coach, June 1983), Birmingham City (reserve-team coach, early 1984), FC Valur/Iceland (manager/coach, August 1984–June 1988); coached in South Africa and Australia (1988 to late 1991); Huddersfield Town (manager, March 1992–May 1993); later licensee of the Gardener's Arms, Timperley near Altrincham, Cheshire

The versatile Ian Ross proved to be a fine professional, a 100 per cent trier who simply never gave up the ghost, battling through each and every game with grim determination and willpower. Used effectively as a marker by manager Bill Shankly, he was nicknamed 'Roscoe' by the fans and made almost 70 senior appearances for Liverpool during his nine years at Anfield, the first against Sheffield Wednesday at Hillsborough in January 1967 when he was called off the bench to replace Ian Callaghan in a 1–0 win. After leaving Anfield he made 205 appearances for Aston Villa, skippering them to victory in the 1975 League Cup final, having three years earlier helped them win the Third Division title. He had three other Merseysiders with him at Villa Park – full-back John Gidman, striker Alun Evans (q.v.) and goalkeeper Jimmy Cumbes, ex-Tranmere Rovers. He added over 100 more games to his collection with Peterborough and then, as manager, took FC Valur to the Icelandic League title in 1985, following up by leading Huddersfield into the promotion play-offs in 1992. As a player, Ross made over 400 League and Cup appearances and in 1976 had the distinction of turning out for four different clubs in four months. Former Liverpool manager Bill Shankly once said of Ross: 'He is a sort of liaison man – a buffer wedged between people who take weight off other players . . . A good marker who can be used for a specific purpose.'

ROSS, JAMES DANIEL
Inside-right: 85 apps, 40 goals
Born: Edinburgh, 28 March 1866 – *Died*: 12 June 1902
Career: Edinburgh St Bernard's (1882), Preston North End (amateur, August 1884; professional, September 1885), LIVERPOOL (£75, July 1894), Burnley (March 1897), Manchester City (February 1899 until his death at the age of 36)

Said to have been as 'clever as a monkey', fast, brilliant on the ball with a stunning right-foot shot, Jimmy Ross, with a flamboyant Hercule Poirot-like moustache, was certainly a star performer during the 1880s and 1890s. He helped Preston complete the League and Cup double in 1889 and added a second League championship medal to his collection in 1890, having lost in the final of the FA Cup in 1888. Believed to be the first player to score seven goals in an FA Cup tie, doing so for Preston against Hyde in October 1887 (won 26–0), he was also the first man to hit four goals in a League game, for Preston against Stoke in September 1889. Ross went on to notch up well over 150 goals in all competitions during his ten years at Deepdale, including 85 in 130 First Division games. He was Preston's leading marksman on seven occasions between 1885 and 1894. He continued to find the net on a regular basis with Liverpool, scoring on his debut against Bolton Wanderers and going on to claim 13 goals in his first season and 24 in his second. Amazingly Ross was never capped by Scotland (simply because he played for English clubs) but he did represent Lancashire in county matches, played for the Players v. the Gentlemen and the Football League v. the Scottish League. At Manchester City he played alongside the great Welsh international Billy Meredith who later stated that 'He [Ross] would always be my favourite hero – what he didn't know about football wasn't worth knowing.' Ross's brother, Nicholas John Ross, played for Hearts, Preston North End, Everton and Linfield, while three other relatives were all professional or semi-professional footballers.

ROSS, SIDNEY
Goalkeeper: 23 apps
Born: Liverpool, *circa* 1870 – *Deceased*
Career: LIVERPOOL (August 1892–April 1893)

Local-born goalkeeper Arthur Ross played for the Reds during the 1892–93 season, gaining a Lancashire League winner's medal for his efforts. He conceded 21 goals in his 23 games.

ROWLEY, ANTHONY ARTHUR
Inside-left: 13 apps, 1 goal
Born: Liverpool, 9 May 1933
Career: Florence Melley Boys' Club, LIVERPOOL (professional, May 1951), Wrexham (November 1954), Crewe Alexandra (February 1957), Tranmere Rovers (September 1958), Burscough Rangers (August 1959–May 1961); went into the printing business with another ex-Liverpool player, Doug Rudham (q.v.)

A small, skilful inside-forward, Arthur Rowley's career at Anfield coincided with that of Welsh international Antonio Rowley's (see below). He made just 13 senior outings in six years, the first against Preston North End (home) in August 1952 when he partnered Billy Liddell on the left wing in a 1–1 draw. His League career realised 88 appearances and 15 goals.

ROWLEY, ANTONIO CAMILIO
Inside-right: 61 apps, 38 goals
Born: Porthcawl, Glamorgan, 19 September 1929
Career: Wellington Town (Shropshire), Birmingham City (professional, January 1949), Stourbridge (August 1951), LIVERPOOL (October 1953), Tranmere Rovers (£3,500, March 1958), Bangor City (July 1961), Northwich Victoria (January 1962), Mossley (September 1963–April 1964)

Born of Italian extraction, Tony Rowley failed to make the breakthrough with Birmingham City and spent two years in non-League football, completing his national service before joining Liverpool at the age of 24, having impressed the club's scouting party in a Birmingham Senior Cup tie. He seemed at times to lack the necessary class to make it to the top but he did have the pleasure of scoring a hat-trick on his First Division debut for the Reds against Doncaster Rovers in a Second Division match in August 1954, two of his goals coming in the last four minutes to clinch a 3–2 victory in front of almost 50,000 fans at Anfield. In the absence of Roy Vernon, he was also capped once by Wales against Northern Ireland in 1959, having netted four goals for Tranmere the weekend prior to that international to secure his place! He and his namesake, Arthur Rowley (above), were colleagues together at Prenton Park (1958–59).

RUDDOCK, NEIL
Defender: 146+6 apps, 12 goals
Born: Wandsworth, London, 9 May 1968
Career: Millwall (apprentice, May 1984; professional, March 1986), Tottenham Hotspur (£50,000, April 1986), Millwall (£300,000, June 1988), Southampton (£250,000, February 1989), Tottenham Hotspur (£750,000, July 1992), LIVERPOOL (£2.5m, July 1993), Queens Park Rangers (loan, March 1998), West Ham United (£100,000, July 1998), Crystal Palace (July 2000), Swindon Town (free, player-manager under Director of Football, Roy Evans, August 2001, quit as manager, December 2001, retired as a player, March 2003); later worked in the media and also acted as team captain against Ally McCoist's trio on the popular BBC TV programme *A Question of Sport*

John Aldridge, champion marksman whose career realised over 400 goals at senior level

Stig-Inge Bjornebye, Norwegian international full-back who later played for Blackburn Rovers

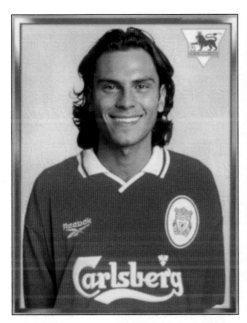

Patrik Berger, Czech Republic attacking midfielder who joined Liverpool after Euro '96

Peter Beardsley, another player who served with both Everton and Liverpool, scored 59 goals in 175 appearances for the Reds

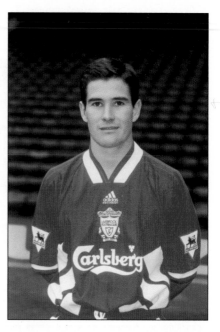

John Barnes moved to Anfield from Watford in 1987 and 12 months later was voted PFA Footballer of the Year as Liverpool won the League title

Nigel Clough, son of the late Brian, who, like his father, was a very talented centre-forward

Polish international goalkeeper Jerzy Dudek was the hero of Liverpool's 2005 European Champions League final win over AC Milan, saving two spot-kicks in the penalty shoot-out

Kenny Dalglish, the first player-manager in Liverpool's history and the first man to lead the Reds to the FA Cup and League double

Robbie Fowler, another of Liverpool's great strikers, netted 170 goals in 330 games for the club before leaving in 2001, returning five years later

Alan Hansen, brilliant Scottish international defender who starred in 620 first-class games for Liverpool over a period of 13 years

Swiss international defender Stephane Henchoz made over 200 appearances in six years for Liverpool

Roger Hunt, a member of England's 1966 World Cup-winning side, scored 286 goals in almost 500 senior appearances for Liverpool

Rob Jones, a full-back signed from Crewe Alexandra, was forced to retire through injury at the age of 27

Kevin Keegan, a star performer in Liverpool's ranks for six years, scored 100 goals in 323 competitive games for the club

The versatile Ray Kennedy was the
last signing made by Liverpool
manager Bill Shankly before
he retired in 1974

Jan Molby scored a hat-trick of penalties for
Liverpool against Coventry City in a League
Cup-tie in November 1986

Chris Lawler was Liverpool's right-back for
almost a decade, being an ever-present in
the side four seasons running and six times
in all between 1966 and 1973

Steve McManaman left Anfield for Real Madrid
in 1999 after making 360 appearances
for the Reds

Scottish international Steve Nicol served Liverpool for over 13 years, making 483 senior appearances in defence and midfield

Michael Owen, like McManaman before him, left Anfield for Real Madrid after scoring 158 goals in 307 appearances for Liverpool

Neil 'Razor' Ruddock played at the heart of Liverpool's defence from 1993 to 1998, making over 150 appearances

Liverpool's greatest-ever marksman, Welsh international Ian Rush netted 346 goals in 659 outings in his two spells at Anfield

Midfielder Jamie Redknapp played in more than 300 games in his 11 injury-interrupted years at Anfield

Steve Staunton is the Republic of Ireland's most capped player, appearing in 102 full internationals between 1989 and 2002

Paul Stewart went out on loan to four different clubs as a Liverpool player and during his career scored over 150 goals in 650 appearances

Peter Thompson, one of the finest wingers of his day, made over 400 appearances for Liverpool following his transfer from Preston North End in 1963

England international defender Phil Thompson was a registered player with Liverpool for 15 years and later was coach, assistant manager and caretaker manager at Anfield

Barry Venison is the youngest player ever to captain a team at Wembley, leading Sunderland against Norwich City in the 1985 League Cup final. He joined Liverpool a year later

Ronnie Whelan spent 15 years at Anfield, making 493 appearances and gaining 45 caps for the Republic of Ireland

Midfielder Nigel Spackman had two spells with Chelsea and also played for Glasgow Rangers and Queens Park Rangers

During an excellent career, stopper centre-half Neil 'Razor' Ruddock appeared in 466 League and Cup games and scored 44 goals. He also gained one full, one 'B' and four under-21 caps for England and represented his country at youth team level. As tough as steel and utterly reliable at the heart of the defence, he starred in over 150 first-team matches for Liverpool, collecting a League Cup winner's medal in 1995 when he partnered Phil Babb at the back in a 2–1 win over Bolton Wanderers. Signed by manager Roy Evans, whom he later worked under at Swindon, Ruddock made his Premiership debut for the Reds against Sheffield Wednesday at Anfield in August 1993 (alongside Mark Wright) and bagged his first goal for the club in the fourth-round League Cup replay against Wimbledon four months later, which Liverpool lost on penalties.

RUDHAM, KENNETH ROBERT

Goalkeeper: 66 apps
Born: Johannesburg, South Africa, 3 May 1926 – *Died*: Johannesburg, 13 August 1991
Career: Johannesburg Rangers (1945), LIVERPOOL (amateur, October 1954; professional, August 1955), Johannesburg Ramblers (May 1960, retired, May 1963); returned to England and went into partnership in the printing business with another ex-Liverpool player, Arthur Rowley (q.v.)

Capped by South Africa as an amateur, goalkeeper 'Doug' Rudham was so impressive on a tour to Great Britain with his country's FA party in 1954 that he was signed by Liverpool – just as his fellow countrymen Gordon Hodgson and Arthur Riley had been some 30 years earlier. He made over 40 of his 66 appearances for Liverpool over a period of 12 months between November 1954 and November 1955. His debut was at home to Nottingham Forest (won 1–0) and after that he shared the first-team duties with Dave Underwood before acting as deputy to Scotsmen Tommy Younger and Bert Slater, returning home in 1960. He was a fine shot-stopper, brave, with a good, clean kick.

RUSH, IAN JAMES

Striker: 629+30 apps, 346 goals
Born: St Asaph, North Wales, 20 October 1961
Career: Deeside Primary Schools XI, Flint Comprehensive School, Flintshire under-19s, Chester (apprentice, April 1978; professional, September 1979), LIVERPOOL (£300,000, May 1980), Juventus (£3.2m, July 1986), LIVERPOOL (loan, July 1986–May 1987, signed for £2.8m, August 1988), Leeds United (free, May 1996), Newcastle United (free, August 1997), Sheffield United (loan, February–March 1998), Wrexham (free, August 1998), Sydney Olympic/Australia (June 1999, retired, May 2000), Chester City (manager, August 2004–May 2005); LIVERPOOL (Academy coach); also worked in the media; acted as advisory-coach to Northwich Victoria (2006)

One of the great goalscorers in the history of Liverpool Football Club and, indeed, one of the finest marksmen in world soccer during the 1980s/early '90s, Ian Rush netted some 425 goals at club and international level during his 22 years in the game (1978–2000) including 346 for the Reds (in 659 games out of a career total of 900). He was only 18 when he joined Liverpool for what was to prove a bargain fee of just £300,000 in 1980 (signed by Bob Paisley). Surprisingly, however, during his early days at Anfield he struggled to find the net for the second XI and at one point there were a few rumblings within the camp that he might make an early departure. But he stuck in there, improved his game significantly and started to score on a regular basis. He hit 30 senior goals in 1981–82, netted 31 the following season (including an impressive four-timer in a 5–0 League win over Everton at Goodison Park and a treble v. Coventry City a week later) and when he weighed in with 48 in 1983–84, he equalled the club's individual scoring record with 5 in one game against Luton Town as he continued to torment defenders (and goalkeepers). After that the goals continued to come thick and fast, from all angles, and at the same time he started to pile up his tallies of team medals and international caps. Standing 6ft 2in. tall and weighing 12st. 6lb, he was relatively slim, supremely mobile and was blessed with speed and awareness in and around the penalty area – but above all was a deadly finisher! He seemed to score goals out of nothing . . . some were welcome tap-ins, a few smart and well-directed headers and a lot were cracking drives, mainly fired home with his trusty right foot. He made the first of his 73 senior appearances for Wales soon after joining Liverpool, lining up against Scotland in May 1980. In fact, his total number of caps was a Welsh record for an outfield player which he shared with another ex-Liverpool star, Dean Saunders (q.v.) and Peter Nicholas until Gary Speed gained his 74th in 2004. Rush then had to wait until December of that same year before making his League debut for the Reds against Ipswich Town at Portman Road when he wore the number 7 shirt in a 1–1 draw.

During the 1980s he was unstoppable in terms of finding the back of the net – becoming the first British footballer to win Europe's 'Golden Boot' award in 1983–84 – and there's no doubt that his goals helped Liverpool win many prizes. In all, Rush collected winners' medals for four First Division triumphs (1982, 1983, 1984 and 1986), four successive League Cup final wins (1981, 1982, 1983 and 1984), successes in the FA Charity Shield, European Cup and FA Cup (in 1982, 1984 and 1986 respectively) and victory in the Screen Sport Super Cup (1986). In the summer of 1988 he moved to Italy for a then British record fee and although he didn't play in Serie 'A' for a year, remaining at Anfield on loan as part of the deal, when he finally pulled on the famous black and white striped shirt of Juventus, he became an instant hit with the supporters, more so after scoring four times in a cup tie against Pescara.

On the eve of the 1988–89 season, Liverpool boss Kenny Dalglish surprised the soccer world by bringing Rush back to Anfield for a British record fee. The Welshman, who got a hero's welcome on his return, took a while to readjust to life in England because of illness and niggling injuries. He eventually participated in 32 games (all competitions) and proved his worth by scoring some important goals (as always) including 2 in the 1989 FA Cup final against Everton after coming on as a substitute which earned him a second winner's medal in this competition. A third Cup triumph followed in 1992, while he also captured a fifth League championship medal (1990) and added another League Cup winner's prize to his collection in 1995 as well as having further success in the FA Charity Shield of 1989. Rush was voted both the PFA and FWA 'Player of the Year' in 1984.

Rush fired in his 300th competitive goal for Liverpool in August 1993 (against QPR) and then followed up ten days later with his 200th strike in League action for the Reds against his future club, Leeds United, leaving Anfield for Elland Road after a tedious cartilage injury had cost him his place in the starting line-up.

Succeeded by his former Anfield teammate Mark Wright as manager of Chester City in 2004, Rush was one of ten children – seven of them boys. The son of a former steelworker, he actually supported Everton as a youngster, attending Goodison Park as often as he could. He actually had a preference to join Manchester City (from Chester) but chose Liverpool instead – a good choice indeed.

RUSSELL, COLIN
Forward: 0+1 app.
Born: Liverpool, 21 January 1961
Career: Merseyside junior football, LIVERPOOL (apprentice, April 1976; professional, April 1978), Huddersfield Town (£15,000, September 1982), Stoke City (loan, March–May 1984), AFC Bournemouth (£10,000, August 1984), Doncaster Rovers (£7,000, July 1986), Scarborough (loan, October 1987, signed permanently, free, November 1987), Wigan Athletic (free, July 1988), Colne Dynamos (May 1989), Bangor City/Wales (July 1991), Morecambe (August 1992), Droylsden (1993), Warrington Town (season 1994–95)

Reserve forward Colin Russell's only first-team appearance for Liverpool was as a second-half substitute for Howard Gayle against Sunderland (home) in May 1981. His career eventually realised a total of 210 League appearances (49 goals). He had his best spells with Huddersfield and Bournemouth, having over 70 senior outings for each club.

ST JOHN, IAN
Inside-/centre-forward: 421+5 apps, 118 goals
Born: Motherwell, 7 June 1938
Career: Central School (Motherwell), Motherwell Bridge Works FC, Douglas Water Thistle, Motherwell (professional, August 1956), LIVERPOOL (£37,500, May 1961), South African football (briefly in 1971), Coventry City (August 1971, assistant manager, December 1971–March 1972), Tranmere Rovers (player, October 1972), Motherwell (manager, July 1973–September 1974), Portsmouth (manager, September 1974, sacked May 1977), Sheffield Wednesday (coach, July 1978–May 1979); became deeply involved with TV, linked up with Jimmy Greaves to form a great double-act (the *Saint and Greavsie* show) on London Weekend; did other media work

Ian St John struck the quickest hat-trick ever recorded in Scottish football, for

Motherwell against Hibernian on 15 August 1959, his three goals coming in the space of 150 seconds. A shade on the short side for a forward, he was nevertheless a 'Spring-heeled Jack', excellent in the air, reaching unbelievable heights when jumping for the ball. He was also decisive on the ground and as well as scoring plenty of goals he created opportunities for his colleagues with some deft touches and superb lay-offs. Brave and aggressive when he had to be, St John was not the quickest of players but he was a smart thinker who certainly had a wonderful career. He gained 21 full caps for Scotland between 1959 and 1963 (it would have been more had he not had a dust-up with the selectors in the mid-'60s), represented the Scottish League on four occasions, played twice for his country's under-23 side and as a Liverpool player won the Second Division title (1962), two First Division championships (1964 and 1966) and the FA Cup (1965) when he stooped to net the crucial winning header in extra-time v. Leeds United. He was in the Reds side that lost in the final of the European Cup-Winners' Cup in 1966. A record signing, he made the first of his 426 senior appearances for Liverpool against Bristol Rovers at Eastville in August 1961, having netted a hat-trick against Everton in the Liverpool Senior Cup shortly after moving to Anfield. Having taken over the centre-forward position from Dave Hickson, he netted his first 2 goals in a 4–1 win at Sunderland a fortnight later and ended that season with 22 to his name, second in the charts behind Roger Hunt who claimed 42. In fact, St John and Hunt as well as Jimmy Melia and Geoff Strong (with others) were excellent together in the Liverpool attack. Teaming up with two former Liverpool stars, Ron Yeats (q.v.) and Tommy Lawrence (q.v.), at Tranmere, his playing career ended after he suffered a fractured leg . . . although he recovered sufficiently well to play in his own testimonial match in 1973 when almost 30,000 fans at Anfield saw the Reds beat Chelsea 4–2, St John scoring twice. St John's name will always be emblazoned in Liverpool's Hall of Soccer Fame, ranking alongside Elisha Scott, Billy Liddell, Ian Rush and others.

Unfortunately as a manager St John didn't have much success. He was in charge of Portsmouth when the club were £300,000 in debt and, in fact, was sacked by Pompey just after the team had escaped relegation to the Third Division.

SALISBURY, WILLIAM
Centre-forward: 17 apps, 3 goals
Born: Glasgow, 23 February 1899 – *Died*: 12 January 1965
Career: St Anthony's FC (Glasgow), Partick Thistle (August 1919), LIVERPOOL (£1,200, October 1928), Bangor/Northern Ireland (August 1929–May 1931), Shelbourne/Ireland (seasons 1931–33)

A tall, long-legged centre-forward, Bill Salisbury started his career on the left wing before switching to centre-forward with Partick Thistle with whom he did exceedingly well, appearing in almost 300 first-team matches (256 in the Scottish League) and scoring more than 50 goals. He won the domestic Cup with Partick in 1921 but was never able to reproduce the form he had shown north of the border with Liverpool and spent only 10 months at Anfield before joining the Irish League club Bangor. The first of his 16 outings for the Reds was against Arsenal at Highbury in October 1928 when he set up 2 of his side's goals in a thrilling 4–4 draw. He was the fourth different player to lead Liverpool's attack that season.

SAMBROOK, JOHN HENRY
Centre-forward: 2 apps
Born: Wednesfield near Wolverhampton, 10 March 1899 – *Died*: Heathtown, Wolverhampton, 30 December 1973
Career: Willenhall Town (1917), Wolverhampton Wanderers (professional, August 1919), LIVERPOOL (December 1922), Stockport County (August 1923), Southport (1924–May 1926); later with Willenhall Swift and C and L Hills FC (retired 1937)
Jack Sambrook was a speedy and thoughtful centre-forward who netted 7 times in 21 games for Wolves before joining Liverpool as cover for 'Tosh' Johnson. He deputised in the front-line in successive League games against Chelsea around the turn of the year (1922) but after that he weaved away in the reserves before moving to Stockport, later switching to Southport for whom he claimed 31 goals in 65 League games. His brother, Chris Sambrook, played for West Bromwich Albion, Coventry City and Nuneaton Town (1919–24), while his son, Ray Sambrook, played for Coventry City, Manchester City, Doncaster Rovers and Crewe Alexandra between 1953 and 1963.

SATTERTHWAITE, CHARLES OLIVER
Forward: 46 apps, 12 goals
Born: Cockermouth, Cumbria, April 1877 – *Died*: Workington, 25 May 1948
Career: Black Diamond FC (1894), Workington Town (1895), Bury (professional, July 1895), Burton Swifts (August 1897), LIVERPOOL (November 1899), New Brompton (June 1902), West Ham United (1903), Woolwich Arsenal (April 1904, retired, May 1910); became a licensee in Workington
Charlie Satterthwaite was a big, strong inside- or wing-forward who packed a thunderous left-foot shot and during his career scored some superb goals, many from outside the penalty area. He made his League debut for Bury in 1895 and had a handful of games for Burton before joining Liverpool, for whom he played his first game in December 1899 away at Nottingham Forest when he occupied the outside-right position in the absence of Jack Cox. He was switched to the inside after four outings and ended the season as partner to Jack Robertson on the left wing. In 1900–01 he scored 5 goals in 22 games as the Reds won the League title. He moved on after Andy McGuigan, Sam Raybould and John Walker had taken charge of the three central forward positions.

Satterthwaite, who was an England trialist in his first season with Arsenal, was the scorer of the Gunners' first ever goal in top flight football v. Wolves in September 1904 (won 2–0). He also let fly with a 25-yard drive for the Londoners against Notts County; the ball bent the crossbar and flattened the goalkeeper as it bounced down onto his head before finding its way over the line.

He netted 48 goals in 141 games for Arsenal before retiring at the age of 33. His younger brother, Joseph Norman Satterthwaite, born in 1885, also played for Woolwich Arsenal, Workington Town and Grimsby Town.

SAUL, PERCY

Full-back: 83 apps, 2 goals
Born: Rotherham, 1881 – *Died*: Sheffield, *circa* 1960
Career: Thornhill (Sheffield), Gainsborough Trinity (professional, May 1901), Plymouth Argyle (1904), LIVERPOOL (May 1906), Coventry City (August 1909), Rotherham Town (July 1911), Rotherham County (1912); did not play after WW1

After more than 70 appearances for Gainsborough and 36 for Plymouth, Percy Saul took over from Alf West at right-back in Liverpool's League side but in his second season at Anfield he was switched to the left where he performed with zest and commitment. A strong, powerful defender, he made his debut for the Reds against Birmingham in September 1906 and had his last outing for the club against Manchester United at Anfield in January 1909. With four other worthy full-backs at the club in Tom Chorlton, Bob Crawford, Billy Dunlop and West, Saul was allowed to move to Coventry. His brother, Ernest Saul, played for Sheffield United (1900–01).

SAUNDERS, DEAN

Striker: 62 apps, 26 goals
Born: Swansea, 21 June 1964
Career: Gwyrosydd and Penlan Schools (Swansea), Swansea Schools, Swansea City (apprentice, July 1980; professional, June 1982), Cardiff City (loan, March 1985), Brighton and Hove Albion (free, August 1985), Oxford United (£60,000, March 1987), Derby County (£1m, October 1988), LIVERPOOL (£2.9m, July 1991), Aston Villa (£2.3m, September 1992), Galatasaray/Turkey (£2.35m, July 1995), Nottingham Forest (£1.5m, July 1996), Sheffield United (free, December 1977), Benfica/Portugal (£500,000, December 1998), Bradford City (free, August 1999, retired, June 2001), Blackburn Rovers (coach, July 2001), Newcastle United (coach, September 2004)

The son of Roy Saunders (below), Dean Saunders was one of the game's most prolific marksmen. After having both cartilages removed from his left knee as an 18 year old he scored his first League goal for Swansea City against Oldham Athletic in March 1984 and his last some 16 years later for Bradford City against Arsenal in February 2000. A positive, all-action, unselfish striker who simply knew where the net was, he retired with a superb record to his credit of 806 senior appearances and 277 goals – and at one time, along with Ian Rush and Peter Nicholas, he was Wales' most capped outfield player with a total of 73, later surpassed by Gary Speed in 2004.

Surprisingly in a wonderful career, during which he consulted his father on many occasions, he gained only two club medals – helping Liverpool win the FA Cup in 1992 and Aston Villa lift the League Cup in 1994 when he scored twice in the final against Manchester United. His best performances on the whole came with Derby (57 goals in 131 outings) and also with Villa (49 goals in 144 games). Wherever he played the fans loved him (to a certain degree). He scored a dramatic goal just 16 seconds from the end of a League game against Luton Town in May 1987 to save Oxford United from relegation and during his only full season at Anfield he certainly produced the goods, top-scoring with 23 goals, 9 coming in the UEFA Cup, including a four-timer in a 6–1 home win over Kuusysi Lahti and a hat-trick in the same competition against Swarovski Tirol. He made his debut for the Reds against Oldham Athletic in August 1991 and struck his first goal for the club against QPR later that month. He was coach under ex-Liverpool player Graeme Souness at both Ewood Park and St James' Park. Saunders was also a very good club cricketer.

In 1994, a case began at the High Court (London) involving defender Paul Elliott (Chelsea) and Saunders (Aston Villa). It revolved around a tackle by Saunders (playing for Liverpool) on Elliott that effectively ended the latter's playing career. Elliott lost the case and was faced with a legal bill of £500,000.

SAUNDERS, ROY

Half-back: 144 apps, 1 goal
Born: Salford, 4 September 1930
Career: Hull City (amateur, April 1946), LIVERPOOL (professional, May
    1948), Swansea Town (£4,000, player-exchange deal involving Des Palmer,
    March 1959, retired, May 1963, served club as coach and assistant trainer);
    Ammanford FC (manager, July 1968–April 1971), Swansea Town (trainer,
    seasons 1971–74, coach, seasons 1975–77)

An England youth international, Roy Saunders was a very capable, hard-working footballer who could play in all three half-back positions, preferring the right. He had the redoubtable Phil Taylor, Bill Jones, Bob Paisley and also Geoff Twentyman to contend with for first-team football at Anfield but he battled on well and made almost 150 senior appearances for the Reds in 11 years before moving to Swansea with whom he won the Welsh Cup in 1961 and played in the European Cup-Winners' Cup the following year. His League debut for Liverpool was at centre-half against Middlesbrough in February 1953 when he came in for Bill Jones in a 3–2 win at Ayresome Park. He occupied both wing-half positions later that season and had his best campaign in 1955–56 when he appeared in 42 senior matches. He played in over 100 games for Swansea.

SAVAGE, ROBERT EDWARD

Inside-left/right-half: 105 apps, 2 goals
Born: Louth, Lincolnshire, February 1912 – *Died*: Wallasey, Cheshire, 30
    January 1964
Career: Louth Grammar School, Stewton FC (Lincolnshire), Lincoln City
    (October 1928; professional, May 1929), LIVERPOOL (May 1931),
    Manchester United (December 1937), Wrexham (November 1938); guest for
    Carlisle United, Chelsea, Fulham, Millwall, Southport, West Ham United
    and York City during WW2; retired May 1945; coached in Holland (briefly),

South Liverpool (manager, during the 1950s); entered the motor trade before taking over as licensee of the Primrose Hotel, Wallasey, 1960 until his death Tall, handsome and well built, Ted Savage made his League debut for Lincoln City at the age of 17. Fast, resourceful and a good judge in defence or attack, he amassed almost 100 appearances for the Imps (and was an ever-present in 1930–31) before transferring to Liverpool for whom he scored twice in his first game against Grimsby Town at Anfield in September 1931 (won 4–0). He moved to wing-half later that season and had his best spell with the Reds in the mid-1930s before transferring to Old Trafford. He helped United win promotion from the Second Division in his first season. During WW2, Savage played for the Eastern Command v. the London Command in April 1942. As well as playing football, Savage also excelled at swimming and was a competent track runner with the Grimsby Harriers AC.

SCALES, JOHN ROBERT
Defender: 93+1 apps, 4 goals
Born: Harrogate, Yorkshire, 4 July 1966
Career: Leeds United (apprentice, July 1982), Bristol Rovers (free, July 1985), Wimbledon (£70,000, July 1987), LIVERPOOL (£3.5m, September 1994), Tottenham Hotspur (£2.6m, December 1996), Ipswich Town (free, July 2000, retired on leaving the club by mutual consent, April 2001); later gained coaching qualifications and worked as a match summariser on Sky Sport and BBC TV; also involved in his own business
Capped twice by England 'B' team and on three occasions at senior level, defender John Scales failed to get into Leeds United's first XI but made 85 appearances for Bristol Rovers and 288 for Wimbledon, with whom he gained an FA Cup winner's medal (1988). He spent a little over two years at Anfield, helping Liverpool win the League Cup in 1995 while having 94 senior outings, all in defence and occupying four different positions. Well built and mobile with two good feet, at his best he had pace, was powerful in the air and proved dangerous at set-pieces. His sheer presence on the field lifted the team and he certainly gave the Reds' supporters value for money. He made his debut for Liverpool against West Ham United in September 1994 and after leaving the club he had a further 37 games with Spurs, adding a second League Cup winner's medal to his collection in 1999 while at the same time passing the personal milestone of 400 League and Premiership appearances.

SCOTT, ALAN
Centre-forward: 4 apps, 2 goals
Born: Birkenhead, June 1910 – *Deceased*
Career: Liverpool Pemblians, LIVERPOOL (professional, April 1929), Swindon Town (June 1932), Gillingham (June 1933–May 1935), London Paper Mills FC (until outbreak of WW2)
Alan Scott made his League debut for Liverpool against Middlesbrough in August 1929 while still a teenager. He scored his first goal for the club in his third game 16 months later to help earn a point at Blackburn Rovers (3–3) and

his only other goal came at Old Trafford in a 4–1 defeat by Manchester United. Reserve to Jim Smith and David Wright at Anfield, he was certainly a useful performer who did reasonably well with Swindon and Gillingham, netting 11 times in 25 games for the latter club.

SCOTT, ELISHA
Goalkeeper: 468 apps
Born: Belfast, Ulster, 24 August 1894 – *Died*: Belfast, 16 May 1959
Career: Belfast Boys Brigade (1909), Linfield (August 1911), Broadway United/Belfast (May 1912), LIVERPOOL (professional, November 1912); guest for Belfast Celtic during WW1 (1917–19); returned to Anfield; Belfast Celtic (as player-manager, June 1934, retired as a player, May 1936, continued as manager until May 1949)

One of the greatest goalkeepers of all time, certainly as far as Liverpool and Northern Ireland were concerned, Elisha Scott – a legend in his own lifetime – was lithe, brave and acrobatic with cat-like reflexes, confident within his own area and above all, very consistent, amassing almost 470 appearances for the Reds during his near 22-year association with the club. Besides his first-class outings he also played in 15 WW1 games and gained the first of his 31 international caps (4 for Ireland, 27 for Northern Ireland) collecting his first in 1920 and his last in 1936 at the age of 41.

An article in a local Liverpool newspaper stated that Scott . . . 'Had the eye of an eagle, the swift movement of a panther when flinging himself at a shot and the clutch of a vice when gripping the ball.' He actually had a fidgety style as he patrolled his six-yard area, often jumping about when play was confined to the other end of the field. Yet this was no nervous trait. Scott confessed in later years that moving about continuously kept his reflexes in sharp readiness for any attack launched upon him. The Anfield faithful adored Scott and during a game against Blackburn Rovers, after he had pulled off a brilliant save, a delighted spectator ran onto the pitch and kissed him. He also starred for his country, producing an immaculate display of goalkeeping against Scotland at Firhill Park in February 1928 when the Irish won 1–0 to claim their first victory over the Scots for 18 years, and represented the Irish League.

Scott's first game for Liverpool was against Newcastle United (away) in January 1913, keeping a clean sheet in a 0–0 draw. He established himself in the side during the 1914–15 campaign but it wasn't until 1920–21 that he once again claimed the number one position. Thereafter, injuries and international calls apart, he was first choice for most of the time, being an ever-present in 1922–23 and 1923–24 and gaining two League championship winner's medals (1922 and 1923). As a guest, Scott gained both runners-up and winner's medals with Belfast Celtic in the Irish Cup finals of 1917 and 1918. He later spent a further 15 years with that club until Celtic folded in 1949. His brother, Billy Scott, played for Everton and Northern Ireland and appeared as a guest for Liverpool during WW1. Early in 1913, Newcastle United had a bid of £1,000 turned down by Liverpool boss Tom Watson and 11 years later, in 1934, Everton came in with an offer of £250 for his services. Liverpool again refused to sell . . . but only after a flood of letters from supporters had said 'don't sell'. In fact, Scott had been turned away from Goodison Park as a 17 year old, the Blues feeling that he was too young for them. What a mistake! Always a miser with his money (he was known as 'Careful Leese'), Scott never wasted a penny and he even preferred walking to the ferry en route to his Wirral home rather than paying for a tram ticket.

SCOTT, JAMES EDGAR
Utility: 10 apps
Born: Stevenston, Ayrshire, Scotland, April 1892 – *Died*: USA, *circa* 1945
Career: Ardeer Thistle (1908), LIVERPOOL (professional, May 1911), Dumbarton (October 1912), Third Lanark (1913), New York Giants/USA (1914); remained in the USA after WW1
Jim Scott was 19 years of age when he joined Liverpool, having been watched by several leading clubs north of the border prior to that. He made the first of his ten senior appearances for the Reds against Bradford City (away) in April 1912 when he deputised at inside-right for McDonald in a 2–0 victory. His second game was at inside-left, the next two at centre-half and his last four at left-half – such was his versatility.

SCOTT, THOMAS
Forward: 18 apps, 4 goals
Born: Newcastle-upon-Tyne, 6 April 1904 – *Died*: Bootle, 24 December 1979
Career: Swifts FC/Tyneside (August 1919), Pandon Temperance FC (1921), Sunderland (professional, December 1922), Darlington (May 1924), LIVERPOOL (February 1925), Bristol City (October 1928), Preston North End (June 1930), Norwich City (June 1932), Exeter City (October 1934), Hartlepools United (November 1936–May 1937), Bangor City (briefly, during season 1937–38); did not play during or after WW2; became a licensee in Liverpool and was a regular spectator at Anfield
The versatile Tom Scott appeared in four different positions in Liverpool's forward-line during his three and a half years at Anfield. He started off on the left wing (making his debut there against his future club, Preston North End, in March 1925), appeared at centre-forward and inside-left during the next season and starred at inside-right after that. He scored over 80 goals in 220 senior games including 76 in his 204 League outings. He had his best spells with Norwich (26 goals in 55 starts) and Exeter (18 in 61). He was said to have been the brains of the Norwich attack – the best footballer the Canaries had seen for 20 years. Scott's father was Liverpool's scout in the north-east of England.

SEAGRAVES, MARK
Defender: 2 apps
Born: Bootle, 22 October 1966
Career: LIVERPOOL (apprentice, April 1982; professional, November 1983), Norwich City (loan, November–December 1986), Manchester City (£100,000, September 1987), Bolton Wanderers (£100,000, September

1990), Swindon Town (£300,000, 1995), Barrow (June 1998)
An England schoolboy and youth international defender, Mark Seagraves made just two senior appearances for Liverpool, both in February 1986, the first against QPR at Loftus Road in the League Cup semi-final first leg and the second v. York City (away) in a fifth-round FA Cup tie. Each time he deputised for Gary Gillespie and wore the number 11 shirt. Released after spending five years at Anfield, during which time he was a permanent reserve, Seagraves went on to make 50 appearances for Manchester City, 195 for Bolton and 79 for Swindon, helping the latter club win the Second Division championship in 1996.

SEALEY, ARTHUR JOHN
Inside-right: 1 app, 1 goal
Born: Wallasey, 27 December 1945
Career: Warrington Town, LIVERPOOL (professional, December 1963), Chester (June 1966), Wigan Athletic (April 1968–May 1970)
Reserve forward John Sealey had the pleasure of scoring in his only First Division outing for Liverpool against Wolves at Molineux in April 1965 when changes were made ahead of the FA Cup final v. Leeds United. He deputised for Roger Hunt in a 3–1 win. He hardly figured at all with Chester (4 games) before entering non-League football with Wigan.

SHAFTO, JOHN
Centre-forward: 20 apps, 7 goals
Born: Humshaugh, Northumberland, 8 November 1918 – *Died*: 1978
Career: Hexham FC (1934), LIVERPOOL (professional, November 1936); served in the Army and played as a guest for Brighton and Hove Albion and Bradford City during WW2; did not feature after 1946
Recruited to Anfield as a sturdy 18 year old, John Shafto did exceedingly well in the second XI before making the first of his 20 senior appearances against Leicester City in October 1937 when he was named at centre-forward in the absence of Jack Balmer and Fred Howe, Arthur Smith having been given an outing without success. He scored 6 League goals in 13 games that season but was restricted to just 4 in the next campaign before WW2 severely disrupted what looked like being a promising career. He netted three times in nine appearances for the Reds during the hostilities.

SHANNON, LESLIE
Centre-forward/wing-half: 11 apps, 1 goal
Born: Liverpool, 12 March 1926
Career: Merseyside junior football, LIVERPOOL (amateur, August 1943; professional, November 1944), Burnley (£6,150, November 1949), Everton (youth team coach, August 1959), Arsenal (reserve coach, July 1962, chief scout and assistant manager, May 1963–May 1966), Bury (manager, July 1966–May 1967, re-engaged two months later), Blackpool (manager, May 1969–October 1970), PAOK Salonika/Cyprus (trainer-coach, January

1971–April 1974), Irakalis/Greece (manager), Olympiakos Piraeus/Greece (manager, seasons 1976–78), returned to live in Liverpool and was an adviser for the Channel 4 series *The Manageress* (early 1990s); Luton Town (coach, briefly)

One can say that Les Shannon was a player Liverpool allowed to escape ... after leaving Anfield he spent 10 years with Burnley, for whom he scored 41 goals in 282 senior appearances, and gained three England 'B' caps. Auburn-haired, he started out as a centre-forward but was switched to wing-half because it was thought he was too lightweight. He developed into a strong and determined tackler and was annoyed not to gain a regular place in the first team at Anfield, eventually asking for, and being granted, a transfer. The first of his 11 games for the Reds was against Manchester City (home) in April 1948 when he led the line in place of Albert Stubbins. He became a qualified FA coach when based at Turf Moor. Then, as a manager he guided Bury to promotion from the Third Division in 1968, also achieving promotion with Blackpool, taking the Seasiders into the top flight in 1970 having succeeded former England centre-forward Stan Mortensen in the hot seat at Bloomfield Road.

SHEARS, ALBERT EDWARD
Half-back: 16 apps
Born: Newcastle-upon-Tyne, 12 May 1900 – *Died*: Lancashire, 1954
Career: Spen Black and White, Preston North End (professional, August 1921), Doncaster Rovers (September 1923), Aberaman (February 1924), LIVERPOOL (August 1924), Tranmere Rovers (May 1930), Wigan Athletic (July 1931), Barnsley (trial, December 1931, signed January 1932), Aldershot (May 1932), Morecambe (April 1933–May 1935)

Albert Shears didn't make much headway at Deepdale but was leading scorer for Preston's reserve side in 1921–22 (28 goals) and 1922–23 (20). Failing to impress at Doncaster, he then drifted into non-League football where he was switched to half-back before returning with Liverpool at the age of 24. Fast and direct with a strong right-foot shot, he was given 16 outings by the Reds, the first against Bury (away) in April 1926 when he deputised for Bill Cockburn at centre-half in a 1–0 win. He made 27 League appearances for Tranmere after leaving Anfield but achieved nothing elsewhere.

SHEEDY, KEVIN MARK
Midfield: 3+2 apps, 2 goals
Born: Builth Wells, 21 October 1959
Career: Hereford Lads' Club, Hereford United (apprentice, April 1975; professional, October 1976), LIVERPOOL (£80,000, July 1978), Everton (£100,000, August 1982), Newcastle United (free, March 1992), Blackpool (July 1993–May 1995), Blackburn Rovers (assistant coach, August 1995), Tranmere Rovers (assistant coach, July 1996), Hartlepool United (assistant coach, season 2002–03)

After leaving Anfield for near-neighbours Everton in 1982, Kevin Sheedy added a further 426 senior appearances to his career total and netted another 104 goals.

He won two First Division championships (1985 and 1987), the European Cup-Winners' Cup (1985), two FA Charity Shields (1984 and 1987) and gained one under-21 and 45 full caps for the Republic of Ireland. Then, after moving to Kevin Keegan's Newcastle, he helped them gain promotion to the Premiership as First Division Champions (old Second Division) in 1993. He developed into one of the finest left-sided midfield players on the European circuit – all this after having a rather frustrating time with Liverpool for whom he made his debut on St Valentine's Day, February 1981. Another player who did superbly well after being allowed to leave Anfield for practically nothing! Indeed, he was the first name to go on the team-sheet at Goodison Park when fit.

SHELDON, JOHN
Outside-right: 147 apps, 20 goals
Born: Clay Cross near Chesterfield, 11 February 1888 – *Died*: Manchester, 19 March 1941
Career: Clay Cross Boys' Club (1904), Nuneaton (1906), Manchester United (professional, November 1909), LIVERPOOL (November 1913, retired, injured, May 1922)
Jackie Sheldon was only 5ft 6½in. tall and 10st. 6lb in weight – fairly small and lightweight for an elusive winger who seemed to enjoy his encounters with the tough defenders who marked him. Owing to a certain Billy Meredith, he had limited opportunities at Old Trafford, scoring once in 26 games for Manchester United before transferring to Liverpool. Recruited to replace the ageing Arthur Goddard, he made his debut for the Reds against Tottenham Hotspur in November 1913 and at the end of his first season at Anfield appeared in the FA Cup final defeat by Burnley – the first time in the competition's history that two teams from Lancashire were involved. Unfortunately the following season Sheldon was one of several players who were involved in a match-fixing scandal which surrounded the 1915 Good Friday League clash between the Reds and his former club, Manchester United, who were on the brink of relegation from the top Division. Sheldon, in fact, failed to convert a penalty awarded to Liverpool and the game ended in a 2–0 win for United. Tom Fairfoul, Tommy Miller and Bob Pursell (all q.v.) were the other Liverpool players involved. Sheldon's suspension was lifted in time for him to continue playing after WW1.

SHEPHERD, JOHN WILLIAM
Right-back: 57 apps
Born: Liverpool, 25 September 1920
Career: Elm Park FC (Liverpool), LIVERPOOL (professional, December 1945), Wigan Athletic (June 1952)
A regular in the Liverpool defence during the 1948–49 season when he missed only one League game, Bill Shepherd had to work hard at his game to get further recognition in the senior side. But he battled on gamely and remained loyal to the Reds until the summer of 1952 when he joined Wigan Athletic. The first of his 57 first-class outings for the club came in August 1948 when he partnered Ray Lambert at full-back in a 2–1 League defeat at Villa Park. His

brother, Arthur Shepherd, scored 11 goals in 8 WW2 games for Liverpool. He later joined New Brighton.

SHIELD, JOHN GEORGE

Left-half: 1 app.

Born: Whitburn, 10 April 1915 – *Died*: 1981

Career: South Shields schoolboy football, Durham University (1931–33), Bishop Auckland (amateur, May 1933), LIVERPOOL (amateur, August 1935), Wolverhampton Wanderers (amateur, August 1937), West Bromwich Albion (amateur, May 1938–May 1939); did not play after WW2

A teacher by profession and an amateur throughout his career, left-half Jack Shield's only League appearance in the four years after leaving Bishop Auckland was for Liverpool against Preston North End (away) in April 1936 when he stood in for Jimmy McDougall in a 3–1 defeat.

SHIELDS, SAMUEL MILLER

Inside-right: 1 app.

Born: Denny, Stirlingshire, 21 March 1929

Career: Dunipace Juniors/Stirling (August 1945), Cowdenbeath (professional, September 1947), LIVERPOOL (£1,500, May 1949), Airdrieonians (£700, May 1951), Darlington (June 1952), Horden Colliery (May 1953–May 1955)

Sam Shields, very skilful with a strong right-foot shot, understudied Kevin Baron, Willie Fagan and Jack Balmer during his two seasons at Anfield, making his only first-team appearance in the 1–1 draw with Wolves in front of 55,000 fans at Molineux in November 1949. He was plagued by injuries at Airdrie but came back to play in 21 Third Division (N) games for Darlington.

SHONE, DANIEL

Forward: 81 apps, 26 goals

Born: Cheshire, 27 April 1892 – *Died*: 1974

Career: Earle FC (Liverpool Zingari League), LIVERPOOL (amateur, May 1915), Grayson's (Garston, season 1920–21), LIVERPOOL (professional, May 1921), West Ham United (June 1928), Coventry City (in exchange for James Loughlin, January 1929, released April 1930)

Short and stocky with good skills and a powerful left-foot shot, Danny Shone had two moderate seasons and one excellent one during his seven years with Liverpool. Surprisingly he did not make a single appearance for the first team between 19 December 1925 and his transfer to West Ham in August 1928. Referred to in some quarters as the 'forgotten man' at Anfield, Shone made his debut for the Reds against Sunderland (away) in August 1921, scoring his first goal for the club to earn a point in the Merseyside derby at Everton in his third game three months later. He gained a League championship medal that season but played in only one game the following year when the crown was retained. He was an ever-present in 1924–25, forming an excellent left wing partnership with Fred Hopkin, and went on to score 5 goals in 12 games for West Ham and one in 9 for Coventry.

SIDLOW, CYRIL
Goalkeeper: 165 apps
Born: Colwyn Bay, Denbighshire, 26 November 1915 – *Died*: Codsall near Wolverhampton, 12 April 2005
Career: Colwyn Bay (August 1931), Abergele (season 1933–34), Colwyn Bay United (August–November 1934), Stoke City (amateur, briefly), Llandudno Town (January 1935), Wolverhampton Wanderers (professional for £100, May 1937); guest for Burnley, Darlington, Hartlepools United, Notts County and Wrexham during WW2; LIVERPOOL (£4,000, February 1946), New Brighton (August 1952), Wolverhampton Wanderers (coach, August 1953, retired May 1955); subsequently returned to Codsall and worked in the building trade until 1980

Said to have been one of the finest goalkeepers ever to play for Wolves, despite appearing in only four League games, Cyril Sidlow's career was severely interrupted by WW2. He had done very well in Welsh football, starring for the North Wales Coast FA representative side and representing his country at amateur level. He signed as a professional at Molineux at the age of 21 and in 1942 helped Wolves win the Wartime League Cup (v. Sunderland). During the hostilities, when he served in the Duke of Wellington's Regiment, stationed initially in the north of England, he also played in 11 internationals for Wales, lining up against his teammate Bert Williams when Wales played England at The Hawthorns in 1945. He went on to add seven full caps to his tally (1947–50), appearing three times against England. After moving to Anfield he helped Liverpool clinch the First Division championship in 1947, playing in 34 of the 42 League matches, having his best game against his former club Wolves when the Reds clinched the title on the last day of the season at Molineux. Three years later Sidlow gained a runners-up medal when Liverpool lost to Arsenal in the FA Cup final. One of the first goalkeepers to make a practice of throwing the ball out to an unmarked colleague, he was agile, brave and possessed tremendous reflexes, although at times he seemed rather too casual in tight situations!

SINAMA-PONGOLLE, FLORENT
Forward: 21+43 apps, 9 goals
Born: Saint Pierre, France, 20 October 1984
Career: Le Havre/France (apprentice, April 2000; professional, October 2001), LIVERPOOL (July 2003), Blackburn Rovers (loan, January–May 2006)
French under-21 international Sinama-Pongolle scored twice in 11 League games for Le Havre before joining Liverpool at the age of 19. Initially a fringe player at Anfield, he made his Premiership debut as a substitute against Tottenham Hotspur (away) on the opening day of the 2003–04 season and became a hero in a League Cup tie against the same London club in the November with two vital spot-kicks – an equaliser in the 27th minute of extra-time to take the game into a penalty shoot-out and then a decisive 12-yard strike which sent the Reds through to the semi-finals. Unfortunately damaged knee ligaments ended his first season prematurely, meaning he missed the final against Chelsea.

SISSOKO, MOHAMMED

Midfield: 37+7 apps

Born: Mont Saint Agnain, France, 22 January 1985

Career: Auxerre/France (amateur, 2001; professional August 2002), Brest/France (loan, late 2002), Valencia/Spain (May 2004), LIVERPOOL (£5.6m, July 2005)

Born in France of Malian parents, Sissoko opted to play international football for Mali in preference to France and has already gained seven full caps (one goal scored). A strong, aggressive and totally committed midfield player, Mohammed Sissoko scored 50 goals for Auxerre's youth team before Rafael Benitez signed him for Valencia. He then followed his manager to Anfield and made his debut for Liverpool against FBK Kaunas in the first leg of the Champions League second qualifying round. He had a sound first season at Anfield, assisting Steven Gerrard, Alonso Xabi and others in centre-field. Celebrated an excellent first season at Anfield by helping Liverpool beat West Ham in the 2006 FA Cup final.

SLATER, ROBERT

Goalkeeper: 111 apps

Born: Musselburgh, Midlothian, 5 May 1936

Career: Airth Castle Rovers (Stirling), Tranent Juniors (1952), Falkirk (professional, July 1953), LIVERPOOL (player-exchange deal involving Tommy Younger, June 1959), Dundee (July 1962), Watford (May 1965, retired May 1968, coach to May 1975); later worked for a company involved in the design, construction and development of golf courses

On the small side for a goalkeeper, 'Bert' Slater nevertheless had a fine career which realised over 350 club appearances. Capped by Scotland at under-23 level, he helped Falkirk win the Scottish Cup in 1957 and Liverpool the Second Division championship five years later. He then returned 'home' and collected a Cup runners-up medal with Dundee in 1964. Sound and very consistent, the first of his 111 outings for the Reds came in the 2–2 draw at Cardiff City in August 1959. He conceded three goals in his second game and gave way to Doug Rudham before regaining his place in late November. An ever-present in 1960–61, he played in 29 games the following season and left Anfield after losing his place to Jim Furnell.

SLOAN, DONALD

Goalkeeper: 6 apps

Born: Rankinston, Ayrshire, 31 July 1883 – *Died*: Northern Ireland, *circa* 1960

Career: Ayrshire junior football, Distillery (professional, August 1903), Everton (May 1906), LIVERPOOL (June 1908), Distillery (player-manager, July 1909–May 1913); not involved in football after WW1

An Irish League representative and Irish Cup winner with Distillery, Don Sloan made just six appearances for Everton and the same number with Liverpool before rejoining Distillery as player-manager in 1909, collecting a second Irish Cup winner's medal in 1910. Competent and composed, Sloan's career clashed with two of the game's finest pre-war goalkeepers, Billy Scott at Goodison Park and Sam Hardy at Anfield. He made his debut for the Reds against Leicester Fosse (away) in October 1908 and conceded 13 goals in his 6 outings.

SMICER, VLADIMIR
Midfield: 110+74 apps, 19 goals
Born: Decin, Czech Republic, 24 May 1973
Career: SK Slavia Praha/Czech Republic (amateur, August 1991; professional, May 1992), RC Lens/France (August 1996), LIVERPOOL (£3.75m, July 1999), Bordeaux/France (free, July 2005)

Vladimir Smicer holds the record for most substitute appearances for Liverpool in first-class football (74), putting him ahead of Danny Murphy (71), David Fairclough (62), Ronny Rosenthal (57) and Emile Heskey (47). An under-21 international, he was capped once by the old Czechoslovakia and has now played in more than 75 full internationals for the Czech Republic (25 goals) whom he helped reach the semi-finals of Euro 2004. Prior to moving to Anfield, Smicer netted 42 times in 172 League games while playing in his home country and in France. He gained four Czech League championship winning medals in succession with Slavia Praha (1993–96 inclusive), also winning the domestic Cup final in the latter year. He then added a French League winner's medal to his collection in 1998 and was thereafter twice a League Cup winner with the Reds (2001 and 2003) as well as gaining FA Cup and UEFA Cup winner's medals in 2001 plus a Champions League winner's prize in 2005. He came on for the injured Harry Kewell during the first half, scored a crucial goal and then netted from the spot in the penalty shoot-out which enabled Liverpool to go on and win the trophy. Troubled with niggling injuries during his last two seasons at Anfield, on his day Smicer was a valuable player to have in the side. He always gave a good account of himself and produced several excellent displays in the centre of the field or as a wide player. Out of contract in 2005, he chose to return to France with Bordeaux.

SMITH, ARTHUR
Centre-forward: 1 app.
Born: Buckie, Banffshire, 21 January 1915 – *Deceased*
Career: Buckie Thistle (semi-professional, 1935), LIVERPOOL (February 1937), Crewe Alexandra (August 1939); did not play after WW2

A reserve at Anfield, Arthur Smith's only League appearance of his career was for Liverpool against Wolverhampton Wanderers at Molineux in October 1937 when he deputised for Fred Howe in a 2–0 defeat. WW2 ruined his career.

SMITH, JAMES TERENCE
Centre-forward: 62 apps, 38 goals
Born: Old Kilpatrick, Dunbartonshire, 12 March 1902 – *Died*: Bridgepoint near New York, USA, 1975
Career: Dumbarton Harp Juniors (1919), Clydebank (professional, July 1925), Glasgow Rangers (April 1926), Ayr United (May 1927), LIVERPOOL

(£5,500, September 1929), Tunbridge Wells Rangers (July 1932), Bristol
Rovers (May 1933), Newport County (May 1935), Notts County (June
1936), Dumbarton (player-manager, August 1937, retired as a player January
1939, remained as manager until May 1941, director, June 1941—April 1943);
did not continue in football after WW2; emigrated to USA in 1950

Eager-beaver centre-forward Jamie Smith created a British record when he
scored 66 goals for Ayr United as they ran away with the Scottish Second
Division title in 1927—28. He netted 6 more in Cup games to finish with 72 —
an amazing tally. He retained his goal-touch with Liverpool, netting twice on his
debut to earn victory over Manchester United at Old Trafford in September
1929. He was the Reds' top marksman that season with 23 goals and hit 14 the
year after. He retired as a player with a very impressive record of 155 goals in 220
senior appearances.

SMITH, JOHN

Forward: 14 apps, 6 goals

Born: Ayrshire, Scotland, *circa* 1866 – *Died*: Byker, Newcastle-upon-Tyne, 3
   February 1911

Career: Kilmarnock (professional, April 1885), Newcastle East End (March
   1887), Kilmarnock (September 1887—June 1888), Sunderland (£75, August
   1889), LIVERPOOL (£100, May 1892), The Wednesday/Sheffield (£100,
   August 1893), Newcastle United (£50, August 1894—May 1896); later a
   licensee in Byker, Newcastle

Jack Smith was a well-known and popular player in the North-east, a tricky,
hard-working forward who helped Sunderland win the League title in 1892,
making 13 appearances on the left wing. He immediately joined Liverpool and
scored twice on his debut in an 8–0 Lancashire League win over Higher Walton
in September 1892. He was only 44 when he died after a short illness. Some
reference books list Smith as also playing for Albion Rovers during his career.

SMITH, JOHN THOMAS

Centre-forward: 59 apps, 14 goals

Born: Birkenhead, 21 December 1927 – *Deceased*

Career: Bromborough Pool (Cheshire), LIVERPOOL (professional, March
   1951), Torquay United (£1,500, May 1954), Bideford (June 1957),
   Bromborough Pool (August 1961—May 1964)

Jack Smith spent just over three years at Anfield during which time he averaged
a goal every four games, including one on his debut against Derby County in
September 1951 when he deputised at centre-forward for Albert Stubbins in a
2–0 win. Moving on after Sammy Smyth had arrived at the club to partner Louis
Bimpson in attack, Smith scored 22 goals in 73 games for Torquay United before
reverting back to non-League football with Bideford.

SMITH, SYDNEY WARWICK

Centre-forward: 2 apps, 1 goal
Born: Liverpool, 1875 – *Died*: *circa* 1938
Career: Merseyside junior football, LIVERPOOL (amateur, August 1903), Southport Central (April 1904–May 1907)

A respected amateur around the Liverpool area during the late 1800s/early 1900s, Syd Smith was a reserve at Anfield for one season, making just two senior appearances, both in September 1903 against Nottingham Forest (scoring on his debut) and Sheffield Wednesday. He was replaced by John Carlin who quickly gave way to Jack Parkinson. Smith scored over 40 goals for Southport Central in the Lancashire Combination.

SMITH, THOMAS, MBE

Midfield/defender: 636+2 apps, 48 goals
Born: Liverpool, 5 April 1945
Career: Archbishop Godfrey High School (Liverpool), Liverpool Schools, LIVERPOOL (amateur, May 1960; professional, April 1962), Swansea City (August 1978, player-coach, August 1979–October 1979), LIVERPOOL (coach, seasons 1979–81)

Rock-solid, built the size of an over-sized baby elephant, Tommy Smith was a human tank out on the field, a player who never shirked a tackle, was honest as the day is long and gave his all for Liverpool Football Club. As his ex-manager, Bill Shankly, famously said: 'Anyone who plays against Tommy knows he has been in a match.' Some people said he was a rugged, uncompromising destroyer, rather slow at times and somewhat dogged and cumbersome. OK, that was fair enough, but he could also play a bit, too, and proved to be a wonderful servant to the club. A Liverpudlian through and through with a wonderful broad 'Scouse' accent, he was an inspiration to everyone who wore a red shirt and will go down in folklore as one of the all-time greats at Anfield. He made the first of his 638 senior appearances against Birmingham City (away) in May 1963, standing in for the injured Gordon Milne at right-half. Soon afterwards manager Bill Shankly played him as an extra defender, and then switched him into the centre of the defence where he quickly became an integral part of the 'red machine' that dominated the English game for well over a decade. With his colleagues Smith gained medals galore: four League championship triumphs (1966, 1973, 1976 and 1977), two FA Cup final wins (1965 and 1974), European Cup glory (1977 – missing out on another winner's medal after dropping a pick-axe on his foot) and victory in the UEFA Cup finals of 1973 and 1976 . . . and he also collected a handful of runners-up prizes as well. Captain of the England youth team in 1963, he represented the Football League, played in ten under-21 internationals and gained one full cap versus Wales in May 1971, the same year he led Liverpool in the FA Cup final (beaten by Arsenal) and was named runner-up in the 'Footballer of the Year' poll behind Arsenal's Frank McLintock. After turning down an extra one-year contract with Liverpool, Smith moved south to The Vetch Field in 1978 where he was reunited with four of his former Anfield colleagues, Phil Boersma, Ian

Callaghan, John Toshack and Alan Waddle. He helped the Welsh club gain promotion to the Second Division in his first season, before a knee injury ended his playing career after he had added another 45 senior appearances to his tally with the Swans. Following a brief spell as a coach, Smith became a well-respected and admired after-dinner speaker, working mainly in the north-west of England. There have been an awful lot of exceptionally tough, robust, hard-tackling defenders in the game of football, but only one Tommy Smith – the 'Anfield Iron'. He was awarded the MBE for services to football.

SMYTH, MARK MICHAEL

Midfield: 0+1 app.
Born: Liverpool, 9 January 1985
Career: LIVERPOOL (apprentice, April 2001; professional, April 2002; released, May 2005)

Young midfielder Mark Smyth graduated via the Anfield Youth Academy and made his debut for Liverpool against Tottenham Hotspur in the quarter-final of the League Cup in December 2004. Not considered to be Premiership material, he was released after four years with the club.

SMYTH, SAMUEL

Inside-left: 45 apps, 20 goals
Born: Belfast, 25 February 1915
Career: Distillery (amateur, April 1942), Linfield (amateur, May 1944), Dunella (professional, June 1947), Wolverhampton Wanderers (£1,100, July 1947), Stoke City (£25,000, September 1951), LIVERPOOL (£12,000, January 1953), Bangor/Northern Ireland (£2,000, January 1955, retired, June 1955); returned to Belfast where he got married and took a full-time job, later working as a bookmaker prior to running his own sports shop business and becoming an agent for the sportswear company Halbro and Falcon

For five years Sammy Smyth was an amateur footballer in his native Northern Ireland. He had international trials as a schoolboy before going on to gain four amateur caps, while also representing the Irish League. He then signed professional forms for Dunella to allow him to move to England, joining Wolves, where he quickly made an impact, going on to score 43 goals in 116 games and gaining an FA Cup winner's medal in 1949 when he netted twice (one a beauty) in a 3–1 win over Leicester City. He also won nine full caps for his country before going on to net 19 times in 44 outings for Stoke. He spent just over two years at Anfield before joining Bangor for an Irish record transfer fee of £2,000. He made the first of his 45 appearances for the Reds against his former club, Stoke, in January 1953 when he partnered Billy Liddell on the left wing and struck home his first goal a month later v. Middlesbrough. He claimed a total of 72 goals in 187 League games in English football before returning to his homeland. Also an enthusiastic golfer, Smyth was both captain and president of the Clandeboye 36-hole golf complex near Belfast and is believed to be one of the oldest former Liverpool footballers alive today, still living in Ireland.

SONG, BAHANAG RIGOBERT

Defender: 30+8 apps
Born: Nkanglicock, Cameroon, 1 July 1976
Career: Tonnerre/Cameroon, Yaounde/Cameroon, Metz/France (professional, August 1994), Salernitana/Italy (July 1998), LIVERPOOL (£2.72m, January 1999), West Ham United (£2.5m, November 2000), FC Köln/Germany (loan, November 2001–May 2002), Racing Club Lens/France (July 2002)

Cameroon international defender Rigobert Song, who helped his country win the 2000 African Nations Cup, gave some competent displays for Liverpool when asked to play in a variety of positions. He started off very well but then became a fringe player at Anfield and in November 2000 was transferred to West Ham, going on to play in only 21 games for the London club before returning to France. He also helped Cameroon qualify for the 2002 World Cup finals and as captain, took his tally of full caps past the 75 mark. The first of his 38 outings for Liverpool was against Coventry City (away) in January 1999, being substituted in the second half by Steve McManaman in a 2–1 defeat.

SOUNESS, GRAEME JAMES

Midfield: 357+2 apps, 56 goals
Born: Edinburgh, 6 May 1953
Career: Carrickvale School (Edinburgh), Edinburgh Schools, Tottenham Hotspur (apprentice, April 1969; professional, May 1970), Montreal Olympic/Canada (loan, June–October 1972), Middlesbrough (£32,000, January 1973), LIVERPOOL (£352,000, January 1978), Sampdoria/Italy (£650,000, July 1984), Glasgow Rangers (player-manager, April 1986, later director and part-owner), LIVERPOOL (manager, April 1991–January 1994), Galatasaray/Turkey (manager, season 1994–95), Southampton (manager, July 1995–June 1997), Torino/Italy (coach/manager, 1998), Benfica/Portugal (coach/manager, August 1999), Blackburn Rovers (manager, March 2000), Newcastle United (manager, September 2004, sacked February 2006)

A Scottish schoolboy international at the age of 15, Graeme Souness went on to gain 54 full (37 with Liverpool), two under-23 and three youth caps for his country and during his playing career amassed over 750 first-class appearances, scoring almost 100 goals. A tough-tackling but creative midfielder, he played in only one game for his first club, Spurs, as a substitute in a UEFA Cup game against Keflavik (Iceland) in September 1971. After assisting Montreal Olympic in the NASL, he became frustrated at not being given an opportunity at White Hart Lane and walked out – leading to his transfer to Middlesbrough, whom he helped win the Second Division title in 1974 under the leadership of Jack Charlton. He developed into an outstanding performer at Ayresome Park and Liverpool boss Bob Paisley had no hesitation in signing Souness in 1978. Nicknamed 'Souey' he quickly became the midfield focal point and had the ability to totally dominate games, taking control and dictating play with his strength, awareness and pinpoint passing ability that often split defences in two. At times he strolled through a game with almost regal arrogance and he could also deliver a powerful shot, often finding the net from distance. With the Reds he won almost every honour available during his six and a half years at Anfield, gaining five League championship winning medals (1979, 1980, 1982, 1983 and 1984), four League Cup winning prizes (1981, 1982, 1983 and 1984, although he missed the replay of the 1981 final) and three European Cup successes (1978, 1981 and 1984), plus victories in the 1979, 1980 and 1982 FA Charity Shield games. He also received a handful of runners-up medals. After reaching the pinnacle of his career he chose to spend two years in Italy's Serie 'A' with Sampdoria, collecting an Italian Cup winner's medal, before returning to Britain as player-manager of Rangers. In his first season at Ibrox, the 'Gers won the Scottish League and League Cup, claimed the League Cup again in 1988, completed the League and Scottish Cup double in 1989 and won the League title and League Cup once more in 1990 and 1991 respectively. He also became part-owner and director of the club whose supporters adored him – but he was deeply unpopular with opposing fans because of his abrasive and arrogant approach. However, success in Europe eluded Souness and in April 1991, after one of the most turbulent, controversial, yet enthralling periods in Rangers' history, he left Glasgow and returned to Liverpool to take over as manager from his former teammate Kenny Dalglish. Unfortunately he failed as boss at Anfield, spending a fortune on 15 players (around £21.25m) during his 33 months in office, in which time he got over the shock of undergoing major heart surgery. He also had a tough time at Southampton but had varying degrees of success in Turkey, Italy and Portugal before easing Blackburn Rovers back into the Premiership in 2001. He then had his work cut out again at Newcastle after taking over the hot-seat from Sir Bobby Robson in 2004. After an initial bright start under his leadership Newcastle finished a disappointing 14th in the 2005 Premier League, then after a poor run the following season chairman Freddie Shepherd's patience finally snapped and Souness was sacked in February 2006. The only trophy Souness failed to win as a player (in England) was the FA Cup but although he has his shortcomings as a manager, as a footballer he was certainly one of the finest in his field for a decade. Souness attended the same Edinburgh School as Dave Mackay who played for Hearts, Spurs and Derby County and Scotland.

SOUTH, ALEXANDER JAMES WILLIAM
Centre-half: 7 apps, 1 goal
Born: Brighton, 7 July 1931
Career: Whitehawk Boys' Club (Brighton), Brighton and Hove Albion (amateur, August 1946; professional, March 1949); served in the RAF; LIVERPOOL (£5,000, December 1954), Halifax Town (£2,500, October 1956, retired, May 1965; became club's Pools promoter)
An England Boys' Club international, capped against Wales in 1946, Alex South also represented the RAF while on national service and made 81 League appearances for Brighton before joining Liverpool as cover for Lawrie Hughes. He made the first of his seven appearances for the Reds against Fulham in February 1955 and scored his only goal for the club in his fourth game to earn a point in a 4–4 draw with Luton Town at Anfield. After leaving Liverpool, South,

strong and physical, played in more than 300 first-class matches for Halifax Town, 296 in the Football League, which stood as a club record until 1974.

SPACKMAN, NIGEL JAMES
Midfield: 50+13 apps
Born: Romsey, Hampshire, 2 December 1960
Career: Andover (August 1976), AFC Bournemouth (professional, May 1980), Chelsea (£40,000, June 1983), LIVERPOOL (£400,000, February 1987), Queens Park Rangers (£500,000, February 1989), Glasgow Rangers (£500,000, November 1990), Chelsea (£485,000, September 1992), Sheffield United (player/assistant manager and coach, July 1996; later caretaker-manager, August 1997–March 1998; left club May 1998); since worked as a soccer summariser/analyst on Sky Sport

Nigel Spackman made his League debut for Bournemouth in a 4–0 win over York City in 1980 – the first of 430 in the League and 557 competitive outings overall at club level. A Second Division championship winner with Chelsea in 1984, he also helped the Londoners win the Full Members' Cup at Wembley two years later before joining Liverpool, who handed him his debut against Southampton (won 1–0) in February 1987. At the end of the following season he celebrated with a League championship winning medal. A strong midfielder with a terrific engine, he was a splendid man-marker and having won the ball, fed his front men with a simple pass, never overdoing the clever stuff. After leaving Anfield for a short spell at QPR, he then moved up to Ibrox Park (signed by Graeme Souness), where he gained three Premier League winner's medals with Rangers as well as winning both Scottish Cup and League Cup medals. The joker in the pack, he was unlucky not to receive international recognition. He failed in his efforts as a manager, having to sell key players when in charge of Sheffield United which triggered off friction and uneasiness in the Bramall Lane camp.

SPEAKMAN, JAMES
Outside-right: 8 apps, 1 goal
Born: Huyton Quarry, Liverpool, 1888 – *Died*: 1962
Career: Merseyside junior football, LIVERPOOL (August 1908–May 1913)
Brother of Samuel (below), Jimmy Speakman was a reserve outside-right at Anfield for five years during which time he appeared in only eight first-team matches, making his League debut in October 1909 when he deputised for Arthur Goddard in a 3–2 home win over Manchester United. His only goal came in his sixth game which helped the Reds beat Bradford City 2–0.

SPEAKMAN, SAMUEL
Full-back: 26 apps, 1 goal
Born: Huyton Quarry, Liverpool, 9 August 1884 – *Died*: Liverpool, 1934
Career: Colne FC (Lancashire Combination), LIVERPOOL (professional, January 1912), South Liverpool (free, August 1920, retired, May 1923)
Sam Speakman's career at Anfield was split in two by WW1 during which time

he made a further 31 appearances for the Reds. A versatile full-back, able to play on both flanks, he made his debut for the club in the Merseyside derby against Everton at Goodison Park in September 1913 when he partnered Ted Crawford in a 2–1 win in front of 40,000 fans. He and his younger brother never played together in Liverpool's first XI.

SPEEDIE, DAVID ROBERT
Forward: 9+5 apps, 6 goals
Born: Glenrothes, Scotland, 20 February 1960
Career: Ardwick School, Barnsley (apprentice, August 1977; professional, October 1978), Darlington (£5,000, June 1980), Chelsea (£70,000, June 1982), Coventry City (£780,000, July 1987), LIVERPOOL (£675,000, February 1991), Blackburn Rovers (£450,000, August 1991), Southampton (£400,000, July 1992), Birmingham City (loan, October 1992), West Bromwich Albion (loan, January–February 1993), West Ham United (loan, March–April 1993), Leicester City (free, July 1993, retired, January 1995; joined coaching staff at Filbert Street); made a brief comeback with Crook Town (season 1996–97); now footballers' agent

Before joining Liverpool at the age of 31, the fiery, unpredictable David Speedie had already scored 121 goals in 468 club matches and played in one under-21 and 10 full internationals for Scotland. An all-action forward, cocky at times, with good pace and finishing power, he was a Second Division championship and Full Members' Cup winner with Chelsea in 1984 and 1986 before Kenny Dalglish brought him to Anfield. Despite scoring with a superb volley on his debut at Old Trafford to earn a point and netting twice in the derby win over Everton to keep the Reds in the title hunt, he failed to maintain his form and after Dalglish had been replaced by Graeme Souness, Speedie was used in midfield. He found this not to his liking and it came as no surprise when he was sold to Blackburn. One of the game's characters, he aggravated a previous injury when playing for Leicester and he retired early in 1995 with 175 goals to his name in 611 club and international appearances.

SPICER, EDWIN
Full-back: 168 apps, 2 goals
Born: Liverpool, 20 September 1922
Career: Liverpool Schools, LIVERPOOL (amateur, September 1937; professional, October 1939); served in the Royal Marines during WW2; retired, injured, October 1953

Full-back Eddie Spicer made 51 appearances for the Reds during WW2, his senior debut coming in the second leg of a fourth-round FA Cup tie against Bolton Wanderers in January 1946. He followed up with his League bow against Sheffield United seven months later. Strong on both flanks, he twice suffered a broken leg, the first on tour to Sweden in 1951 (which caused him to miss the whole of the next season) and second at Old Trafford when he collided with his own goalkeeper, Dave Underwood, and Manchester United's centre-forward Tommy Taylor. He never recovered from this set-back and retired at the age of

31. An England schoolboy international, capped at the age of 14, there was nothing flashy about his play. He was a tenacious tackler, quick in recovery with a powerful kick, often sending the ball upwards of 70 yards, one bounce, downfield. He missed out on a League championship winning medal in 1947 (playing in only 10 games), played well without success in the 1950 FA Cup final and was an ever-present in the side the following season. Spicer was decorated with a bravery award while serving with the Marines during the war.

STANIFORTH, FREDERICK WALTER
Outside-right: 3 apps
Born: Kilnhurst near Rotherham, 1884 – *Died*: Bristol, 23 May 1955
Career: Kilnhurst Town, Rotherham Main, Mexborough Town, Bristol City (August 1906), Grimsby Town (1911), LIVERPOOL (May 1913–May 1914); served in Army during WW1; did not play after 1919; became a shopkeeper in Bristol

An FA Cup finalist with Bristol City in 1909 (beaten by Manchester United), Fred Staniforth had five excellent years at Ashton Gate, a stay that coincided with the club's first spell in the top flight of English League football. A clever dribbler and brainy with it, he netted 15 goals in 156 games for the Bristol club and 8 in 69 for Grimsby before having a season at Anfield when he deputised in three games for Arthur Goddard, making his debut against Sheffield Wednesday at Hillsborough in October 1913. He played in the second XI from December 1913 onwards following the introduction of John Sheldon.

STAUNTON, STEPHEN
Defender: 127+23 apps, 8 goals
Born: Drogheda, County Louth, Ireland, 19 January 1969
Career: Gaelic football (Louth), Dundalk (May 1985), LIVERPOOL (£20,000, professional, September 1986), Bradford City (loan, November 1987–January 1988), Aston Villa (£1.1m, August 1991), LIVERPOOL (free, July 1998), Crystal Palace (loan, October–November 2000), Aston Villa (free, December 2000), Coventry City (free, August 2003), Walsall (free, player-coach, August 2005–January 2006), Republic of Ireland (manager, January 2006)

Able to play in a variety of defensive positions (and, indeed, in midfield) Steve Staunton preferred the left-back berth. Capped a record 102 times by the Republic of Ireland between 1989 and 2002, he also represented his country in three youth and four under-21 matches and prior to his retirement had amassed almost 750 appearances for his five English clubs and his country at competitive level. Strong in the tackle with grand anticipation and good pace, he made his debut for Liverpool against Tottenham Hotspur in September 1988, having previously spent two years in the second team. He helped the Reds win the FA Cup that season and followed up with a League Championship winner's medal in 1990. After spending seven years with Aston Villa, during which time he twice won the League Cup in 1994 and 1996, he returned to Anfield for a second but much quieter spell. After another trip to Villa Park, he spent two years with Coventry City before taking over as player-coach under Paul Merson at Walsall in 2005. He was still associated with the Saddlers when the FAI appointed him as manager of the Republic of Ireland national team early in 2006 but his club agreed a settlement and released him from his position as player-coach. Staunton was then delighted when Sir Bobby Robson was named as his aide and consultant. Kevin MacDonald, ex-Liverpool, became Staunton's assistant.

STEEL, WILLIAM GILBERT

Full-back: 128 apps
Born: Blantyre, Lanarkshire, 6 February 1908 – *Died*: Scotland, *circa* 1990
Career: Bridgton Waverley, St Johnstone (professional, August 1926), LIVERPOOL (trial, August 1931, signed, September 1931), Birmingham (£5,000, March 1935), Derby County (£1,275, February 1939, retired, May 1940); Airdrieonians (trainer, April 1950, manager April 1954), Third Lanark (manager, January 1963–June 1964)

An ever-present at full-back for three successive seasons as a St Johnstone player, Billy Steel joined Liverpool at the age of 23 but had to wait four months before making his debut for the club, lining up against Derby County at Anfield a week before Christmas 1931 as partner to Jimmy Jackson, who had switched flanks. A resilient and highly respected defender with a footballing brain, he had taken his League appearance tally in English and Scottish football to 345 games by the time war broke out in 1939. As a qualified masseur (trainer), he served the Scottish national team during the early 1950s and after his four-year stint as manager of Airdrie, that club's chairman rated him as the best the club had ever had.

STEVENSON, GENERAL

Right-back: 23 apps
Born: Padiham near Burnley, December 1877 – *Died*: Burnley, 1945
Career: Hapton FC (1893), Padiham (1895); LIVERPOOL (professional, August 1898), Barnsley (July 1900), Wellingborough (May 1902), Millwall Athletic (May 1903–April 1910); returned to assist Accrington FC (1912–13); became a licensee in Padiham

A small but powerful full-back with a strong kick, General Stevenson spent two seasons at Anfield, having his best spell in the first team at the start of the 1899–1900 campaign when he partnered Billy Dunlop in 13 League games, having made his debut for the Reds against Nottingham Forest (away) in November 1898. He played in 54 League games for Barnsley before becoming a huge favourite with the Millwall supporters. As captain, he made 318 senior appearances for the London club (9 goals scored), had two trials for England (in South v. North matches in 1904 and 1905), won both London League championship and Southern Professional Charity Cup winner's medals in 1904 and helped the team win successive Western League titles in 1908 and 1909. His loyal service to the Lions was rewarded with a benefit match in 1909 v. Northampton Town in front of a 10,000 crowd, just prior to that second title win.

Some reference books state that Stevenson had another Christian name, William (unconfirmed), while his brother, Admiral Stevenson, was also an amateur footballer. His son, Arthur Stevenson, played for Wigan Rugby League Club.

STEVENSON, WILLIAM

Wing-half: 240+1 apps, 18 goals
Born: Leith, 26 October 1939
Career: Edinburgh Schools, Edna Hearts (1955), Dalkeith Thistle (1956), Glasgow Rangers (professional, November 1957); played briefly in Australia (early 1962); LIVERPOOL (£20,000, October 1962), Stoke City (£48,000, December 1967), Tranmere Rovers (free, July 1973), Vancouver Whitecaps/NASL (May 1974, retired September 1974); went into business in Newcastle-under-Lyme with another former Stoke City player, Eric Skeels

Willie Stevenson was a stylish footballer, superb in possession, a fine passer of the ball who could tackle strongly and aggressively when required. Twice a League championship winner with the Reds, in 1964 and 1966, he also won the FA Cup in 1965 and played in the losing European Cup-Winners' Cup final also in 1966. He made the first of his 241 appearances for Liverpool against Burnley (home) in November 1962 when he took over at left-half (number 6) from Tommy Leishman and retained that position in the side until the end of the 1966–67 season, subsequently replaced by Emlyn Hughes. One of the few players sold by manager Bill Shankly to another First Division club, he continued his good form with Stoke City, for whom he made over 100 first-class appearances before a broken leg disrupted his game prior to him joining Tranmere Rovers in 1973, signed by Ron Yeats (q.v.). As a Glasgow Rangers player, Stevenson collected a Scottish League championship winner's medal in 1959 and a Cup winner's medal 12 months later. He made 103 appearances for the Ibrox Park club, represented his country at schoolboy level and also played for the Scottish League side. He was replaced in the 'Gers team by the legendary Jim Baxter.

STEWART, JAMES MUNRO

Inside-forward: 68 apps, 27 goals
Born: Dumbarton, 1885 – *Died*: before 1965
Career: Dumbarton junior football, Motherwell (professional, August 1907), LIVERPOOL (April 1909), Hamilton Academical (October 1913, retired May 1920); later a member of the Portsmouth training staff

A short, stocky inside-right, clever on the ball with a powerful right-foot shot, Jimmy Stewart spent four and a half years at Anfield, having a wonderful first season (1909–10) when he netted 18 goals in 37 League games as the Reds claimed second place in the First Division table. He made his debut for the club at Chelsea (lost 2–1) on the opening Saturday and struck his first goal in his third game to set up a 3–1 win over Blackburn. Injuries and an occasional loss of form affected his game during the next three seasons and after Sam Gilligan and then John Bovill had been introduced into the team to play alongside Jack Parkinson, Ronald Orr and then Tommy Miller, he moved back to Scotland.

STEWART, PAUL ANDREW
Forward: 39+4 apps, 3 goals
Born: Manchester, 7 October 1964
Career: Blackpool (apprentice, August 1980; professional, October 1981), Manchester City (£200,000, March 1987), Tottenham Hotspur (£1.7m, June 1988), LIVERPOOL (£2.3m, July 1992), Crystal Palace (loan, January–March 1994), Wolverhampton Wanderers (loan, September–November 1994), Burnley (loan, February–March 1995), Sunderland (loan, August–September 1995, signed, free, March 1996), Stoke City (free, June 1997), Workington (free, August 1998–May 2000)

In an excellent 20-year career, striker Paul Stewart netted over 150 goals in more than 650 club appearances (145 coming in 600 major League and Cup games). He also gained three full, five 'B', one under-21 and three youth caps for England, was an FA Cup winner with Spurs in 1991, won the First Division championship with Crystal Palace in 1994 and Sunderland in 1996 and then helped Workington clinch the North-Western Trains League title in his twilight days of 1999.

A totally committed player, using both aggression (when called for) and quality, he was a top-rate finisher who had his best spells with Blackpool (62 goals in 225 outings) and Spurs (37 in 172). He was almost 28 years of age when he joined Liverpool, scoring an unfortunate own goal on his debut for the Reds in a friendly against Rosenborg BK before having his first League outing v. Nottingham Forest (away) on the opening day of the 1992–93 season, when he teamed up with Dean Saunders and Ian Rush in attack. He scored his first goal in his second game to earn a 2–1 victory over Sheffield United. After a pretty good initial season, thereafter he struggled to get into the side and with Nigel Clough, Robbie Fowler and Ian Rush seemingly the main strike-force, he moved north to Sunderland, following a series of moderate loan spells up and down the country.

STORER, HAROLD
Goalkeeper: 121 apps
Born: Butterley, Ripley, Derbyshire, 24 July 1870 – *Died*: Holloway, Derbyshire, 25 April 1908
Career: Ripley Town (September 1886), Derby Midland (June 1888), Derby County (professional, February 1891), Gainsborough Trinity (July 1892), Loughborough Town (May 1893), Woolwich Arsenal (May 1894), LIVERPOOL (£75, December 1895–May 1901)

A very clever and competent goalkeeper with a safe pair of hands, strong kick and reassuring to his defenders, Harry Storer spent 15 years in the game before injury forced him into an early retirement at the age of 30. He had made 41 senior appearances for Arsenal before joining Liverpool immediately after serving a four-week suspension with the Gunners. A Football League representative in 1895, he was handed his debut by the Reds against Manchester City (home) on New Year's Day 1896 when he took over from the versatile Matt McQueen who later played at left-half. Storer conceded only 8 goals in 11 games that season, earning himself a Second Division championship medal. He played in 23 League matches the following season, was an ever-present in 1897–98 and after missing only three games in 1898–99 he shared the keeping duties with Bill Perkins until he left Anfield in 1901. Storer also played county cricket for Derbyshire (appearing in six matches in 1895). His son, Harry junior, was a footballer with Notts County, Grimsby Town, Derby County, Burnley and England and a cricketer for Derbyshire, scoring 13,513 runs at an average of 27.63 over a period of 16 years from 1920. He also took 200 wickets and won a County Championship medal in 1936. He later managed Coventry City, Birmingham City and Derby County and was a scout for Everton. Harry's brother William was a Derby County, Glossop North End and Loughborough Town footballer and a Derbyshire and England cricketer. Harry Storer was only 37 when he died.

STORTON, TREVOR GEORGE
Defender: 11+1 apps
Born: Keighley, Yorkshire, 26 November 1949
Career: Tranmere Rovers (apprentice, April 1966; professional, October 1967), LIVERPOOL (£25,000, August 1972), Chester City (£18,000, July 1974, retired, March 1984)
Central defender Trevor Storton played in more than 100 senior games for Tranmere before joining Liverpool, principally as a reserve. Then after leaving Anfield, having failed to make headway in the first XI, he amassed a record 493 League and Cup appearances for Chester and, in fact, was only 12 short of Ray Gill's all-time record of 396 League games for that club which he set between 1951 and 1962. Obviously better suited to life in the lower divisions, Storton was nevertheless a splendid defender whose debut for the Reds was against Leeds United in September 1972, when he deputised for Tommy Smith in a 2–1 win at Elland Road. His brother, Stan, also played for Tranmere Rovers as well as Bradford City and Darlington and after retiring managed FA Cup giant-killers Telford United.

STOTT, JAMES
Wing-back/inside-left: 18 apps, 14 goals
Born: Darlington, 1871 – *Died*: Gosforth, Newcastle-upon-Tyne, 8 October 1908
Career: South Bank FC (1887), Middlesbrough (amateur, August 1891), LIVERPOOL (professional, August 1893), Grimsby Town (June 1894), Newcastle United (£15, June 1895), Middlesbrough (July 1899, retired, May 1900); became a licensee in Newcastle
A key member of Liverpool's Second Division championship and promotion winning side of 1894, Jimmy Stott was an inspiring player, clever and quick over the ground, an all-rounder, who was not afraid to tackle or shoot at goal, hence

his terrific strike record. He made his debut for the Reds against his former club Middlesbrough in September 1893 (won 2–0) and later fired home a hat-trick in the return fixture which was won 6–0. He top-scored that season with 14 goals, playing brilliantly up front with David Henderson and his wing partner, Hugh McQueen. Moving to Grimsby after losing his place to John Givens and then Harry Bradshaw, Stott had one season with Grimsby before taking over as captain of Newcastle United. The scorer of 11 goals in 131 appearances during his time with the Geordies, he helped them gain promotion to the top flight in 1898. Unfortunately he lost his temper occasionally and in 1896 was censured by United's Board of Directors for 'continually fouling opponents'. He made only one appearance in his two spells with Middlesbrough. A snappy dresser, said to be the 'Beau Brummell' among professional footballers, he often wore a top hat and frock coat when he attended church on a Sunday, and after retiring he became a popular licensee of The Star Hotel on Westgate Street, Newcastle. He sadly died in a lunatic asylum, the victim of a brain tumour.

STRONG, GEOFFREY HUGH

Forward/midfield/left-back: 195+5 apps, 32 goals
Born: Kirkheaton, Northumberland, 19 September 1937
Career: Northumberland Boys, Throckley Juniors (from 1952), Stanley United (Northern League, April 1954), Arsenal (£100, amateur, November 1957; professional, April 1958), LIVERPOOL (£40,000, November 1964), Coventry City (£29,500, August 1970; retired, May 1972); later ran a hotel interior furnishing company on Merseyside

A machine-tool fitter by trade, Geoff Strong did his national service in the Royal Army Ordnance Corps (1959–61) and played for the Army in representative games. He scored 77 goals in 137 senior appearances for Arsenal and also netted 118 times in 130 intermediate and second XI matches during his seven years at Highbury. Initially an inside-left, he was switched to wing-half by Gunners manager Billy Wright and that he didn't like, choosing to join Liverpool when Bill Shankly made an offer. He quickly established himself at Anfield, linking up in attack with Roger Hunt. He helped Liverpool win the FA Cup at the end of his first season, deputising for the injured and unlucky Gordon Milne against Leeds United. He followed up by gaining a League championship winner's medal in 1966, playing in 22 First Division matches, half of them at right-half. In fact, he wore seven different numbered shirts that season – truly a man for all seasons. Unfortunately he didn't play in the European Cup-Winners' Cup final defeat by Borussia Moenchengladbach, despite grabbing the winning goal that knocked out Celtic in the semis. Nevertheless, he proved to be a key member of the senior squad and showed his versatility by performing very efficiently at left-back. All told Strong, in name and commitment, gave Liverpool six years' excellent service, making 200 League and Cup appearances, the first against Fulham (away) in November 1964 when he partnered Peter Thompson on the left wing in a 1–1 draw. Ivan Ponting wrote in his *Player by Player* book of 1996 . . . 'When Strong left Anfield he didn't leave one gap – he left ten.' He added a further 41 senior appearances to his career tally with Coventry City before retiring.

STUBBINS, ALBERT

Centre-forward: 180 apps, 83 goals

Born: Wallsend-on-Tyne, 13 July 1919 – *Died*: Cullercoats near Newcastle, 28 December 2002

Career: Whitley and Monkseaton FC (April 1934), Sunderland (amateur, briefly in 1935), Newcastle United (amateur, March 1936; professional, April 1937); guest for Sunderland (1941–42), LIVERPOOL (£12,500, September 1946), Ashington (September 1953, retired May 1954), LIVERPOOL (scout, seasons 1954–60); New York Americans (coach, July 1960, also coach to the USA national team); returned to England, November 1960, became a well-known and respected journalist with the *Sunday People* as well as working on local radio, resided in Wideopen near Newcastle until shortly before his death

Red-haired Albert Stubbins, a former shipyard draughtsman, was a prolific marksman for Newcastle United during WW2, netting 231 goals in only 188 appearances. It was a pity that the hostilities came when they did, for he would surely have set the world on fire with his all-action displays from the centre-forward position. Brought up in America as a youngster, moving to New York in 1923 and later Detroit, he was tall and forceful and loved to run at defenders, scaring some of them to death at times. He possessed frightening pace and packed a ferocious right-foot shot, as well as being a useful header of the ball, too. Wearing size 11 boots, he claimed 33 goals in 1941–42 (when he also played for the FA XI against the Army), netted 42 the following season and grabbed 43 in each of the 1943–44 and 1944–45 campaigns. His wartime tally included 29 hat-tricks – one turning into a five-timer struck with venom against Middlesbrough in December 1941. Defenders, some of the best in the game, simply couldn't contain him. He failed to win a full cap for England (due to the presence, really, after WW2 of Tommy Lawton) but he did represent his country against Wales in a Victory international at The Hawthorns in October 1945 and played three times for the Football League, scoring five goals against the Irish League in 1950. After his services at St James' Park, Stubbins joined Liverpool for a club record fee and was immediately taken to by the supporters who loved his every move (and goal). He scored on his debut for the Reds in a 3–1 win at Bolton in September 1946 and went on to become a legendary figure at Anfield. Joint top scorer in 1947 when the League title was won, he also played in the 1950 FA Cup final defeat by Arsenal. Unfortunately he fell out with the Liverpool hierarchy in the later 1940s over his wish to move back to Tyneside and, indeed, train there (with Newcastle), as his wife could not settle on Merseyside. Things were sorted out to a degree but after a series of niggling injuries, Stubbins eventually went back home to sign for Ashington. Once nicknamed the 'Smiling Assassin', Stubbins was a gentleman on and off the field and was featured on the cover of the Beatles' hit album *Sgt Pepper's Lonely Hearts Club Band*. He was also honoured at the House of Commons and is certainly listed as a Liverpool all-time great.

TANNER, NICHOLAS

Defender: 47+3 apps, 1 goal

Born: Kingswood, Bristol, 24 May 1965

Career: Kingswood Boys (1981), Mangotsfield United (August 1982), Bristol Rovers (professional, June 1985), LIVERPOOL (£30,000, July 1988), Norwich City (loan, March–April 1990), Swindon Town (loan September–October 1990); returned to Anfield (retired, injured, May 1993)

A very competent defender, a stopper in the old regime, standing 6ft 1in. tall and weighing 13st. 10lb, Nicky Tanner could also play in midfield (in an emergency) and made well over 100 senior appearances for Bristol Rovers before joining Liverpool at the age of 23. He spent five years at Anfield, acting as a reserve most of the time, having his best season of first-team action in 1991–92 when he appeared in 32 League games, 26 in succession. He made his debut for the Reds as a substitute in a 4–1 win at Manchester City in December 1989 and started his first game at Charlton four months later. A back injury forced Tanner into early retirement.

TAYLOR, HENRY

Left-half/forward: 71 apps, 6 goals

Born: Hanley, Stoke-on-Trent, January 1912 – *Died*: *circa* 1985

Career: Stoke-on-Trent schoolboy football, Stoke St Peter's FC, Stoke City (amateur, February 1929; professional, June 1929), LIVERPOOL (June 1932, released, May 1936)

Harry Taylor was more effective as a winger than a half-back. Initially reserve to two Bobbys at the Victoria Ground (Liddle and Archibald), he scored 11 goals in 26 games for Stoke before joining Liverpool. He then had to wait five months before making his debut for the Reds against Leeds United in November 1932. He was switched to left-half later in the season and performed very well before reverting back to the wing in 1933–34. During his five years at Anfield, Taylor occupied five different positions, four in the forward-line.

TAYLOR, PHILIP HENRY

Right-half/inside-/wing-forward: 345 apps, 34 goals

Born: Bristol, 18 September 1917

Career: Greenback Council School (Bristol), Bristol Boys, Bristol Rovers (amateur, May 1932; professional, September 1935), LIVERPOOL (£5,000, March 1936); guest for Bristol Rovers, Brighton and Hove Albion, Leeds United and Newcastle United during WW2; (retired as a player, July 1954; joined LIVERPOOL coaching staff, became chief coach, then acting manager, May 1956 and manager from April 1957, resigned November 1959); later worked as a sales representative and was then a local businessman in the Liverpool area

Besides his excellent peacetime record with Liverpool, Phil Taylor also scored 24 goals in 92 WW2 games for the Reds and during the hostilities he played in three games for Western Command (1944–45). An England schoolboy international, he went on to win three full caps for his country, against Wales,

Northern Ireland and Sweden in 1947, the same year he won the League title with the Reds, later adding an FA Cup runners-up medal to his collection after defeat by Arsenal in the 1950 final. He also represented the Football League and England 'B'. As a youngster Taylor was a clever, weaving inside- or wing-forward who was switched to half-back in 1946 to replace Matt Busby. There he developed into a class performer, exhibiting wonderful ground passes and always giving his forwards (and at times his defenders) terrific support. He made the first of his senior appearances for Liverpool against Derby County (away) in March 1936 when he played on the left wing in place of Syd Roberts. After retiring he did great things behind the scenes at Anfield, just failing as manager to get the team back into the top flight. He did however see the Reds knocked out of the FA Cup by non-League side Worcester City! He subsequently handed over his duties to Bill Shankly. Also a useful cricketer, Taylor played in one first-class County match for Gloucestershire in 1938. Taylor is believed to be still alive – making him one of Liverpool's oldest surviving players.

TENNANT, JOHN WILLIE
Left-back: 42 apps
Born: Newcastle-upon-Tyne, 3 August 1907 – *Died*: 1978
Career: Washington Colliery (County Durham), Newcastle United (reserves), Stoke City (1927), Torquay United (1932), LIVERPOOL (May 1933), Bolton Wanderers (January 1936), Stoke City (November 1938); guest for LIVERPOOL, Southport and Wrexham during WW2; did not play football after 1946

A versatile defender who occupied both full-back berths with confidence, Jack Tennant was, in fact, a goalkeeper as a lad and he also led the Washington Colliery attack after coming up from the pit. During his career he played in every position but preferred a full-back role overall. He made his senior debut for the Reds in a 4–2 League defeat at Aston Villa in September 1933 and 28 of his appearances for the club came the following season, all at left-back, mainly as partner to Tommy Cooper. Guesting from Stoke City during WW2, Tennant made a further 15 appearances for the Reds.

THOMAS, MICHAEL LAURISTON
Midfield: 128+35 apps, 12 goals
Born: Lambeth, London, 24 August 1967
Career: Henry Thornton School, South London Schools, Arsenal (associated schoolboy forms, September 1982; apprentice, August 1983; professional, December 1984), Portsmouth (loan, December 1986), LIVERPOOL (£1.5m, December 1991), Middlesbrough (loan, February–May 1998), Benfica/Portugal (July 1998)

On the last day of the 1988–89 League season Arsenal travelled to Anfield needing to win by two clear goals (2–0) to steal the title from under the noses of Liverpool. They did just that thanks to a dramatic second goal scored in the very last minute by Cockney-born Michael Thomas. Two years later, however, all was forgiven as the 24-year-old strong-running midfielder moved to Merseyside, signed by Reds manager Graeme Souness who, in truth, had been watching the player (along with other managers and scouts) for quite some time before moving in to secure his services. Injuries had plagued Thomas at various times as an Arsenal player but he was still able to amass an impressive record during his eight years with the Gunners, scoring 31 goals in 210 appearances. He also gained a League Cup winner's medal and a second League championship medal as well as collecting 2 full, 2 'B', 12 under-21, six under-19 and 14 youth caps for England, having earlier represented his country as a schoolboy. He later starred in three more 'B' internationals as a Liverpool player and was the recipient of another FA Cup winner's medal in 1992, as well as winning the League Cup three years later. The first of his 163 senior outings for Liverpool was against Tottenham Hotspur (away) in December 1991; he came on as a second-half substitute in a 2–1 win. He was a regular in the side after that, forming a very useful midfield department with Jan Molby, Steve McManaman, Ray Houghton and others. Unfortunately a snapped Achilles tendon didn't help matters as injury again affected his game. Thankfully he recovered and went on to serve the Reds impressively until leaving for the sun of Portugal in 1998, turning down Bayern Munich to rejoin his old boss, Souness, at Benfica following a short loan spell with Middlesbrough.

THOMPSON, CHARLES

Half-back: 6 apps
Born: Forest Hall, April 1909 – *Died*: Cumbria, *circa* 1979
Career: Wallsend-on-Tyne (North-Eastern League, 1926), LIVERPOOL (professional, May 1929), Blackpool (April 1931), Barrow (May 1932, released May 1933); emigrated to South Africa before returning to live in Cumbria until his death

Signed after impressing with Wallsend, Charlie Thompson proved to be a very reliable reserve during his two seasons at Anfield. A strong tackler, he made the first of his six senior appearances for the club against Newcastle United in April 1930, starring at centre-half in a 0–0 draw. He failed to make Blackpool's first team and on his release from Barrow went into business in Carlisle.

THOMPSON, DAVID ANTHONY

Midfield: 31+25 apps, 5 goals
Born: Birkenhead, 12 September 1977
Career: LIVERPOOL (apprentice, September 1993; professional, November 1994), Swindon Town (loan, November 1997–January 1998), Coventry City (£3m, August 2000), Blackburn Rovers (£1.5m, August 2002), Wigan Athletic (free, January 2006)

David Thompson spent seven years at Anfield but was never a regular in the first team, owing, of course, to the enormous amount of midfield talent at the club. However, when called into action he certainly gave a good account of himself with some excellent performances. An FA Youth Cup winner in 1996, he made his debut for the Reds against Arsenal (as a substitute) in August of that same year and scored his first goal for the club in a 7–1 home Premiership win over

Southampton in January 1999. An England youth international who later added seven under-21 caps to his collection, Thompson, a real live-wire who was aggressive, tenacious and industrious, played in 72 senior games for Coventry before re-entering the Premiership with Blackburn Rovers in 2002, signed by another ex-Liverpool star, Graeme Souness. He was plagued by injuries during his first two and a half years at Ewood Park but came back strongly in 2005 (after Mark Hughes had taken over as manager) and re-established himself in the side, taking his career appearance record past the 250 mark before moving to Wigan.

THOMPSON, MAXWELL STUART
Defender: 1+1 apps
Born: Liverpool, 31 December 1956
Career: Liverpool junior football, LIVERPOOL (apprentice, April 1973; professional, January 1974), Blackpool (loan, December 1977; signed for £80,000, March 1978), Dallas Tornado/USA (loan, summer of 1980), Seattle Sounders/NASL (loan, March–July 1981), Swansea City (£20,000, August 1981), AFC Bournemouth (free, August 1983), Port Vale (loan, November–December 1983), Baltimore Blast/USA (June 1984); later with Coimbra FC/Portugal (1985), Northwich Victoria (1986), Caernarfon Town, Fleetwood, Newport County, Kramfors/Sweden, Southport, Knowsley United (manager), LIVERPOOL (physiotherapist), Southport (physiotherapist)
Tall central defender Max Thompson made only two senior appearances for Liverpool, the first against Tottenham Hotspur (away) in May 1974 – four days after the FA Cup final. Unable to get regular first-team action, he left for Blackpool, initially on loan in 1977, and played in 109 competitive games for the Seasiders, following up with over 30 more for Swansea with whom he gained a Welsh Cup winner's medal in 1982 by playing in the first leg of the final against Cardiff City.

THOMPSON, PETER
Outside-left: 408+8 apps, 55 goals
Born: Carlisle, Cumbria, 27 November 1942
Career: Carlisle and District Schools, Preston North End (amateur, August 1958; professional, November 1959), LIVERPOOL (£37,000, August 1963), Bolton Wanderers (loan, November 1973; signed for £18,000, January 1974; retired, March 1978); later ran a Blackpool caravan park, was director of a garage and, along with his wife, ran a hotel on Lake Windermere
Peter Thompson was an orthodox winger who preferred playing on the left rather than the right. Fast and clever with a myriad of tricks, he teased and tormented full-backs at the highest level for almost 20 years. A gifted performer – adored by Reds boss Bill Shankly – 'Thommo' delighted the Anfield faithful for a decade, producing many outstanding performances. He could cross a ball inch-perfect, high or low and, in fact, some newspaper pundits (and indeed, older supporters) compared him at times to the great Tom Finney who was a legend at Deepdale where, of course, Thompson began his career. Finney and

Thompson were club colleagues together at Preston for two years before the former retired in the summer of 1960. 'Thommo' went on to score 31 goals in 146 first-class games for North End before joining Liverpool for what was to prove a bargain fee. He made the first of his 416 appearances for the Reds at Blackburn in August 1963 and at the end of his first season gained a League championship winner's medal as an ever-present. Thereafter Thompson – and Liverpool – continued to produce the goods and win trophies: lifting the FA Cup in 1965 and securing a second League victory in 1966, while runners-up medals were gained in the European Cup-Winners' Cup, also in 1966, and the FA Cup in 1971. Recognised by England at schoolboy level, Thompson went on to win 16 full and 4 under-23 caps and he also represented the Football League. After leaving Anfield he appeared in 132 senior games for Bolton (2 goals scored) before retiring at the age of 35. Thompson was an entertainer – one of the finest in the game during the 1960s.

THOMPSON, PHILIP BERNARD
Defender: 459+7 apps, 12 goals
Born: Kensington, Liverpool, 21 January 1954
Career: Kirkby Schools (Liverpool), LIVERPOOL (apprentice, April 1970; professional, February 1971), Sheffield United (loan, December 1984; signed permanently, March 1985; retired May 1986), LIVERPOOL (coaching staff, July 1986–May 1992 and summer 1999–June 2004; acting also as caretaker-manager and assistant manager at various times); now a soccer pundit/reporter on Sky Sport

Tall and gangly, Phil Thompson didn't look like a footballer on the training pitch – but when kitted out he certainly gave Liverpool wonderful service over a period of 15 years before moving to Sheffield United. Strong in the tackle, confident with the ball, powerful in the air, he was called 'matchstick legs' by manager Bill Shankly but had the heart of a lion, developing into one of the finest defenders the club has ever had, amassing well over 450 senior appearances. Surprisingly, he did not figure in the first team on a regular basis until 1973–74, having had just 25 outings prior to that – his debut coming against Manchester United in April 1972 when he came on as a second-half substitute for John Toshack in front of 54,000 fans at Old Trafford, a game Liverpool won 3–0. Playing alongside Emlyn Hughes (initially) and then Alan Hansen, Thompson was eventually replaced by Mark Lawrenson – but not until after he had helped the Reds win five League titles (1976, 1977, 1979, 1980 and 1982), the European Cup twice (1978 and 1981), the UEFA Cup (1976), the FA Cup (1974) and the League Cup (1981 and 1982) as well as tasting success in the European Super Cup (1977) and claiming the FA Charity Shield five times (1974, 1976, 1979, 1980, 1982), sharing it once (1977). He also gained a handful of runners-up medals, while on the international front he was capped 42 times at senior level by England, played in one under-23 match, helped his country's youth team win the 'Little World Cup' in Spain in the summer of 1972 (with Everton's Mick Buckley) and played for the Football League side. As a youngster Thompson stood on the Kop at Anfield cheering the Reds to League glory in the 1960s, not knowing that in years to come he would skipper his favourite team to major success in England and Europe. He was coach at Liverpool under four different managers. Ironically Thompson's father is a keen Everton fan.

THOMSON, ROBERT
Right-back: 7 apps
Born: Menstrie, Clackmannanshire, 21 November 1939
Career: Sauchie FC, Partick Thistle (professional, August 1957), LIVERPOOL (£7,000, December 1962), Luton Town (£3,000, August 1965–May 1967)
After doing very well in Partick Thistle's second team, Bobby Thomson was lured to Anfield by Liverpool manager and fellow Scot Bill Shankly as cover for right-back Gerry Byrne. He made just seven senior appearances in less than three years on Merseyside, the first against Fulham (away) in April 1963 when he partnered Ronnie Moran. Thomson played in 74 League games for Luton in two seasons.

TOMLEY, FREDERICK WILLIAM
Centre-half: 2 apps
Born: Liverpool, 11 July 1931
Career: Litherland FC (Liverpool), LIVERPOOL (amateur, August 1951; professional, September 1953), Chester (July 1955, free transfer, May 1956)
One of five different centre-halves used by Liverpool during the 1954–55 season, 6ft 2in. giant Fred Tomley made his debut for the club in a 4–3 win at Bury in March 1955. He played in only one Third Division (N) game for Chester.

TOSHACK, JOHN BENJAMIN, MBE
Forward: 237+9 apps, 96 goals
Born: Cardiff, 22 March 1949
Career: Radyr Junior School XI, Canton High School Rugby XV, Pegasus FC (all in Cardiff), Cardiff Schools, Cardiff City (apprentice, June 1965; professional, March 1966), LIVERPOOL (£111,000, November 1970), Swansea City (free, player-manager, March 1978; resigned, October 1983; re-appointed as manager, December 1983–March 1984), Sporting Lisbon/Portugal (manager-coach, May 1984–May 1985), Real Sociedad/Spain (manager-coach, August 1985–May 1989), Real Madrid/Spain (manager, May 1989–November 1990), Real Sociedad/Spain (general manager, February 1991; manager, May 1991); thereafter Deportivo La Coruña/Spain (manager, two spells), Real Madrid (manager for a second time), Besiktas/Turkey (manager), St Etienne/France (manager), also Wales (manager, two spells, the second from November 2004)
After netting a hat-trick for Wales against Northern Ireland in a schoolboy international and grabbing 47 goals in 22 matches for the Cardiff Schools team, John Toshack became one of the youngest players ever to appear in a League game for Cardiff City, making his debut as a 16 year old against Leyton Orient in November 1965 – scoring to celebrate the occasion. Turning professional at Ninian Park in 1966, he became a star performer with the Welsh club, going on

to claim 75 goals in 162 League games and gaining three Welsh Cup winner's medals before joining Liverpool – this after Cardiff boss Jimmy Scoular had turned down substantial bids from both Birmingham City and Fulham. Making his debut against Coventry City, Toshack scored and set up the winner for Chris Lawler in his first Merseyside derby soon afterwards. But despite these efforts he still made a tentative start to his Liverpool career. Not undaunted, he worked hard at his game, eventually drawing up a wonderfully successful partnership with Kevin Keegan . . . and it was commonplace to see big 'Tosh' rising high to knock the ball down into the path of his colleague. It was a combination of the tall, muscular front man (Toshack) and the mercurial, elusive predator (Keegan) . . . and what a terrific understanding they had between them. Not everyone liked Toshack – he had many critics – but as his boss, Bill Shankly, once said: '. . . his record speaks for itself and that is all I am interested in'.

During his seven and a half years at Anfield, Toshack helped the Reds win three League championships (1973, 1976, 1977), the FA Cup (1974) and the UEFA Cup twice (1973, 1976) while collecting runners-up medals in the League (1974, 1975) and FA Cup (1971). He was capped 26 times by Wales as a Liverpool player and in all represented his country in 40 full and 3 under-23 internationals.

When he left Anfield in 1978, Toshack didn't anticipate what was in store for him . . . but what a superb job he did at The Vetch Field, transforming the Swans from an ordinary Fourth Division side into a decent, hard-working First Division outfit, the Welsh club achieving promotion in 1978, 1979 and 1981 by virtue of winning their final game of each season in their respective divisions. In fact, it was the first time in the club's history that top-line football had been staged at The Vetch Field and Toshack, besides his marvellous League exploits, also saw his charges claim a hat-trick of Welsh Cup final victories, in 1981, 1982 and 1983.

He signed quite a few more ex-Liverpool players to boost the squad but in 1983 things started to go wrong and he resigned – only to return to the fray in double-quick time, before leaving for good in March 1984 after results had failed to improve. Out of work for a while, Toshack returned as boss of Sporting Lisbon and after that did well in Spain, steering the San Sebastian side Real Sociedad to victory in the Spanish Cup final of 1987 and guiding Real Madrid to the La Liga title in 1990, later adding further trophies to his collection when in Spain. Sadly, from his point of view, he didn't achieve a great deal when in charge of the Welsh national team. He was awarded the MBE in March 1982 for services to soccer. He was also the subject of the BBC TV programme *This Is Your Life*.

TOSSWILL, JOHN SPEARE
Inside-right: 11 apps, 1 goal
Born: Eastbourne, 6 August 1890 – *Died*: Brighton, 28 September 1915
Career: Eastbourne FC (September 1905), Hastings and St Leonard's (1906), Aberdare Athletic (1907), Tunbridge Wells Rangers (1908), Maidstone United (1910), Queens Park Rangers (1911), LIVERPOOL (June 1912),

Southend United (August 1913), Coventry City (1914); served with the Royal Engineers as a dispatch rider during the early part of WW1; taken ill and sent home (to Brighton), he died after an operation, aged 25

Although having served with six different clubs, Jack Tosswill was nevertheless an inexperienced inside-forward with only three Southern League games under his belt when he arrived at Anfield. He spent just one season with Liverpool, having almost a dozen outings, scoring on his debut against Oldham Athletic in September 1912 when he partnered Arthur Goddard on the right wing. He failed to hold his place (replaced by the converted Don McKinlay) and had brief spells with Southend and Coventry before his demise.

TRAORE, DJIMI

Defender: 120+19 apps, 1 goal

Born: Laval, France, 1 March 1980

Career: Laval FC/France (semi-professional, April 1997), LIVERPOOL (£550,000, February 1999), Racing Club Lens/France (loan, during season 2001–02)

Djimi Traore was still only 18 years of age when he joined Liverpool in 1999. With limited experience behind him, he made only eight Premiership appearances in his first four seasons at Anfield but then got to grips with the English game and after that became a key member of the senior squad, having by far his best run in the first XI in 2002–23 when he played in 49 competitive games, mostly as an attacking left-back and some at the heart of the defence. He made his debut for the Reds against Hull City in the League Cup in September 1999 and having represented France in both youth and under-21 internationals, Traore 'changed' countries and has since been capped five times by Mali at senior level. He helped Liverpool win the League Cup in 2003 and the European Champions League two years later. He has now taken his appearance tally past the 150 mark. Was an unused substitute when Liverpool beat West Ham on penalties in the 2006 FA Cup final.

TWENTYMAN, GEOFFREY

Half-back: 184 apps, 19 goals

Born: Carlisle, 19 January 1930 – *Died*: Southport, 16 February 2004

Career: Swifts Rovers (Carlisle), Carlisle United (amateur, August 1945; professional, February 1947), LIVERPOOL (£10,000, December 1953), Ballymena United (player-manager, March 1959), Carlisle United (as a player, June 1963), Morecambe (player-manager, June 1964), Hartlepools United (June–October 1965), Penrith (manager-coach, July 1966), LIVERPOOL (chief scout and part-time coach, August 1967–1970)

Geoff Twentyman was one of Carlisle United's finest discoveries and after producing some superb displays there was a lot of speculation as to which First Division club would sign him. In the end, after more than 150 appearances for the Cumbrians, it was struggling Liverpool who secured his services halfway through the 1953–54 season but his presence in defence failed to keep the Reds in the top flight. He played very well in what was a moderate Liverpool team and despite a couple of near misses, promotion was not forthcoming. Twentyman, strong in the air with a very powerful and sometimes unexpected shot, made his debut for the club in December 1953 in a 5–1 defeat at Manchester United. Another five goals were conceded in his second outing at top-of-the-table West Brom but in his third game Liverpool drew 0–0 with the Albion at Anfield.

He captained the Irish League when associated with Ballymena and he was replaced by a certain Brian Clough in the hot seat at Hartlepool.

UNDERWOOD, EDMUND DAVID
Goalkeeper: 50 apps
Born: St Pancras, London, 15 March 1928 – *Died*: Hertfordshire, 6 January 1989
Career: Edgware Town (1945), Queens Park Rangers (amateur, September 1949; professional, December 1949), Watford (February 1952), LIVERPOOL (£7,000, December 1953), Watford (£1,250, July 1956), Dartford (free, August 1957), Watford (free, part-time professional, April 1960), Fulham (free, July 1963), Dunstable Town (July 1965), Hastings United (August 1966, appointed player-manager, June 1967), Barnet (Chairman, 1970s); also ran his own haulage contractor's business

Making his debut for Liverpool in place of Russell Crossley on the same day as Geoff Twentyman (q.v.) in December 1953, Dave Underwood wondered what had hit him when he let in five goals. He missed the next game but came back for the draw with the Albion on Boxing Day and held his place until September 1954 when Charlie Ashcroft took over, followed by Doug Rudham. He languished in the reserves after that but came back strongly during the second half of 1955–56 before losing his place again, this time to Scotsman Tommy Younger. On his day Underwood was a very efficient keeper who in his three spells with Watford amassed 176 League appearances. He joined Fulham at the age of 35 as cover for Tony Macedo. He was a record sale by Watford back in 1953.

UREN, HAROLD JOHN
Outside-left: 46 apps, 2 goals
Born: Barnet Regis, Bristol, 23 August 1885 – *Died*: 7 April 1955
Career: Millbank Juniors (Bristol), Northern Nomads (1903), Hoylake FC (1905), LIVERPOOL (amateur, May 1907; professional, September 1909), Everton (in exchange for Bill Lacey and Tom Gracie, February 1912), Wrexham (May 1913, retired, injured, October 1913)

Harold Uren was a splendid dribbler, hard to dispossess but a player who had the annoying habit of overdoing the clever stuff! A shade on the hefty side for a winger, he was exchanged for two players from Goodison Park after scoring twice in almost 50 senior appearances for Liverpool for whom he made his debut against Manchester City (away) in November 1907 when he lined up at inside-right as partner to Robbie Robinson. He took up his usual position on the left wing in his next game (v. Preston). Unfortunately due to injury he never got a game with Wrexham.

VAN DER BERG, HARMAN HUBERT CHRISTOPHER

Outside-left: 22 apps, 4 goals

Born: Cape Town, South Africa, 13 August 1912 – *Died*: Transvaal, South Africa, 7 June 1977

Career: Peninsula FC (Cape Town), LIVERPOOL (professional, October 1937; retired, injured, May 1941); returned to South Africa where he worked in the diamond industry

Harman Van der Berg was an exceptionally tall, long-striding outside-left, quick over the ground with an eye for goal. He was signed as cover for Alf Hanson but then had Bill Kinghorn to compete with for a first-team place during the last season before WW2. Making his League debut for the Reds in the Merseyside derby against Everton in February 1938 (won 3–1), he scored for the first time in a 2–2 draw at Leicester eight months later and then netted one of the quickest goals ever by a Liverpool player (after just 33 seconds) against Huddersfield Town at Leeds Road in October 1938 (3–3 draw). Van der Berg, whose brother played cricket in South Africa, claimed 4 goals in 17 WW2 games for the Reds.

VENISON, BARRY

Full-back/midfield: 145+20 apps, 3 goals

Born: Stanley, County Durham, 16 August 1964

Career: Consett schoolboy football, Stanley Boys (seasons 1977–79), Sunderland (apprentice, May 1979; professional, January 1982), LIVERPOOL (£250,000, July 1986), Newcastle United (1992), Galatasaray/Turkey (£750,000, June 1995), Southampton (£850,000, October 1995, retired, injured, May 1997); became a national TV presenter for ITV Sport

Barry Venison won three youth and ten under-21 caps for England and made 205 senior appearances in his 7 years at Roker Park, making his League debut at the age of 17 years 55 days v. Notts County in October 1981. He is also the youngest player to captain a team at Wembley, leading Sunderland, in the absence of Shaun Elliott, against Norwich City in the League Cup final of 1985, a game the Canaries won 1–0. He joined Liverpool in 1986 after helping the Wearsiders avoid relegation to the Third Division and was immediately included in the Reds' line-up at the start of the new campaign against Newcastle United (away) when he partnered Gary Gillespie at full-back in a 2–0 win. A composed player who could also man midfield very efficiently, Venison had a determined and positive attitude towards the game. He was never overrun by an opposing winger, always linked up well with his front men and delivered, most of the time, accurate crosses. As new defenders such as Gary Ablett, Steve Staunton and David Burrows came to the fore, Venison's position in the Reds' back division was not guaranteed and in the summer of 1992 he moved back to the North-east with Newcastle (signed by Kevin Keegan). He won successive League championships with Liverpool (1988 and 1989), was also a member of the Reds' 1989 FA Cup winning team, won four FA Charity Shields (1986, 1988, 1989 and 1990) and the Screen Sport Super Cup (1986). After leaving Anfield he did well at St James' Park, helping the Magpies gain promotion to the Premiership as First Division champions in 1993 and gaining two full caps for his country.

Another ex-Liverpool star, Graeme Souness, signed him for the Turkish side Galatasaray and when Venison was a Southampton player, Souness came along to The Dell as his manager. During his career, which ended a shade prematurely due to a back problem, Venison amassed 563 appearances at club and international level. He became a television presenter after hanging up his boots and was often seen wearing a flashy shirt and matching tie!

VIGNAL, GREGORY
Defender: 14+6 apps
Born: Montpellier, France, 19 July 1981
Career: Montpellier Herault Sport Club/France (professional, August 1998), LIVERPOOL (£500,000, September 2000), Sport Club Bastia/Corsica (loan, September–December 2002), Stade Rennais FC/France (loan, August 2003–May 2004), Glasgow Rangers (loan, July 2004–May 2005), Portsmouth (free, July 2005)

Not too many players have been loaned out for two and a half seasons, but Liverpool's promising young Frenchman Gregory Vignal was – and he did well with each club he served, gaining both Scottish Premier League and League Cup winner's medals with Rangers in 2005, making 30 appearances in the former competition and scoring a vital goal in the Old Firm derby win over Celtic in February. A strong competitor with good pace, he was a non-playing substitute when Liverpool won the FA Cup, UEFA Cup and European Super Cup in 2001 and two years later lifted the League Cup. He made his debut for the Reds in a third-round FA Cup tie against Rotherham United in January 2001, replacing Vladimir Smicer in the second half of a 3–0 win.

WADDLE, ALAN ROBERT
Centre-forward: 26+6 apps, 1 goal
Born: Wallsend-on-Tyne, 1 December 1954
Career: Wallsend Boys' Club, Halifax Town (professional, October 1971), LIVERPOOL (£50,000, June 1973), Leicester City (£45,000, September 1977), Swansea City (£24,000, May 1978), Newport County (£80,000, December 1980), Gloucester City (free, September 1981), Mansfield Town (free, August 1982), Happy Valley FC/Hong Kong (December 1982), Hartlepool United (free, August 1983), Peterborough United (£6,000, October 1983), Hartlepool United (non-contract, January 1985), Swansea City (non-contract, March 1985), Barry Town (part-time professional, March–May 1986), Swansea City (commercial operations manager, June 1986), Port Talbot (1987), Maesteg Park (1988), Bridgend Town (November 1989), Llanelli (December 1989–May 1993)

Cousin of the former England forward Chris Waddle, Alan Waddle's nomadic career in League football brought him 76 goals in 289 appearances. Standing almost 6ft 4in. tall and exceptionally good in the air, he had the pleasure of scoring the winning goal for Liverpool in his first Merseyside derby in December 1973 in front of more than 56,000 fans at Anfield – this after an impressive debut the week before against West Ham. Never quite hitting it off with the Reds, he went on to become a very efficient striker who certainly did the business in the lower divisions.

Bill Shankly declared: 'He [Waddle] is so tall they will have to lift the crossbar when he plays.'

WADSWORTH, HAROLD

Outside-right/-left: 54 apps, 3 goals
Born: Bootle, 1 October 1898 – *Died*: Chesterfield, 2 November 1975
Career: Bootle St Matthews (Bootle League), Tranmere Rovers (amateur, April 1914), LIVERPOOL (amateur, January 1918; professional, August 1918), Leicester City (June 1924), Nottingham Forest (April 1927), Millwall Athletic (June 1928, retired May 1932)

Harold Wadsworth joined his long-serving brother Walter (below) at Anfield during the 1917–18 wartime season and soon etched a reputation as a fast-raiding winger by scoring 11 goals in 34 regional appearances for Liverpool before normal League football resumed in August 1919. He had to wait until the eighth match of that season (at Newcastle in early October) before making his senior debut, deputising for Bert Pearson on the left flank. He was, however, confined to the reserves for long periods before having a good 1920–21 season, netting 3 times in 25 First Division matches. After leaving Anfield he helped Leicester win the Second Division championship in 1925 and was a key member of Millwall's side for three years before spending his last season in the treatment room. His career realised 252 League appearances (28 goals).

WADSWORTH, WALTER

Centre-half: 241 apps, 8 goals
Born: Bootle, 7 October 1890 – *Died*: Cheshire, 12 October 1951
Career: Lingdale FC (West Cheshire League), Ormskirk (1911), LIVERPOOL (professional, June 1912), Bristol City (May 1926), Flint Town (player-manager, June 1928), New Brighton (player, January 1929), Oswestry Town (September 1930, retired May 1931)

Walter Wadsworth – known as 'Big Waddy' – started out as a full-back before developing into a first-class centre-half. Outstanding when Liverpool won successive League titles in 1922 and 1923, he drew up an excellent understanding with his co-defenders and goalkeeper. Strong in the air and on the ground (in the tackle), he did, however, have the tendency to give the ball far too much height when clearing his lines. He made the first of his 241 senior appearances for the Reds against Middlesbrough (away) in March 1915 when he deputised at left-half for Don McKinlay. He had 112 first-team outings during WW1 and after the hostilities became the club's first choice centre-half, retaining his position (injuries allowing) until 1925 when he gave way to David Pratt. A Football League representative, Wadsworth came close to winning a full England cap in 1923 but was pipped for a place by Jimmy Seddon of Bolton Wanderers.

WALKER, JOHN

Inside-right: 133 apps, 31 goals

Born: Coatbridge, 31 May 1874 – *Died*: Scotland, 1940

Career: Armadale FC, Heart of Midlothian (professional, August 1893), LIVERPOOL (£350 with Tom Robertson, April 1898), Glasgow Rangers (May 1902), Greenock Morton (August 1904; retired, injured, April 1905)

John Walker could, and would, play in any forward position for Liverpool but preferred the inside-right berth where he performed admirably for four seasons before returning to Scotland. He made his debut in the Football League in a 4–0 home win over Sheffield Wednesday in September 1898 and netted six goals that season as the Reds finished runners-up in the First Division behind Aston Villa, pipped for the title by just two points. He made up for that disappointment in 1901 when he gained a winner's medal himself as Liverpool took the title ahead of Sunderland. Given the chance, Walker would try a shot from anywhere (within reason) and he was also an individualist, often going on a mazy run through the opposing defence. Capped five times by Scotland (three with Hearts, two with Rangers) between 1895 and 1904, he also represented the Scottish League on five occasions and played in one international trial. Twice a League championship winner with Hearts in 1895 and 1897, he also gained a Scottish Cup winner's medal in 1896 and after leaving Anfield, helped Rangers win the Cup in 1903, finishing runners-up the following season.

WALL, THOMAS PETER

Left-back: 42 apps

Born: Westbury, Wiltshire, 13 September 1944

Career: Local junior football, Shrewsbury Town (apprentice, April 1961; professional, September 1962), Wrexham (£3,000, November 1964), LIVERPOOL (£26,000 plus Stuart Mason, October 1966), Crystal Palace (£35,000, May 1970), Leyton Orient (loan, December 1972–March 1973); returned to Palace (released, March 1978)

During an excellent career, full-back Peter Wall accumulated 258 League appearances, having his best spell with Crystal Palace with whom he was registered for eight years. He had done very well as a youngster with Wrexham before joining Liverpool at the age of 22, making his debut for the Reds against Burnley in March 1968 when he replaced the injured Gerry Byrne. He partnered Chris Lawler in nine League games at the end of that season and in 13 at the start of the next before reverting to second-team football. With Geoff Strong switched to left-back Wall found it hard to get into the senior side after that and was transferred to Selhurst Park in 1970.

WALLACE, GORDON HENRY

Inside-left/midfield: 21+1 apps, 6 goals

Born: Lanark, 13 June 1944

Career: Central School (Motherwell), Lanarkshire junior football, Motherwell (trialist, 1958), LIVERPOOL (amateur, June 1959; professional, July 1961), Crewe Alexandra (£5,000, October 1967–May 1972)

A pupil at the same school which produced Ian St John, Gordon Wallace could play in both inside-forward positions and on the left wing but found life tough at Anfield owing to the depth of players of similar ability. He made the first of his 22 senior appearances for Liverpool in a 1–0 defeat at West Bromwich Albion in October 1962, partnering Jimmy Melia on the left wing. After leaving the club he scored 20 goals in 94 League outings for Crewe.

WALSH, JAMES ARTHUR
Inside-/centre-forward: 76 apps, 27 goals
Born: Stockport, 15 May 1901 – *Died*: 1971
Career: Edgeley Park Juniors, Stockport Lads' Club, Stockport County (amateur, July 1919; professional, April 1920), LIVERPOOL (June 1922), Hull City (June 1928), Crewe Alexandra (briefly in 1931), Colwyn Bay (August 1932–May 1933)
A clever footballer who could also occupy a wing-half position, Jimmy Walsh had a useful career in League football, scoring 38 goals in 188 appearances. He had his best spell with Hull after giving Liverpool good service for six years. He netted twice on his debut for the Reds against Birmingham in August 1923 (won 6–2) and played in 42 League and Cup games that season, all at centre-forward, finishing up as top scorer with 19 goals. He was later converted into a very capable right-half by Hull City and at the time was said to be 'keen in tackling . . . a ready wit and a ready kick'. Walsh toured Australia with the FA party in 1925, playing in three Test matches against the Aussie national team.

WALSH, PAUL ANTHONY
Forward: 92+20 apps, 37 goals
Born: Plumstead, South London, 1 October 1962
Career: Blackheath Schools, South London Schools, London Schools, Charlton Athletic (professional, October 1979), Luton Town (July 1982), LIVERPOOL (May 1984), Tottenham Hotspur (February 1988), Queens Park Rangers (loan, September 1991), Portsmouth (£400,000, June 1992), Manchester City (£750,000, March 1994), Portsmouth (£500,000 exchange deal involving Gerry Creaney, September 1995; retired, knee ligament injury, December 1997); later a soccer summariser on Sky Sport
From his early days as a teenager which saw him win ten England youth caps, Paul Walsh showed a natural talent. He made his first-class debut for Charlton in 1979 and played his last competitive match for Portsmouth in 1996, an injured knee eventually ending his career. In-between times, he prospered to the full as a thirsty, all-action, ball-playing and goalscoring forward. He became the youngest-ever Charlton player to net a hat-trick (aged 20 v. Brentford in August 1980), appeared in five full (his first on tour to Australia in 1983) and four under-21 internationals for his country, starred for the London FA XI (v. England at Highbury) in 1981, was voted PFA 'Young Player of the Year' in 1984, collected a runners-up medal when Liverpool lost the 1985 European Cup final to Juventus at the Heysel Stadium, earned League championship and Screen Sport Super Cup winner's medals a year later, received a League Cup

runners-up prize in 1987 and finally won both the FA Cup and FA Charity Shield with Spurs in 1991 . . . not forgetting that he also netted 162 goals in 633 club matches. He made the first of his 112 senior appearances for Liverpool as a substitute at Wembley, in the 1984 FA Charity Shield defeat by Everton, following up a week later with his League baptism against Norwich City (away) when he set up one of his side's goals in a 3—3 draw. Very popular among the fans and blessed with a terrific work-rate, during his time at Anfield the likeable Walsh underwent cartilage and hernia operations, suffered a broken wrist, damaged ankle ligaments and a twisted knee, an injury which flared up again in February 1996 when he was playing for Portsmouth v. Leicester. He never recovered full fitness, announcing his retirement at the age of 35 after a wonderful innings. Plucky and determined, he was sidelined for a total of 12 months as a Liverpool player but always bounced back. He gave the Reds almost four years' service before transferring to White Hart Lane.

WALTERS, MARK EVERTON
Wing-forward: 83+42 apps, 19 goals
Born: Birmingham, 2 June 1964
Career: Hampton Junior and Holte Grammar Schools (Lozells, Birmingham), Aston and District Boys, Birmingham Schools, Birmingham City (trialist, during season 1979—80), Aston Villa (apprentice, June 1980; professional, May 1982), Glasgow Rangers (£650,000, December 1987), LIVERPOOL (£1.25m, August 1991), Stoke City (loan, March—April 1994), Wolverhampton Wanderers (loan, September—October 1994), Southampton (free, January 1996), Swindon Town (free, July 1996), Bristol Rovers (free, November 1999), Ilkeston Town (August 2002), Dudley Town (September 2003—May 2004)

Mark Walters could play on both wings but preferred the left. Fast and tricky with an excellent body swerve and telling shot, he could cross a ball with great precision, sometimes when in full flight, and was also an expert at dead-ball situations. He had one favourite trick where he used to interrupt his run by dragging his foot over the ball before gliding past his bemused opponent. After representing England at both schoolboy and youth team levels, he went on to win one full, one 'B' and nine under-21 caps. An FA Youth Cup winner with Aston Villa in 1980 and a European Cup victor two years later, he made 225 appearances for the Birmingham club before joining Rangers, where he became a hero with the Ibrox faithful as he helped the 'Gers win three Scottish League titles and two League Cup finals. He netted 52 goals in 143 games in Scottish football before signing for Liverpool, for whom he made his debut as a substitute against Oldham Athletic at Anfield in August 1991 (won 2—1). That season Walters gained an FA Cup winner's medal and three years later added a League Cup winner's prize to his collection. One third of his appearances for the Reds came as a substitute. His career realised more than 750 senior appearances and over 170 goals.

WARK, JOHN

Midfield: 98+16 apps, 42 goals

Born: Glasgow, 4 August 1957

Career: Ipswich Town (apprentice, August 1973; professional, August 1974), LIVERPOOL (£450,000, March 1984), Ipswich Town (£100,000, January 1988), Middlesbrough (£50,000, August 1990), Ipswich Town (free, September 1991, player-coach, August 1994, retired, May 1997); later became a keen after-dinner speaker

John Wark was a professional at the highest level for almost 23 years. During that time he served with three different clubs and amassed a total of 829 senior appearances and scored 225 goals – and also gained 4 youth, 8 under-21 and 29 full caps for Scotland (8 goals). Listed as one of Ipswich Town's all-time greats, he had three spells at Portman Road, netting 181 goals in 678 outings for the Suffolk club whom he helped win the FA Youth Cup (1975), the FA Cup (1978) and the UEFA Cup (1981), all when Bobby Robson was manager. Voted 'Footballer of the Year' also in 1981, he later added a Second Division championship medal to his collection (1992). A European Cup runner-up with Liverpool in 1985 (horrified at what took place prior to kick-off with Juventus in the final at the Heysel Stadium in Brussels) a year later, when the Reds were heading for the League and FA Cup double, Wark sadly broke his leg and missed out on both prizes, as well as Scotland's trip to the World Cup finals in Mexico, although he did help the Reds win the Screen Sport Super Cup (v. Everton). On his day Wark was, without doubt, a tremendous box-to-box player who could defend, create and attack, often combining all three in the space of 90 minutes. A manager's dream, he spent almost four years at Anfield, averaging more than a goal every three games, although he admitted that he was disappointed with his overall performances in a red shirt. Replacing Craig Johnston in the team, he scored on his debut for Liverpool against Watford in March 1984 (won 2–0). However, the strong-running midfield performances he had shown with Ipswich never really shone through at Anfield, although, having said that, he still gave the club good service. Incidentally, Wark was the first player to score a hat-trick of penalties in a major European Cup tie, for Ipswich Town against Aris Salonika of Greece in the 1980–81 UEFA Cup competition.

WARNOCK, STEPHEN

Defender: 40+20 apps, 1 goal

Born: Ormskirk, 12 December 1981

Career: LIVERPOOL (apprentice, April 1998; professional, April 1999), Bradford City (loan, September–November 2002), Coventry City (season loan, July 2003–May 2004)

An England schoolboy and youth international left-back, Stephen Warnock was nurtured through the Academy ranks by Liverpool's efficient coaching staff. He then had a successful spell in the second XI before establishing himself as a vital member of the senior squad at Anfield during season 2004–05, having gained valuable experience as a loan player with first Bradford City and then Coventry City, for whom he made 49 appearances and was voted the Sky Blues 'Player of

271

the Year'. He finally made his first-class debut for the Reds as a substitute against Tottenham Hotspur (away) in August 2004 and then as the season wore on, he was given more outings in place of Djimi Traore. He is not (as some references indicate) related to Neil Warnock (manager of many clubs including Notts County, Oldham Athletic and Sheffield United).

WATKINSON, WILLIAM

Outside-right: 24 apps, 2 goals

Born: Prescot, Lancashire, 16 March 1922

Career: Prescot Cables (August 1939); served in forces during WW2; LIVERPOOL (professional, February 1946), Accrington Stanley (£3,100, January 1951), Halifax Town (£2,500, September 1954), Prescot Cables (August 1956–May 1958)

Bill Watkinson's career took off after he left Anfield – not that he did badly with Liverpool. Far from it – he was a useful player, signed initially as a centre-forward. He was strong, reasonably quick and possessed a powerful right-foot shot. He was mainly kept in reserve by Liverpool, whose main wingers during his time at the club were Harry Eastham, Jimmy Payne, Bob Priday and of course, Billy Liddell. After scoring from the inside-left berth on his League debut against Aston Villa in April 1947 (when the title race was hotting up) Watkinson missed out on a championship medal but made 11 appearances the following season, all on the right wing. Signed by Third Division (N) side Accrington Stanley for a club record fee in 1951, he was outstanding at Peel Park, netting 45 goals in 105 outings in three and a half years – including an 18-minute hat-trick v. Oldham – and finished as their leading scorer in 1952–53. He also had a decent spell with Halifax, claiming 24 goals in 60 games.

WATSON, ALEXANDER FRANCIS

Defender: 7+3 apps

Born: Liverpool, 5 April 1968

Career: LIVERPOOL (apprentice, May 1984; professional, May 1985), Derby County (loan, August–September 1990), Bournemouth (£150,000, January 1991), Gillingham (loan, September–November 1995), Torquay United (£50,000, November 1995, later player-coach), Exeter City (free, July 2001), Taunton Town (June 2003)

Alex Watson's opportunities of first-team football with Liverpool were restricted owing to the presence of so many other fine defenders. An England youth international, he started only seven senior games for the Reds, the first against QPR (away) in March 1988 when he deputised for Barry Venison. He did, however, help the Reds win the Charity Shield that same year. After leaving Anfield, Watson, who developed into a powerful and commanding centre-half, made 182 appearances for Bournemouth and 230 for Torquay, and when he quit top-class football at the age of 35, his overall appearance record stood at 485. His younger brother, Dave Watson, was a junior at Anfield who went on to play for Norwich City (251 appearances) and Everton (529 games) as well as winning 12 full and 7 under-21 caps for England.

WELFARE, HENRY
Outside-right/-left: 4 apps, 1 goal
Born: Liverpool, August 1888 – *Died*: Rio de Janeiro, Brazil, 1961
Career: St Helens Recreationalists, Southport Central (amateur, July 1911), Northern Nomads (amateur, October 1911), LIVERPOOL (amateur, June 1912–May 1914), Corinthians/Brazil (August 1914), Fluminese/Brazil (May 1916, retired *circa* 1924)

A well-known amateur around the Merseyside area before WW1, Harry Welfare made only four League appearances – all for Liverpool – the first against Sheffield Wednesday in February 1913 when he deputised on the left wing for Irish international Billy Lacey. Emigrating in 1914, Welfare – nicknamed 'Cellos' by the South American fans – became a star performer in Brazil. He made over 150 appearances in ten years with Corinthians and Fluminese, helping the latter club (based in Rio de Janeiro) record a hat-trick of League championship wins (1917–18–19). He was 72 when he died.

WELSH, JOHN JOSEPH
Midfield: 3+7 apps
Born: Liverpool, 10 January 1984
Career: LIVERPOOL (apprentice, May 2000; professional, January 2001), Hull (exchange deal involving Paul Anderson, January 2006)

Captain of Liverpool's successful reserve team, John Welsh, 5ft 7in. tall and weighing 11st. 6lb, made his first-team debut as a substitute against Middlesbrough in a fourth-round League Cup tie in November 2004 and he later converted from the spot in a penalty shoot-out with Tottenham Hotspur that propelled the Reds into the semi-finals of that competition. His form was superb and it earned him a call-up to the England under-21 squad, winning four caps to go with those he had earlier gained at youth team level. Unfortunately for Welsh, he couldn't get going the following season and joined Hull City in the deal that brought Paul Anderson to Anfield when the transfer window opened in January 2006.

WEST, ALFRED
Right-back: 140 apps, 6 goals
Born: Nottingham, 15 December 1881 – *Died*: Nottingham, 3 March 1944
Career: Nottingham Boys, Nottingham Jardine FC, Radford Congregationalists, Ilkeston FC (August 1900), Barnsley (professional, May 1902), LIVERPOOL (November 1903), Reading (June 1909), LIVERPOOL (May 1910), Notts County (July 1911), Mansfield Town (August 1919), Shirebrook FC (December 1919, retired, injured, January 1920)

Alf West made exactly 300 appearances in the Football League – his first for Barnsley against Leicester Fosse in September 1903 and his last for Notts County v. Aston Villa in April 1915. Although a Nottingham man, he began his career in Yorkshire, being signed by Barnsley two years after captaining The Rest of the Midland League against the Tykes in a representative match. Not a showy defender, he was consistently cool and reliable, clean-kicking, resourceful and never afraid to tackle. He gave Liverpool excellent service, especially during his first spell at Anfield, making his debut for the Reds in November 1903 against his future club, Notts County, when he was introduced at right-back, his best and favoured position. The recipient of a Second Division championship winner's medal the following season, he helped Liverpool clinch the First Division title twelve months later, missing only one game and scoring three vital penalties, two in one game at Newcastle (won 3–2) and the other to earn a point in the Merseyside derby with Everton (1–1). A regular in Notts County's side for three seasons, he made 134 appearances for the Magpies and gained another Second Division championship medal in 1914. West was also a very fine golfer, securing a handicap of seven.

WESTERVELD, SANDER
Goalkeeper: 103 apps
Born: Enschede, Holland, 23 October 1974
Career: FC Twente Enschede/Holland (amateur, April 1992; professional, November 1993), Vitesse Arnhem/Holland (August 1996), LIVERPOOL (£4m, June 1999), Real Sociedad/Spain (December 2001), Portsmouth (free, June 2005), Everton (loan, February 2006)
A Dutch international, capped by his country at youth, under-21 and senior levels, gaining six caps in the latter category, 6ft 3in. goalkeeper Sander Westerveld played in Liverpool's successful team of 2001, gaining FA Cup, League Cup, UEFA Cup, European Super Cup and FA Charity Shield winner's medals. After enjoying an excellent first season at Anfield, he was even a shade better in his second campaign, producing many outstanding performances, being particularly impressive in the UEFA Cup games against AS Roma and Barcelona. Occasionally uncertain on crosses and corners, he was nevertheless a fine shot-stopper, his huge frame denying the opposition time and again when a goal looked certain. After losing his place to Jerzy Dudek and with Chris Kirkland also signed, he reluctantly left Anfield for Real Sociedad. Westerveld made exactly 100 League appearances for Vitesse before joining Liverpool.

WHEELER, JOHN EDWARD
Right-half: 177 apps, 23 goals
Born: Crosby, Liverpool, 26 July 1928
Career: Carlton FC (Liverpool Combination), Tranmere Rovers (amateur, August 1944; professional, April 1946), Bolton Wanderers (in exchange for Vince Dillon plus £1,500, February 1951), LIVERPOOL (£9,000, September 1956), New Brighton (appointed player-manager, May 1963, but did not take up his position), Bury (assistant trainer, May 1963, head trainer July 1967, assistant manager, September 1969–September 1970)
Also able to play effectively and with flair at inside-right, the gifted Johnny Wheeler was, in fairness, at his best in the right-half position. Possessing loads of stamina, a crunching tackle and strong kick, he enjoyed pushing forward behind the front players and scored some excellent goals, many from long range. Having chalked up over 100 appearances for Tranmere, he then gave Bolton

Wanderers five years' service, playing in the 1953 FA Cup final, one of 205 outings he made for the Burnden Park club, netting 18 goals, including a hat-trick against Blackpool as an emergency centre-forward. He also won five England 'B' caps and represented the Football League in 1955. The first of his 177 senior appearances for Liverpool was against Stoke City (home) in September 1956 when he partnered Brian Jackson on the right wing. He occupied both inside-forward and the two wing-half positions that season before settling down in the number 4 shirt in 1957. His last four seasons with the Reds were under manager Bill Shankly, who replaced him in the side with Gordon Milne, signed from Shankly's former club, Preston.

WHELAN, RONALD ANDREW
Midfield: 475+18 apps, 73 goals
Born: Dublin, 25 September 1961
Career: Home Farm/Dublin (from September 1976), Manchester United (associated schoolboy forms, three spells), LIVERPOOL (free, professional, October 1979), Southend United (free, September 1994, player-manager, June 1995–May 1997)

During his 15 years at Anfield, Ronnie Whelan ('Mr Loyalty' as he was called) won six League championships (1982, 1983, 1984, 1986, 1988 and 1990), three successive League Cup finals (1982, 1983 and 1984), two FA Cup finals (1986 and 1989 as captain), the European Cup final (1984), the FA Charity Shield at Wembley (1982 and 1988, sharing the prize in 1986) and the Screen Sport Super Cup (1986). After representing the Republic of Ireland at schoolboy and youth team levels, he went on to gain one under-21, one 'B' and 45 senior caps (later adding six more to his tally as a Southend player). He was also voted PFA 'Young Player of the Year' in 1982 and appeared in almost 500 competitive games for Liverpool, scoring 73 goals. A workaholic, he covered acres of ground every time he played for the Reds and, indeed, for his country. After spending three summers with Manchester United he signed professional forms with Liverpool as an 18 year old. Classed as a midfielder, he occasionally slotted in as an emergency defender and there's no doubt that he gave his all for the Merseyside club. In the 1950s/60s, Whelan would have been described as an attacking wing-half but in modern times he was the classic goalscoring midfielder, a creator and taker of chances, a fine passer of the ball and very consistent. He packed a powerful shot in his right foot and over the course of time scored some stunning goals for the Reds, including one on his League debut against Stoke City in April 1981 (won 3–1). He eventually replaced Ray Kennedy in the engine-room and went on to captain the team. Injuries interrupted his performances in the early 1990s before he started a new life with Southend, taking his first steps in management in 1995. Whelan's father, Ron senior, played for St Patrick's Athletic and Drogheda in the League of Ireland and was also capped at full international level.

WHITBREAD, ZAK BENJAMIN

Defender: 6+1 apps
Born: Houston, USA, 4 March 1984
Career: LIVERPOOL (apprentice, April 2000; professional, May 2003), Millwall (on loan, November 2005–June 2006)

Central defender Zak Whitbread came successfully through the Anfield Academy to make his senior debut against Millwall in a League Cup tie in October 2004. He made four appearances that season, performing solidly each time.

WHITE, RICHARD

Centre-half/right-back: 217 apps, 1 goal
Born: Scunthorpe, 18 August 1931 – *Died*: Nottingham, 15 June 2002
Career: Scunthorpe Sea Cadets (August 1946), Brumby Amateurs (April 1947), Scunthorpe Sports Club (August 1948), Scunthorpe United (amateur, May 1949; professional August 1950); served in the RAF (on national service); LIVERPOOL (£8,000, November 1955), Doncaster Rovers (£4,250, July 1962), Kettering Town (player-manager, April 1964–April 1966); later worked in a garage

Dick White, a former joiner, played for Scunthorpe United at both non-League and Football League levels. Initially a centre-half, he made 145 senior appearances for the 'Irons' in six years and continued to perform well for the Reds following an impressive debut in a 5–0 win at Barnsley in March 1956 when he deputised for Lawrie Hughes. He finally established himself at the heart of the Liverpool defence in 1957 and after Ron Yeats had been signed, he was successfully switched to right-back, gaining a Second Division championship winner's medal in 1962. Calm, cool and constructive, always a solid figure at the heart of the defence, White made a further 92 appearances for Doncaster and amassed 454 League and Cup appearances in total, before having a two-year spell as player-manager of Kettering Town in the old Southern League.

WHITE, WILLIAM

Inside-right/outside-left: 6 apps, 1 goal
Born: Edinburgh, 1872 – *Died*: Scotland, before 1960
Career: Edinburgh Thistle (1890), Heart of Midlothian (professional, August 1891), Woolwich Arsenal (May 1897), New Brompton (March 1899), Queens Park Rangers, LIVERPOOL (August 1901), Sandyford FC (May 1902, retired, May 1909)

Billy White made a terrific start to his career with Liverpool, scoring inside two minutes when making his debut in the Merseyside derby against Everton at Anfield in September 1901 when 30,000 fans witnessed the 2–2 draw. Strong and forceful, he was better suited to playing through the middle but when he was asked to occupy the left wing position he always produced the goods. He broke through with Hearts before scoring 16 goals in 42 games for Arsenal. He played in the Southern League with both New Brompton and QPR (8 goals in 25 starts) and was 30 years of age when he joined the Reds, spending only one season with the club before returning to Scotland.

WHITEHEAD, JOHN

Goalkeeper: 3 apps
Born: Liverpool, *circa* 1871 – *Died*: after 1935
Career: Bootle (1890), Everton (November 1892), LIVERPOOL (March 1895–April 1896)

Reserve goalkeeper Jack Whitehead spent only one full season at Anfield, acting as cover for Billy McCann and Matt McQueen. He made the first of his three senior appearances in a vital Test match against Bury in April 1895 which was lost and as a result Liverpool suffered relegation to the Second Division. He conceded five goals in his last game against Newton Heath six months later. He had just two outings with Everton.

WHITEHURST, ALBERT JOHN

Centre-forward: 8 apps, 2 goals
Born: Fenton, Stoke-on-Trent, 22 June 1898 – *Died*: Birkenhead, 1976
Career: New Haden FC, Stoke (June 1920), Rochdale (June 1923), LIVERPOOL (May 1928), Bradford City (February 1929), Tranmere Rovers (June 1931, retired, May 1934)

Bert Whitehead was a fine centre-forward who played competitive football for 13 years, having his best spell with Rochdale for whom he netted 116 goals in 168 Third Division (N) appearances, heading that section's scoring charts in 1926–27 with 44 strikes in 42 matches. Unfortunately he failed to impress during his nine months at Anfield, despite making a scoring debut against Bury in August 1928. He won a Third Division (N) championship medal with Bradford City in 1929 and after serving Tranmere (sometimes as a centre-half) he retired with an impressive League record under his belt of 180 goals in 313 appearances.

WHITHAM, JOHN

Forward: 16 apps, 7 goals
Born: Burnley, 8 December 1946
Career: Lancaster Juniors, Holy Trinity FC (Burnley), Sheffield Wednesday (trial, October 1964; signed as a professional, November 1964), LIVERPOOL (£57,000, May 1970, contract cancelled by mutual consent, December 1973), Cardiff City (loan, January 1974, signed March 1974), Reading (July 1975–April 1976), Worksop Town (August 1977), Hallam (August 1979), Oughtbridge (1982), Hallam (December 1983); returned to Sheffield where he became licensee of the Wadsley Jack pub and police social club steward

Jack Whitham made 111 League appearances during his 12-year career, 15 with Liverpool. An England under-23 international, capped against Wales in 1968, his goalscoring exploits made him a popular figure with Sheffield Wednesday – but the moderate appearance tally (71) in a total of 5 years with the Owls is explained by the fact that he spent several periods on the treatment table, his courageous style taking its toll. After his surprise transfer to Anfield, he found the competition fierce at Liverpool. He made his debut for the Reds against Newcastle United (away) in September 1970 and recorded his first goal against West Ham United (away) three months later. Whitham battled hard at Cardiff, gaining a Welsh Cup winner's medal (1974). His grandfather was awarded the VC in 1917.

WHITWORTH, GEORGE GEOFFREY
Right-half: 9 apps
Born: Eckington, Derbyshire, 22 September 1927
Career: Stanton Iron Works, LIVERPOOL (professional, February 1950, released, May 1953)
Although primarily a full-back, George Whitworth made all his senior appearances for Liverpool in the right-half position in place of the injured Phil Taylor towards the end of the 1951–52 season, the first against Fulham (away) in early March.

WILKIE, THOMAS
Left-back: 65 apps, 2 goals
Born: Edinburgh, 1876 – *Died*: Perth, Western Australia, 8 January 1932
Career: Edinburgh junior football, Heart of Midlothian (professional, August 1893), LIVERPOOL (May 1895), Portsmouth (June 1899–May 1904); later emigrated to Australia
One of Heart of Midlothian's first professionals, Tom Wilkie took over the left-back position from Duncan McLean at Anfield and gained a Second Division championship winner's medal in 1896. A footballing defender, he was also strong in the tackle and kicked long and accurately. He made almost 150 senior appearances for Portsmouth, and when gaining a Southern League championship winner's medal in 1902 two of his teammates were also ex-Liverpool stars, Tom Cleghorn and Bobby Marshall.

WILKINSON, GEORGE BARRY
Wing-half: 79 apps
Born: Bishop Auckland, 16 June 1935
Career: West Auckland (amateur, August 1951), Bishop Auckland (amateur, May 1952), LIVERPOOL (professional, June 1954, having been registered with the club as an amateur since August 1953 whilst still playing for the Bishops), Bangor (August 1960), Tranmere Rovers (trial, August 1963, signed, September 1963), Holyhead Town (October 1964–May 1966)
An England amateur youth team player, George Wilkinson gained an FA Amateur Cup runners-up medal with Bishop Auckland in 1954 when technically a Liverpool player – being allowed to assist the non-League club in that competition. Able to play in both wing-half positions, he made his First Division debut for the Reds against the FA Cup holders Blackpool at Anfield in December 1953. He made 18 League appearances that season and 15 the next

before having long periods in the reserves. He moved on after John Wheeler and Tommy Leishman had established themselves as the two half-backs alongside Dick White at centre-half.

WILLIAMS, ROBERT BRYAN
Utility: 34 apps, 5 goals
Born: Liverpool 4 October 1927
Career: South Liverpool (1943) LIVERPOOL (amateur, March 1944; professional, August 1945), South Liverpool (player-coach, July 1953), Crewe Alexandra (July 1954), Rhyl (August 1958–April 1961)
Bryan Williams could play in a variety of positions from right-back to inside-left. A very versatile performer, he possessed an exceptionally long throw and one of his deliveries was measured at 55 yards, from touchline to the far side of the penalty area. He made his debut for Liverpool against Birmingham City (home) in March 1949 when he deputised at right-half for Phil Taylor. After leaving Anfield he appeared in over 150 first-class games for Crewe.

WILSON, CHARLES
Wing-half: 90 apps, 3 goals
Born: Stockport, February 1877 – *Deceased*
Career: Cheshire junior football, LIVERPOOL (professional, 1897, retired May 1905; remained at Anfield in scouting and coaching capacities; appointed head trainer in 1929, a position he held for ten years); did not participate in football after WW2
Charlie Wilson, one of Liverpool's greatest-ever servants, was associated with the Reds for some 40 years. As a player he preferred the right-half berth but also starred as an inside-forward and occasionally left-half. He made the first of his 90 senior appearances for the club against Bolton Wanderers in March 1898, gaining a regular place in the side in 1899–1900 and collecting a League championship winner's medal the following season. A broken leg, suffered in 1903, clearly upset his rhythm and although he fought hard to regain his fitness, he was forced to retire at the age of 28.

WILSON, DANIEL
Outside-right: 2 apps
Born: Liverpool, 1875 – *Deceased*
Career: East Bontas FC (1895), LIVERPOOL (with Robert McNaven, July 1899–May 1900)
Dan Wilson was reserve to Jack Cox at Anfield and both of his senior outings for Liverpool were against two other Lancashire clubs, Burnley and Preston North End, on successive Saturdays in December 1899.

WILSON, DAVID CHARLES
Outside-right: 0+1 app.
Born: Nelson, Lancashire, 24 December 1942
Career: Burnley Schools, Preston North End (amateur, April 1958; professional,

April 1960), LIVERPOOL (£20,000, February 1967), Preston North End (£4,000, May 1968), Bradford City (loan, March–April 1972), Southport (loan, October–November 1973), Telford United (April 1974–May 1976)

Capped by England at schoolboy level, fast-raiding winger David Wilson went on to gain under-23 recognition for his country and in his two spells at Deepdale made over 300 senior appearances for Preston North End, 281 in the Football League. He played in their 1964 FA Cup final defeat by West Ham and in 1971 gained a Third Division championship winner's medal. He failed to make much of an impact at Anfield, having just one substitute outing for the Reds against Blackpool in May 1967.

WOAN, DONALD
Outside-right: 2 apps
Born: Liverpool, 7 November 1927
Career: Bootle FC (1945), LIVERPOOL (£1,100, October 1950), Leyton
    Orient (£6,500 plus Brian Jackson, November 1951), Bradford City (October
    1952), Tranmere Rovers (February 1954), Yeovil Town (July 1955–May
    1957)

Unable to make headway at Anfield owing to the form of Jimmy Payne, Don Woan only played in two games on the right wing, the first against Derby County (away) in January 1951. He made 73 League appearances after leaving Liverpool unlike his older brother, Alan Woan, who between 1953 and 1964 scored 140 goals in 289 games in the same competition as an inside-forward with Norwich City, Northampton Town, Crystal Palace and Aldershot.

WORGAN, ARTHUR
Centre-/inside-forward: 2 apps, 2 goals
Born: Liverpool, 1871 – *Died*: Liverpool, 1934
Career: LIVERPOOL (September 1893–April 1895)

Arthur Worgan was a reserve forward at Anfield for two seasons. He had the pleasure of scoring twice on his League debut against Burton Swifts (home) in March 1894 when he took over at inside-right from Malcolm McVean. His other senior game was against Sheffield United seven months later.

WRIGHT, DAVID
Utility forward: 100 apps, 35 goals
Born: Kirkcaldy, Fife, 5 October 1905 – *Died*: Kirkcaldy, 1955
Career: Scottish junior football, Raith Rovers (professional, November 1923),
    East Fife (May 1924), Cowdenbeath (June 1926), Sunderland (£8,000, April
    1927), LIVERPOOL (March 1930), Hull City (£1,000, July 1934), Bradford
    Park Avenue (May 1935–May 1936); later ran his own bakery in Kirkcaldy

The bald-headed Dave Wright could play in any of the five forward positions and did so very effectively, averaging a goal every three games for Liverpool and one in every four throughout his career. Besides finding the net himself, he also helped create chances for his colleagues with subtle passes and excellent prompting. Described as a 'smart dribbler and hard worker' by a scribe in 1933, he had done exceedingly well in Scotland before joining Sunderland. He replaced Dick Edmed on the right flank when making his debut for the Reds at Bolton in March 1930 and also that season deputised for Fred Hopkin on the left. The following term he occupied the inside right and centre-forward berths, leading the attack superbly for two years, notching up 27 goals. A great favourite with the fans, he eventually moved to inside-left and after Sam English and Gordon Hodgson had established themselves as the main strikers, Wright switched his allegiance to Hull City.

WRIGHT, ERNEST VICTOR
Inside-forward: 85 apps, 33 goals
Born: Bloxwich near Walsall, 24 January 1909 – *Died*: Wednesbury, 4 March 1964
Career: Bloxwich Strollers (1926), Bristol City (professional, February 1929), Rotherham County (June 1929), Sheffield Wednesday (October 1930), Rotherham United (February 1933), LIVERPOOL (March 1934), Plymouth Argyle (June 1937), Chelmsford City (June 1938); guest for Crystal Palace, Millwall and Walsall during WW2; retired 1945
Vic Wright was a lively inside-forward who established a fine reputation during his two spells with Rotherham. Blessed with a powerful right-foot shot, he never wasted time in getting in a strike at goal and during his career scored over 75 goals in League and Cup football. Deputising for Berry Nieuwenhuys in a re-jigged attack, he made the first of his 85 appearances for Liverpool against Birmingham in March 1934, setting up one of Gordon Hodgson's four goals in a 4–0 win. The following season he was second-top scorer behind Hodgson with 20 goals and after that he was in and out of the side before his transfer to Plymouth Argyle. Wright was the nephew of the former Aston Villa, Small Heath and England winger Charlie Athersmith.

WRIGHT, MARK
Defender: 207+4 apps, 7 goals
Born: Dorchester, 1 August 1963
Career: Oxford United (apprentice, August 1979; professional, August 1980), Southampton (£80,000 with Keith Cassells, March 1982), Derby County (£760,000, August 1987), LIVERPOOL (£2.2m, July 1991, retired, injured, Sept 1998) Chester City (manager, January 2002–May 2004), Peterborough United (manager, May 2005, sacked due to gross misconduct, January 2006), Chester (manager, February 2006)
In an excellent career that spanned almost 20 years, central defender Mark Wright amassed a total of 664 club and international appearances and scored well over 30 goals. He made his debut for Oxford United as a 17 year old in a second-round FA Cup tie against Plymouth Argyle in December 1980, following on with his League baptism against Bristol City ten months later. Spotted by Southampton scout Joe Mallet, he moved to The Dell when still a teenager and quickly bedded himself into the Saints' line-up. After some splendid displays he was called into England's under-21 side (eventually winning four caps at that level) and as time rolled by he went on to appear in 45 full

internationals, making his debut against Wales in 1984, and was all set to play in the 1986 World Cup finals but unfortunately missed the tournament after breaking his leg playing against Liverpool in the FA Cup semi-final. He regained his fitness and went on to have 216 outings for Saints before joining Derby County in readiness for the 1987–88 campaign. Four years later he was snapped up by manager Graeme Souness for Liverpool and over the next seven years gave the Reds great service. A precise tackler, strong and dominant in the air, Wright – who was nicknamed 'Bonner' – was a class act when on top of his game. He made his debut at Anfield against Oldham Athletic in August 1991 but was hurt in his second game. Returning to the side at the end of November, he held his position comfortably (injuries and suspension apart) and won an FA Cup winner's medal that season. Having formed an excellent partnership at the heart of the Reds' defence with first Nicky Tanner and then Neil Ruddock, when Phil Babb and John Scales arrived Wright continued to pull his weight and although he lost his place, he battled back, regained it and went on to make 211 appearances for the club. Unfortunately, like his Anfield teammate Rob Jones (q.v.) Wright missed the European Championships in 1996 through injury. He was succeeded as manager at Chester in 2004 by another ex-Liverpool star, Ian Rush.

WRIGHT, STEPHEN
Right-back: 15+6 apps, 1 goal
Born: Liverpool, 8 February 1980
Career: LIVERPOOL (apprentice, April 1996; professional, October 1997), Crewe Alexandra (loan, August 1999–May 2000), Sunderland (£3m, August 2002)

Honoured by England at youth and under-21 levels (six caps gained in the latter category), Stephen Wright gained a UEFA Cup winner's medal with Liverpool in 2001 and four years later helped Sunderland win the Football League championship and a place back to the Premiership. A tall right wing-back, strong and mobile, combative in style with a terrific engine, he found it tough to get into the first team at Anfield and went on loan to Crewe for a season to gain experience and, indeed, keep fully match fit. He returned to Liverpool fresh and eager to succeed, and was handed his debut as a substitute against Stoke City in a League Cup tie in November 2000. Unfortunately he still couldn't secure a place in the team and subsequently left Anfield for the Stadium of Light. He became a regular in the Sunderland side, reaching the milestone of 100 senior appearances for the Wearsiders in 2005.

WYLLIE, THOMAS GEORGE
Outside-right: 29 apps, 16 goals
Born: Maybole, Ayrshire, 5 August 1897 – *Died*: Bristol, *circa* 1955
Career: Maybole FC, Glasgow Rangers (April 1888), Everton (December 1890), LIVERPOOL (September 1892), Bury (season 1893–94), Bristol City (August 1897–May 1898); became a Football League linesman, then a referee; later ran a thriving newsagent's shop in Bristol

Scottish international Tom Wyllie (capped once v. Ireland in 1890) was a very competent outside-right who scored 5 times in 11 games for Rangers and 5 in 21 for Everton before becoming Liverpool's first professional player, moving to Anfield when the team were members of the Lancashire Combination. He made his debut for the Reds against Higher Walton (won 8–0) and hit his first goal in his third game against West Manchester. Unfortunately he left before League football came to Anfield, having been second top scorer in season 1892–93 behind Jimmy Miller. Wyllie also starred in seven Inter-City games for Glasgow v. Sheffield and Edinburgh.

XAVIER, ABEL

Full-back: 20+1 apps, 2 goals

Born: Mozambique, 30 November 1972

Career: Estrella Amadora FC/Portugal (professional, May 1990), Benfica/ Portugal (June 1993), Bari/Italy (September 1995), Real Oviedo/Spain (August 1996), AS Roma/Italy (briefly, March 1998), PSV Eindhoven/ Holland (June 1998), Everton (£1.5m, September 1999), LIVERPOOL (£800,000, January 2002), Galatasaray/Turkey (loan, January– May 2003), Hannover 96/Germany (season 2004–05), Middlesbrough (free, August 2005)

Attacking Portuguese international full-back Abel Xavier, capped at youth, under-16, under-18 and 20 times at senior level, represented his country in the 1998 European Championships and the 2000 World Cup finals. Signed by manager Gerard Houllier after an injury-plagued spell at Goodison Park, he appeared in only 15 competitive games in his first 18 months at Anfield, scoring on his debut in a 6–0 Premiership win at Ipswich in February 2002 and later adding a second goal to his tally, a crucial one at that, in the Champions League quarter-final clash with Bayer Leverkusen. Standing 6ft 2in. tall and weighing 13st. 6lb, he moved on after a loan spell in Turkey and when he joined Middlesbrough in 2005 that made it 11 different clubs in 14 years for a player who loves to change his hairstyle and its colour! In October 2005, Xavier was suspended from playing football indefinitely by FIFA for failing a routine post-match drugs test, requested after Middlesbrough's UEFA Cup game against the Greek side Xanthi, at the end of the previous month. He appealed, was unsuccessful and as a result was banned from 22 November 2005 for 18 months. While all this was going on Xavier was also in the process of taking his former employers, Hannover 96, to the Court of Arbitration for Sport, accusing the German's club's coach, Ewald Lienen, of racial discrimination.

YEATS, RONALD

Centre-half: 453+1 apps, 16 goals

Born: Aberdeen, 15 November 1937

Career: Causeway End School (Aberdeen), Aberdeen Lads' Club (1955); national service in the Royal Army Service Corps (Aldershot); Dundee United (professional, May 1957), LIVERPOOL (£22,000, July 1961), Tranmere Rovers (player/assistant manager, December 1971, player-manager,

April 1972–April 1974, then manager to April 1975), Stalybridge Celtic (player, October 1975), Barrow (player-manager, August–December 1976); later LIVERPOOL (chief scout, from season 1986–87 to date)

Standing 6ft 2in. tall and weighing almost 14st., Ron Yeats was described by Liverpool manager Bill Shankly as 'the colossus of the defence'. In fact, he was one of Shanks' greatest-ever signings and became an integral part of the Reds' superb 'spine theory' evolved by Shankly – Lawrence in goal, Yeats at centre-half and St John at centre-forward. A natural leader, he was dominant in the air, hardly missed a header or, indeed, a tackle and rarely had a bad game. He was 23 years of age when he left his native Scotland for Merseyside and made the first of his senior appearances for the Reds against Bristol Rovers (away) in August 1961. He gained a Second Division championship medal that season, claimed a First Division winner's medal 12 months later, helped Liverpool win the FA Cup in 1965 and added another First Division medal to his collection in 1966, the same year his own goal won the European Cup-Winners' Cup final for Borussia Dortmund. As manager of Tranmere he signed many ex-Liverpool players to boost the squad and he also introduced a certain Steve Coppell to the game. In anticipation of promotion, attendances rose considerably at Prenton Park but all his efforts were in vain and in 1975, with relegation looming, he was sacked. Honoured by Scotland at schoolboy level, Yeats ('Big Ron' to the fans) went on to win two full caps for his country, against Wales (1965) and Italy (1966). Originally a slaughterman, working at an Aberdeen abattoir, after leaving football he became involved in first the haulage business and then in catering on Merseyside. Bill Shankly once said: 'With him [Yeats] at centre-half we could play Arthur Askey in goal.' And replying to one reporter after being asked what Yeats had to offer, Shanks said: 'Come outside and I'll give you a walk round him.'

YOUNGER, THOMAS

Goalkeeper: 127 apps

Born: Edinburgh, 10 April 1930 – *Died*: Edinburgh, 13 January 1984

Career: Hutchison Vale FC (Edinburgh); served in the Army during WW2; Hibernian (professional, June 1946), LIVERPOOL (£9,000, June 1956), Falkirk (in exchange for Bert Slater, June 1959; appointed player-manager, October 1959, semi-retired, February 1960); returned with Stoke City (March 1960), Leeds United (September 1961, retired, October 1962; appointed scout at Elland Road to 1964), Toronto City/Canada (coach, 1964–66), Hibernian (as Public Relations Officer, October 1969); took over a pub in Edinburgh (January 1970); later joined the board of directors at Easter Road after becoming a successful partner in a vending machine company in Scotland; was President of the Scottish Football League until his death

Tommy Younger kept goal for the British Army of the Rhine XI while serving with the Royal Scots Greys in Germany during WW2. When peacetime football returned he became a professional with Hibernian, winning two League championship medals (1951 and 1952), a Scottish Cup runners-up medal (also in 1951) and gaining the first of 24 full caps for Scotland (1955). He spent three fine years at Anfield, taking over between the posts from Doug Rudham (and Dave Underwood), his debut coming against Huddersfield Town in August 1956 (lost 3–2 at Anfield). Despite his burly frame, Younger was agile and dependable with good reflexes and a safe pair of hands. He secured further international honours as a 'Red' and represented the Football League before moving back to Scotland with Falkirk, in exchange for Bert Slater who took over his position at Anfield. Younger, in fact, returned to Liverpool to 'spy' on the team and check out their players on behalf of Hibernian, ahead of the 1970–71 European Fairs Cup clash. He didn't quite get things sorted as the Reds won both legs – 1–0 at Easter Road and 2–0 at Anfield.

ZENDEN, BOUDEWIJN
Midfield: 10+6 apps, 2 goals
Born: Maastricht, Holland, 15 August 1976
Career: Leonadis/Holland (junior club), MVV Maastricht/Holland (seasons 1992–94), PSV Eindhoven/Holland (professional, August 1994), CF Barcelona/Spain (July 1998), Chelsea (£7.5m, August 2001), Middlesbrough (loan, August 2003, signed free, July 2004), LIVERPOOL (free, July 2005)

Enterprising wide and central midfielder 'Bolo' Zenden has now netted 8 goals in 54 full internationals for his country. Prior to him entering English football in 2001, he scored 23 goals in 111 Dutch First Division games for PSV, gaining a League championship medal in 1997 and successive Cup winner's medals in 1996 and 1997 and netted 3 times in 64 outings for Barcelona, helping them win La Liga in 1999 and finish runners-up in 2000. In and out of the Chelsea side, he made 59 first-class appearances, half of them as a substitute, but did much better with Middlesbrough, claiming 15 goals in 88 outings and receiving a League Cup winner's medal in 2004. He was recruited by Liverpool boss Rafael Benitez to add spice to the midfield and to provide more options if an orthodox wing man was required. He made his debut for the Reds in the first leg of the Champions League first qualifying round against Total Network Solutions of Wales in July 2005 and netted his first goal in their 2–0 home victory over West Ham in October 2005. Unfortunately, injury ruined the rest of the season for the Dutchman.

ZIEGE, CHRISTIAN
Left-back: 20+12 apps, 2 goals
Born: Munich, Germany, 1 February 1972
Career: Bayern Munich/Germany (apprentice, May 1988; professional, April 1990), AC Milan/Italy (£2m, August 1997), Middlesbrough (£4m, August 1999), LIVERPOOL (£5.5m, August 2000), Tottenham Hotspur (£4m, August 2001), Borussia Moenchengladbach/Germany (January 2004)

A very talented and cultured left wing-back, Christian Ziege scored almost 50 goals in close on 200 appearances (41 in 172 at League level) for Bayern Munich whom he helped win the German Bundesliga in 1994 and 1997 and the UEFA Cup in 1996. He followed up by netting 4 times in 39 Serie 'A' games for AC

Milan. A player with a strong attacking instinct, he had one good season with Middlesbrough but struggled with his form and, indeed, with injuries at both Anfield and White Hart Lane, making only 121 senior appearances for his three Premiership clubs in five years. Winning the first of his 62 full caps in 1993, he helped Germany win the European Championship in 1996 and in 2001 was a League Cup winner with Liverpool, for whom he made the first of his 32 appearances as a substitute against Manchester City three weeks into his only season on Merseyside. He returned to his homeland in 2004.

LATE SIGNINGS

GONZALEZ, MARK
Midfielder: yet to make his senior debut for Liverpool
Born: Durban, South Africa, 10 July 1982
Career: Universidad Catolica Santiago/Chile (1999), Albacete/Spain (August 2004), LIVERPOOL (season-long loan from July 2005, signed July 2006*)
Chilean international with 13 caps to his credit (plus three goals), Mark Gonzalez, who can play on both flanks, was injured playing in La Liga against Levante in May 2005 and as a result his loan move to Anfield was severely interrupted. He remained in rehabilitation in Spain for quite a while before moving to Liverpool on regaining full fitness. Fast and clever, he was watched by several major European clubs including Real Madrid and Barcelona before choosing Liverpool. Outstanding with relegated Albacete in 2004–05, he was recommended to Reds manager Rafael Benitez by the club's chief scout, Pace Herrera.

*Depends on Liverpool (and Gonzalez) being able to secure a work permit

PALETTA, GABRIEL
Defender:
Born: Bueonos Aries, February 1986
Career: Banfield/Argentina (April 2002; professional, March 2003), LIVERPOOL (£2m, July 2006)
Liverpool boss Rafael Benitez beat off a challenge from River Plate to land Argentinian under-20 international centre-back Gabriel Paletta. The transfer was initially agreed in principle in February 2006 and the formalities completed five months later. A strong tackler, highly rated in his home country, Paletta is looking forward to winning trophies with the Reds. He has an Italian passport.

WARTIME FOOTBALL

During both World War periods (1915–19 and 1939–46) Liverpool recruited several guest players, some of them full internationals, some moderate lower Division performers, a few amateurs and the odd local non-League footballer. They also handed outings to various youngsters associated with the club. Here are details of most of the players who represented the Reds in wartime football.

NB: Players who starred for Liverpool in League and FA Cup games pre- and post-war and who have been detailed elsewhere in this book are not included.

GUESTS AND OTHER PLAYERS DURING WWI, 1915–1919

- Jim ASHCROFT, Tranmere Rovers and England international goalkeeper (three senior caps won) who had earlier starred for Woolwich Arsenal and Blackburn Rovers. He also played as a forward in an emergency.
- Steve BEATTIE, an outside-right from Runcorn, scored 12 goals in 25 WW2 games for the Reds.
- Joe BUTLER, goalkeeper from Lincoln City, who also played for Stockport County, Clapton Orient, Glossop, Rochdale and Sunderland, with whom he won the League and played in the FA Cup final in 1913.
- Tom CAPPER, goalkeeper from Dundee, once of Southport Central who later played for Southend United and Wigan Borough.
- Billy CONNELL, Liverpool-born goalkeeper who later made seven League appearances for Wrexham and also played for Crewe Alexandra.
- Benny CROSS, utility forward from Runcorn, an England schoolboy international and both an FA and Football League representative, he scored 61 goals in 255 games for Burnley (1920–28) with whom he won a First Division championship medal in 1921.
- Frank CURTIS, a versatile forward from Llanelli who later played for Wolves, Reading and Kidderminster Harriers.
- Joe DONNACHIE, winger from Everton whose other League clubs included Morton, Newcastle United, Oldham Athletic, Glasgow Rangers, Blackpool and Chester, the latter as player-manager.
- Horace FAIRHURST, reserve left-half from Darwen, previously with Bolton Wanderers who later played for Blackpool (1919–20).
- Arthur GEE, a former England schoolboy international inside-forward from Oldham Athletic who also played as a guest for Everton and later

served with Stalybridge Celtic, Rochdale and Crewe Alexandra among others.

- Robert GODDARD, 20-year-old goalkeeper who went on to play for his home-town club Bristol City and also Reading.
- Tommy GREEN, a centre-forward from local junior football who went on to play for West Ham United, Southport Central, Accrington Stanley, Stockport County, Clapton Orient, Hearts and Third Lanark. He scored 19 goals in 19 games for Liverpool.
- Charlie HAYES, amateur right-back in local football who later signed for Tranmere Rovers (1921).
- Jim HENDERSON, inside-right from Cardiff City who later served with Ashington and Spennymoor United. He played in 11 games for the Reds, scoring 1 goal.
- Cyril HOUGHTON, goalkeeper from Walsall, who made 14 appearances for the Reds.
- Edwin HUGHES, a Welsh international half-back (16 caps won) who was signed from Manchester City. Previously with Wrexham and Nottingham Forest, he later assisted Aberdare Athletic, Colwyn Bay and Llandudno Town.
- James KENNEDY, inside-right from Preston North End.
- Joe LEE, inside-forward from Barnsley, later with Rotherham County, Lincoln City, Halifax Town, Scunthorpe United and Newport County.
- James MIDDLEHURST, a full-back from Hull City who played 27 times for the Reds.
- Billy 'Spud' MURPHY, outside-left from Crewe Victoria who played for Manchester City, Southampton, Oldham Athletic and Tranmere Rovers after the war.
- Arthur NEWMAN, centre-forward from Smethwick Highfield who also played for Stockport County and Kidderminster Harriers.
- Fred OSBORNE, a forward from Preston North End, previously with Leicester Fosse, also played for Leicestershire CCC.
- John PAGE, full-back from neighbours Everton who also served with Rochdale, Cardiff City and Merthyr Town.
- Tom PAGE, inside-forward and brother of John Page, who was recruited from St Mirren having earlier assisted Everton and Liverpool (on trial); later with Port Vale and New Brighton.
- Willie PATTERSON, Scottish-born wing-half, whose clubs included Sheffield United and Gainsborough Trinity.
- Reggie PHILLIPS, outside-left from Brighton and Hove Amateurs who later joined Brighton and Hove Albion.
- Ernie PINKNEY, an outside-right from Everton who also assisted Barrow, Gillingham, Tranmere Rovers, Halifax Town and Accrington Stanley. He scored 3 goals in 28 games for the Reds.
- Clement RIGG, a defender from Todmorden who assisted Burnley, before making 254 League appearances for Nelson between 1921 and 1928 and then moving on to Newcastle United.

- George RITCHIE, an inside-forward from Preston North End, whose other clubs included Chester, Norwich City, Brighton and Hove Albion and Reading.
- Alex ROBERTSON, Liverpool-born centre-half from Northern Nomads who was a reserve at Anfield after the war and also played for Oldham Athletic and New Brighton.
- George SCHOFIELD, a junior forward from Southport who later played for Bury, Manchester United and Crewe Alexandra. He scored 4 goals in 46 games for the Reds.
- Billy SCOTT, Northern Ireland international goalkeeper (25 caps won between 1903 and 1913). Also played for Cliftonville, Linfield and Everton, and was recruited from Leeds City. The older brother of Elisha Scott, he won the FA Cup in 1906 with Everton for whom he made 289 appearances. He had 27 outings with Liverpool.
- Walter Ernest SMITH, goalkeeper from Manchester City who had earlier starred for Leicester Fosse and later assisted Port Vale, Plymouth Argyle and Grimsby Town. He played for the Football League side and made 15 appearances for the Reds.
- Jimmy STANSFIELD, a left-back from Bury.
- Charlie SUTCLIFFE, goalkeeper from Leeds City who served with Rotherham County and Sheffield United in the 1920s.
- Jack SWANN, ex-Northern Nomads and Manchester City goalkeeper.
- Edward 'Teddy' TAYLOR, was an England international goalkeeper from Oldham Athletic (capped eight times at senior level) who gained three League championship medals after WW1, two with Huddersfield Town (1923 and 1924) and one with Everton (1928). He also played for Wrexham and Liverpool Balmoral (in the Zingari League), represented the North v. the South and made 17 WW1 appearances as guest for Liverpool.
- Jack WAINE, outside-right from local junior football who scored 8 goals in 39 games for Liverpool.
- Davey WATSON, from Sunderland, ex-Falkirk and Bo'ness who went on to score 61 goals in 276 League games for Portsmouth between 1920 and 1929. He netted 13 times in 28 outings for Liverpool.
- David WILLIAMS, a forward from Notts County, formerly with Glossop, who also played for Luton Town, Brighton and Hove Albion and Maidstone United.
- Ted WINN, a half-back from South Liverpool, later with Tranmere Rovers.
- Other players: Jack HANNAWAY (outside-right), Jack LOVELL (goalkeeper) and Jock McTAVISH (right-back).

WW1 STATS AND FACTS

Top appearance-makers (including 'regular' players): McKinlay 134, E. Longworth 120, W. Wadsworth 112, Lewis 99, Metcalf 91, J. Bamber 85, Bennett 70, Jenkinson 59, Cunliffe 53, Pagnam 49, Goddard 48, Schofield 46, Lucas 41, Waine 39, K. Campbell 37, H. Wadsworth 34, Speakman 31, Watson 28, W. Scott 27.

Top goalscorers: Bennett 77, Lewis 56, Pagnam 43, Metcalf 42, McKinlay 26, Green 19, Watson 13, H. Wadsworth 11, Miller 9, Waine 8.

GUESTS AND OTHER PLAYERS DURING WW2, 1939—1946

- George AINSLEY, centre-forward from Leeds United, formerly with Sunderland and Bolton Wanderers and later with Bradford Park Avenue. His League career, either side of the war, realised 59 goals in 146 games.
- Peter BAINES, inside-forward from Wrexham, later with Crewe Alexandra, Hartlepools United and New Brighton.
- Sam BARTRAM, the Charlton Athletic goalkeeper who made 623 appearances for the London club between 1934 and 1956. Later manager of York City and Luton Town, he played in 16 games for the Reds.
- Bob BATEY, wing-half from Preston North End, previously with Carlisle United and later with Leeds United and Southport. He played 138 League games in total and featured in 12 WW2 fixtures for the Reds. He also assisted Newcastle United, Gateshead, Hartlepools United, Millwall, Barrow and Southport as a guest player during the war.
- Bob BEATTIE, Scottish international inside-left from Preston North End who helped Liverpool win the League (N) Cup in 1944. He scored 49 goals in 264 League games during his 17 years at Deepdale (1937–54), gaining an FA Cup winner's medal in 1938.
- Andy BLACK, Scottish international centre-forward from Heart of Midlothian who scored 47 goals in 139 League games for Manchester City (1946–50) and 38 in 94 for Stockport County (1950–53). He won a Second Division championship medal in 1947.
- Jack BLOOD, full-back from Notts County who later played for Exeter City (1946–47).
- Jack BREEZE, amateur forward whose brother played for Port Vale in the 1930s.
- Cliff BRITTON, right-half from neighbours Everton, an England international with 21 full and 12 wartime caps to his credit, he made 242 peacetime appearances for the Blues, gaining a First Division championship medal in 1931 and FA Cup winner's medal two years later. He also played for Bristol Rovers and Burnley, was manager at Turf Moor and Goodison Park, as well as boss of Hull City and Preston North End.
- Allan Winston BROWN, centre-half from Huddersfield Town who played for Burnley and Notts County after the war. He later managed Burnley, Sunderland and Sheffield Wednesday and made four WW2 appearances for the Reds.
- Ronnie BURKE, utility forward from Luton Town who later served with Manchester United, Huddersfield Town, Rotherham United and Exeter City.
- Stan BUTLER, outside-left from West Bromwich Albion, previously with Scunthorpe and Lindsey United and later with Southport.
- Billy CAIRNS, inside-forward from Newcastle United, later with Grimsby Town for whom he scored 120 goals in 211 League games.
- Jimmy CAMPBELL, outside-right from Celtic who was also a guest with

Leicester City. He helped Liverpool win the League (N) Cup in 1944 and scored 18 goals in 61 WW2 appearances for the Reds.

- Johnny CAREY, brilliant full-back from Manchester United for whom he made 344 League and FA Cup appearances in 17 years, 1936–53. He won 36 caps for the Republic of Ireland and also captained the Rest of Europe against Great Britain in 1947. He gained an FA Cup winner's medal a year later and won a League championship medal in 1952. Voted 'Footballer of the Year' in 1949, he later managed Blackburn Rovers, Nottingham Forest, Everton and Leyton Orient. He had one game for Liverpool.
- George CARTER, local-born right-half who later assisted Marine.
- Stan CHARLESWORTH, centre-half from Grimsby Town who played for Barnsley and Gainsborough Trinity after the war.
- Doug COLE, centre-half from Chester City, previously with Sheffield United.
- George COLLISTER, Liverpool-born amateur outside-left.
- Douglas COOK, versatile defender from the Liverpool area who scored 3 goals in 24 WW2 games for the Reds.
- Stan CULLIS, centre-half and captain of Wolverhampton Wanderers and England who played in 152 League games plus 12 full and 20 wartime internationals. As a manager, he guided Wolves to three League titles in the 1950s and two FA Cup final victories (1949 and 1960) and was later in charge of Birmingham City (1960s). He played in eight games for Liverpool.
- Horace CUMNER, outside-left from Arsenal who also played for Hull City, Notts County, Watford, Scunthorpe United and Bradford City, retiring in 1954 with 254 League appearances under his belt.
- Ronnie DIX, England international inside-forward from Tottenham Hotspur who had previously starred for Bristol Rovers, Blackburn Rovers, Aston Villa and Derby County. He was also a guest for Blackpool, Bradford Park Avenue, Bristol City, Chester, Wrexham and York City during the war and ended his career with Reading. He was only 15 when he scored on his League debut for Bristol Rovers in 1928, the first of almost 450 club appearances. He gained two full caps, won the League (N) Cup with Blackpool in 1943 and netted twice in six games for Liverpool.
- Peter DOHERTY, brilliant Northern Ireland international inside-forward from Manchester City whose career spanned 20 years during which time he also played for Glentoran, Blackpool, Derby County, Huddersfield Town and Doncaster Rovers. He appeared in 403 League games, scored 197 goals and won 16 full caps. He also managed Doncaster, Bristol City and the Northern Ireland national team and acted as assistant manager and coach at several other clubs.
- Dicky DORSETT, inside-forward from Wolves who was later converted into a defender with Aston Villa. He scored 23 goals in 22 games for Liverpool, becoming assistant trainer at Anfield in 1957.
- Jim DOUGAL, inside-forward from Preston North End, previously with Falkirk and later with Carlisle United and Halifax Town. He gained one full cap for Scotland.

- George DRURY, inside-forward from Arsenal who also played for Sheffield Wednesday, West Bromwich Albion and Watford, making almost 150 League appearances in total.
- Stan EASTHAM, right-half who joined Liverpool as a professional in 1938 and later played for Exeter City and Stockport County.
- Maurice EDELSTON, an England amateur international centre-forward from Reading who had earlier played for Fulham and Brentford and later assisted Northampton Town. He scored 93 goals in a career total of 267 League appearances and after retiring became a BBC broadcaster.
- Bill FAIRHURST, goalkeeper from Bury who had been at Anfield in 1929 prior to joining Wigan Athletic. He also played for Rhyl Athletic and Bristol City.
- George FARROW, wing-half from Blackpool who had earlier served with Stockport County, Wolverhampton Wanderers and Bournemouth. After the war he played for Sheffield United and made a total of 267 League appearances between 1930 and 1948.
- Charles FAZACKERLEY, half-back, and the son of the former Everton player Stan Fazackerley.
- Tom GARNER, outside-right, recruited from local non-League football.
- Bill GORMAN, international full-back, capped 13 times by the Republic of Ireland and 4 times by Northern Ireland, he played for Bury until 1938 and Brentford after that, making 180 League appearances in all.
- Jack GRAINGER, England 'B' international outside-right from Rotherham United who hit 112 goals in 352 League games for the Millers before joining Lincoln City in 1957.
- Arthur GROSVENOR, an England international inside-right who made 183 League appearances while serving with Birmingham, Sheffield Wednesday and Bolton Wanderers before the war. He had one game for Liverpool in 1941.
- Jack GRUNDY, an inside-forward or wing-half previously with Newcastle United.
- Joffre GULLIVER, a well-groomed full-back from Reading who had earlier played for Southend United and Leeds United. After the war, he assisted Swindon Town and made 172 League appearances in all, 161 for Reading. He helped Liverpool win the League (N) Cup in 1944 and played in 93 matches for the Reds.
- Ron GUTTRIDGE, full-back from Aston Villa who made 47 appearances for Liverpool. He was also a guest for Notts County and Nottingham Forest and later played for Brighton and Hove Albion.
- Harold HALL, amateur goalkeeper, serving in the armed forces.
- Willie HALL, winger who joined Liverpool in 1943 and later played for Southport.
- Walter HALSALL, defender, once on Liverpool's books (1929) who went on to play for Bolton Wanderers, Blackburn Rovers, Birmingham and Chesterfield, guesting for the Reds from the latter club.
- Tom HARTLEY, inside-forward from Chesterfield, previously with

Gateshead and Bury and later with North Shields, Leicester City and Watford. He had nine outings with the Reds.

- Freddie HAYCOCK, inside-forward from Aston Villa who scored twice in 34 games for the Reds. He also played for Waterford and Blackburn Rovers and guested for 11 different clubs during the war.
- George HINSLEY, half-back from Bradford City who also played for Barnsley and Halifax Town, making 153 League appearances in total.
- Alf HOBSON, goalkeeper from Chester who had previously appeared for Liverpool (1936–38).
- Steve HUGHES, defender from New Brighton, previously with Liverpool (1936) and Oldham Athletic.
- Mick HULLIGAN, signed by Liverpool as a winger in 1942 and the scorer of 24 goals in 46 appearances for the Reds during the war. He joined Port Vale (with Stanley Polk) for a record fee of £10,000 in 1947 and netted 23 goals in 209 games for the Valiants.
- George HUNT, centre-forward from Bolton Wanderers who had previously scored 138 goals in 198 games for Tottenham Hotspur, he also played for Chesterfield, Arsenal and Sheffield Wednesday and became a coach at Bolton. He netted five times in seven games for Liverpool.
- Lloyd ICETON, outside-left from Preston North End who made 77 League appearances for Carlisle United and 140 for Tranmere Rovers after the war.
- George JACKSON, full-back from Everton, who made 19 appearances for the Reds.
- Bobby JOHNSTONE, wing-half from Raith Rovers who helped Liverpool win the League (N) Cup in 1944. He later played for Tranmere Rovers.
- John JONES, full-back from Everton who played for Sunderland (1945–47).
- Errington Ridley Liddell KEEN, an England international left-half who played in 17 WW2 games for the Reds. Initially with Newcastle United, he also assisted Derby County, Chelmsford City, Hereford United (as player-manager, 1939–45) and Leeds United and later coached in Hong Kong.
- Denis KIRBY, played right-back or wing-half and was recruited from Leeds United in 1942.
- Albert LEADBETTER, an amateur outside-right from Accrington Stanley who scored once in four WW2 games for the Reds.
- Archie LIVINGSTONE, an inside-forward from Bury who played for Everton and Southport after the war having assisted Newcastle United at the start of his career. As a guest he scored seven goals in a match for Wrexham v. Tranmere in September 1943 (won 9–0).
- Charlie LONGDON, wing-half from Brighton and Hove Albion who appeared in League games for Bournemouth and Rochdale after the war.
- Jock LORAN, outside-right, recruited by the Reds from Scottish junior football while serving in the forces.
- Tom LYON, centre-forward or outside-left from Chesterfield, played for Albion Rovers and Blackpool before the war and for New Brighton afterwards.
- Joe McCORMICK, an outside-right from Tottenham Hotspur who served

with Rotherham United and Chesterfield before moving to White Hart Lane and after the war played for Fulham, Lincoln City and Crystal Palace. He made 256 League appearances in total and after several coaching positions, managed York City in 1953–54.

- Jimmy McINTOSH, a centre-forward from Preston North End who played for Blackpool either side of his spell at Deepdale. He later assisted Everton (1948–50) and scored 47 goals in a career total of 149 League appearances.
- Andy McLAREN, Scottish international inside-forward from Preston North End who went on to play for Burnley, Sheffield United and Barrow after the war, scoring 52 goals in 155 League games for the latter club.
- Eric Holmes MANSLEY, goalkeeper, signed from Chester in 1939.
- Alf Woolley MASSEY, right-half from Stoke City who later played for Stafford Rangers.
- Harold MATHER, full-back from Burnley who appeared in 329 first-class games for the Clarets over a period of 10 years (1945–55). He also played for Hull City and Accrington Stanley.
- George MILLS, centre-forward of Chelsea who scored 123 goals in 239 appearances for the London club (1929–43). He netted a hat-trick on his England debut v. Northern Ireland in 1937 and added two more caps to his tally against Wales and Czechoslovakia that same year. He registered nine goals in nine WW2 games for the Reds.
- Jack MOLYNEUX, local-born centre-half, who played in seven WW2 games for the Reds.
- Jimmy MULVANEY, right-back from Dumbarton who played for Luton Town, Brighton and Hove Albion, Bradford City, Bath City and Halifax Town after the war.
- George MURPHY, centre-forward from Bradford City who scored once in three WW2 appearances for the Reds. He netted 43 goals in 180 League games for the Tigers and later assisted Hull City.
- George MUTCH, inside-left from Preston North End who played once for the Reds in 1942. Previously with Manchester United (49 goals in 120 games) and also assisted Arbroath and Southport. He scored Preston's last-ditch penalty winner in extra-time v. Huddersfield Town in the 1938 FA Cup final.
- Frank O'DONNELL, Scottish international centre-forward, six caps won, who played for Celtic, Preston North End, Blackpool, Aston Villa and Nottingham Forest between 1933 and 1947, scoring 130 goals in 244 League games. He served with 11 different clubs during the war.
- Hugh O'DONNELL, outside-left and younger brother of Frank who also played for Celtic, Preston North End and Blackpool as well as Rochdale and Halifax Town, retiring in 1948 after netting 73 goals in 285 League appearances.
- Arthur OWEN, left-back and left-half from Everton who had played for Tranmere Rovers from 1936.
- Patrick OWENS, left-back, recruited from Stockport County.
- Tom Usher PEARSON, Scottish international outside-left from Newcastle United who scored 46 goals in 212 League games during his time at St James' Park (1933–48).

- Jack PICKSTOCK, amateur outside-right, signed in an emergency in March 1941.
- Jack PILLING, left-half, signed in September 1942 who helped Liverpool win the League (N) Cup in 1944. He scored 3 times in 116 appearances for the Reds during the war and later played for Southport.
- Alf POPE, full-back from Heart of Midlothian, formerly with Leeds United and Halifax Town.
- Bob PRYDE, centre-half of Blackburn Rovers for whom he appeared in 323 League games in 15 years from 1933. He also played for St Johnstone, Brechin City and Wigan Athletic.
- Frank RAWCLIFFE, centre-forward from Notts County. Previously with Tranmere Rovers, Wolverhampton Wanderers and Colchester United, he served with Newport County, Swansea Town and Aldershot after the hostilities.
- Sid RAWLINGS, outside-right from Millwall whose career started with Preston North End in 1932 and ended at Plymouth Argyle in 1948. In between times he also assisted Huddersfield Town, West Bromwich Albion, Northampton Town and Everton and made over 200 senior appearances in total.
- Dennis RIDGE, right-back, son of the former Nelson and Scarborough player of the same name.
- Frank RIST, defender from Charlton Athletic who later moved to Colchester United.
- Jack ROBINSON, goalkeeper recruited from Manchester City in 1940–41 who also played for Accrington Stanley, Bury and Southend United.
- Jimmy SANDERS, goalkeeper from Charlton Athletic who went on to win an FA Cup winner's medal with West Bromwich Albion (1954) and later assisted Coventry City.
- John SEARCH, centre-forward, recruited from Runcorn who was registered with Liverpool in 1933 and also played for Lucerne in Switzerland and New Brighton.
- Ken SEDDON, right-back, recruited in 1943 as an amateur from Notts County.
- Bill SHANKLY, Scottish international right-half, capped five times at senior level who was recruited from Preston North End after an initial spell with Carlisle United. He made 300 League appearances in 15 years at Deepdale and later became a great manager at Anfield. (See under Managers.)
- Arthur SHEPHERD, centre-forward or winger, signed by Liverpool in 1943, later with New Brighton.
- Jack SMITH, centre-forward from Manchester United who had two games for Liverpool in 1944. He also played for Huddersfield Town, Newcastle United, Blackburn Rovers and Port Vale and scored 129 goals in 244 League games.
- Bob STUART, full-back from Middlesbrough and later with Plymouth Argyle. He had 15 outings for the Reds and during his career amassed 269 League appearances, all but 20 with 'Boro.

- Frank SWIFT, brilliant Manchester City and England goalkeeper who played twice for the Reds. He made 376 League and Cup appearances during his 17 years at Maine Road (1932–49) and won 19 full caps. He became a reporter and was sadly killed in the Munich air disaster in 1958.
- Bill TEASDALE, local non-League goalkeeper.
- Willie TENNANT, ex-Liverpool left-back, guest from Stoke City.
- Sam THORPE, right-half from Sheffield United.
- Norman TURNER, centre-half, recruited from Liverpool non-League football, brother of Arthur Turner (Stoke City).
- George WALTON, inside-left from Walsall, previously with Accrington Stanley, Bolton Wanderers and Cardiff City. He hit 39 goals in a career total of 192 League appearances.
- Don WELSH, centre-forward who helped Liverpool win the League (N) Cup in 1944, playing in the second leg of the final v. Bolton Wanderers. He netted 42 goals in 41 appearances for the Reds as a guest from Charlton Athletic for whom he struck 50 goals in 216 first-class games. He also played for Torquay United and was later manager of Brighton and Hove Albion and Liverpool. (See under Managers.)
- Jack WESTBY, full-back, signed from Blackburn Rovers in 1942, he helped Liverpool win the League (N) Cup in 1944. He scored once in 78 regional games for the club and played for Southport after leaving Anfield, having failed to make the League side. He represented the Western Command v. the Scottish Command in January 1944.
- Dennis WESTCOTT, centre-forward from Wolverhampton Wanderers for whom he netted 124 goals in 144 senior appearances. He also netted 91 goals in 76 WW2 games for the Molineux club as well as scoring for Blackburn Rovers, Manchester City and Chesterfield. He played for England in four Victory internationals, gained an FA Cup runners-up medal in 1939 and notched six goals in three games for the Reds, four in one game v. Chester in 1940 (won 9–1).
- Bert WHALLEY, right-half from Manchester United who was killed in the Munich air crash in 1958.
- Jackie WHARTON, winger from Preston North End who had previously starred for Plymouth Argyle and after the hostilities did likewise for Manchester City, Blackburn Rovers and Newport County, scoring 25 goals in a total of 262 League appearances.
- Arnold WHITESIDE, wing-half from Blackburn Rovers for whom he appeared in 218 League games between 1933 and 1949.
- Bill WHITTAKER, centre-half from Charlton Athletic who had been an amateur with Arsenal. After the war, he played for Huddersfield Town and Crystal Palace, and made nine appearances for the Reds.
- Fred WILLIAMS, wing-half from Southampton who went on to play for Stockport County and Altrincham.
- Jimmy WOODBURN, a Scottish-born left-half from Newcastle United whom he helped gain promotion from the Second Division in 1948. He later made 132 League appearances for Gateshead.

- Arthur WOODRUFF, centre-half from Burnley for whom he appeared in 292 first-class matches. He also played for Bradford City reserves and later Workington (1952–53).
- Albert YOUNG, defender from Arsenal and later with Swindon Town for whom he appeared in 123 League games (1946–50).
- Others include Stan WILLIAMS (wing-half), Richard WILLIS (forward), Jack WOOD (left-back) and Albert YOXON (goalkeeper).

WW2 STATS AND FACTS

Top appearance-makers (including 'regular' players): Hobson 172, Kaye 170, Liddell 149, Nieuwenhuys 136, Done 135, Pilling 116, Lambert 113, Hughes 111, Fagan 110, Balmer 105, Gulliver 93, Taylor 92, Westby 78, Campbell 61, Polk 61, Paisley 60, Spicer 51, Guttridge 47, M. Hulligan 46, Harley 45, Welsh 41, F. Haycock 34, Carney 33, Beattie 25, Busby 24, R. Dorsett 22, Van der Berg 17, Bartram 16.

Top goalscorers: Done 148, Liddell 83, Fagan 68, Balmer 66, Nieuwenhuys 61, Welsh 42, Hulligan 24, Taylor 24, Dorsett 23, Campbell 18, Carney 15, Polk 14, Beattie 12, Mills 9.

LIVERPOOL MANAGERS

Liverpool FC has had 16 different managers in 114 years (10 in the first 90 seasons). Tom Watson has served the club the longest in this capacity, 18 years, 9 months until his death. When he retired George Kay had been in office for 14 years, 9 months (technically losing 7 years due to WW2) which puts Bill Shankly in second place, having been in charge for 14 years, 7 months. Remarkably, no manager has had less than three years in the job apart from Joe Fagan, who retired out of choice after two magnificent seasons.

The practice of promoting internally at Anfield did not begin with Shankly's successor. In fact, five of the first nine managers – Watson, Shankly himself, Kay, Ashworth and Welsh – had never really been associated with the Reds, although Welsh and Shankly had played as guests during WW2. The two recent foreign imports, Houllier and Benitez, also follow this line whereas McQueen, Taylor, Paisley, Dalglish, Souness and Evans had all played competitively for the club prior to becoming team manager.

Every manager apart from Patterson, Taylor and Welsh (who was the last to be in charge when the Reds suffered relegation) had some silverware to show for their efforts. Paisley won more trophies than the others, and indeed, only Sir Alex Ferguson (Manchester United) has bettered Paisley's triumphs in terms of winning more prizes at club level in England; (in Scotland, Jock Stein did great things with Celtic).

Watson and Souness both enjoyed success as managers before arriving at Anfield while Dalglish was the club's first player-manager and, indeed, the first to win the double. He was also the first to win honours as a boss after leaving Anfield.

MANAGER	APPOINTED	LEFT
John McKenna	August 1892	August 1896
Walter Barclay*	August 1892	August 1896
Tom Watson	August 1896	May 1915
David Ashworth	December 1919	February 1923
Matt McQueen	February 1923	February 1928
George Patterson	February 1928	May 1936
George Kay	May 1936	February 1951
Don Welsh	March 1951	May 1956

Phil Taylor	May 1956	November 1959
Bill Shankly, OBE	December 1959	July 1974
Bob Paisley, OBE	July 1974	June 1983
Joe Fagan	June 1983	May 1985
Kenny Dalglish, MBE	June 1985	February 1991
Graeme Souness	April 1991	January 1994
Roy Evans +	January 1994	November 1998
Gerard Houllier, OBE +	July 1998	May 2004
Rafael Benitez	June 2004	

* Barclay was McKenna's right-hand man
+ Evans and Houllier were joint managers from July to November 1998
NB: There was no manager during WW1

MANAGERS' NOTES

- Irishman John McKENNA was one of the great figures in Liverpool's early history, earning the nickname 'Honest John'. Although never officially listed as the club's manager, he performed all the necessary jobs a manager would have done and at one point acted as both secretary-manager and chairman of the club. He was President of the Football League for 26 years (from 1910 until his death in March 1936, aged 82). Elected to the Football League Management Committee in 1902, he became vice-president of the Football Association in 1908 and took over as President of the Football League in 1910. He had two spells as Chairman at Anfield, the first from 1909 to 1914 and the second from 1917 to 1919. As straight as a die, he never shirked an issue, his concern for the poorest clubs was constant and sincere, and he did the job in his own inimitable style. McKenna was instrumental in defeating the proposed two-referee system. A plaque in his memory still hangs in the stairway of Anfield.
- Walter BARCLAY was McKenna's main assistant, the club's general secretary-manager (if you like) who was not too involved with team affairs as such. A football enthusiast, he was the organiser of contracts, the necessary and urgent paperwork, fixtures and travel, and was always a willing worker. When Liverpool gained entry into the Football League (for the 1893–94 season) Barclay, who had been opposed to this venture, received a telegram from McKenna which read: 'Liverpool elected. Come to London at 3 p.m. tomorrow to arrange fixtures.' He travelled south without any questions. A former Everton employee (before the split), he was always on the lookout for new players and along with McKenna brought many great stars to Anfield. Besides his footballing activities, Barclay was a headmaster of the Industrial Schools in Everton Crescent.
- Tom WATSON was born in Newcastle-upon-Tyne in April 1859 and died in May 1915. He didn't play football seriously and managed Rosehill, Willington Quay, Newcastle West End, Newcastle East End and Sunderland (1889 to August 1896) before taking over at Anfield. He took Sunderland to three First Division titles (1892, 1893 and 1895) and then steered Liverpool

to two championship triumphs in 1901 and 1906 as well as Second Division glory in 1905 and FA Cup runners-up spot in 1914. A much-liked gentleman, he was still in office when he died and scores of players attended his funeral.

- David 'Little Dave' ASHWORTH was born in Waterford, Ireland, and played intermediate football for Newchurch Rovers. He then became a League referee before taking over as manager of Oldham Athletic in 1906, moving to Stockport County in 1914 and then to Anfield in the same capacity in 1919. After leaving the Reds he returned to Boundary Park and later managed Manchester City, Walsall, Caernarfon and Llanelli, and scouted for Blackpool. He guided Liverpool to the League title in 1922 and the reasons for his departure from Anfield have never been fully explained. Ashworth died in March 1947, aged 79.

- Matt McQUEEN – see under player profile.

- George PATTERSON was born and bred in Liverpool. He played for Marine before becoming assistant to manager Tom Watson at Anfield in 1908, taking over as the club's secretary in 1915. He then assisted Dave Ashworth until eventually being appointed manager himself in 1928, retaining office for eight years with the Reds almost being relegated in his last season. He was associated with the club for 28 years and died in Liverpool in May 1955.

- George KAY was born in Manchester in September 1891 and was a centre-half with Eccles, Bolton Wanderers, Distillery, West Ham United, Stockport County, Luton Town (player-coach) and represented the Irish League before taking over as manager of the latter club in 1928. He was then in charge of Southampton (for five seasons to May 1936) before spending almost 15 years in the hot seat at Anfield. A man of fine mettle and a great talker, he never donned a track suit, always preferring to wear a collar and tie and a suit (or blazer and trousers) no matter what the circumstances. His bark was far worse than his bite and he certainly got the players wound up before a game. He guided Liverpool to the First Division title in 1947 and then took them to the FA Cup final three years later, dropping Bob Paisley from the line-up against Arsenal. He appeared in 259 games for West Ham, captaining them to the Second Division championship and in the first FA Cup final at Wembley in 1923. Kay died in Liverpool in April 1954.

- Don WELSH was born in Manchester in February 1911 and died in Stevenage, Herts, in February 1990. A strong, forceful forward, he served in the Royal Navy (playing for Valetta in Malta) before joining Torquay United in 1932. He was sold to Charlton Athletic for £3,250 in 1935 and went on to score 50 goals in 216 games for the Londoners, gaining a Third Division (S) championship medal in 1935 and an FA Cup winner's medal in 1947, having collected a runners-up prize the year before. He also helped the Addicks win the Football League (S) Cup in 1944. Six months after retiring he was appointed manager of Brighton and Hove Albion, before taking over as Liverpool boss in 1951. On leaving Anfield he bought a hotel in Bovey Tracey (Devon) but returned to club management with Bournemouth in 1958. He later became the boss of Wycombe Wanderers before returning to Charlton in 1964 to work in the administration offices. Welsh won three full caps for England and when serving as a company sergeant major instructor in the Army, he scored 11 goals (including 4 against Wales in 1941) in 9 wartime internationals. He also played in representative games during WW2 for the Army Physical Training Corps (v. the RAF), the Army (12 times, including one game against an England XI), an Army XI, twice for the British Army (v. the French Army), for the Army (England) v. the Army (Scotland), the FA XI 3 times and on 4 occasions for the Western Command.

He captained Charlton for eight years and is listed as one of the greatest ever players to represent that club. As Liverpool manager he spent heavily in the transfer market but sadly his efforts were all in vain as relegation was suffered to the Second Division in 1954. He came within a whisker of promotion in 1956, taking the Reds into third spot, but there his Anfield days ended.

- Phil TAYLOR – see under player profile.
- Bill SHANKLY was born in the Scottish coalmining village of Glenbuck, near to the Ayr racecourse, in September 1913. He worked down the pit and was a wing-half for two junior sides north of the border before joining Carlisle United in July 1932. After spending a frustrating season in the reserves, he was transferred to Preston North End for £500 a year later. He remained at Deepdale until 1949 when he retired, having starred as a guest for Northampton Town, Liverpool (one game v. Everton in May 1942), Arsenal, Cardiff City, Bolton Wanderers, Luton Town and Partick Thistle during WW2. Capped five times by Scotland in peacetime football and seven times during the war, he won the FA Cup and the Football League Wartime Cup with Preston in 1938 and 1941 respectively (both at Wembley) and, in fact, during the hostilities he also played for a Scottish XI (1941), the Football League (1942), and the RAF on four occasions (1941, 1942, 1944 and 1945), the latter v. Wales.

Soon after hanging up his boots, he took over as manager of Carlisle United, bossed Grimsby Town from 1951 to 1954 and was then in charge of Workington before becoming assistant manager at Huddersfield, rising to manager in December 1955. His career at Anfield began just before Christmas 1959 (after he had agreed an annual salary of £2,500 with the club's chairman Tom Williams and director Harry Latham) and was to last almost 15 years, during which time Liverpool won the Second Division championship (1962), three League titles (1964, 1966 and 1973), the FA Cup twice (1965 and 1974) and the UEFA Cup (1973) while taking the runners-up prize in the 1966 European Cup-Winners' Cup and 1971 FA Cup finals. He was also voted 'Manager of the Year' in 1973. Shankly, who had the great ability to instil his own brand of confidence into players, made some terrific signings for Liverpool, including fellow Scots Ian St John, Willie Stevenson and Ron Yeats, goalkeepers Ray Clemence and Tommy Lawrence, defenders Emlyn Hughes, Alec Lindsay and Larry Lloyd, wing-half Gordon Milne, winger Peter Thompson and forwards Kevin Keegan, John Toshack and Tony

Hateley, among others. He also launched the careers of Ian Callaghan, Brian Hall, Steve Heighway, Roger Hunt, Chris Lawler and Tommy Smith. He made very few bad signings, Alun Evans perhaps one of them. Shankly surprised everyone when he announced his retirement in 1974, the same year he was awarded the OBE for services to football. His autobiography was published and simply called *Shankly*. The great man, who did so much for Liverpool FC, died in his adopted Merseyside city in September 1981.

Shankly was notorious for his brilliant one-liners, comments and quips. Some of his finest were . . .

'When the ball's down the Kop end, they frighten it and sometimes suck it into the back of the net' . . . 1960s

'Liverpool was made for me and I was made for Liverpool' . . . 1965

'I'm a people's man. Only the people matter' . . . 1965

'Football is not a matter of life and death. It's much more important than that' . . . 1967

'My life is my work. My work is my life' . . . 1968

'Tommy Smith would start a riot in a graveyard' . . . 1972

'There are two great teams in Liverpool: Liverpool and Liverpool reserves' . . . 1972

'I don't drop players – I make changes' . . . 1973

'I was the best manager in Britain because I was never devious or cheated anyone. I'd break my wife's legs if I played against her, but I'd never cheat her' . . . 1974

'I had to say I was retiring, though I believe you retire when you're in a coffin and the lid is nailed down and your name is on it' . . . on his retirement, also in 1974

'Don't overeat and don't lose your accent' . . . talking to Kenny Dalglish in 1977

- Joe FAGAN was born in Liverpool in March 1921 and was 80 years of age when he died in the same city in June 2001. His brief managerial tenure at Anfield provided continuity to Liverpool's remarkable success story of the 1970s and '80s. A former centre-half with Manchester City (with whom he won a Second Division winner's medal in 1947), Bradford Park Avenue, Altrincham and Nelson (player-manager), he was Rochdale's trainer for a short while before becoming a member of Anfield's famous 'boot room' team in 1958. He was appointed assistant manager in July 1974 and succeeded Bob Paisley as boss in 1983 at the age of 62, thus becoming the oldest-ever debutant manager of a Football League club. He guided the Reds to three major honours in his first season, becoming the first manager to achieve such a treble – League championship (ahead of Southampton), League Cup (v. Everton after a replay) and European Cup (v. AS Roma on penalties). Sadly the following season there came the Heysel disaster – just after Fagan had announced his intended retirement. Fagan was distraught after seeing 39 people lose their lives ahead of Liverpool's 1–0 defeat by Juventus in that 1985 European Cup final – it is doubtful he ever got over the trauma.

- Kenny DALGLISH – see under player profile.

- Graeme SOUNESS – see under player profile.
- Roy EVANS – see under player profile.
- Gerard HOULLIER was born in Therouanne, France, on 3 September 1947. A former coach of the French national team and technical director of the French Football Federation, he took time to bed himself in as joint manager at Anfield with Roy Evans. Indeed, at one time the Frenchman came under fire from certain groups of supporters. But he remained strong, soaked up the pressure and after Evans had left in November 1998 he got down to serious business. In 2001 Liverpool won five trophies – the FA Cup, the League Cup, the UEFA Cup, the European Super Cup and the Charity Shield. Later in 2001 Houllier had major surgery after a heart attack – which triggered off speculation about his future. But he silenced the doubters as Liverpool finished runners-up in the Premiership in 2002 and won the League Cup again a year later. With his health seemingly not what it should have been, he left Anfield in 2004. He rested for a while and was then placed in charge of the French club Olympique Lyonnaise, guiding them to their fourth French League title win in the club's history in 2005 as they finished eight points clear of Lille. Houllier said his fondest memories with Liverpool included the 2001 FA Cup and UEFA Cup triumphs over Arsenal and Alaves respectively, and the fans' tribute at Anfield when he was recovering from heart surgery. When he left the club he said: 'I arrived at Anfield a Liverpool supporter and I leave as an even bigger supporter. I will return to watch the team as a fan.' He was awarded the OBE in 2001 after Liverpool's terrific trophy-winning campaign.
- Rafael BENITEZ, in his first season in charge, saw Liverpool lose in the final of the League Cup 3–1 to Chelsea and then go on and lift the coveted European Champions League trophy after a thrilling victory over AC Milan in Istanbul, a nervous penalty shoot-out going in favour of the Reds who had been 3–0 down to the Italian club in the first half, before fighting back to level the scores at 3–3. Born in Madrid on 16 April 1960, Benitez became the first Spaniard to manage Liverpool. He immediately introduced some new 'foreign' faces to Anfield, although it must be said that a few eyebrows were raised with regard to some of his signings. Taking it in his stride, he proved everyone wrong by turning things round in a short period of time . . . just like he had done at his previous club, Valencia, whom he guided to a first Spanish La Liga title for 31 years in 2002. Two years later they won the same League competition again and also added the UEFA Cup to their prize collection after beating Olympique Marseille 2–0 in the final in Gothenburg. It was quite an achievement for Benitez to outwit mighty Real Madrid and Barcelona.

  During his playing days he had a spell with Real Madrid. He never played for their first team, spending most of his career in the lower Leagues in Spain with Parla and Linares. He started coaching with Real in 1986, being in charge of the youth team at the Bernabeu Stadium. After similar spells with four other Spanish clubs, Valladolid, Osasuna, Tenerife and CF Extremadura, he returned as head coach of the then Second Division side Tenerife in

August 2000 and a year later started a fairytale success story with Valencia. His appointment as successor to Hector Cuper was met with mixed reaction and was questioned by fans and pundits alike. However, Benitez was to have the last laugh, guiding Valencia to the La Liga title. The following season was somewhat disappointing and, like Liverpool, Valencia finished fifth in the League. However, they did have a good run in the Champions League, reaching the quarter-finals after beating Liverpool twice, 2–0 at the Mestalla Stadium and 1–0 at Anfield. And not many people argued with how Valencia played in those matches! Guided Liverpool to their seventh FA Cup final victory in 2006 (v. West Ham).

SIGNIFICANT OTHERS

- Local businessman Edward BAINBRIDGE had the distinction of being a director of both Everton and Liverpool at the same time before WW1. He alternated Saturday to Saturday, sitting in the directors' boxes at the clubs' respective grounds. His emotions were greatly strained on derby days! He died in 1927, aged 92.
- Merseyside solicitor Edwin BERRY played briefly for Everton and was also that club's treasurer (from 1884) before the famous split in 1892. He later assumed the role of chairman of Liverpool FC, holding office from 1904 to 1909. His son, Arthur, played for Liverpool (q.v.).
- Walter CARTWRIGHT was Liverpool chairman from 1932 to 1935 and was followed by his son, Harold CARTWRIGHT, who was chairman of the club from 1967 to 1969.
- William J. HARROP was a brilliant legislator who was chairman at Anfield in two separate spells – before WW2 and just after it. The first Liverpool director to become a member of the Football League management committee since John McKenna, he was automatically elected as a member of the FA Council. He also served as vice-president of the Football League until his death.
- Cecil HILL, an Anfield director during the 1950s, '60s and '70s, was the son of a former club director.
- John HOULDING, a former Lord Mayor of Liverpool, was instrumental in the birth of Liverpool FC in 1892. A dispute arose between him and other members of the Everton club whose ground was then at Anfield. One faction left and moved to the present site (Goodison Park) but Houlding remained put and built another team – Liverpool.
- Cliff LLOYD, born in Ellesmere Port in 1916, had three short spells at Anfield (between 1931 and 1935) without ever getting into the first XI. He turned professional with Wrexham and then moved to Fulham in 1943 prior to becoming player-manager of Margate (1949). He also assisted Bristol Rovers before being employed by his former club, Wrexham, as assistant secretary, then secretary and finally secretary-manager (1955–57). He had become a respected legislator with the PFA in 1950 of which he was secretary from 1953 to 1981. He made 12 League appearances for Wrexham and 2 for Fulham.

- Chairman Billy McCONNELL was a grand Liverpudlian whose business drive and acumen took Liverpool to the League title in 1947. The principal of a catering firm serving the docks, he held office for three years from 1944 and it was he who clinched the signing of Albert Stubbins. He was taken ill during the run-in to winning the League crown but ensured he was fit enough to attend the official party in London when the trophy was presented. Sadly he died shortly afterwards, allowing his brother, Tom, to be elected to the board in his place (1948).

- Robert Lawson MARTINDALE was a leading figure in the coal industry when he was co-opted to the Liverpool board in April 1931. Blessed with a mind for administration and finance, he was the son of Richard MARTINDALE who had been the club's chairman from 1924 to 1926. Followed into office by his son Lawson MARTINDALE in 1941, he was one of the founders of the Liverpool Sportsmen's Association and was awarded the MBE for his efforts.

- Goalkeeper George POLAND, born in Penarth in 1913, played for Swindon Town (as an amateur), Cardiff City and Wrexham and gained two full caps for Wales before joining Liverpool in July 1939. WW2 disrupted his career at Anfield but he did represent his country in four wartime internationals (1941–43), played for a Welsh XI and for Northern Command (1942–43) while also guesting for Brentford and Leeds United, returning to Ninian Park in 1946. He did not play in the Reds' first team and became a postman after retiring.

- Ted RAY, an amateur with Liverpool in 1921–22, was bitterly disappointed when he was told by the club that he would not be getting a contract. He buckled down and became one of the best comedians in the business – an all-time variety great.

- Sydney REAKES was Chairman of Liverpool FC when they won the FA Cup in 1965 and the League title the following year. A quarry owner and club director, he was a very assured businessman who supported the Reds all his life.

- Henry Robson ROBERTS, a former Liverpool vice chairman, was followed by his son Eric ROBERTS as chairman in 1970.

- First engaged in the Anfield offices in the summer of 1965, Peter ROBINSON was appointed secretary of Liverpool Football Club in 1973, signing a seven-year contract – a clear indication of his general organisational and administrative efficiency. He had started out in football as secretary of Crewe Alexandra, moved next to Scunthorpe United and then to Brighton and Hove Albion, his last club before Liverpool. His contract at Anfield was later extended and he remained as the club's secretary until 1997 when he was replaced in office by Bryce Morrison.

- Tom SAUNDERS was, for many years, youth development officer at Anfield. A former schoolteacher who became a headmaster, he managed the Liverpool and England schoolboy teams for several seasons before getting deeply involved with the youth set-up at the club. He nurtured many youngsters who went on to become superstars in their own right . . . and his work was much appreciated by the various managers under whom he worked.

- Thomas Valentine WILLIAMS, a former postman, was the man who spotted Ronnie Moran as a 15 year old when he was scouting for the club in his spare time. Two years later, after Liverpool had monitored the player's progress, Moran was signed by manager Don Welsh. Williams, a life-long supporter of the club who stood on The Kop in 1905 and joined in the first Liverpool song, was asked by Mr John McKenna to become a director of the club in the late 1920s. For business reasons, Williams had to refuse, but in 1948 he was elected to the board and eventually became chairman, a position he held for eight years. In 1962, and by now a retired cotton broker, he was elected as Liverpool's first-ever President, later Life President, a position he retained for many years. He was also a member of the FA Council and the FA International Selection Committee.
- Walter R. WILLIAMS was Liverpool's chairman from 1919 to 1924, and was followed into the 'chair' by his son, Samuel R. WILLIAMS.

THOSE WHO GOT AWAY . . .

Here are details of players who did well in competitive football after failing to make much headway at Anfield, for one reason or another.

- Benjamin Howard BAKER was one of the greatest of all England amateur goalkeepers, who was mainly associated with the Corinthians (176 appearances) and Chelsea, although he did serve Liverpool briefly in 1920 (second XI but no first-team outings), Blackburn Rovers reserves, Preston North End, Oldham Athletic and Everton (13 games). A superb athlete, he was born in Aigburth, Liverpool, in February 1892 (the year Liverpool FC was formed) and competed in the high jump for Great Britain in the 1912 Olympic Games in Stockholm and Antwerp in 1920, finishing sixth in the latter before going on to beat the American Jess Landon in the GB v. USA athletics meeting a year later with a leap of 6ft 3½in. He later established a new British record of 6ft 5in. He also played cricket for Liverpool CC (obliging with two centuries) and once turned out at centre-half for Lancashire County in a soccer match. Also a fine swimmer, hurdler, tennis player, long jumper and water polo goalkeeper, he appeared in ten amateur internationals for England at football (between 1921 and 1929) as well as winning two full caps for his country v. Belgium in 1921 and Ireland in 1926. He won the Welsh Cup with Northern Nomads in 1921 and was 94 years of age when he died in September 1987.
- Full-back John GIDMAN, born in Liverpool in January 1954, was released after spending just two seasons as an apprentice at Anfield. He joined Aston Villa in 1971, moved to Everton for £650,000 in 1979, switched to Manchester United for £450,000 in 1981, went across to Maine Road on a free in 1986, assisted Stoke City in 1988–89 and then became player-manager of Darlington before taking charge of King's Lynn. He made 432 League appearances during his career, represented England at youth, 'B', under-23 and senior levels, won the FA Youth Cup and League Cup with Villa in 1972 and 1977 respectively and added an FA Cup winner's meal to his collection with Manchester United in 1985. He now runs a café/bar on Spain's Costa del Sol.
- Alan HARPER, an England youth international midfielder, joined Everton in 1983 at the age of 22, having failed to make the first team at Liverpool. He won two League championship winner's medals with the Blues in 1985 and

1987 before joining Sheffield Wednesday, later assisting Manchester City, Everton (again), Luton Town, Burnley and Cardiff City. He retired in 1996 with over 500 senior appearances under his belt, 440 in the Football League (178 with Everton).

- John JEFFERS, an England schoolboy international, was a hard-working left-sided midfielder (winger) who failed to make headway at Anfield. However, after leaving Liverpool for £30,000, he did extremely well with Port Vale for whom he made 220 appearances and scored 11 goals. He also assisted Shrewsbury Town on loan (three games) and Stockport County, having 57 League outings (1995–97).

- Attacking midfielder Paul JEWELL was born in Liverpool on 28 September 1964 and as a teenager used to clean the boots of all the international stars at Anfield before turning professional in 1982. He was sold to Wigan Athletic for £15,000 in December 1984, having failed to make the Reds' first team, and from that point on his career took off. He scored 47 goals in 171 appearances for Wigan, followed up with 66 strikes in 308 outings for Bradford City (1988–95) and also played on loan with Grimsby Town before taking over as manager at Valley Parade in 1998, a position he held until 2000 when he was appointed boss of Sheffield Wednesday. Taking charge of his former employers, Wigan, in June 2001 and backed all the way by the club's millionaire-owner Dave Whelan (ex-Blackburn Rovers full-back), Jewell did a terrific job with the Latics, guiding them to the Second Division title in 2003, promotion to the First Division (via the play-offs) the following year and then into the Premiership as Football League champions in 2005. Then, with two ex-Liverpool players in his side – Stephane Henchoz and Ian Mellor – he guided Wigan to the 2006 League Cup final (v. Manchester United).

- Ted MacDOUGALL played in Liverpool's third and second teams between 1964 and 1967 before being released to join York City. His career took off and over the next decade or so he served with Bournemouth, Manchester United, West Ham United, Norwich City and Southampton, played in Australia, South Africa, the USA and Canada and also assisted Blackpool, scoring well over 300 goals, 256 in the Football League. He was capped seven times by Scotland, played in a League Cup final at Wembley (with Norwich) and created a record by netting nine goals in an FA Cup tie for Bournemouth against Margate in November 1971. Who let him go – surely not Bill Shankly?

- Forward Frank McGARVEY was born in Kilsyth, Scotland, in March 1956 and in five years scored over 60 goals in 175 games for St Mirren (52 in 132 League outings), helping them win the First Division title in 1977 before joining Liverpool in the summer of 1979 for £300,000. Honoured by his country in one under-23 and two full internationals, he also represented the Scottish League, but never made the first XI at Anfield. In March 1980 he moved to Celtic for £275,000 and won the Scottish Cup and League championship with the Bhoys in 1980 and 1981 respectively. He returned to St Mirren in 1985 aftrer netting a further 109 goals in 235 appearances. Certainly one who was allowed to escape from the Anfield net.

- James MAGILTON, a midfielder who was born in Belfast, 6 May 1969, failed to get a first-team outing with Liverpool. He moved to Oxford United for £100,000 in October 1990, switched to Southampton for £600,000 in February 1994, joined Sheffield Wednesday for £1.6m in September 1997 and ended up at Ipswich Town for £682,500 in January 1999. By 2006 he had amassed well over 650 club appearances, scored more than 80 goals and gained 52 full caps for Northern Ireland, while also representing his country in one under-21 and two under-23 internationals.
- Right-half Jim MILLER joined Liverpool in 1927 from Felling Colliery in the north-east of England. Failing to get into the first team, he moved to Crewe Alexandra and later appeared in 161 League games for Carlisle United (1928–34).
- Des PALMER, born in Swansea in September 1931, played for his local club for nine years before joining Liverpool (in a deal involving Roy Saunders) in March 1959. Due to a knee injury, he failed to make a first-team appearance for the Reds and moved to Johannesburg Ramblers in 1960. He later assisted Derby County, Wellington Town, Slavia Melbourne and Yugal Sydney (both in Australia) and Llanelli (player-manager). Capped three times by Wales (as a Swansea player) he netted a hat-trick in his second international v. East Germany.
- Abe ROSENTHAL, an ice-cream manufacturer by profession, was released by Liverpool in 1938 at the age of 17 without appearing in the first team. A local-born inside-forward, dark haired and stocky with a genial character, he went on to have three spells with both Tranmere Rovers and Bradford City and also assisted Oldham Athletic as a trialist. He scored 79 goals in a total of 228 League games before retiring in 1956.
- Giant goalkeeper Bob SCOTT was released by Liverpool in 1933 after failing to make the first XI. He went on to appear in 57 League games for Burnley, 119 for Wolves and 44 for Crewe Alexandra. He also appeared in the 1939 FA Cup final. Born in Liverpool in 1913, he died in 1962.
- England youth international striker Peter SPIRING joined Liverpool for £60,000 at the age of 22 in March 1973, having scored 16 goals in 63 League games for Bristol City. He never got a single outing in the Reds' first team and left Anfield in November 1974 for Luton Town. He netted twice in 15 starts for the Hatters before going on to score another 20 goals in 227 League appearances for Hereford United (1976–83).
- Merseyside-born striker Tommy TYNAN signed apprentice forms for Liverpool on his 16th birthday (17 November 1971). Spotted by manager Bill Shankly playing in the finals of a local soccer competition organised by the *Liverpool Echo* which was entered by 1,000 youngsters, he reached the final 20 and soon afterwards joined the Reds. Unfortunately he failed to make the grade at Anfield and after six League outings for Swansea (on loan) he joined Sheffield Wednesday, here making the decisive breakthrough. He switched from Hillsborough to Lincoln City and then assisted Newport County, Plymouth Argyle (three spells), Rotherham United, Torquay United and Doncaster Rovers before retiring from top-line football. He gave tremendous

service to Plymouth for whom he scored 148 goals in 310 games. His career spanned 21 years (1971–92) and during that time he amassed 740 League and Cup appearances and netted a staggering 306 goals – a magnificent set of statistics. He played in the 1984 FA Cup semi-final for Plymouth v. Watford.

- Goalkeeper Tony WARNER (born in Liverpool in May 1974) joined the apprentice ranks at Anfield at the age of 18, turned professional in January 1994 but never made the first XI at Anfield, being transferred to Millwall in 1999 after loan spells with Swindon Town, Celtic and Aberdeen. In 2004 he signed for Cardiff City, having made 225 senior appearances during his five seasons at The Den. Standing 6ft 4in. tall, he helped the Lions win the Second Division title in 2001.

- Centre-half Dave WATSON (born in Liverpool on 20 November 1961), brother of Alexander Francis Watson (q.v.), was a junior and then professional at Anfield in the late 1970s. He was released without ever tasting first-team action and went on to make 251 senior appearances for Norwich City (1980–86) and 529 for Everton (1986–2001) as well as winning 12 full and 7 under-21 caps for England. He was manager of Tranmere Rovers from April 2001 to September 2002. During his career Watson gained winner's medals for triumphs in the First and Second Divisions of the Football League, the FA Cup, the League Cup and the FA Charity Shield. Why was he allowed to escape from the Anfield enclosure?

- Frank WORTHINGTON had trained and, indeed, had played in two trial games for Liverpool and was all ready to sign for the Reds in the summer of 1972. However, after a routine medical, he was stunned when told that he was suffering from high blood pressure and would not be joining the club. Elvis Presley fanatic Worthington went on to become one of the great characters in the game, scoring almost 300 goals in 905 appearances at club and international level. He played for Huddersfield Town initially and after being rejected by Liverpool served, in turn, with Leicester City, Bolton Wanderers, Birmingham City, Philadelphia Fury, Leeds United, Southampton, Brighton and Hove Albion, Tranmere Rovers, Preston North End, Stockport County and Cape Town Spurs before venturing around the non-League grounds. He gained eight full and two under-23 caps for England.

SUPPORTERS

- In April 1966, ardent Liverpool supporter Peter O'Sullivan, a 35-year-old bricklayer, had his daughter officially named St John Lawrence Lawler Byrne Strong Yeats Stevenson Callaghan Hunt Milne Smith Thompson Shankly Bennett Paisley O'Sullivan. The offspring had one other Christian name, which was eventually accepted as the regular one . . . Paula.
- Michael Sutton gave his son a similar list to commemorate Liverpool's 1973 League Championship and UEFA Cup successes. His youngster was named: Kirk Lee Keegan Heighway Cormack Toshack Hughes Callaghan Hall Lloyd Smith Lindsay Lawler Clemence Shankly Sutton.
- Neville Ross gave his son the following names after Liverpool's 1974 FA Cup final victory over Newcastle United: Kevin Stephen Emlyn Alexander Philip Peter Thomas Ian St John Raymond Brian William (after manager Bill Shankly) Ross.
- Reds fanatic Gwyn Edwards gave his daughter the players' second names (also after that 1974 triumph): Victoria Shankly Clemence Smith Lindsay Thompson Cormack Hughes Keegan Hall Heighway Toshack Callaghan Lawler Edwards.

BIBLIOGRAPHY

Whilst compiling this Who's Who of Liverpool FC, I have referred to several publications including many hardback football books, club and supporters' handbooks, soccer annuals, hundreds of home and away programmes featuring the club, various football magazines (from 1933 onwards) and an assortment of newspapers, nationwide.

In respect of ascertaining information regarding players' statistics, personal details (i.e. dates of births and deaths) there are some conflicting references, certainly relating to the older players (pre WW1) and therefore I have made judgements as to what is likely to be correct when several possibilities have been forthcoming.

The list of items referred to:

Barwick, B. and Sinstadt, G. *The Great Derbies: Everton v. Liverpool: 1962–1988* (BBC Books, London, 1988)

Davies, G.M. and Garland, I. *Welsh International Soccer Players* (Bridge Books, Wrexham, 1991)

Farror, M. and Lamming, D. *A Century of English International Football, 1872–1972* (Robert Hale and Co., London, 1972)

FA Yearbook 1951–2000, published annually (The Football Association, London)

Gibbs, N. *The Football Facts* (Facet Books, Exeter, 1988)

Gibson, A. and Pickard, W. *Association Football and The Men Who Made It* (4 vols) (Caxton Publishing Company, London, 1906)

Goldsworthy, M. *The Encyclopaedia of Association Football* (Robert Hale and Co., London, 1969)

Goldsworthy, M. *We Are The Champions* (Pelham Books, London, 1972)

Hargreaves, I. *Liverpool Greats* (John Donald Publishers Ltd, Edinburgh, 1989)

Hill, Jimmy *Great Soccer Stars* (Hamlyn, 1978)

Horsnell, B. and Lamming, D. *Forgotten Caps* (Yore Publications, Harefield, Middlesex, 1995)

Hugman, B.J. (ed.) *PFA Footballers' Factfile 1996–97 to 2000–01* (Queen Anne Press, Hertfordshire, 1996–2000)

Hugman, B.J. (ed.) *PFA Footballers' Factfile 2001–02* (AFS, Basildon, 2001)

Hugman, B.J. (ed.) *PFA Footballers' Factfile, 2002–03 to 2005–06* (Queen Anne

Press, Hertfordshire, 2002–2006)

Hugman, B.J. (ed.) *PFA Premier and Football League Players' Records: 1946–1998* (Queen Anne Press, Hertfordshire, 1998)

Johnson, F. *Football Who's Who* (Associated Sporting Press, London, 1935)

Joyce, M. *Football League Players' Records: 1888–1939* (Tony Brown/Soccer Data, Nottingham, 2002)

Keith, J. and Thomas, P. *The Daily Express A–Z of Mersey Soccer* (Beaverbook Newspapers Ltd, London, 1975)

Kelly, S. F. *You'll Never Walk Alone – The Hamlyn Illustrated History of Liverpool, 1892–1997* (Hamlyn/Reed International Books Ltd, London, 1997)

Lamming, D. *Who's Who of Scottish Internationalists: 1872–1982* (AFS, Basildon, 1982–83)

Pead, B. *Liverpool: A Complete Record 1892–1988* (Breedon Books Sport, Derby, 1988)

Ponting, I. *Liverpool: Hamlyn Player By Player* (Hamlyn/Reed Consumer Books Ltd, London, 1996)

Pringler, A. and Fissler, M. *Where Are They Now?* (Two Heads Publishing, London, 1996)

Rollin, J. *Soccer At War: 1939–45* (Willow Books Collins, London, 1985)

Spiller, R. (ed.) *AFS Football Who's Who: 1902–03, 1903–04, 1907–08, 1909–10* (AFS, Basildon, 1990)

Whitney, S. *The Ultimate Book of Non-League Players: 2002–03* (Baltic Publications Ltd, Newcastle, 2003)

Williams, T. (ed.) *Football League Directory: 1992–1995* (Daily Mail, London, 1992–95)

OTHER PUBLICATIONS

AFS Bulletins (various)

Charles Buchan Football Monthly: 1951–1969

Goal magazine: 1966–78

Liverpool Daily Post (newspaper) various: 1955–2006

Liverpool Echo (newspaper) various: 1949–2006

Liverpool FC handbooks, reviews, magazines, supporters guides; 1954–2006

Liverpool FC official programmes: 1905–2006

Rothmans Football Yearbooks (1970–2006), vols. 1–36 (various editors)

Shoot magazine: 1990–2004

Soccer Star magazine: 1963–67

Sports Argus Football Annuals: 1949–68

I have also referred to several other national and local newspapers, various club histories and Who's Who books, autobiographies and biographies of players and managers, scores of general football books and magazines and hundreds of assorted programmes.